KLONDIKERS

KLONDIKERS

DAWSON CITY'S
STANLEY CUP CHALLENGE
AND HOW A NATION FELL
IN LOVE WITH HOCKEY

TIM FALCONER

Purchase the print edition and receive the eBook free. For details, go to ecwpress.com/eBook.

This book is also available as a Global Certified Accessible™ (GCA) ebook. ECW Press's ebooks are screen reader friendly and are built to meet the needs of those who are unable to read standard print due to blindness, low vision, dyslexia, or a physical disability.

LIBRARY AND ARCHIVES CANADA CATALOGUING IN PUBLICATION

Title: Klondikers : Dawson City's Stanley Cup challenge and how a nation fell in love with hockey / Tim Falconer.

Names: Falconer, Tim, 1958– author.

Description: Includes bibliographical references.

Identifiers: Canadiana (print) 2021021967X | Canadiana (ebook) 20210219688

ISBN 978-1-77041-607-9 (softcover)
ISBN 978-1-77305-821-4 (ePub)
ISBN 978-1-77305-822-1 (PDF)
ISBN 978-1-77305-823-8 (Kindle)

Subjects: LCSH: Dawson City Nuggets (Hockey team)—History. | LCSH: Stanley Cup (Hockey) (1905 January 13-16 : Ottawa, Ont.) | LCSH: Hockey—Yukon—Dawson—History.

Classification: LCC GV848.D39 F35 2021 | DDC 796.96209719/1—dc23

Copyright © Tim Falconer, 2021

Published by ECW Press
665 Gerrard Street East
Toronto, Ontario, Canada M4M 1Y2
416-694-3348 / info@ecwpress.com

Editor for the Press: Michael Holmes
Cover design: David A. Gee
Cover photo: Yukon Archives, Paul Forrest fonds, 88/25, #1.

This book is funded in part by the Government of Canada. *Ce livre est financé en partie par le gouvernement du Canada.* We also acknowledge the support of the Government of Ontario through the Ontario Book Publishing Tax Credit, and through Ontario Creates.

MIX
Paper from responsible sources
FSC® C103567

PRINTED AND BOUND IN CANADA   PRINTING: MARQUIS   5 4 3 2 1

For the guys in the dressing room

CONTENTS

Part Two

PART THREE

- PROLOGUE -

The Canadian Pacific Railway's Continental train was nearly three hours late when it pulled up to the station in Winnipeg. Given what the hockey players had been through since leaving the Klondike, this barely counted as a complication. After all, inconvenient forces had started conspiring against them even before they headed out of Dawson City. First, one of the team's stars decided to stay behind with his injured wife. Then the captain and most accomplished player realized he had to stay a little longer for work. He'd try to catch up with others as soon as he could. The team's luck did not improve once the journey began.

Setting out to capture the Stanley Cup, and the fame that went with it, the players figured it would be a straightforward eighteen-day trip. Straightforward by Yukon standards, anyway. Three left on foot on December 18, 1904; four others followed on bikes the next day, though they all eventually abandoned their wheels. After 330 miles, the team arrived in Whitehorse two days after Christmas, only to watch a blizzard shut down the narrow-gauge trains on the White Pass & Yukon Route Railway. When they finally reached Skagway, Alaska, they'd missed their steamer to Vancouver by two hours and had to wait days to board a Seattle-bound ship for a voyage that left the players severely seasick.

They believed the hardship was worth it. Since 1893, the reward for being Canada's best amateur team was the Dominion Hockey Challenge Cup, a silver bowl donated by Lord Stanley of Preston, the governor general at the time. Known from the beginning as the Stanley Cup, it quickly became the most prestigious trophy in the land. While the trustees wouldn't allow just any team to contend for the honour, they did approve a challenge from Dawson City's all-stars. To win the Cup, the Yukoners would have to defeat the formidable Ottawa Hockey Club—a team known in lore as the Silver Seven—and the sport's original superstar, "One-Eyed" Frank McGee. Few hockey people considered the Klondikers a serious threat. The team was from a small subarctic town and no squad from west of Brandon had yet challenged for the Cup, let alone won it. When accepting the challenge, Ottawa insisted the Dawson team not play any exhibition matches en route. Rather than an attempt to ensure their opponents would arrive unprepared, this was to avoid any losses to weaker teams that might discourage ticket sales for the Cup series.

The original plan, as set out by Joe Boyle, the brash businessman managing the tour, was for a layover in Winnipeg to do some training. But the team was so far behind schedule, that was no longer an option. With just a two-hour stop before continuing on to Ottawa, the players didn't have enough time to do much more than stretch their legs and assure reporters their challenge was no joke. Despite the team's lack of star power, the cross-country trek charmed Canadians. Though the codified version of the sport was only three decades old, passion for hockey had swept the nation since Lord Stanley had donated the Cup and was only intensifying. But there was more to the enthusiasm for the underdogs from the Yukon than a love of the game. The Klondike Gold Rush was over, but people contin- ued to romanticize the North. And the long journey from that faraway land to the nation's capital fit into that mystique. All along the route, fans had cheered the Yukon team. And it was no different in the home of the champions, where the *Citizen* reported, "The matches are creating the greatest interest of any Stanley Cup contests yet played in Ottawa."

At a quarter to five on January 11, 1905, three and a half weeks after leaving Dawson City, the hockey players stepped off the train and onto the platform at Ottawa's Central Station, where a large and appreciative crowd gave them "a right hearty recep- tion." Bob Shillington, the manager of the Cup-holding team, and other club executives led the players away to the Russell House. A throng overflowed the hotel's rotunda in hopes of catching a glimpse of the exotic visitors. But the cordial welcome didn't mean the hosts were about to grant Dawson's request for a one-week postponement before starting the best-of-three series. Meanwhile, the challengers denied a newspaper report that they'd default the series opener and focus on the second and third matches rather than play unprepared. The first game would go ahead as scheduled, with Earl Grey, the new gover- nor general, "facing the puck" at 8:30 p.m. on Friday the 13th. After nearly a month on the road, the exhausted and far-from- game-shape Klondikers would take on the reigning Stanley Cup champions before a sellout crowd of 2,500 fans at Dey's Rink in just over forty-eight hours.

Part One

- ONE -

"It looks like any other trophy,
I suppose"

Still just twenty years old, the boyishly handsome and clean-cut Weldon Champness Young was already a veteran star with the Ottawa Hockey Club when he went to the Russell House for a formal banquet. The March 1892 evening, hosted by the Ottawa Amateur Athletic Club, was to celebrate his team's season. So it was fitting that when Weldy, as everyone called him, and the other guests sat down at the elegant place settings, they found menu cards that told two tales. One side, as usual, set out the fine fare the hotel would serve that Friday night. The other showed the names of the OHC players and an account of another impressive season. In ten matches that winter, the squad had won nine times, scoring fifty-three goals and allowing only nineteen. "This was the record," according to the *Evening Journal*, "of a genuine amateur team playing for pure love of sport and treating all comers as they wished to be treated themselves." More than seventy-five sportsmen had gathered in the dining room to honour the players, but by the end of the night they'd have something else to cheer about.

Located a short walk from Parliament Hill, on the south-east corner of Sparks and Elgin streets, the five-storey Russell

House was the city's finest hotel. Popular with Ottawa's high society, who enjoyed the luxurious public rooms and excellent food, the establishment was the obvious choice for a banquet that attracted many distinguished local gentlemen, as well as guests from Montreal and Toronto, and featured music from the Governor General's Foot Guards band. Women joined the festivities around 9:30 p.m., taking seats in a wing of the dining room, and the hotel staff served coffee and ices. At ten o'clock, OAAC president J. W. McRae began the evening's formal proceedings. A lengthy round of toasts was a regular part of such gatherings and, by tradition, the host always led off with one to the Queen. After McRae had done so, Philip Dansken Ross, the *Evening Journal* publisher and OAAC past president, drew cheers for his toast to the health of the governor general, including complimentary remarks about the Englishman's staunch support of sports, especially hockey.

In 1888, an aging Queen Victoria had tapped Frederick Arthur Stanley, the forty-seven-year-old son of a former Tory prime minister, to be her Canadian representative. After serving two decades in Parliament, where he held several portfolios, including Secretary of State for the Colonies, Baron Stanley of Preston entered the House of Lords in 1886. Yet his career always seemed overshadowed by the political accomplishments of his father and brother. The viceregal position in Ottawa, not exactly the most glamorous, or warmest, city in the British Empire, sure wasn't about to change that. In fact, it sounded more like a retirement posting. Initially, he declined the Queen's offer, but Lord Salisbury, his prime minister, talked him into becoming the Dominion of Canada's sixth governor general.

When he arrived in Ottawa in June 1888, Stanley was a middle-aged aristocrat about five feet, ten inches tall with a stout build. He kept a grizzled beard and above his broad forehead, his hair was thinning and starting to grey. *The New York Times* described him as having "a commanding and soldier-like appearance" and being "decidedly good looking." He came from a sporting family. In 1780, his great-grandfather, the 12th Earl of Derby, created The Derby, the second and most prestigious of the three horse races that make up the British Triple Crown. Although he showed less interest in art and literature than his father had, Stanley shared his family's passion for horse racing as well as its love of hunting, fishing and cricket. He and his wife, Lady Constance, had ten children, eight of whom survived to adulthood. Four of the offspring arrived in Canada with their parents and others followed. The family quickly embraced winter, snowshoeing, tobogganing and, most of all, the nascent sport of hockey.

Unable to attend the banquet, Stanley sent his aide-de-camp, Lord Kilcoursie. During his time in the Grenadier Guards, Frederic Rudolph Lambart had been known as Fatty because he was short and stocky and his "trousers were too short and a yard too broad in the seat." Having racked up gambling debts, he left England in 1891 to work for Stanley. He quickly took to hockey, playing regularly with members of Ottawa's elite and his boss's sons, and occasionally with his boss himself. Responding to the toast, he noted that while Stanley might not have the agility of OHC captain Herbert Russell or the speed of Weldy Young, he was a decent player and a clever bodychecker. Then Kilcoursie read a letter from His Excellency: "I have for some time past been thinking that it would be a good thing if there were a challenge cup which should be held from year to year by the championship hockey team in the Dominion. There does not appear to be any such outward or visible sign of the championship at present, and considering the interest that hockey matches now elicit, and the importance of having the games fairly played under rules generally recognized, I am willing to give a cup that shall be held from year to year by the winning club."

Thrilled, the dinner guests applauded enthusiastically and the good mood in the room rose some more. When McRae proposed a toast to "the hockey team," friends and supporters stood on their chairs to drink it. Then each player responded. Russell went first with a much-appreciated humorous speech. Young earned a special round of applause for raising a glass to the good fellowship among the OAAC clubs and their members. The last player to speak, Chauncey Kirby, added emphasis by standing on the table. Eventually, Kilcoursie was on his feet again with a song he'd composed. Called "The Hockey Men," it began:

> There is a game called hockey—
> There is no finer game,
> For though some call it "knockey"
> Yet we love it all the same.

> 'Tis played in this Dominion,
> Well played both near and far;
> There's only one opinion,
> How 'tis played in Ottawa.

Verses about the Ottawa players followed and were, if possible, even cornier than the first two. The stanza about Young, who played cover point, one of two defence positions, went:

> At cover point—important place—
> There's Young, a bulwark strong,
> No dodging tricks or flying pace
> Will baffle him for long.

The audience hooted and clapped at the mention of each player. Everyone loved the performance. After more songs, toasts and speeches, the guests sang "God Save the Queen" and then belted out "Auld Lang Syne" before heading home, or moving on to the next party, at midnight. The evening had been a great success.

The delight at Stanley's promised gift had come from hockey people, including players, league and club officials and other hangers-on. Still, their excitement over a trophy to recognize the nation's championship team revealed a lot about the growing ardour for the sport. And having been among the first people to hear about it, Weldy Young would never shake his desire to win the honour.

Although Canada had its own fine silversmiths, Stanley opted for an imported trophy. He asked Captain Charles Colville, his former military secretary, to handle the arrangements in England. Colville, who'd also played hockey with Stanley's sons, visited George Richard Collis & Company on Regent Street, even then a high-end shopping strip in London's West End. He paid ten guineas for a late-Victorian punch bowl, with gold gilding inside, on a pedestal base. The trophy was slightly more than seven inches high and eleven across. Engraved on one side was "Dominion Hockey Challenge Cup"; the other side read "From Stanley of Preston" above his family crest. After the small crate arrived at Rideau Hall in April 1893, the donor told a British sportswriter who'd asked him to describe the cup: "It looks like any other trophy, I suppose." Still, he was pleased enough that he invited John Sweetland to pick it up. A doctor and the sheriff of Carleton County, Sweetland was one of two Ottawa gentlemen Stanley had asked to be trustees of the Cup. P. D. Ross, the newspaper publisher, was the other.

Although Stanley was popular and remains among the country's best-known governors general, conventional historical thinking has it that he was an unimaginative, even inconsequential, viceroy who served a largely uneventful term. In *Lord Stanley: The Man Behind the Cup*, Kevin Shea and John Jason Wilson argue against that take. "Stanley's endorsement of hockey," they write, "may have contributed more to cultural identity in Canada than any other figurehead, never mind governor general, in Canadian history." For sure, he'd picked just the right moment in the development of the sport to donate a trophy. But there was more to it than good timing. The nation that had emerged out of a collection of colonies in 1867 was technically just a self-governing dominion and definitely still part of the Empire. In fact, people born in Canada or naturalized immigrants were British subjects (this didn't change until 1947, with the Canadian Citizenship Act). So colonial thinking lived on. Most English Canadians were ardent Anglophiles and monarchists, and if the Queen's own representative approved of this new game enough to donate a trophy, people took it seriously: hockey must be something Canadians should enjoy. So they did. No one had any idea the sport would help speed the development of a new, more independent and less British culture in the country.

The letter Kilcoursie read didn't include the word amateur, but the line about "the importance of having the games fairly played under rules" revealed Stanley's thinking. Sportsmanship was a crucial tenet of amateurism, and the governor general clearly wanted to support and reward amateurs, which by its original definition meant white men with some degree of wealth. Professionalism wasn't a concern in hockey yet—the game was too new for that—but pay-for-play had invaded more established activities such as baseball and boxing, causing concern within the elites. In the nineteenth century, the country's attitude to sports was, predictably, based on the British one and reflected Victorian England's view of honour, fair play and manliness as well as its preoccupation with social class. But Canada was going through a period of profound social and technological change, which helped spread the game. Hockey proved so popular that before long, people from other classes and ethnic groups would pick up the sport.

Stanley's daughter Lady Isobel and other women also enjoyed hockey, but his trophy was meant to encourage boys and men at a time when the British believed society was facing a crisis of manliness. While Arthur Wellesley, the first Duke of Wellington, never actually said, "The battle of Waterloo was won on the playing fields of Eton"— he said, "It is here that the battle of Waterloo was won!" while at the posh boys' school— the misquotation revealed a lot about the British attitudes toward sports, war and empire even decades later. Hockey players valued sportsmanship, but violence was a controversial part of the sport from the beginning.

Over the years, many people have tried to explain the game's brutal side. Six decades after Stanley left Canada, Hugh MacLennan, who wrote about the nation's linguistic and cultural duality in his novel *Two Solitudes*, eloquently captured part of the appeal of the game in "Fury on Ice," a 1954 magazine article. "To spectator and player alike, hockey gives the release that strong liquor gives to a repressed man," he wrote. "It is the counterpoint of the Canadian restraint, it takes us back to the fiery blood of Gallic and Celtic ancestors who found themselves minorities in a cold new environment and had to discipline themselves as all minorities must." But "this combination of ballet and murder," as an Al Purdy poem puts it, has always been about much, much more than on-ice mayhem for Canadians. French-born American historian and cultural critic Jacques Barzun noted, "Whoever wants to know the heart and mind of America had better learn baseball, the rules and realities of the game—and do it by watching first some high school or small-town teams." He could have switched out America and baseball for Canada and hockey and achieved similar wisdom.

Stanley's simple gift—just an unremarkable silver bowl, much like any other trophy, by his own admission—may have been more symbolic than anything else, but symbols are often powerful. And before the decade was out, Canadians across the country, as far away as the Yukon, dreamed of winning the Stanley Cup. Seven years after attending the banquet that launched an obsession, Weldy Young moved to the Klondike, leaving behind his team and his hometown, but not his hunger for the Cup. The Gold Rush had already peaked, but there were still opportunities worth pursuing and he was hardly the only delayed stampeder. During his first couple of years in the sub-arctic, he offered occasional updates on life in Dawson for people "Outside," as Yukoners called everywhere south of the territory. In a summer 1900 letter, he covered local politics, a mild small-pox outbreak and the doings of several former Ottawa residents. He also made an announcement that must have seemed particularly outlandish given the northern town hadn't even existed five years earlier. "And now, by way of warning, let me break the news gently, a challenge from the Dawson Hockey club, for the possession of the Stanley Cup, is now being prepared," Young wrote. "And let me further inform you 'outsiders' that if a team is sent you do not want to hold us too cheaply."

- TWO -

*"I think we could
beat those fellows"*

I t was a great day for hockey. Spring comes late in Montreal and in early March of 1875, winter's end seemed a long way off. The mercury barely made it up to eighteen degrees on the third day of the month. James George Aylwin Creighton welcomed the cold. The ice at the Victoria Skating Rink would be hard and since it was indoors, he didn't have to worry about all the snow that had fallen the past two days. Creighton wasn't looking forward to just another late-season match. He'd organized the sport's first indoor game, an event that would come to represent the beginning of modern hockey.

Basketball has a widely accepted creation myth. James Naismith, originally from Almonte, a mill town in Ontario's Ottawa Valley, became an athletics instructor at McGill University while studying theology at Montreal's Presbyterian College. After moving to the International YMCA Training School in Springfield, Massachusetts, he invented the indoor game in 1891 as a form of winter conditioning for athletes. Hockey, on the other hand, has ancient roots and evolved slowly and then all at once. Humans have played stick-and-ball games at least since the Egyptians, and hockey grew out of a tradition that includes Ireland's hurling or hurley; Scotland's shinty; England's field hockey; and bandy, an on-ice game played for centuries in Russia and northern Europe. Rugby and lacrosse—which was based on the Indigenous game of baggataway, and codified into the modern settler sport by Montrealer William George Beers in the 1860s—were also crucial influences.

The argument over hockey's birthplace may never be settled, especially since much of the wrangling hinges on the definition of hockey. So contentious is the debate that the Society for International Hockey Research's official position, enshrined in a 2016 constitutional amendment, is to take no official position on the matter. Too many towns and cities—including Windsor, Nova Scotia; Kingston, Ontario; and Montreal—have made claims, and there's also evidence of early hockey in New England. The oldest reference appears in the papers of calamitous explorer John Franklin, whose men played a version of the game on a lagoon at Déline, an Indigenous settlement just south of the Arctic Circle on Great Bear Lake. "We endeavour to keep ourselves in good humour, health and spirits by an agreeable variety of useful occupation and amusement," wrote Franklin in an October 1825 letter. "Till the snow fell, the game of hockey, played on the ice, was the morning's sport."

Less contentious than the birthplace are the details of the first indoor contest: March 3, 1875, at the Victoria Skating Rink. Born in 1850, Creighton had grown up in Halifax and enjoyed sports such as rugby football, figure skating and a hockey variant with roots in hurling played on the city's frozen harbour. He started studying at Dalhousie University when he was fourteen. After graduating with an honours engineering degree, he worked on the Intercolonial Railway, which would soon connect the Maritime provinces with central Canada. In 1872, he moved to Montreal, where his assignments included the Lachine Canal expansion, the Montreal Harbour and other infrastructure projects. In his spare time, he made friends with fellow athletes and joined the Montreal Football Club, which played under rugby union rules, and the Victoria Skating Rink.

Tall and lean, just 145 pounds in his twenties, he was starting to lose the hair on his head, but he kept his walrus moustache. While he was competitive as an athlete, he was a humble, gentle and unassuming man. But not so unassuming that he couldn't convince his football friends that hockey would be a good way to train during the winter. He introduced them to the sport, and given Montreal winters, the players must have dreamed of moving inside, away from the wind and snow.

The Victoria Rink offered a sheltered venue. The plain but imposing two-storey red brick building was located on Drummond below St. Catherine Street and stretched all the way to Stanley Street. From the outside, it looked mostly functional, like it might be an armoury or something, but inside it offered some elegance. Wooden trusses curved over the rink to a height of fifty-two feet. All around the ice, a promenade eight inches high and ten feet wide offered standing room for spectators and resting skaters. There was also a director's gallery and a bandstand so musicians could play waltzes for the swarms on blades. The rink was open from eight o'clock in the morning until ten o'clock at night. During the day, light came in through the fifty large arched windows on three sides of the building; several hundred gas jets produced a soft light—more of a glow, actually—at night. For well-heeled Montrealers of Scottish and English descent, the club quickly became a popular spot. The skating masquerades and fancy-dress carnivals were much-anticipated social events.

The ice surface was 202 feet long and 80 feet wide and the decision by the Montreal architectural firm of Lawford & Nelson to support the pitched roof with the arches—a technique used in European train stations at the time—meant no columns. Aside from the square corners, it was ideal for hockey. Since opening on Christmas Eve in 1862, the rink had operated primarily for one purpose: figure skaters, speed skaters and pleasure skaters were all welcome. But in order to keep the place financially viable, the club occasionally allowed other activities such as snowshoe races and lacrosse on ice. That may have provided an opening for Creighton. As a figure skating judge, he was sufficiently well connected to be able to cajole or bribe a caretaker or someone else in authority to allow hockey practices when the rink would otherwise be closed. Soon, the players decided to arrange a formal game.

An indoor match required some rule tweaks. Outdoor games sometimes featured dozens of players, the limits being how many skaters were available and the size of the pond, slough or river. For the smaller ice surface, Creighton and his pals, some of them McGill students, settled on nine a side. Many of the basic rules were based on field hockey, but the players used an idea from lacrosse and stood two six-foot sticks in the ice, eight feet apart, to create goals. They also agreed on an offside rule that prevented passing to teammates who were ahead of the play.

The leading skates at the time were made by the Starr Manufacturing Company of Dartmouth, Nova Scotia. The blades attached to boots with a spring apparatus and required no screws. For sticks, Creighton arranged for Halifax friends to send two dozen of the best, which were handcrafted by Mi'kmaq carvers. A rum barrel plug had served as a puck for Franklin's men. Other early players used a variety of objects, including lacrosse balls, blocks of woods or even hunks of horse dung. While an unwieldy lacrosse ball was adequate on large ice surfaces, it posed a danger to both spectators and the Victoria Rink's windows. An announcement in Montreal's the *Gazette* promised, "Good fun may be expected, as some of the players are reputed to be exceedingly expert at the game." The paper added, "Some fears have been expressed on the part of intending spectators that accidents were likely to occur through the ball flying about in too lively a manner, to the imminent danger of lookers-on, but we understand that the game will be played with a flat circular piece of wood, thus preventing all danger of its leaving the surface of the ice." Hockey players quickly discovered they could handle this projectile with much greater control than they ever had with a ball. The *Gazette* first called it a puck in 1876. One fanciful but charming etymological theory suggests the disc's tendency to dart about unpredictably, appearing and disappearing without warning, was reminiscent of Puck, the mischievous sprite in William Shakespeare's *A Midsummer Night's Dream*.

The next day, the *Montreal Star* reported on "an interesting game of Hockey," which suggested faint praise. The *Gazette* made it sound a bit more entertaining: "The match was an interesting and well contested affair, the efforts of the players exciting much merriment as they wheeled and dodged each other." Both papers said the crowd was large, though that was a relative assessment. This was a new sport and only about forty people stood on the platform surrounding the ice surface that night. By about 9:30 p.m., Creighton's team had won and "the spectators then adjourned well satisfied with the evening's entertainment."

The *Gazette* didn't mention any violence, but the Montreal *Daily Witness* did. Some kids, perhaps frustrated their usual ice time had been hijacked, started skating even as play continued. "An unfortunate disagreement arose," according to the paper. "One little boy was struck across the head, and the man who did so was afterwards called to account, a regular fight taking place in which a bench was broken and other damage caused." A few days later, the story perhaps having grown with time and retelling, Kingston's *Weekly British Whig* ran this front-page brief: "A disgraceful sight took place at Montreal in the Victoria Skating Rink over a game of hockey. Shins and heads were battered, benches smashed, and the lady spectators fled in confusion." It would hardly be the last time a Canadian newspaper expressed outrage at violence in hockey.

Despite that ill will, the rink hosted another match two weeks later. This time, Creighton's team of Montreal Football Club members and a skating club team wore uniforms and already strategy was crucial to success. "Captain Creighton, whose individual play deserves special encomium, did all he could to get his men together and make them play into each other's hands, but to no purpose," reported the *Gazette*. "They seemed to have lost that organized system which distinguished their play at the beginning of the afternoon, and the result was a well-deserved victory for their opponents, who certainly did play exceedingly well and with remarkable science."

Two years later, the McGill University Hockey Club became the sport's first organized team. The Montreal Victorias soon followed and their secretary mailed contacts in other cities for guidance on the rules but received no replies. Team captains typically agreed on how they'd play beforehand. But in February 1877, the *Gazette* published hockey rules along with a game summary. That Creighton, who'd played in the match, wrote for the newspaper at the time may not have been a coincidence. Hockey didn't become a popular pastime right away, but the participation of McGill students in these early matches helped spread the game because the out-of-towners took their passion for it, along with the new rules, back to their hometowns.

Meanwhile, other amateur sports thrived, especially snowshoeing and tobogganing—which, like lacrosse, had come from Indigenous culture—and curling. In 1881, local cycling, lacrosse and snowshoe clubs joined together to create the Montreal Amateur Athletic Association, which organized the first Montreal Winter Carnival. It took place over five days in January 1883 and, as hoped, attracted lots of tourists, including many Americans, to Montreal. They participated in skating parties and sleigh rides and other social events; visited the massive ice palace in Dominion Square; and watched competitions in sports, including a novelty called hockey. McGill, the Victorias and Quebec City played a round-robin tournament on the St. Lawrence River. The games featured two thirty-minute periods, a ten-minute intermission and just seven players a side because Quebec showed up with only seven men and the Montreal teams agreed to drop two from their squads.

Two Ottawa visitors, Jack Kerr and Halder Kirby, watched McGill battle Quebec on the river. People had played shinny in the nation's capital, on the canal and the rivers, but this game was different. Not so different that they were intimidated, though. "I think we could beat those fellows," one of them said and the other responded, "I think so, too." When they returned home, they organized a team, and in early March, the Ottawa Hockey Club played its first game at the Royal Skating Rink. The next year, the OHC joined four Montreal teams at the Winter Carnival. This time, organizers requested a seven-a-side tournament and that became the standard. Except for one demonstration game at the Victoria Rink, where a large ice-grotto "slightly interfered with" the play, the matches were outdoors on the McGill campus. The 1885 tournament, indoors at the Crystal Rink near Dominion Square, included Ottawa and five local teams. The MAAA's just-formed Montreal Hockey Club won its first championship.

A smallpox epidemic meant no Winter Carnival in 1886, so the MHC, McGill, the Victorias and the Crystals created a schedule of games and agreed to a set of updated rules. The goal would be six feet high and six feet wide; sticks could be any length but not more than three inches wide at any point; and the puck "must be one inch thick and three inches in diameter, and of vulcanized rubber." A team consisted of seven players with no substitutions allowed; in the event of injury, the usual solution was for the other team to remove a player to even up the sides. This helped shape hockey's play-through-injuries code. Goalkeepers had to stand—no lying, kneeling or sitting on the ice allowed.

In December 1887, the four Montreal teams and the Ottawa Hockey Club formed a proper league called the Amateur Hockey Association of Canada; Quebec City joined the next year. Following another cancellation in 1888, the Carnival returned for a final year before collapsing under the weight of high costs and infighting among the organizers. In February 1889, several members of the Stanley family and their aides attended the opening day of the Carnival as special guests of the organizers. By the time the entourage arrived at the Victoria Rink at 9:05 p.m., the MHC and the Victorias were already twenty minutes into their match. When Stanley entered, a trumpet blared, the game stopped and the players lined up at centre ice. The band performed "God Save the Queen" and the Vics' captain called for three cheers in honour of the governor general, with the spectators joining in.

The viceregal party then made its way to the director's gallery to watch what was an especially entertaining match. "One of the finest exhibitions of the Canadian national winter game took place last night at the Victoria rink before an immense crowd," reported the *Gazette*. "Such a surging, swaying mass of dense humanity has seldom packed the gallery and promenades of the rink." Although the paper was premature in declaring hockey Canada's national winter game, the sport was a hit in Montreal. At 10 p.m., before the Vics had eked out a 2-1 victory, Stanley left the building. He and his retinue had enjoyed the match and been impressed by the skill of the players. Hockey had made a few more fans in high places.

As it turned out, a skating rink was already an annual feature on the eighty acres of rolling estate that surrounds Rideau Hall, or more formally, Government House, where governors general live. Lord Dufferin had first requested the installation of a rink in 1872 (the tradition continues today and the ice is open to the public on weekends). Shortly after his family returned from the Carnival, Arthur Stanley organized a five-on-five game.

One team consisted of three Stanley boys—Arthur, Edward and Victor—and two of their father's aides-de-camp, including Aubrey McMahon, who'd seen the game in Montreal with the Stanleys and quickly became an avid hockeyist, as players were often called in those days. They took on a team that featured at least two members of Parliament. The rink would soon be the site of many enjoyable games.

Meanwhile, hockey began to spread across the country. By the mid-1890s, more and more places in Canada had built covered skating rinks. Electric lights were safer and not as hot as gas ones, making the ice better and the growing number of fans more comfortable. In 1899, less than a quarter-century after Creighton organized the first indoor game, Arthur Farrell wrote *Hockey: Canada's Royal Winter Sport*, the first book about the game. "Played in every city, town, village, hamlet, it has aroused more public interest, more enthusiasm, than any athletic pastime that the votaries of sport have yet enjoyed, and as each succeeding year glides by, it grows in popular favor," observed Farrell, a member of the Montreal Shamrocks, Stanley Cup holders from 1899 to 1900. "Rinks are springing up everywhere, and even their greatest capacity cannot accommodate the enthusiastic crowds of spectators who rush to witness an exciting match. Like the Klondyke gold fever, the love of hockey spreads." Canadians were making hockey their favourite game.

- THREE -

"Best game I know of, hockey"

In the spring of 1879, a year after graduating from McGill, P.D. Ross was working for the Montreal Harbour Commission's engineering department. But he really wanted to be in newspapers. He'd loved his time as an editor at the McGill College *Gazette* and had, as he put it, "got the bug." Armed with a letter of introduction from a friend, the lanky young man went down to the *Montreal Star* and presented himself to Hugh Graham. The future Lord Atholstan had co-founded the populist paper a decade earlier and quickly built the largest circulation in the country. But he had little interest in hiring this eager engineer and had, he said, no openings. Besides, he took on only junior reporters. When Ross said he'd like to be a junior reporter, the publisher asked how him how much he made at the Harbour Commission.

"Twenty-five dollars a week," Ross told him.

"That is good pay for a young man," Graham pointed out. He looked relieved, figuring he'd a found a way to get rid of the annoying kid. "We don't do anything like that for a start in the newspaper business. We pay inexperienced new reporters $5 a week."

"Thank you very much, Mr. Graham," responded Ross. "When can I come?"

Defeated, the publisher said, "Oh, when you like, I suppose."

Before the new hire left the room, Graham offered some advice. He spoke slowly and with emphasis: "What I want to see in the *Montreal Star* is the sort of news, or item, or story, or article which if you saw in some newspaper or book you would be tempted to read aloud to the next person to you." A few days later, Ross reported to the city editor for work. While the publisher had been reluctant to be taking on a new employee, especially this one, that soon changed. After less than a year, the former engineer became city editor.

Long before that, Ross had "got the bug" for sports. He excelled in rowing, lacrosse, gymnastics, fencing, boxing and speed skating. At McGill, he'd made the rugby football team in his first year and later captained the side. He also played right wing for the university's hockey club, the sport's first team. The squad arranged exhibition games against social organizations such as the Metropolitan Club, whose membership included James Creighton. On his twenty-first birthday, New Year's Day, 1879, Ross began keeping a journal. That winter, he went skating at the Victoria Rink almost daily and sometimes played hockey on the river, the canal or an outdoor rink. On January 23, he wrote: "P.M. Down to the river to play hockey on the ice. Hard at work all afternoon, and came home pretty stiff. Best game I know of, hockey."

A week earlier, he'd watched the Benedicts, a team that included Creighton, play the Bachelors at Victoria Rink and was excited to be asked to serve as one of the umpires. Although he'd already graduated, Ross still occasionally played for the McGill team. "Our men (McGill) were very unfortunate, our skates and sticks breaking promiscuously," he wrote after a match in March. "Also our best player losing his head and thereby the game. Better luck next time." Ross was several years younger than Creighton, but the two must have played with or against each other in Montreal. There just weren't that many players in the city that they could have avoided each other even if they wanted to. Oddly, these two jocks also took eerily similar early career paths. Both graduated in engineering and briefly worked in the field before becoming journalists and doing stints in the Parliamentary Press Gallery. After finishing law school at McGill in 1880, Creighton worked for a Montreal legal firm, then moved to Ottawa, where in 1882, he became Law Clerk to the Senate. Ross stayed in the news business, but also ended up in Ottawa. Both men helped popularize hockey there. Despite his crucial contribution to the first modern match, Creighton's connection to the sport eventually faded, while Ross became increasingly influential.

With $50 in his pocket, Philip Simpson Ross was determined to leave Scotland for Canada. His father hadn't wanted him to go, but realizing his son had made up his mind, had offered him $250. The young man declined it. He crossed in 1851 and after a year in Upper Canada, found work as an accountant in Montreal. A few years later, he wrote a Presbyterian minister in Glasgow, giving him the names of three women and a request: propose to each of them on his behalf and if one says yes, send her to Canada. Within half an hour of landing in Portland, Maine, Christina Chalmers Dansken married Ross (they stayed together until his death fifty years later). Philip Dansken, their first of eight children, was born in 1858.

While still practising as an accountant, Philip Sr. started a company that sold supplies and equipment to ships, and after he'd "made something like a fortune," he bet heavily on real estate. In the 1870s, the chandlery business was in trouble, the victim of fraud by a colleague, and the real estate investments had turned sour. Ross was close to bankruptcy. But he worked his way back, paid off all his debts and, leaving the company to his brothers, he started P.S. Ross and Sons, which grew into one of the largest chartered accounting firms in the country.

Three of the five Ross boys ended up working for their father, but not Philip. Many prominent Montreal families might have disapproved of a university-educated eldest son with journalistic aspirations. After all, to most people from an upper-middle-class background, engineering was a respectable profession, reporting was not. But in an 1880 letter to his son, the family patriarch wrote, "With regard to your change of profession my dear son I never had the slightest objection. I never thought much of the engineers. It is a very exceptional thing to see any of them well off." He went on to add, with the help of a loose biblical quotation, "The warmest wish of my heart is to see my sons and daughters succeed in life and while I do not think great riches is a sine qua non yet I would like to help them even to that if I could. I have trained all of you and your mother has been a true helpmeet in this to 'fear God, honour the King and love the brethren.'"

So, with his father's blessing, P.D. Ross devoted himself to journalism. Shortly after receiving that letter, he left the *Star* for a reporting position at the *Toronto Daily Mail*, the Conservative organ in the Ontario capital. Indeed, it had launched in 1872 as a competitor to George Brown's Liberal paper, *The Globe*, because Sir John A. Macdonald found the city's other Tory publications insufficiently supportive. The *Star* wasn't overly partisan and politics hadn't been his beat, so Ross didn't know much about covering it. He was in for an education when city editor Tom Grogg sent him to a political meeting. The speakers were former Liberal prime minister Alexander Mackenzie and Conservative MP Alfred Boultbee. By the time Ross turned in his story, Grogg had left the newsroom, so the piece ran untouched in the next day's paper. The reporter was pleased when he saw it; the editor was not. "That sure was a rotten job you did last night."

"What's the matter?" sputtered Ross. "Was it too long?"

"It wasn't too long maybe for the right kind of stuff, but a darn sight too long for the sort of slush it is," snarled Grogg. "You gave as much space in your report to that man MacKenzie as you did to Mr. Boultbee. What the devil do you think we publish a Conservative paper for?"

Ross kept his job and had things figured out by the time he met Macdonald at a political meeting. Sir John A., who was serving his second stint as PM, overindulged in red wine at the banquet, so when it was time for him to speak, he was not in good form and kept his address short. Afterwards, Ross received a message that Macdonald wanted to see the *Mail* reporter at his hotel. When Ross arrived, the prime minister was sitting on the bed and had a towel around his head. He seemed completely sober. "Perhaps you haven't got a good report of my speech tonight," he said. "No? Well, I'd better help you. Sit down and take some notes." He then delivered what Ross considered "an admirable little speech" that lasted at least fifteen minutes before asking, "How will that do?"

"Fine," said the reporter, "thank you very much, Sir."

"All right. Send it off."

As Ross was leaving the hotel room, Macdonald added, "Wait a moment, young man. I want to give you a piece of advice." His tone turned stern. "Never again, sir, attempt to report a public speaker when you are under the influence of intoxicating liquor."

It wasn't all politics at the *Mail*. Ross moved from reporter to city editor to what must have seemed the perfect position for him: sporting editor. Celebrity athletes, including prizefighter John L. Sullivan, often dropped by his office; Ned Hanlan, the local boy who'd become the world rowing champion, was a frequent visitor. Sometimes, at the end of the day, half a dozen staffers in no rush to go home would congregate in Ross's shared office on the top floor of the *Mail* building. They'd push the desks aside and, with Ross serving as referee, two men would don boxing gloves and have at it.

Despite working for a Toronto paper, he covered the first Montreal Winter Carnival in 1883 and set the opening-day scene: "The deep blue of the winter sky was not marred by the smallest cloud, and the atmosphere was so keen and dry that the sleighs and cutters as they whirled through the streets raised light clouds of snow as fine and as penetrating as dust. Mount Royal stood out clear and cold against the western sky, fairly glittering in the sunshine over the white, jagged, and barren expanse of the ice-clad St. Lawrence." About the hockey tournament, he informed Torontonians, most of whom knew nothing of the sport, "The game is one of the finest and fastest in the world."

Away from the office, Ross continued to build his reputation as a sportsman. A member of the Toronto Rowing Club and then the Argonaut Rowing Club, he spent a lot of time in Toronto Bay. Six feet tall and wiry, he had long arms and great stamina, an ideal combination for an oarsman. Both as stroke on four-man crews and as a single sculler, he won thirty-two races, including the Canadian fours championship in 1883. He also joined the Toronto Lacrosse Club; was president of the Toronto Press Lacrosse Club; was a member of a fencing club; and served on the executive of the Canadian Rugby Football Union. But while he did skate on occasion, hockey had yet to make it to the Ontario city.

Wanting an evening sibling for their paper, the owners of the *Mail* started the *Evening News* in 1881. It also leaned Conservative, and after a new editor took over in 1883, it became a muckraking paper that was shamelessly low-brow and working-class. Ross did a stint as telegraph editor, and second-in-command, at the *News*. Meanwhile, he continued to write for Montreal's *Star* as a special correspondent and dreamed of other possibilities. One idea was to start a sporting paper, either a daily or a weekly. And he lost a chance to become *Winnipeg Sun* editor over a coin toss with Thomas Preston, then the *Globe*'s city editor. Ross flipped a half-dollar coin, Preston called heads. Preston went west.

Early in the fall of 1884, Ross was in Montreal, visiting family. His father told him that Hugh Graham wanted to see him. The city's *Morning Herald* was in financial trouble and the *Star*'s publisher was considering a plan to set up a company to buy it. If Ross could raise some money to invest in the project, Graham would make him editor. It was, he told his father, "an extraordinary opening for a young man." After his meeting with the publisher, he wrote in his journal that if he could get the money, "I may, at the age of 27, have a powerful position, a fair salary, and unlimited prospects, for I can trust Graham."

That deal didn't work out, but in the spring, Ross returned to the *Star*. He quickly moved from an editor position to parliamentary reporter to managing editor. But he didn't stay long. With bigger ambitions than just writing and editing, he wanted to own a newspaper. Ross had been in the Parliamentary Press Gallery in December of 1885 when Ottawa printer Alexander Smith Woodburn launched the *Evening Journal*. On January 1, 1887, while still in his twenties, he completed the purchase of half of the paper for $4,000, much of it borrowed against his mom's insurance policy. "No one would have paid 4,000 cents for a half interest in *The Journal* at that time had he known anything about the business side of a newspaper," Ross later wrote. The publication was losing money, was several thousand dollars in debt and had no assets. Woodburn had set it up so the *Journal* leased its plant from him and printed the paper on a press owned by his printing business. The circulation was only 1,700, and 600 of those were giveaways.

Unfortunately, the partnership between a printer who knew nothing about journalism and a reporter who knew nothing about business was not the solution to the paper's problems. The *Journal* continued to struggle so badly that Ross finally sought work elsewhere. In 1891, he accepted a job with a paper in Fort Macleod, Alberta, which he considered "the very remote far northwest." But as he was about to pack his trunk, an unexpected investor suddenly appeared.

Believing that everyone should perform some public service, Ross had joined the board of Ottawa's Central Fair. Two years later, Charles Magee, the outgoing president of the board, asked him to assume the role. When Ross said he couldn't because he was leaving town, Magee asked why. "Well—between ourselves," the young newspaperman admitted, "*The Journal* is up salt creek, I'm out, and I've booked a job elsewhere." Magee was the president of the Bank of Ottawa and had a reputation as a tough businessman who was not given to throwing money around. He liked the newspaper, but he must also have seen something he trusted in Ross. After helping him buy out Woodburn—who, despite all evidence to the contrary, insisted his half interest was still worth $4,000—Magee and two others invested $30,000 to set the paper up properly. Within two or three years, the *Journal* was profitable.

In November of 1891, his job and financial situations sufficiently settled, he married Mary Littlejohn, whom he'd met during his Toronto years. In 1893, they moved from the Grand Union Hotel, where Ross had boarded since first arriving in town, to a house in fashionable Sandy Hill. On his birthday, New Year's Day, 1894, he recorded in his journal: "Age, 36. Never better, or better off." Ottawa had been a good choice for Ross. It was no Montreal, of course. Montreal was Canada's largest and most sophisticated city; Ottawa in the mid-1880s was, by his own admission, "an unattractive town of but 36,000 people, distinguished only by the new Parliament Buildings." Yet, the old lumber village was now the fledgling nation's capital and that may have given Ross confidence that it would be a good place to live, to own a newspaper and, soon, to play a lot of hockey.

In Montreal, Ross had been well known among the sporting, social and political elites and it didn't take him long to gain similar stature in Ottawa. He was an easy guy to like: smart, curious and almost as much a fan of theatre, opera and other cultural pursuits as he was of sports; his height, lean face and athletic body made him a handsome man and he was a good dresser. All that helped him forge connections with influential people. By February of 1888, he was accepting invitations to dinners at Rideau Hall. It didn't hurt that influential people liked knowing a man who owned a newspaper and wrote editorials for it. As publisher of the *Journal*, he'd used his contacts to save the moribund paper. Influential connections would also come in handy as he helped revive hockey in Ottawa.

When he started at the *Journal*, the rival *Citizen* welcomed him "to the journalistic circles of the Capital" and added, "Mr. Ross will prove a valuable acquisition to the athletic and rowing clubs of this city, as he stands high among the athletes and oarsmen of the Dominion." Sure enough, despite his troubles at work, he was indeed heavily involved in sports. He was elected to the board of the Ottawa Amateur Athletic Association and then, after being instrumental in the construction of a three-storey clubhouse with a spacious gymnasium, he became president of the Ottawa Amateur Athletic Club. While formally opening the building in November 1889, Sir John A. Macdonald admitted that he wasn't an athlete. Then, in his remarks, Ross teased the prime minister by saying he was welcome to practise on the horizontal bar or have a few rounds, Marquis of Queensberry rules, any time he wanted.

Ross was also president of the bicycle club and the toboggan club and active in various other sporting organizations, including the rowing club. He rowed a lot in the summer and skated often in the winter. The Grand Union Hotel was at the corner of Elgin and Queen, a short walk to both the Rideau Canal and Dey's Rink. He was known for his speed on his blades. One day, he accepted a challenge from a man who bet that no one could skate along the Ottawa River to the town of Buckingham and back in under five hours. Although the skies were clear when Ross skated away from Parliament Hill at ten o'clock on a December morning, a snowstorm moved in during the afternoon. Still, he completed the round trip of forty-seven miles in just three hours and fifty-five minutes. Occasionally, he'd play shinny. In late November 1888, he wrote in his diary: "Rideau canal frozen over. Had a gorgeous skate and a game of hockey in evening."

There wasn't much in the way of formal hockey at the time given that the Ottawa Hockey Club had gone dormant. Despite twice competing in the Winter Carnival tournament and having been a founding member of the Amateur Hockey Association of Canada, the club had gone inactive in 1887 after one season in the new league, due to the departure of a couple of the leading players and problems finding suitable places to play. The Royal Skating Rink had become a roller-skating venue, leaving the Dey brothers with the only indoor ice. Once they had a monopoly, they were not easy to do business with. Also, the city had no other hockey teams, making warm-up matches and developing new talent difficult. Travel was also a problem given that the club competed in a Montreal-based league.

But Ottawa was about to become a hockey town. The establishment of the Rideau Skating and Curling Club, located next to the University of Ottawa, in early 1889 was the seminal event. Eighteen forty-two-foot-high arches supported the curved roof of the elbow-shaped structure that featured a cupola over the entrance. Inside, the building had two ice pads—one for curling and one for skating—as well as dressing rooms, a checkroom, a bandstand and a director's gallery. Lord Stanley, who'd only recently arrived in town, was the club's patron and one of the investors. He officiated at the formal opening, which included a fancy-dress carnival attended by many members of the town's high society.

As its name suggests, the club had originally been built with skating and curling in mind, but it immediately resurrected hockey in the city. Ross went to the rink almost daily, either for pickup hockey games or skating. Meanwhile, the OHC reformed, with the young publisher on the management committee. Several members of the original incarnation of the team were back; one of them, George Young, brought along his seventeen-year-old brother Weldy. The players reserved an hour of ice time on Mondays, Wednesdays and Fridays. By March, they were ready for a serious match and invited the Montreal Hockey Club to town. Ross reffed the game, and if there were any concerns about his impartiality, well, two of his brothers were on the visiting seven.

Although Ottawa lost to the more experienced opponent, Weldy Young made a strong impression. At the time, teams left it to the forwards, including the rover, to generate the offence. The defence pair consisted of a point and a cover point. Even more than the equivalent of what would come to be known as a stay-at-home defenceman, the point was originally almost a second goaltender. The cover point lined up in front of the point and was focused on defence as well. When they gained control of the puck, points or cover points looked to make a lateral pass to a forward or loft it high into the rafters to ease pressure from opponents. The puck might or might not make it down to the other end, depending on what was up there. "In the meanwhile the forwards would skate themselves dizzy trying to be in position for the puck descending from the gloom overhead," according to Charles L. Coleman in *The Trail of the Stanley Cup*. "In the rinks that were festooned with flags and bunting, the high lifts could be trapped and the puck might drop anywhere." But it was a crowd-pleasing move and one the teenage cover point excelled at. "Young got a chance and 'lifted' a hot shot through the Montreal goal from quite a distance up the ice," reported the *Journal*. "Terrific cheering greeted the Ottawa success."

Not everyone cheered this new sport, though. Some skaters complained that hockey chewed up the ice surface and reduced their ice time. Just weeks after the Rideau Rink opened, the

Journal responded to the critics by running a letter signed by "A Humble Votary of the Game" defending hockey under the head-line "A Plea for One of Our Finest Sports" on the front page. The letter contended that the game did minimal, and easily repaired, harm to the ice and took little time from other skaters. It also argued that hockey "strengthens the skating of all who play; it fosters a manly, plucky spirit; it trains the age and strengthens the wrists; makes strong arm and muscular legs and generally increases physical vitality; and when properly played is a game full of interest to onlookers." If Ross didn't write that himself, he no doubt agreed with it.

- FOUR -

*"Mr. Ross was again conspicuous
by his strong, skilful play"*

Although the natural setting was lovely—waterfalls and rapids surrounded by thick forest—the town that developed near the confluence of the Ottawa and Rideau rivers didn't have much charm. Still skittish about an American invasion following the War of 1812, the British began construction of the Rideau Canal. The 126-mile waterway connected Lake Ontario and the St. Lawrence River at Kingston with the Ottawa River. The Corps of Royal Engineers, led by Colonel John By, established a camp at the north end of the canal in 1826. Plentiful Ottawa Valley trees and power from the Chaudiere Falls made Bytown ideal for the lumber industry. But by the middle of the 1860s, the buildings, mostly wooden shanties, were sooty, the streets were muddy and the piles of sawdust were everywhere. The town lacked basic services such as sewers and water and gas systems and, with no police force, boozing and brawling and sometimes deadly clashes between Irish and French-Canadian gangs were rampant. The relentless sound of the sawmills added to the unpleasantness.

Without a wave of Queen Victoria's hand, the gritty working-class community might have, and perhaps should have, remained just another resource outpost. But in 1857, two years after Bytown became Ottawa, the monarch made it the unlikely capital of the united Province of Canada. Her choice, a compromise after parliamentarians couldn't agree, began the transformation of the homely lumber village of 9,000 people. New government buildings went up and educated, upwardly mobile white-collar workers came in. By the time the Gothic Revival Parliament Buildings opened atop the river bluff in 1866, the town's population had doubled. A year later, Ottawa became the capital of the new Dominion of Canada. Most of the politicians spent just four months of the year there and the civil servants numbered only about 350. But they combined with the growing professional class to change the town's culture. Along with more money and new expectations came different ways of socializing and spending leisure time. Soon a string of British governors general, who hosted social events at Rideau Hall, added a dash of pomp to the place.

The Russell House quickly emerged as the favoured spot for politicians, journalists and professionals. After a five-storey brick building, an example of the Second Empire architectural style, replaced the original stone structure in 1880, the hotel's standing rose further. Oscar Wilde stayed at the Russell when he came to town in 1882 to give a public lecture and ended up berating the city for allowing the dumping of so much sawdust into the Ottawa River. Celebrities aside, the hotel became a civic hub. Stores operated on the ground floor, newspapers maintained telegraph offices and just about anyone who mattered hung out, or even lived, there. Wilfrid Laurier called it home for a decade, including during his first year as prime minister. No wonder some people dropped by daily just to see who was around. Beyond its role as a day-to-day hive, it was also a popular venue for special events such as banquets and balls.

Ottawans seeking more privacy joined the Rideau Club. Founded in 1865, with John A. Macdonald serving as the first president, the elite institution admitted only men as members.

And only the right sort of men: doctors were generally more acceptable than dentists, for example. By 1876, the new clubhouse, across the street from the gates of Parliament, was a place for dining and drinking; hosting banquets; playing billiards, backgammon and cards; telling tales; and engaging in general revelry. Livery servants had to wait inside the front entrance and members checked their briefcases and business papers with the porter, though that didn't mean people refrained from discussing business. Officially, the three subjects the club did ban were politics, religion and women, but given the location and the membership, attempts to enforce the first one, in particular, must have been hopeless. And it's hard to imagine the management had much luck with the third one, either. The Ottawa Club, established in 1888, was popular with militia officers and men who couldn't get into the even more exclusive Rideau Club. Some people, including Macdonald and P.D. Ross, joined both. Though these were social institutions, their members were from the class of people that played sports.

Teams representing the two clubs faced each other in the first formal hockey match in the Rideau Skating and Curling Club in mid-February of 1889. James Creighton, who was verging on forty years of age but clearly had a knack for being part of historic games, captained the Rideaus; Ross was the captain of his opponents. The next day, the rink hosted another hockey game full of VIPs: the Military team, with three of Stanley's sons on its roster, lost to the Civilian team. Ross was the referee and Creighton was one of the umpires. A number of games between various loosely assembled parliamentary, military, Government House and civilian teams followed. And in March, Lady Isobel Stanley, a teenager who'd attended the Montreal Winter Carnival with her family, took part in the first recorded women's game. She played for the Government House team that defeated the Rideau Skating and Curling Club on its home ice.

The interest from the city's elite gave the sport some cachet, which meant the new rink did far more than restart the Ottawa Hockey Club. Even in a town where the sport wasn't a big deal yet, throwing together two sides for a friendly pickup match was not much trouble. There were many such games on the rink at Rideau Hall and at the skating club. Though the talent level wasn't always the best, the enthusiasm was high.

Eventually, the Vice-Regal and Parliamentary Hockey Club evolved out of these games. They called themselves the Rideau Rebels. The fluid roster included several political and civil service luminaries and at least two of Lord Stanley's sons plus aide-de-camp Aubrey McMahon. Rather than the Rebels, the Establishment would have been a more apt name. Of course, most early hockey players were from the professional and wealthier classes anyway. Not only were these the people who had the time and money to pursue leisure activities, they tended to go to universities and military schools and join social and athletic clubs—the organizations that fostered many of the first teams.

Creighton had retired from hockey by the time the Rebels lost their first official game in January 1890, but Ross often suited up. Another regular was John Augustus Barron, a Liberal MP whose riding included Lindsay, Ontario. In February 1890, he organized a weekend tour for the team, which adopted a uniform of crimson flannel sweaters, white trousers and white caps. With a lineup that also featured Arthur Stanley, McMahon, fellow MP Henry Ward and Ross, the Rebels beat Lindsay 4-3 on a Friday night. The next morning, the team left for Toronto. Hockey wasn't much of a thing in the provincial capital at the time. The sport had finally made it there two years earlier with a few scrimmages at the Granite Curling Club before the first official match between the Granites and the Caledonian Curling Club. The Rebels' visit generated considerable interest, especially since the governor general's son—who counted as a celebrity to Empire-obsessed Torontonians—was playing.

Sure enough, the Rebels received the royal treatment. After being guests of honour at a luncheon at the home of A. Morgan Cosby, the president of Toronto's Victoria Rink, they played an afternoon match against the Granites. On the strength of a pair of goals by Ross and two more from McMahon, the visitors jumped out to a 5-0 lead before a big, boisterous crowd at Granite Rink. But the Ottawa team nearly let it slip away before winning 5-4. Afterwards, the *Citizen* thought the Toronto team would benefit from avoiding "the rougher methods of lacrosse." But it was even less impressed by the local fans. "While the Granite players were exceedingly pleasant and agreeable," the paper reported, "some improvement on the part of the spectators might be made, especially in the direction of discontinuance of hissing and rushing upon the ice whenever a dispute arose." Meanwhile, the *Mail* expressed consternation over the violence. "It is greatly to be regretted that in a game between amateur teams," whimpered the paper, "some players should so forget themselves before such a number of spectators, a good portion of whom on the occasion referred to being ladies, as to indulge in fisticuffs."

Not everyone in town had such delicate sensibilities. That night, following a dinner in their honour, the visitors played St. George's at Victoria Rink before another large and loud crowd from elite Toronto society. The tired Rebels, playing in their third match in two days, lost 4-1. Still, the *Citizen* reported, "Mr. Ross was again conspicuous by his strong, skilful play." The trip's success led to another: in March, Ross again joined the team as it travelled to Kingston. Unlike Toronto, the Limestone City already had a healthy hockey tradition. As early as the winter of 1886, four teams had competed in a local league. The Rebels took on Queen's University and Royal Military College, losing badly both times.

Although Arthur Stanley didn't play in Kingston, he was a catalyst on the team and in the formation of an Ontario association for the game. Accustomed to England's structured leagues for sports such as cricket, he was dismayed at hockey's lack of organization. During post-game drinks in Toronto, he'd talked to representatives of the Granites and St. George's about a provincial league. Before the winter of 1890 was over, four Toronto teams arranged a tournament to determine a city champion. Late in November, Arthur Stanley, Barron and Ward and thirteen other men gathered at the Queen's Hotel (where the Royal York now stands). Stanley had just turned twenty-one, but most of the others were in their thirties or early forties.

Barron chaired the meeting in an upstairs parlour that smelled of cigar and pipe smoke and featured overstuffed chairs, cherrywood settees and elaborate mirrors. Hockey in the province needed a governing body, he said, because when the Rebels played in Toronto, the host teams, unaware of the rules, had engaged in too much rough play. By the end of the meeting, the sportsmen had unanimously passed Stanley's motion to create the Hockey Association of Ontario, which soon became known as the Ontario Hockey Association. At his son's request, Lord Stanley had already agreed to be the honorary chairman. Unable to attend, Ross sent a letter pledging his support and promising three first-class teams from Ottawa. They would join six from Toronto, three from Kingston and one from Lindsay. The delegates appointed Ross to the committee charged with coming up with rules and bylaws.

That same week, the Ottawa City Hockey League formed at a meeting in the OAAC clubhouse. The Rebels planned to join, then thought better of it after realizing they couldn't compete against Ottawa College, the Dey's Rink Pirates and the OHC. But the team continued to play exhibition games and attract aristocrats to the roster. Lord Kilcoursie joined the lineup in 1892.

That winter, Ross played some games for the team, including when it travelled to Kingston in the governor general's luxurious private railway car. By the time the Rebels disbanded in January 1894, they'd won just eleven of thirty-seven games over four years. But they were far better missionaries than players and helped popularize the sport. Not only were there more people playing the game, more people were watching.

Early in the nineteenth century, a group of Scottish immigrants in Montreal curled on the frozen St. Lawrence River. Afterwards, they'd enjoy a drink and a bite, with the losers paying. During one of these sessions, at Gillis Tavern in January 1807, twenty merchants and a chaplain formed the Montreal Curling Club. Organizations for other sports followed, especially after 1840. But athletics remained the domain of men who were part of the English-speaking elites, mostly middle-class businessmen and professionals. The truly upper class preferred pursuits such as cricket, golf, tennis and horse riding in the privacy of their own restrictive clubs.

Originally, amateur athletic clubs had plenty of their own restrictions. Not welcome were women, people of colour, the Québécois, the Irish, Catholics and anyone in the trades or other working-class jobs. Indeed, traditional British definitions of amateurism specifically excluded artisans and labourers. Some Canadian organizations explicitly banned Black and Indigenous people. Standard thinking in the Victorian era, these classist and racist policies allowed members to hang out exclusively with their own kind. A lot of these clubs were as much social as sporting. The rules also helped make sure no one had to compete against men who might be physically stronger or athletically more gifted. The British and their colonial offspring weren't the only people obsessed with amateurism. When the modern Olympics began in 1896, supposedly pure amateurs from fourteen nations, including Greece, France and Germany—but not Canada—participated in the first Games. Still, Pierre de Coubertin, the French aristocrat who founded the International Olympic Committee, was heavily influenced by what he saw while visiting English schools such as Rugby, where the upper classes sent their sons for the right education.

But the world was changing. The forces of urbanization and industrialization hit Montreal sooner and harder than elsewhere in Canada. Population density grew and working hours began to shrink, leaving more time for leisure activities. While individual competition didn't fade away, starting around 1870, team sports went through a growth spurt. In addition, people outside the elite began to take part. The members of the legendary Shamrock Lacrosse Club, formed in 1868, were Irish Catholic and working class. But even as the participation slowly became broader, the organizers and managers remained the same. A major Victorian-era fear was that urbanization and industrialization were leading to the feminization of society, making boys weak and effeminate because they were spending more time with their mothers while their fathers were away at work in a factory or an office. The response to this perceived crisis of manliness was Muscular Christianity, a dogma that celebrated physical recreation and many traditional male attributes. Sport wasn't just about good health; it fostered qualities such as comradeship, discipline and determination and represented values related to character development, morality and middle-class ideas about honour. The indoctrination started in boyhood, so there was a deeply creepy social engineering aspect to this thinking. (Even today, it remains a powerful force in Canadian society and, especially, hockey culture.)

When the lacrosse, snowshoe and bicycle clubs joined together to create the Montreal Amateur Athletic Association in 1881, they adopted the winged wheel, a symbol of progress, as the emblem. The first group of its kind in the country, it was immediately successful and quickly influential. The initial membership of 600 tripled in three years. Over time, the umbrella organization added several other sports groups, including those dedicated to tobogganing, football and hockey, as either affiliated or connected clubs. The MAAA also approached athletic clubs throughout the Dominion about creating a national organization. More than twenty-five responded positively, which led to the 1884 formation of the Amateur Athletic Association of Canada. The MAAA also served as a model for other local groups, including the Ottawa Amateur Athletic Association and its offshoot, the Ottawa Amateur Athletic Club. These bodies didn't just coordinate competition, they codified rules and regulated behaviour.

By this point, most amateur organizations no longer specifically excluded people from other races or certain jobs. Though the MAAA remained predominantly Anglo-Protestant, it added some francophones and Jewish members. But these associations remained elitist. At the opening of the OAAC clubhouse in 1889, Ross said a member didn't need a fashionable tailor to join, just be a man—whether baronet or mechanic—of good moral standing and be willing to follow the association's rules. But those rules didn't exactly encourage the participation of mechanics, and the cost of sporting equipment and membership fees was a disincentive for many working-class people. So members still tended to be businessmen and professionals. Although the OHC became the OAAC's first connected club, it wasn't strict about jobs or backgrounds and its players didn't have to belong to the umbrella organization.

That was good news for George and Weldy Young. Rather than the sons of a captain of industry, they were the sons of the fire chief, even growing up in a fire hall. Their father, William Young, moved from Quebec City to Ottawa in 1859, finding work with jewellers and joining the volunteer fire brigade. He opened his own jewellery business but sold it in 1872 when he became fire chief. Within two years, he'd turned a volunteer service with outdated equipment into a modern, professional municipal department. One of the perquisites of the job was that he and his family lived at the Central fire station. He and his wife had one daughter and four sons. George and Robert opened Young Bros., a watchmaking, jewellery and engraving shop on Sparks Street, and Weldy later worked with them.

The Youngs were just two of the OHC's twenty-five members, more than enough for two teams without precluding effective practices. In 1890, Ross became the president and Weldy Young joined the management committee. A hockey club's structure generally included a president, a secretary-treasurer, a captain and a management committee of two to four players. This executive group went to league meetings, arranged travel, booked rinks, promoted games, recruited players and handled the accounting. The captain and the management committee were also responsible for selecting who would suit up for the first and second teams before matches. That wasn't always quite as simple as picking the best players, because work commitments and injuries sometimes limited the options. Ottawa played only exhibition games that winter, but the next season, the club rejoined the AHAC and competed in the OHA and the City League. At thirty-three, Ross was a relative old man, especially compared to teenagers such as Young, but often played with the club's top seven.

The Ottawas won the City League after defeating the Dey's Rink Pirates, who wore black uniforms with a white skull-and-crossbones on their sweaters. On March 7, Ross was on the roster when the team clinched the inaugural OHA championship by beating St. George's before a crowd of nearly a thousand people, including Lord and Lady Stanley, at Rideau Rink. The governor general was no casual fan. He often attended matches and even requested changes to the dates or start times of games when they conflicted with social events he was hosting. After Ottawa's victory, the Stanleys threw a reception, commonly known as an at-home, to celebrate and thank St. George's for its sportsman-ship. Ross piled the Toronto players into hacks and took them to Rideau Hall.

The following week, the Ottawas planned to travel to the provincial capital to play two Saturday matches. But a warm spell meant the games were off—until Ross received a telegram from the OHA secretary on Friday afternoon. The weather had turned cold and the matches were on again. With little time to round up his teammates, Ross wielded his charm and his local prominence to talk at least three of their bosses into letting the players go. Among those who cooperated was the president of the British American Bank Note Company, which engraved and printed bank notes, postage stamps and financial documents—and employed Weldy Young. After Ross worked his magic, the team caught a train at 10:45 that night. It pulled into Toronto two hours late, at nine o'clock the next morning. Ross didn't dress for the afternoon defeat of St. George's in the Mutual Street Rink but played in the evening win against Osgoode Hall at the Victoria Rink. At the supper after the games, the Ottawas accepted the new Cosby Cup as OHA champions.

The growing number of paying customers at games injected plenty of money into hockey, but the players weren't getting any of it. Though the opportunities for remuneration in sports weren't plentiful, and certainly not in hockey, amateurs saw pro-fessionalism as a threat to their cherished way of life. Gentlemen competed for the pure love of the sport and participating with honour and goodwill mattered more than winning. At least that's what they maintained, though their actions often belied their words. Not only did amateurs want to win a lot more than they liked to admit, money determined many team and league decisions and was the source of many disagreements. Due to a quarrel with another team, the Gladstones refused to pony up the City League's $3 membership fee. Since the money was going toward the championship banner, the Ottawas paid it. A larger sum was at stake in an OHA conflict. The custom was to share gate receipts to help defray travel costs. When St. George's travelled to the nation's capital, the OHC gave the visitors $60, not to mention the good time Ross had shown them. Wanting a return match, the Toronto team guaranteed Ottawa $25, but then refused to honour that commitment. The OHA executive kicked the club out of the league. Those two incidents contributed to the OHC's $70 deficit for the year, but Ross and another member covered the shortfall. The disputes were especially annoying because as much as the Ottawas were proud of winning those two new leagues, AHAC hockey was better and the championship more prestigious. But in an impressive season with thirteen wins and one loss, the team couldn't knock off the MAAA's Montreal Hockey Club, which held onto the title.

Ross's hockey obsession was as strong as ever. In January 1891, a few days after helping Ottawa beat McGill before over 700 fans at the Rideau Rink, the thirty-three-year-old noted in his diary that he'd played hockey in the evening, and then gone to bed at nine o'clock. "Feeling used up," he wrote. "Too much exercise between hockey and dancing. Determined to quit dancing for a time." The next season, though, he retired from playing for Ottawa. Still, he occasionally practised with his old teammates, became club president again and sometimes lined up as cover point for the Rebels. Most winter days, he managed to work in a practice or a pickup game. Meanwhile, his social and public life remained as active as ever.

Ross caught the 5 p.m. train to Montreal and then took a cab to the Crystal Rink. Instead of playing he'd be reporting, though he paid the admission price of twenty-five cents. The next day, the headline on his story announced, "Champions of Canada." It was only early January and the 1892 season had just begun and "the famous Montreal Amateur Athletic Association hockey team" had lost for the first time in four years. But it was true: the Ottawas were the new champions. Since its inception, the AHAC had operated under a challenge system and despite growing support for switching to a schedule of games, some clubs, including the OHC, argued against any change. Initially, that worked out well for Ottawa. Until the team lost the title, all championship matches were in the Rideau Rink. That meant home-ice advantage, no more train rides to and from Montreal and more money in the team's coffers, because it received $45 from the rink for each game.

The Ottawas managed to stay champs for two months, turning aside two challenges from the MHC, two from Quebec City and one from the Shamrocks. The winning streak attracted more fans to the rink. Two thousand people, the largest crowd yet, watched a mid-February match with Quebec. The crush of humanity was so great that it periodically expelled some spectators from the mass and onto the ice, leaving the hapless patrons to try to squeeze back into the crowd. At one point, according to the *Journal*, "Play had to be stopped for five or ten minutes to give the immigrants a chance to repatriate themselves on the promenade."

Newspaper ads billed the last game of the season as the "Grand Championship Match." Montreal was coming to town for one last crack at the new champs. That's when Ottawa's run came to an end and winning the OHA's Cosby Cup again was small consolation. The club lost only one game all year, to a team it beat three times. But under the system the OHC fought to maintain, the Montrealers finished the season with the title and were, unofficially, the champions of Canada.

The idea of creating an official national championship had been around for a couple of years but no one had done anything about it. During one of the Ottawa-Montreal games, Lord Stanley chatted with Sheriff John Sweetland and mentioned he'd been thinking about donating a trophy to encourage interest in the sport. He invited Sweetland to Rideau Hall to discuss the idea the next day. During that meeting, Stanley asked him to be a trustee of the prize.

Born in Kingston in 1835, Sweetland graduated from Queen's College with a medical degree. After practising as a small-town doctor and county coroner for several years, he moved to Ottawa. He was a popular physician and was a surgeon to the General Hospital and the Carleton County Jail. In 1880, he became the sheriff of the County of Carleton, a position that made him the sheriff of the Supreme Court of Canada. A former president of the Rideau Club, he was an active and respected community member for his leadership in many charities, medical organizations and athletic associations, including serving on the Rideau Skating and Curling Club board. He loved his books, but also sports, particularly golf. At fifty-eight, his civic credentials were impeccable and everyone respected him as a man of integrity. That made him a good choice to be a trustee but, although he was a fan, he wasn't really a hockey guy.

Ross, of course, was most definitely a hockey guy. Perhaps it was no coincidence that he gave the toast to the governor general at the 1892 banquet: some accounts suggest he planted the trophy idea with Stanley. In addition, from his arrival in town, Ross had been a regular at the right parties, and his social standing was higher than ever after the financial turnaround of the *Journal*. Stanley had no way of predicting this, but a publisher and editor was a wise choice given the crucial role newspapers would play in promoting the game and the trophy.

So Ross's credentials to be a Dominion Hockey Challenge Cup trustee were impressive. Maybe too impressive, given that his involvement with the Ottawas meant he might have strong feelings about who should win the trophy. No one seemed to mind the obvious conflict of interest, though, perhaps because he was respected for fearlessness and fairness in both sports and journalism. "Condemn a man's views as much as you like," he believed, "but leave his personality alone." While he was a Conservative, the *Journal* was not a party organ. (When Ross died in 1949, his honorary pallbearers included several Conservative politicians as well as the previous Liberal prime minister, Mackenzie King, and the sitting one, Louis St. Laurent.)

Given his many years as an avid player on the ice and connected executive off it, Ross was the more active guardian of the prize. He hadn't even seen the trophy yet when he invited Kilcoursie to lunch at the Rideau Club on Saturday, April 22, 1893. The next morning, Ross rose at seven, wrote a letter to his wife, who was out of town, and, as he recorded in his journal, "also drafted Hockey Cup rules." If that diary entry makes him seem nonchalant about the responsibility, he probably was. After all, being a trustee for a sports trophy was just one more public service Ross had agreed to take on. And, like everyone else, he had no idea what the Cup would become.

- FIVE -

*"There was 'siss-boom-ah,' 'rah-rah-rah'
and several other audible tokens of imbecility
and enthusiasm mixed"*

John Sweetland carried a beautiful mahogany box with him on the train to Montreal in mid-May of 1893. He was on his way to the MAAA's annual meeting in the gymnasium of the Mansfield Street clubhouse. Putting aside the usual order of business, association president James Taylor introduced the trustee. After the "handsome looking elderly gentlemen" talked about Lord Stanley's great interest in hockey, he joked that while he'd have preferred Ottawa won the league championship, Montreal was his second choice. Then Sweetland opened the mahogany box and officially presented the Stanley Cup to Taylor, who accepted it with "a brief but very appropriate speech." The ceremony was so genteel the trustee had no idea he was stumbling into the trophy's first controversy.

A couple of weeks earlier, on the Sunday after drafting the rules for Stanley's bowl, P.D. Ross saw it for the first time when he visited Sweetland after breakfast. A week after that, the *Journal* and the *Gazette* published His Excellency's five conditions and the trustees' nine rules. The governor general decreed that winners must "give bond for return of the Cup in good order"; teams had to arrange, and pay for, engraving their name and the year on a silver ring fitted on the trophy; it must stay a challenge cup even if a club won it more than once; the trustees had the final say in disputes, with "their decision being absolute"; and if a trustee left the position, the other was to nominate a new one. The most significant condition was that it remain a challenge cup. At the time, teams, especially repeat winners, often kept trophies. A new one would appear the next year or the next tournament. But Stanley didn't want his gift to become the property of one club. Beyond that, the governor general left everything to the trustees.

Like Sweetland, Stanley was a fan of the Ottawas and wanted—maybe even expected—his favourite team to be the Cup's first winner. That was not to be. The best hockey was played in two leagues: the Ontario Hockey Association and the Amateur Hockey Association of Canada, though with teams in Montreal, Quebec City and Ottawa, the loop was far more regional than its name suggested. For the 1893 season, the AHAC dropped its challenge system and moved to an eight-game schedule. Although Ottawa beat the Montreal Hockey Club early in the season, the MHC kept the league championship with the help of a 7-1 victory over Ottawa at home in mid-February. But Ottawa won the OHA's Cosby Cup for the third straight year and the trustees' seventh rule stated that a league champion could challenge for the Cup even if it had been defeated in the other league. "The object of this," Ross added in parentheses, "is to continue the interest in the game up to the very close of the season." The Ottawas were the only club in both leagues. Offering just one team—a trustee's former club—two routes to vie for a championship might have ignited the trophy's first dispute. But no one seemed to mind.

If Ross had devised the rules before the end of the 1893 season, Ottawa and Montreal could have faced each other. But the Cup didn't arrive from England until April so it had been too late for that. Stanley and the trustees decided to award the trophy to Montreal. Their logic was sound: the team had shown its superiority by finishing two points ahead of Ottawa. If the OHC was disappointed, the winners were about to become downright unhappy.

In early May, Lord Kilcoursie wired the MAAA asking for the date of the annual meeting. A letter from Ross then informed the association that Sweetland would attend. A sub-committee had arranged to present gold rings to the nine men who'd competed for the senior team that year. The engravings read "MHC" and "Champion 1888-1893" to celebrate six straight years atop their league. (Whether or not they count as the first Stanley Cup rings is a matter of some debate.) The MAAA also planned to present a Heintzman piano to Tom Paton, the long-time goaltender, team captain and a founder of the association. With the rings, the piano and the Cup, the annual meeting should have been a great tribute to the hockey club. That's not the way it turned out.

Sweetland's visit disrupted more than the meeting's usual order of business, as it soon became clear the association's warm feelings for the hockeyists were unrequited. The players were upset that the trustees didn't communicate with them and that Sweetland would present the trophy through the MAAA. James Stewart, the hockey club president and senior team player, declared that no one should accept the Cup on behalf of the MHC, until "the proper representatives of said club had an opportunity of learning the conditions upon which said trophy was to be held." He asked the association to convey that decision to the trustees. An enraged Taylor refused to relay anything to the trustees, and if the team wouldn't receive the trophy, he would. The minutes of the annual meeting note that Taylor accepted the trophy "owing to the unavoidable absence of Mr. Stewart," though the absence was a completely avoidable boycott. Worse, the trustees handled the engraving and the silver ring around the wooden base of the bowl read: "Montreal AAA 1893."

Living in Ottawa, Kilcoursie and the trustees were unaware of the nuances of the relationship between the MAAA and the MHC. In 1884, Paton proposed creating a hockey club and won approval from his fellow directors. Although the players wore the winged bicycle wheel emblem in white on their navy blue sweaters, the team—sometimes called the Winged Wheelers—was technically just a "connected club." Unlike affiliated clubs, the MHC received no money from the association beyond small loans to buy equipment or book ice, which the team always repaid. The players maintained an independent spirit and a chip on their shoulders about their second-class status.

As the dispute dragged on into November, the MAAA considered returning the trophy to the trustees, but decided against it. The directors didn't want to offend Stanley, who'd returned to England in July, a couple of months before his five-year term as governor general was up. With his brother's death in April, he became the 16th Earl of Derby and he needed to deal with family matters. His Excellency never saw a Stanley Cup game. Nor did the directors want to do anything that "would tend to lower the name of this Association in the eyes of the general public at large." Instead, they struck a subcommittee to meet with the MHC. After the team refused to accept the Cup unless the MAAA directors apologized for receiving it, the association executive decided to hold the trophy in trust until Ross and Sweetland decided what to do with it.

In mid-February, with the conclusion of the 1894 hockey season fast approaching and nothing resolved, Ross performed a little shuttle diplomacy in Montreal. His agenda included: an AHAC meeting; a discussion with the MHC's Stewart; and attendance at a hockey game with his brother James, who was on the MAAA board. Three days later, Ross and Sweetland sent a letter to Stewart that noted, "The trustees of the Stanley hockey challenge cup learn that through an accidental misunderstanding the cup has not yet come into the possession of the Montreal

Hockey club, whose team last year won the championship." The reference to "an accidental misunderstanding" was the closest to an official apology the team would get. The same day, the trustees sent two letters to the MAAA confirming the arrangements for the handover of the trophy. The hockey club finally took possession of the Cup in March, shortly before defending it.

Just as that squabble ended, another erupted. If Ottawa successfully defended the Cosby Cup again, it would challenge for the Stanley Cup even if it didn't win the AHAC. That might have drawn unwelcome attention to the unfairness of Ross's seventh rule, but OHA politics saved him. Clubs from the provincial capital—sometimes known as Hogtown—controlled the eighteen-team league to such an extent that critics called it the Toronto Hoggey Association. In 1894, the entire executive was made up of representatives from the six Queen City teams except for one from Hamilton, and he'd recently moved there from Toronto. They finessed things such as scheduling to their teams' advantage, including having to do little or no travelling. Out-of-town squads often suffered. After winning 4-1 in the first match of a two-game, total-goal semi-final series against Queen's, the Ottawas learned they had to play the second match in Toronto's Mutual Street Rink on February 24. It didn't matter that they were the defending champions or that they had an AHAC game scheduled for that day.

The club's executive met and unanimously decided to pull out of the league in protest. Weldy Young, the captain that season, said the players realized they'd never get fair treatment from the OHA. Others agreed. "When Toronto's chances for a championship become slim, something has to bust," noted the *Kingston News*, while the *Hamilton Herald* said the league's stance "was a case of hoggey again." The departure was probably for the best. Trying to compete in two senior leagues wasn't practical and the Ottawas cared more about the eastern loop. Their fans felt the same way, showing up in larger numbers for games against AHAC opponents. And, for the Ontario league, it meant other teams finally had a chance to win the championship. Still, the heavy-handed and self-interested actions of the Toronto-run executive were a reminder that for all the blather about amateur ideals, the desire to win was powerful and often made men behave in unseemly and unsportsmanlike ways. Bitterness lingered over the Cosby Cup. The league wanted it back, but the Ottawas, having won it three times, believed it was theirs to keep. "Why, they are even asking for the return of a cup which is our property," said Young. "But we will not give it up, unless Mr. Cosby says our contention is incorrect." Although Ottawa returned the trophy in the end, the incident showed the wisdom of Stanley's insistence that no team ever took permanent possession of his Cup.

The governor general's conditions would hold up much better than trustees' rules. Ross could hardly have imagined that his first rule for the trophy would create the fewest problems and survive the longest. That Canadians never really knew the Dominion Hockey Challenge Cup by its proper name was no accident of history or something that happened slowly over time. Ross's rules began: "1. That the cup be called the Stanley Hockey championship cup."

The Victoria Rink was ready to burst. Fans brandished team colours: much blue and white for the hometown Montrealers; less red, black and white for the visiting Ottawas. Everyone made as much noise as possible. Some came armed with five-cent horns, which they blew with abandon. "It would not be right to say that tin horns tintinnabulated, but they made a much more certain sound, which the acoustic properties of the Victoria rink despatched back in heart-rending reverberations," said the *Gazette*. The paper reported the attendance as 5,000 spectators, the largest crowd the rink had ever held, and observed, "There was 'siss-boom-ah,' 'rah-rah-rah' and several other audible tokens of imbecility and enthusiasm mixed."

Ross had taken a 4:45 p.m. train from Ottawa that afternoon and eaten on the way so he could go directly to the rink. His *Journal* story said, "The excitement in the densely crowded rink was electrical." He put the crowd at 3,000, probably closer to the truth given the building's size. Either way, on a mild March 22 in 1894, two years after first learning about the Stanley Cup, Young was playing for it. Instead of an official challenge match, though, it was a game to decide the AHAC championship.

The trustees' rules included a request that the two senior leagues end their seasons no later than the first Saturday of March, leaving enough time for the champions to face each other before the ice melted. But the eastern league's 1894 season had ended with four of the five teams—Ottawa, Quebec, the Victorias and the MHC—tied. The fifth team, the Montreal Crystals, lost all eight of its games. Unwilling to travel, Quebec dropped out and, in return for a bye, Ottawa agreed to play the winner of the Vics and the MHC on the road. Whoever triumphed in that match would then meet Osgoode Hall. The Legalites, who'd won the Ontario league after Ottawa's departure, wanted to play March 17. But determining an AHAC champion dragged on too late. Even if Montreal's winter hung on long enough for decent ice at the end of March, the Toronto team realized that competing for the Cup after not playing for nearly a month made no sense and dropped its challenge.

Although the decisions by Quebec and Osgoode Hall must have seemed reasonable at the time given that trophies came and went with great regularity, it's hard to imagine Young making a choice like that. He didn't know what the Cup would come to mean, either—though he did have a special connection to it, having heard Lord Kilcoursie read the governor general's letter—but he was too competitive to give up on a chance to win something.

Even as a teenager, Young had excelled at lifting the puck, but as early as 1893, he helped changed the game when he became among the first cover points to begin scoring, or setting up, goals after making end-to-end rushes. This development meant cover points increasingly contributed to the offence. Starting in the 1893-94 season, he was most often paired with point Harvey Pulford. The way Young, whose nickname was Chalk, moved the puck and Pulford, the Bytown Slugger, slammed bodies made the duo an intimidating force. If the cover point was caught up ice after a rush, his partner took care of things in his own end. Neither fast nor fancy, Pulford didn't worry about adding to the offence: he played for seven seasons before scoring his first goal and notched only eight during his fourteen-year career.

While Pulford, who was big, strong and fit, was the more fearsome checker, nobody pushed Young around. Although he wasn't particularly large—he was a wiry 165 pounds, about average at the time—he loved to indulge in a physical game and could be hot-headed. Many opponents felt his stick across their ankles and he regularly received penalties. He also often found himself at the centre of brawls and other incidents. And he wasn't above being a little devious. When the Ottawas were under pressure from their opponents or found themselves in penalty trouble, he would fall into a faint to stop the game and buy some time. But by the mid-1890s, Quebec's high-scoring forward Albert "Dolly" Swift had seen enough of this tactic. Before a home game against the OHC, he hid a bucket of cold water. When Young slumped on the ice, Swift dumped the bucket on the prone cover point.

In March 1894, the cover point and his teammates were more focused on the AHAC title, though winning the new trophy would be a welcome bonus. All the captain of the Ottawas had to do to was lead his club over the defending champs. The papers agreed that the quality of play was high, the ice was soft and that the referee wasn't strict enough, with the *Gazette* noting,

"Hockey is not necessarily synonymous with homicide." After the home team won 3-1, excited Montreal fans spilled onto the ice and carried star rover Billy Barlow away on their shoulders. Meanwhile, Young had to be carried to his team's dressing room because between the hour of hard hockey and getting caught in the crush of fans as he tried get off the ice, he'd begun to faint, presumably for real this time, since the game was over. "Thus ended the most exciting hockey season on record," said the *Journal*, "and one which established the game in Canada in a popularity second only to lacrosse." The Cup's first champions had held onto the prize, but this time the team handled the engraving itself. It read simply: "Montreal 1894."

Ross and Sweetland surely had no idea what they were getting themselves into when they agreed to be trustees. The job must have seemed simple enough: approve challenges and ensure the honour of Stanley's donation. Before long, though, complications arose. The trustees wanted the AHAC and the OHA to sort out challenge matches between themselves, but the two leagues couldn't agree on much. Which left it up to Ross and Sweetland.

In late February of 1895, the OHA secretary wrote the trustees to inform them that Queen's had gone undefeated and won the league championship. Not wanting a repeat of 1894 when no challenge took place, Ross decided Queen's would play the MHC, which still held the Cup from the previous year, on March 9. In a bit of cruel timing, the AHAC season ended March 8, with the Victorias atop the standings. That made them, at least temporarily, the new Cup champions. The Vics were willing to play Queen's the next day, but Ross stuck to his original plan. After all, the MHC had already rented the rink, paid for advertising and made the other necessary arrangements. Switching everything at the last minute just wasn't practical. The bizarre situation may have diminished interest in the match or, more likely, no one thought it would be much of a game since Montrealers weren't about to take any OHA challenger seriously. Indeed, the MHC had already made plans to hand the Cup over to the Vics after the game. Whatever the reason, only about 400 people showed up at the Victoria Rink.

Play in the two leagues was mostly the same. A hockey match or contest lasted one hour with a ten-minute break between the two halves. When a team scored a goal, it was called a game, as in Montreal beat Ottawa three games to one. With no substitutions, players couldn't just step off the ice to rest, so they paced themselves, which reduced the tempo of games. The restriction on passing to a player ahead of the puck carrier also slowed play. Initially, with less passing, individual skills, including stick-handling and rushing ability, were at a premium. As the sport became more sophisticated, the forwards moved down the ice as a unit, making lateral passes back and forth—combination plays, they called them. The rover, the fourth forward, who was also responsible for helping out the point and cover point, often followed close behind to accept a back pass or pick up the puck if the carrier overskated it or the other team checked him. When Ottawa defeated the MHC in a January 1894 match, the *Journal* description was: "The four white jerseys would go up the ice like snow birds, with the puck twittering between them."

One difference between the two leagues involved the offside rule. Under the OHA's interpretation, a player could pass the puck ahead as long as he could "skate his fellow-players on side," by moving fast enough to be in front of his teammates before the pass was completed. But Queen's and Montreal played their match under AHAC rules. The students didn't get the referee they wanted, either. They'd asked for Young, but the trustees opted for his teammate, goalie Fred Chittick. With Barlow out, Montreal dressed Clarence McKerrow at rover, even though he hadn't played during any of the team's regular season games.

Queen's didn't complain and the first ringer in Cup history scored what ended up being the winning goal in the 5-1 game.

While the press was dismissive of the challengers' performance, the *Queen's University Journal* argued that the game was closer than the score. "We do not usually make excuses when we are defeated, and would not depart from our custom on this occasion were it not that the Toronto and Montreal papers, without exception, have given one-sided reports of the match," the paper said, before noting that the team missed J.S. Rayside's goal-scoring abilities, struggled to adjust to the larger rink and, most of all, was crushed by offside calls. By the *Journal's* reckoning, the school team scored three disallowed goals that would have counted in an OHA game.

Regardless, the Winged Wheelers had done the trustees a huge favour by dispatching the Ontario team and ensuring the Victorias were the new champions. Already facing criticism for their handling of the predicament, Ross and Sweetland would have been mightily unpopular in hockey circles if a club had won the Cup by defeating a team that no longer held it. That would have been a huge embarrassment for both the trustees and the trophy.

- SIX -

"Montrealers are keeping the puck at Winnipeg goal and raining shot after shot"

Jack Armytage arrived in Winnipeg before formal hockey did. Shinny had been popular on the Assiniboine, Red and other rivers and during the winter of 1887, teams called the Bankers and the All-Comers played a few indoor games in the Royal Rink. In January 1890, the *Manitoba Free Press* ran a short article about young men enjoying hockey every afternoon on the open-air Street Railway Rink, adding whimsically that "the ambulances wait outside for the victims." Armytage may or may not have participated in those pickup games, but the eighteen-year-old did join several other men, mostly from the business community, at an early November meeting that launched the Victoria Hockey Club of Winnipeg. Within two weeks, the Vics had a rival: the Winnipeg Hockey Club. The two squads faced each other for the first time the following month. In the fall of 1892, representatives from the Vics, the Pegs and a military team from the Fort Osborne Barracks met in the Manitoba Hotel to establish a league. They adapted the AHAC constitution and adopted a version of OHA rules. About fifty spectators had paid to watch the city's earliest games, but now several hundred fans showed up.

Armytage, who'd been elected captain of the Victorias in the fall of 1891, was "the king of the Manitoba hockeyists," according to the *Winnipeg Daily Tribune*. Originally from Fergus, Ontario, he was a multi-sport athlete who excelled at lacrosse and rugby football and was a member of the rowing four that would win the Canadian championship in 1896. He was also renowned as a physical trainer, keeping himself and his teammates in excellent shape with rigorous drills. On at least one occasion, he "was carried triumphantly off the ice by his fellow players and members of his club." In 1893, he led an all-star team that travelled east for more competition. Shortly before leaving, the Vics on the squad lost their skates, sticks and uniforms when a fire broke out in the McIntyre Rink. That might have seemed a bad omen for the tour, but the *Tribune* was full of bravado: "Hockey is not the product of a land of orange groves and miasmas, and the men who play it bear about with them the breath of salt sea spray that clung to the vikings, and the spirit of the wild north wind, and Winnipeg sends off her warriors with the warning that it must be a case of death or victory."

As it turned out, the tour was mostly a case of victory. Their hosts, who'd been reluctant to agree to the games because they couldn't imagine a hinterland team at their level, were stunned. Armytage and his teammates won eight of eleven matches, often by lopsided scores. Their first loss was to Weldy Young and the OHC, with P.D. Ross as referee, but Ottawa hockey people were impressed. "The men from the Manitoba capital are exceptionally fast skaters and good stick handlers and understand the game pretty well," observed the *Citizen*, "but they lack in team play, and it was in this the Ottawas showed their superiority." The next day, the all-stars beat the Rideau Rebels, though Ross and his teammates "made an unexpectedly good stand," losing only 3-1. When the all-stars returned home, an enthusiastic crowd met them at the CPR station and Armytage led the team through the onslaught of fans who wanted to shake hands. By the end of 1893, the city had two indoor rinks, hockey had "attained an immense hold in the public estimation" and games attracted as many as 1,000 people.

When Ross sat down to write the rules, he knew Stanley wanted his bowl to be held by the "champion hockey team in the Dominion," which meant accounting for the possible future growth in the game and the rise of other leagues. A couple of months earlier, the Winnipeg all-stars had provided Ross with evidence that the game's spread was more than just theoretical. While the trustee's regulations specifically mention the AHAC and the OHA, the eighth rule read: "Should any representative provincial hockey association outside of Quebec and Ontario desire to compete for the cup, the trustees shall endeavour to arrange means whereby its champion team may secure an opportunity to play for it." Good thing, too, because an outside challenge would come soon.

The all-star tour boosted the western province's enthusiasm for hockey, and by the middle of the decade, people played the game in just about every Prairie village. At the senior level, the Manitoba and North West Hockey League expanded to include Brandon, Portage La Prairie and the northwestern Ontario town of Rat Portage (later known as Kenora) along with the Victorias and the Winnipegs. Even with the increased competition, the Vics dominated, winning or tying the league every year in its first decade. They were ready to prove they were among the best in the country. In 1895, the Vics toured the east and won four of five games. Back home, the players attended a banquet in their honour. More than 150 gentlemen filled the Manitoba Hotel dining room. After the toast to the Queen, club vice-president Abe Code gave one billed as "The Champions of the World." He argued that before any eastern team could legitimately call itself the champions of Canada, it would have to reckon with the westerners.

Armytage felt the same way. After a 5-1 victory over the Montreal Hockey Club, a team that had beaten the Winnipeg all-stars handily two years earlier, the Vics went to the post-game festivities at the MAAA clubhouse. The captain spied the Stanley Cup in a trophy case. Central Canadian hockeyists arrogantly saw themselves as the best in the world, and Armytage knew that to prove them wrong, his Vics would have to take that bowl from them. He was determined to win it.

The arrival of the main line of the Canadian Pacific Railway in 1885 transformed Winnipeg. Grain and livestock heading east moved through the Prairie city, as did everything—from lumber to farm implements to household furniture—necessary for the settlement of the west. Eleven years later, the city's population had grown to more than 31,000 permanent residents and the business community thrived. Winnipeggers were understandably proud of what they'd built and a good way to show off would be to capture the Stanley Cup, which had yet to leave Montreal. Armytage, his teammates and a handful of hardcore fans shared that optimism when they hopped on an eastbound train in February 1896. The Winnipeg Victorias would play the Montreal Victorias in a Valentine's Day match at Victoria Rink. Sure, two teams named after the Queen playing each other in a building named after the Queen sounds like a royal parody, but Canada was just really devoted to the monarch.

Adding to the fun, the two teams wore similar colours. Garnet with gold trim and a gold buffalo on the left chest for the westerners, which is why some people called the team the Bisons; maroon with distinctive yellow Vs on the front of the sweater for the easterners. In the gloomy light of a rink, bright scarlet and deep red wouldn't seem that different, so the home team would end up wearing white sweaters.

The off-ice confusion was less amusing. For Ross and Sweetland, even naming referees had become contentious. Early on, Montreal proposed Weldy Young and Winnipeg suggested Ross. The trustee appointed Alexis Martin of Toronto. Montreal wasn't pleased, wiring, "Want Young or Chittick of Ottawa. We refuse all others." Ross didn't budge. Then the eastern team asked for a postponement because of three injured players, but the western club was already en route so the trustee decreed the game would go ahead as planned. Montreal had to play or forfeit the trophy.

Despite the quibbling, and the impressive showing of westerners on previous tours, Montrealers liberally placed bets on the assumption that the champions would school the challengers. The packed rink included twenty-five Manitobans who "gave an excellent exhibition of Western lung power" in a vain attempt to match the volume of the 2,000 or so locals. The fans in Winnipeg were no less excited. The *Manitoba Morning Free Press* newsroom's phones kept ringing as people called for the score. Hundreds of other people congregated in three hotels—the Manitoba, the Queen's and the Clarendon—to await updates.

Only a few years old, the Manitoba Hotel was the city's poshest. The Northern Pacific and Manitoba Railway built it in the French Chateau style, setting the tone for many future railway hotels in the country. Numerous towers, turrets and gables adorned the roofline of the large red sandstone and brick building. The highlight of the interior was a large, high-ceilinged rotunda. That's where John Tait, a man with a distinctive Scottish burr, disappointed the fans by announcing an early Montreal lead. Tait was the city manager of the CPR Telegraphs, which had a branch office in the hotel. But he soon read another bulletin indicating the goal had been disallowed because the play was offside. Eleven minutes into the match, the fans cheered when Armytage scored. The Bisons added a second goal nine minutes later. The telegrams tracked major developments, such as goals and injuries, so there were often stretches of anxious wondering what was going on more than 1,100 miles away. In the second half, there was a long, worry-filled wait until word came that Higgy—Winnipeg's big and talented cover point Fred Higginbotham—had broken his suspenders, leading to a delay until someone could find a new pair for him.

Once the game resumed, Montreal's Vics pressed hard to score, but couldn't get the puck past Winnipeg's George "Whitey" Merritt. One of four original club members in the game, he'd developed his "quick and reliable eye" as a lacrosse goalkeeper. He wore a walrus moustache and white cricket pads, becoming the first to take advantage of such protection in a Stanley Cup game. Given his performance in the match, it's no surprise that eastern goalies soon adopted the gear. Finally, at 9:50 p.m., Tait made an announcement "in stentorian tones, which reverberated through the great rotunda." Winnipeg had won 2-0. The assembled fans responded with triumphant cheers and exuberant handshakes all 'round before sending many congratulatory telegrams to Montreal. The announcement of the final score during the performance of *Princess Toto* at the Bijou Opera House elicited "a perfect shriek of delight." In Montreal, supporters of the western Vics made their way to the Windsor Hotel to collect at least $2,000 in winnings from their wagers.

After the traditional dinner with the host team, the Bisons left in a private railway car. They took with them $160, which was their share of the gate, and the Stanley Cup. Most of the players stopped in Toronto for a few days of celebration, so they didn't make it home until February 24. A crush of fans packed the platform and watched as the train chugged into the CPR depot. It flew the Union Jack and had hockey sticks and brooms, denoting a clean sweep, in its cowcatcher. As a brass band played "See the Conquering Heroes Come," the players climbed into open sleighs. The Cup sat in full view in the lead sleigh as the procession—including the band and the fans—made its way along Main Street, creating the first Stanley Cup parade.

A crowd of several thousand greeted them at the Manitoba Hotel. After the mayor and the club president made speeches from the bunting-draped balcony, Armytage stood up in his sleigh. The captain said he was too hoarse to give a speech, which made the crowd laugh, but thanked everyone for the warm welcome. Then the players and dignitaries made for the hotel's smoking room, where they filled the bowl to the brim with champagne. Drinking from the Cup would become a ritual that subsequent winners would gleefully follow.

Losing was a bitter blow for Montreal. A *Free Press* story claimed the Victoria Rink's caretaker "was so worked up over the defeat that he shed enough tears to almost fill the big trophy." The former champs wanted it back as soon as possible and issued a formal challenge in mid-November. The club's president and secretary took the train to Ottawa to present seven conditions to Ross and Sweetland at the Russell House on a Saturday evening. Ross met with them again on Sunday. A challenger with demands was another indication of how the trustees' role was becoming a burden.

Some of the conditions were straightforward: a share of the gate receipts, the appointment of the referee, and so on. But the eastern Vics also wanted a best-of-three series, arguing that because the challenge would take place so early in the season, they wouldn't be in game shape. Given the distance between the two cities and the prospect of more entertainment and greater revenue from more games, the trustees liked the idea. But Winnipeg refused because, everyone assumed, Montreal had denied a similar request from the Bisons before the February match. At the time, the Cup holders said it couldn't play a series because of its league schedule, though westerners believed the real reason was that the easterners didn't think the Prairie team was good enough to play more than once. The trustees urged

Winnipeg's Vics to reconsider but didn't force them. The fate of the Cup would be decided in one game on the second last day of the year.

On Christmas, young men in team colours saw the former champions off from Windsor Station. The players, "much be-furred, looked as though they were about to start on an Arctic expedition," according to the *Montreal Daily Herald*. At a stop in Rat Portage, the players began to notice the western enthusiasm and started to hear they had no chance of winning. When the entourage of fifteen, including nine players, reached Winnipeg on December 27, a large crowd greeted them with a cheer. The team rode open sleighs to the Manitoba Hotel, which would be their headquarters for the week. The next morning, 700 people watched their first of three practices at the McIntyre Rink. Their hosts also showed them around town and took them to the opera.

Despite their eagerness to see the Montrealers play, Winnipeggers were so confident that placing wagers on their Vics wasn't easy without giving four-to-one odds. Two days before the match, fans gathered at hotels and newspaper offices to learn who Armytage and Mike Grant, the two captains, had selected for the final lineups. Armytage had to compensate for the loss of Higginbotham. Another original member of the club, the cover point excelled at throwing bodychecks and carrying the puck up ice. At the end of the 1893 all-star tour, his teammates gave him an engraved watch that read: "Presented in commemoration of glorious rushes." He'd been stalwart in February's Cup victory, but died in a freak accident in September. Armytage replaced him with Charlie Johnstone, who'd been playing hockey for only a year. Other than that, Winnipeg's lineup remained the same. Montreal had a new goalie, Gordon Lewis, and Graham Drinkwater went in at forward.

In shops and hotels, and on the streets, people talked about the big game. Montreal's *Star* marvelled at the excitement and predicted police would need to keep order "to prevent the anxious crowds who cannot obtain tickets from storming the rink." The McIntyre Rink managers had been busy making upgrades. They'd removed the gas lighting and added four additional electric arc lights and opened large vents in the roof in hopes of solving the problem of mist obscuring the fans' view. They also increased the capacity from 1,200 to about 2,000. Even that wasn't going to be enough. The price for one of the 250 reserved seats was a steep $2. But that didn't stop scalpers from doing brisk business, getting as much as $25 for a pair. A Calgary man paid $15 for one and another fan traded two and a half tons of coal for a seat. For people fortunate enough to hold a ticket, the rink's doors opened fifteen minutes early, at 6:45 p.m. The lineup for rush seats and standing room started at 4 p.m. and fans of all ages stood in the cold and hoped. Several police officers kept the jostling to a minimum, but there was nothing they could do about the capacity of the building. More than half the fans who'd lined up were out of luck.

When representatives of the challengers had met with Ross and Sweetland, Young had been one of their suggestions for referee. But later, when the trustees asked each team to propose three refs, he wasn't among Montreal's choices. When no name appeared on both lists, the trustees selected Young. It's possible the eastern Vics finessed that outcome by submitting three other names, knowing the Ottawa star would be an ideal compromise candidate. The *Star* claimed both clubs were satisfied: "His record on the ice, and in the lacrosse and football fields, his well-known reputation for squareness, his courage, which has cost him many painful injuries, all go towards creating the greatest confidence in his decisions." Behind the scenes, though, the situation wasn't so rosy. When Young arrived in Winnipeg, he learned the western Vics were unhappy about an eastern man reffing the game and didn't believe they'd get a fair shake. He called on club president E.B. Nixon and told him that if he'd known the feelings against him were so strong, he'd never have left Ottawa. "Mr. Young," Nixon said, "all we want is a good square show and we will be thoroughly satisfied."

Before starting the match at a little after 8:20 p.m., the ref lined up the two teams. He had no interest in giving them a sermon, so he just said, "Gentlemen, you all know the game as well as I do. Take your positions and play." Soon it was hard to hear his "dainty little whistle" above the crowd noise. The play was fast and close and exciting. The Bisons thrilled their fans by storming out to an early lead, firing the first three goals as the visitors struggled to adjust to an unfamiliar ice surface that was eighteen feet shorter than the Victoria Rink and shaped like a long-sided octagon. They had to contend with unusual bounces in the corners. The boards were also much higher than the ones in the Victoria Rink. But in the second half, the visitors roared back and took the lead. When Winnipeg scored late to tie it up at five goals apiece, "the crowd was beside itself with joy and hats, handkerchiefs, muffs and other articles were frantically waved." The eruption impressed even the Montreal seven. "I have played many exciting championship games, but I never heard such a wild burst of cheering as went up when the score was made even," one player said. "It was like a great and prolonged roar of thunder rolling again and again from end to end of the rink."

When the visitors made it 6-5, it put "a damper on the crowd but they could not restrain a cheer for the fine work of the visiting team." The *Free Press* headline the next day announced, "The Other Vics Won." The *Tribune* observed, "Winnipeg is in mourning for her lost Valentine, her Stanley Cup." Maybe a best-of-three series wouldn't have been such a bad idea after all.

An assessment of the referee's performance was a regular part of game reports. After the match in Montreal, the *Herald* argued that Martin should have stepped aside when the eastern Vics protested his appointment and since he "had not the good grace to withdraw, he had the opportunity of making probably the most hopeless exhibition of ignorance of hockey that has yet appeared." The paper added that "nothing short of a triple X cathode ray could tell what was going on in the inner recesses of his brain." Of course, that was the view in the losing city, but even in neutral Toronto, the *Globe* noted, "Both sides were dissatisfied with Mr. Alexis Martin of Toronto as referee, claiming he was utterly ignorant of the rules, an opinion that seemed to be shared by the spectators."

After Winnipeg lost the second match, the hometown reporters refused to blame Young. The *Tribune* said he "performed his duties in a most impartial manner, and his decisions were above reproach." The *Free Press* agreed: "His position was a trying one, but he handled the two teams with such consummate skill that all little unpleasantnesses were absent. It was owing to him that the game was one of the cleanest on record." For his part, Young praised the crowd: "During all my experience in hockey matches both as a player and as an official," he said with some gracious pandering, "I never saw such an intelligent, impartial and well conducted audience."

Whether he knew it or not, the audience was far larger than just the crowd in the rink. The CPR and Great North Western telegraph companies provided detailed coverage of the game with direct wires to the arena. This had been done for other sports, notably boxing, but not for hockey. The Manitoba Hotel had promised "every move of the puck will be announced." Several hundred people made the rotunda reverberate with cheers, and groans, as they followed the play in only slightly delayed real time through frequent CPR bulletins. Late in the game they heard:

"Merritt has just stopped a hot one.

"Grant has just had a run down the rink and made a shot on Winnipeg's goal, which was well stopped by Merritt.

"The play is very fast—and just eight minutes more to play.

"Merritt has stopped several hot ones.

"Montrealers are keeping the puck at Winnipeg goal and raining shot after shot.

"Winnipeg on the defensive. Montreal is playing the best game.

"The Winnipegs are wakening up.

"Another shot on Winnipeg goal was beautifully stopped by Merritt."

At telegraph offices, smaller gaggles of fans listened to the same accounts, and patrons at the Bijou and Grand opera houses also heard updates. In Montreal, the *Daily Star* had set up a twelve-square-foot Star Bulletin Booth in the centre of the ice at the Victoria Rink, which was hosting the skating club's first fancy-dress carnival of the season. News of the game went up on eight large bulletin boards that rotated on pivots to allow one side to be visible to skaters while the other side was being updated. A brass gong sounded with each new telegram, which came so quickly that five *Star* employees struggled to keep up.

The innovation was so popular that by the end of the 1890s, telegraph reconstructions, often written with the help of sports-writers or knowledgeable fans who sat with the operators in press boxes or rinkside, were commonplace. Hotels, theatres and newspapers scrambled to make them available to fans. The only source of play-by-play coverage until the 1920s, when radio stations began to broadcast games, the updates delighted Canadians and helped develop hockey's play-by-play diction.

Not to be outdone, newspapers boosted their coverage. Several papers across the country ran stories on the first game, though often these were just briefs. More devoted more space to the second match. The Cup was now a national story. Not surprisingly, Montreal and Winnipeg papers hyped the games the most. They'd reported on the February game, including the tiff over the choice of referee, and the victory was front-page news in Winnipeg. But for the December match, the increase in reporting was dramatic. Papers in both cities provided extensive coverage of the negotiations over the challenge, the arrival of the challengers and the preparations for the game by the teams, the fans and the rink. The match made the front page again in Winnipeg, and though the victory by the eastern Vics still didn't make the front page in Montreal, there was far more coverage. The *Herald* devoted most of a page to the story, as did the *Star*, which also printed the telegraph play-by-play.

Starting with the first game and increasing with the second, the newspapers ran excerpts of coverage and commentary from the rival city and other hockey towns such as Toronto and Ottawa. As this became common practice, it showed how different fan bases saw the games. Predictably, local bias prevailed: the hometown players were gentlemen, their opponents were ruffians; the referees were too lenient on them and too strict on us. In addition, papers indulged in regional rivalries, taunting the other city with trash talk. In November, the *Gazette* chirped "the Good People of the Boom City of Prairie Province" by suggesting the westerners didn't deserve to win the February match. "The question still remains whether their last victory was a victory of hockey or a victory of luck over hockey," goaded the paper. "We are inclined to the latter opinion, for the Victorias should have won that match."

The *Tribune* responded to the trolling by reprinting the *Gazette* piece, defensively recounting the performance of the Bisons and ending by trying to stay above it all: "Westerners are rather under the impression that the article in question was written by one who has an ounce or two of spite in his make-up and that it does not express the sentiments of Montrealers generally." A few weeks later, when the teams disagreed over whether to play one match or a best-of-three series, the *Tribune* printed a letter from Montreal's Vics arguing that the early date would not allow them enough time to practise. Simply postponing one league game would allow them to go west to compete for the Cup, argued the paper. "And besides, at such a time they would be in the pink of condition, and would not have to [be] making the babyish, unmanly and unsportsmanlike excuse of playing before they were in shape, that they have made to the trustees at the present time."

No doubt the sniping helped sell newspapers and whip up local fans. But part of the subtext was the conflict between what the *Free Press* called the "effete east" and what the *Gazette* called "the Wild and Woolly West." The clash wasn't just east versus west, but old Canada versus new Canada and the urban establishment versus the pioneering spirit of the Prairies. The sport wasn't the root of the country's endless regional squabbles, but it didn't escape the wrangling, either. And yet, by providing different views of hockey, the press helped create a broader national hockey culture.

The first three years of the Stanley Cup had been underwhelming: awarded to a team without a challenge and initially refused; kept by the same club after the rival league's champions dropped their challenge; and won by one team but defended by another. That surely wasn't the way the governor general or the trustees had imagined things would go. But 1896 was the trophy's breakout year. Although Jack Armytage and his Victorias had reigned as Cup champions for less than a year, a team from outside Montreal had finally fulfilled Stanley's desire to create a national honour. The matches in February and December served notice that westerners were just as good at, and just as passionate about, the game as anyone else. Enthusiasm for the sport was exploding, the rinks were packed with fans and, in the press, the Cup was a big story. Stanley's gift mattered now. Best of all, fans in two different cities, in two different provinces—and, indeed, anywhere else in the country—could experience the same game at the same time because of the telegraph. More than an influential precursor to broadcasting, these play-by-play transmissions brought Canadians together through a shared love of hockey.

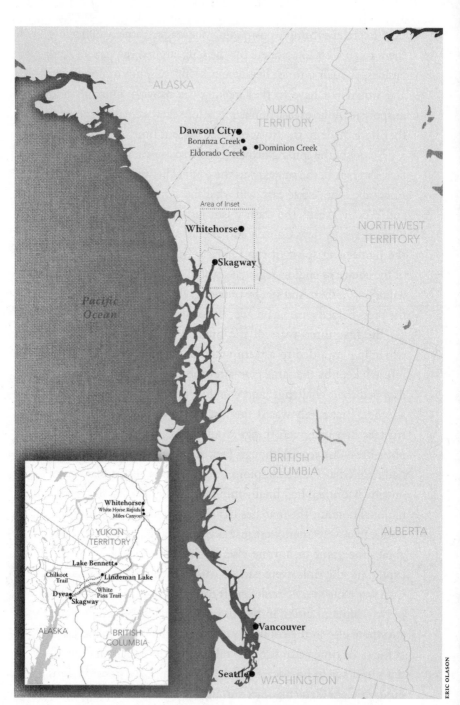

THE KLONDIKE GOLD RUSH.

Dawson City
Bonanza Creek
Eldorado Creek
Dominion Creek

ALASKA
YUKON TERRITORY
NORTHWEST TERRITORY

Area of Inset
Whitehorse
Skagway

Pacific Ocean

BRITISH COLUMBIA
ALBERTA

Whitehorse
White Horse Rapids
Miles Canyon
YUKON TERRITORY
Lake Bennett
Chilkoot Trail
Lindeman Lake
Dyea
White Pass Trail
Skagway
ALASKA
BRITISH COLUMBIA

Vancouver
Seattle
WASHINGTON

ERIC OLASON

PART TWO

- SEVEN -

*"The days were short and cold, the nights longer and colder,
and the trail seemed endless"*

Joe Boyle was restless. He was big and strong, full of energy
and blessed with impressive stamina, but those attributes
seemed like wasted gifts to the teenager. Although he did some
sightseeing during a trip to New York in the fall of 1885, he spent
most of his time down at the docks, watching the loading and
unloading of cargo. He was fascinated by the ships. According
to family lore, a sea captain noticed him there day after day and,
putting his hand on the boy's shoulder, said, "Sonny, what's the
matter? You've been here such a long time. Not in trouble, are
you? This old world isn't such a bad place after all."

"But I don't know about the world. And that's the trouble,"
Boyle told W.A. Smith, the well-built, wind-battered captain of
a three-masted barque called the *Wallace*. At first, the old salt
tried to dissuade the seventeen-year-old. Life at sea was hard, he
warned, while a college education had many benefits. Eventually,
though, he relented and signed the kid on as a common seaman.
With just two hours before he was to ship out, Boyle ran back to
the Kelsey Hotel, where he'd been staying with his brothers. He
left a terse note: "I've gone to sea. Don't worry about me. Joe."
That was the last the family heard of him for nearly three years.

Born in 1867, four months after Confederation, Joseph Whiteside Boyle was the son of a successful breeder, trainer and owner of Thoroughbred horses. Charles Boyle and jockey Charles Littlefield won many races on both sides of the border. In 1862, Palermo, a Thoroughbred Boyle trained and Littlefield rode, won the third running of the Queen's Plate, a stakes race that started fifteen years before the Kentucky Derby and quickly became Canada's premier horse event. Charles Boyle, who was a big, robust and dynamic man from a family of Irish immigrants, and the diminutive Littlefield must have been an odd sight together, but they became business partners and worked out of New Jersey. After returning to Canada, Boyle married Martha Bain, a small, quiet Scottish woman. With three sons and a daughter, the couple left Toronto for Woodstock, a small western Ontario town that was a leading horse racing centre. Boyle, who sported impressively bushy mutton chops, which were stylish at the time, was a leader in the development of modern horse racing. He won the Queen's Plate with his own horse, a three-year-old brown gelding named Roddy Pringle, in 1883. His last two victories in that race came in 1897 and 1898 with horses owned by Joseph Seagram, a wealthy distiller who'd become an avid breeder and owner of Thoroughbreds as well as a hockey team owner with Stanley Cup ambitions.

While Joe was the youngest son, he was the most like his old man. Charles saw that the boy was imaginative, bright and a good talker as well as the toughest of his children; he hoped the kid would grow up to be a lawyer or maybe go into the church. But Joe bristled at imposed discipline and was an academic underachiever. He once told his father that he was second in his class in the one-room school, but then had to admit there was only one other student in his grade. Horses and being outside were far more appealing than his studies. When the family sent him to Woodstock College, he received a solid education but the small boys' school steeped in Baptist traditions couldn't tame him. "I had always been of a roving disposition," he once said, "and though I had a pleasant home and all the comforts necessary, I wanted to travel for adventure."

He'd later admit to some loneliness and feeling like an outsider as a teenager among adults, but his time at sea was no disappointment. He rose through the ranks from deckhand to quartermaster to mate, saw much of the world and collected plenty of tales of danger, hardship and heroism. On his first voyage, the ship landed in Bombay in March 1886, laded cargo bound for Saint Helena Island and set sail again. Off the Cape of Good Hope, they began taking on water. The crew pumped as the ship struggled 4,700 miles back to Bombay. For thirty days, there was never less than ten feet of water in the hold. The ship barely made it into port, where it was condemned, but everyone survived. A family yarn had it that Boyle took command of the seemingly futile pumping efforts, working alongside the other men and keeping their spirits up when they were exhausted and ready to give up.

In an 1897 interview with Rochester's *Democrat and Chronicle*, Boyle didn't mention taking charge there, but told of the time he was on a steamer bound for Alexandria, Egypt, with a load of coal. They encountered a storm—"the most fearful one I ever witnessed"—and suffered significant damage. "For one solid week the seas ran like mountains," he remembered. "From 10 o'clock Sunday night until 7 o'clock Tuesday morning, I was the only man on the bridge. No one could possibly get across the deck to relieve me. On Monday night the binnacle lamp could not be lighted, and in the pitch dark I had to steer by the roll of the vessel." Although two other steamers were lost in the same storm, the reward for saving his ship was merely five pounds and a week's leave of absence.

By the time he returned to New York, the strapping teenager had become a handsome, square-jawed young man. His six-foot frame had filled out and he was a powerful, barrel-chested 200 pounds. He met and quickly married Mildred Raynor, an older, divorced woman with a two-year-old son. It didn't matter that his shy brother Dave was in love with her. Although Boyle was just twenty, he'd saved enough money at sea to start a business. Not enough to breed racehorses, a field he knew and had an affection for, but horses weren't only for racing. In the days before automobiles took over the roads, they were also transportation—and they needed to eat, so he launched a horse-feed and grain-delivery company. The Boyles soon enjoyed a lavish lifestyle, with a Manhattan home and a New Jersey country house, both staffed with servants, and led an active social life. His wife, who insisted on the finer things, earned the nickname Mink because of her fondness for the fur.

Eventually, Boyle became restless again. His daughter Flora believed he was unhappy in his marriage to a woman he considered frivolous—he wanted to read and study; she wanted to socialize with friends he saw as shallow—and bored with his conventional life. But Boyle would later confess that Millie left him, convinced he'd be a failure. Regardless of the reason, the couple split and he fell into a new career in sports management and promotion.

During his time on the ships, Boyle honed his innate promotional skills with a couple of side hustles. Taking advantage of his musical talent, appealing baritone and an ability to improvise new songs and cover many well-known favourites, he put on shows for sailors at port and then passed the hat. He also arranged fighting exhibitions. He was a good boxer, but his shipmates went through the crowd taking wagers "against Joe Boyle" without mentioning the opponent. That way, even if he didn't win, people would remember his name and show up the next time he fought in that town.

Later, in the United States, he balanced running his horse-feed company with his interest in sports. He managed an athletic club in Hoboken, New Jersey, where Frank "Paddy" Slavin defeated Jake Kilrain in an 1891 bout. The tall, long-limbed Slavin was a former Australian heavyweight champion known as the Sydney Cornstalk. After the end of his marriage, Boyle became the manager of the gregarious aging prizefighter and another Australian, middleweight Jim Hall. It wasn't an easy way to make money. Boxing was struggling to gain respectability as a sport and the backlash over professionalism created snags, including cancellations, when arranging fights. Worse for Boyle and Slavin, the crowds were often disappointing. A former Australian champ wasn't exactly a huge draw and the boxer didn't always win. It was a precarious existence. After an unfortunate Canadian tour—a story out of Quebec City described Slavin and Hall as "dead broke and in low spirits"—the three men moved to Rochester early in 1897. They helped establish the National Sporting Club with Boyle as the manager.

He didn't stay long. In late April, he and Slavin chased an offer of a $2,000 purse and $500 in expenses to fight Henry Baker in San Francisco. Once they arrived, though, they discovered that Baker had changed his mind and the bout was off. Instead, the California Athletic Club arranged for Slavin to fight Joe Butler. Although the Australian was the heavy favourite, Butler crushed him in a short, controversial bout. The loss ruined the chance for a fight against Jim Jeffries, who'd just defeated Butler and was on his way to becoming the world heavyweight champion. But Boyle's talent for befriending sports editors and getting stories in newspapers produced other offers. One was to take two boxers and two wrestlers to Japan. Another was in Juneau, where a man was eager to go four rounds with Slavin. If Alaska went well, they'd go back to Rochester; if not, they'd go to Japan. It all depended on how much money they could make. "When we left San Francisco," Boyle later wrote to his family, "Slavin and I had fifty cents between us, but we were as happy and contented as if our fortunes were already made."

They saw between four and twenty whales a day during their voyage up the coast aboard the SS *City of Puebla*. Landing in Victoria just before the four-day Diamond Jubilee celebrations for Queen Victoria, Boyle insinuated himself into the festivities by promoting a boxing exhibition starring Slavin and Frank Raphael, a twenty-two-year-old San Francisco lightweight who'd joined them. Facing challengers from British Navy ships stationed at nearby Esquimalt, Slavin defeated three and Raphael bested two. But in a town full of free events, only about fifty people were willing to pay to watch. In Nanaimo, Boyle offered $25 to anyone who could last four rounds with Slavin or anyone under 135 pounds able to go that long against Raphael. While on Vancouver Island, they contemplated adding the Yukon to their itinerary. Even if they hadn't already heard rumours about a gold strike in the Klondike, it would have been hard to miss "Yukon Riches," a three-part series by Dominion Land Surveyor William Ogilvie that ran in the *Victoria Daily Times* while they were there. Still, Boyle claimed to be focused on the boxing ring rather than the goldfields: several willing fighters awaited them in the subarctic. "It is twenty days' journey over land and river," he wrote from Nanaimo, "but if they put up as much as they say they will, we will go."

The trio sailed up the Inside Passage to Juneau on *The Queen*. Boyle thought it was a "delightful voyage . . . through some of the most beautiful scenery in the world." The steamer passed towering snow-capped mountains and immense glaciers and the sea was surprisingly placid. That was the last calm he'd enjoy for a long time.

Traditionally, the Hän Hwëch´in used the alluvial flat at the mouth of the Tr'ondëk River as a salmon fishing camp. This land, called Tr'ochëk, was also home to moose and migrating caribou. But that all changed abruptly after three men struck gold at Rabbit Creek, a Tr'ondëk tributary, in August 1896. The prospectors were American George Washington Carmack and two men from the Tagish First Nation: Carmack's brother-in-law Keish, known in the non-Indigenous community as Skookum Jim, and their nephew Káa Goox, known as Tagish Charlie or Dawson Charlie. Carmack wasted no time heading fifty miles down the Yukon River to a mining camp called Forty Mile to register the claims they'd staked. Upon seeing the man's shotgun shell full of nuggets, some gold seekers immediately hurried upstream. Others, particularly jaded old-timers, were initially skeptical, but soon followed.

Years before, Joseph Ladue, a veteran prospector originally from upstate New York, had figured out that selling supplies to miners was more lucrative than mining. Before the end of August, he staked a 160-acre townsite on the north side of the Klondike River. The new mining camp was eight and a half miles from the initial discovery, but it was on the Yukon River, which would prove crucial. Since the Klondike was too shallow for bigger boats, Ladue's site became a distribution point for goods going to the outlying gold settlements. The arrival of banks, merchants, hotels, theatres and newspapers would solidify its role as a service centre for the miners. But Dawson was also on a flood plain, which would soon make people realize it was an unwise place to put a town. The population swelled to 1,500 in the spring of 1897, but it was about to grow dramatically.

That summer, in Juneau, Boyle, Slavin and Raphael watched men board boats bound for the Lynn Canal as a band played "A Life on the Ocean Wave" and "The Girl I Left Behind Me." The coastal Tlingit had used five routes to trade dried fish and other marine products for furs, skin clothing and other items with inland First Nations. When fur traders from Britain, America and Russia arrived in the mid-1880s, the trails helped the Tlingit serve as middlemen. The Raven clan of Chilkoot village controlled the Chilkoot trail, which emerged as the preferred route after the U.S. Navy negotiated an 1880 deal to let prospectors climb it to get to the upper Yukon River basin. Starting by the village of Dyea, it rose sharply to the summit.

Before they received their own serenade, the boxing trio was careful to amass a sizeable outfit. The food included pilot bread (300 pounds), bacon (300 pounds), flour (one hundred pounds), beans (one hundred pounds), canned beef (one hundred pounds), corned beef (fifty pounds), canned mutton (fifty pounds), butter (fifty pounds) and sugar (fifty pounds). They also packed coffee, tea, condensed milk, prunes, mustard, oatmeal, baking powder, salt and pepper. The supplies included a sheet iron stove, a tent, a full set of carpenter's tools, a shotgun, a rifle, revolvers, hunting knives, mining tools, spare canvas, rope, matches, soap and a collapsible twenty-foot-long canvas boat. Along with their clothing, it all weighed about 1,200 pounds. They planned to hire Indigenous packers, who would charge $14 per hundred pounds, to help carry everything up the Chilkoot.

But they made a last-minute change after learning surveyors had opened a new route in late June. Starting by Skagway, the White Pass promised to be less daunting than the Chilkoot because it wound its way along the Skagway River valley to a much lower summit. A company advertising the option claimed it was ready for travellers, and Boyle, Slavin and Raphael, along with eleven prospectors, Indigenous packers and twenty-five horses, were the first group to take it. Before they left, Boyle spied a discarded banjo. He grabbed it and put on an impromptu concert, as Slavin passed the hat, before adding the instrument to his kit.

They expected to reach the summit in a day, but the footing was poor and Slavin later described the trek as "tedious, tiresome and treacherous." After three days, they reached the summit only to discover that's where the rudimentary trail ended. Boyle thought Alaska's White Mountains were "wildly, weirdly, magnificently grand," but the conditions were miserable. Between the rain, which rarely stopped, and the cold nights, the party had to use the boat canvas as a tent. And he was astonished by the mosquitos: "They are thicker than you can possibly imagine, and go buzzing about over the snow, and when a poor unhappy mortal comes along they go at him with a will and try to devour him alive." Undaunted, he took five men and went ahead to find Lake Bennett. Once he returned to the summit three days later, they still had to cut a trail so they could move their gear. By August 9, he was at Lake Bennett. Unlike others who'd made it that far, he didn't have to worry about cutting timber to build a vessel that could survive the Yukon River. He had his collapsible boat. But Slavin had been missing for two days. Despite some greatly exaggerated reports in Outside newspapers that he'd died in the wilds, the boxer soon showed up and they made their way down the river to Dawson.

Boyle's experience with both horses and boats was invaluable, but the journey from the coast to the Klondike was still demanding and dangerous. He proved himself a leader and earned the unofficial title of Captain. According to biographer William Rodney, the trip was a seminal event in his life. "Boyle, though clearly a man of firm character, well travelled, experienced, highly independent, had not yet distinguished himself in any striking way," he writes. "But the north is a merciless taskmaster, and Skagway marks a major dividing line in his life. From the moment that the trio stepped or waded ashore to start the back-breaking trek to the Klondike gold diggings, Boyle begins to stand out. In the days and months ahead his fierce determination, strong will, and quick intelligence were tested to the full."

On July 14, just before Boyle and his companions tackled the White Pass, the *Excelsior* docked in San Francisco; three days later, the *Portland* reached Seattle. The two steamships had sailed from St. Michael, Alaska, a port on the Bering Sea about seventy miles north of the mouth of the Yukon River. They carried dozens of Klondike millionaires and their new fortunes. Despite earlier reports of gold in the territory, including Ogilvie's articles, few people paid much attention until the arrival of these two ships. Reporters on tugboats met the *Excelsior* before it even made it through the Golden Gate. Ogilvie was aboard and "to escape the annoyance of several long interviews," he pretended to be a crew member. But the newspapers didn't need the expertise of the respected surveyor for their stories. The headlines in the San Francisco papers became increasingly dramatic: from "Sacks of Gold from the Mines of the Clondyke" on July 15 through "Rush for the Land of the Golden Fleece. Thousands Preparing for the Invasion of the Clondyke" and "Reports from the Far-Away Land Where the Earth Seems Lined with Gold" to "Inexhaustible Riches of the Northern El Dorado" on July 20.

Up the coast, reporters and photographers from the *Seattle Post-Intelligencer* waited two days on a tugboat called the *Sea Lion* in the Strait of Juan de Fuca. Once the *Portland* appeared, their mission was to board it and interview the passengers. The paper initially reported the ship carried one ton of gold, only half of what was actually on the ship. The understatement was surely accidental given the hyperbolic coverage that was to come. The front-page headlines of the 9 p.m. extra edition on July 17 screamed, "Gold! Gold! Gold! Gold!" and "Sixty-Eight Rich Men on the Steamer Portland." In the top left corner of the page, beside those headlines, an ad for Cooper & Levy, a Seattle outfitter, read: "Don't get excited and rush away only half prepared. You are going to a country where grub is more valuable than gold and frequently can't be bought for any price. We can fit you out quicker and better than any firm in town. We have had lots of experience, know how to pack and what to furnish." The Klondike Gold Rush was on.

Sensational, sometimes highly embellished, newspaper reporting stoked a human fetish for gold that goes back thousands of years. As the starting point for many stampeders, Seattle and San Francisco stood to benefit financially and their papers made the most of the news. But publications elsewhere were no less excited. William Randolph Hearst's empire, fresh from helping incite the Spanish-American War, sent five reporters to the Klondike and pumped the story hard with lots of front-page coverage. Publishers and editors engaged in newspaper wars loved the Gold Rush.

While the papers sold the golden dream, government officials worried about famine. As early as August, they urged people not to go. Their warnings held little sway. In the wake of an economic depression that had started in 1893, the Klondike story ignited a get-rich-quick mania. Infected with Klondicitis, thousands quit jobs upon hearing the news; others hatched schemes and touted new technologies. Nikola Tesla, the brilliant engineer who'd played a crucial role in developing the alternating-current electrical supply system, didn't go to the Yukon, but he claimed to have invented a gold-detecting X-ray machine.

For lots of the dreamers, it was about more than money or adventure. Often they were running away from something—bad marriages, bad debts, bad luck or just boring lives—as much or more than running to something. Many left farms and factories, but plenty of others were middle-class with at least some education who departed desk jobs with banks, governments or other dreary places. The Gold Rush was a chance to reinvent themselves, which is a different kind of dream, and required a certain amount of confidence, enough anyway to believe such reinvention is possible.

The Yukon River, with its hazardous sections and unforgiving frigid water, claimed many lives, but if Boyle found navigating the whitewater challenging, he wasn't about to admit it. "The trip down the river is very pleasant," he wrote in a letter, "but the nights are very cold and the mosquitos are very desperate."

When he arrived in the Klondike on August 24, more than a month after leaving Juneau, gold was everywhere and everything was expensive. Labourers made $15 a day, but the cheapest meals cost $1.50. According to his count, Dawson had about 500 tents, eighty log cabins, seventy saloons and restaurants and three stores. He and Slavin began preparing for winter by building a fourteen-by-sixteen-foot log cabin. Anything larger would be too hard to keep warm.

Although Boyle and his companions had carried mining equipment with them, in a letter from Juneau, the boxing manager wrote, "I am not a gold-fever patient and do not expect to dig gold. I have something easier." But as a teenager, Slavin had done some mining in the creeks close to his home near Maitland, New South Wales, and he would later say in his less-than-reliable autobiography that even in California, he realized his fighting career was coming to an end so he was thinking of devoting his energies to gold seeking. In October, the *San Francisco Examiner* reported, "Slavin wishes to remain and do some mining, but Raphael is fidgeting." The young lightweight didn't last long in the Yukon.

While Boyle and Slavin staged boxing exhibitions in Dawson, they learned about placer mining by working on Eldorado Claim No. 13. Then they obtained a Sulphur Creek claim and an interest in some others. All the while, Boyle imagined another way; in fact, it's possible that's what he meant by "something easier." While in California, he'd heard about mining machines called dredges that could do the work of hundreds of men. First developed in New Zealand in 1860, they used the same principles as a gold pan or a sluice box, but on a much larger scale. A dredge floated in a pond as its large bucket, or a series of buckets on a conveyer, scooped up the creek bed and poured it into the machine. Once inside, the gravel and rock moved through the dredge as water sluiced out the gold. The waste rock and water came out the other side, forming giant tailings piles.

Boyle wasn't the only person who figured technology would work in the subarctic. But he wanted to go big with massive machines and work the Klondike River, which no one was mining because the gravel was so deep. First, though, he needed to lease a large chunk of land from the government; he had his eye on thirty-seven-and-a-half square miles of the Klondike River Valley. He also needed to raise money. Before reaching Dawson, he'd said he planned to leave with the first dog team, which would have been a wiser move. Instead, in the fall of 1897, as the Yukon winter was about to set in, Boyle went Outside with William Gates. Hundreds of other people departed Dawson after the summer because of the fear of famine, but Boyle and Swiftwater Bill had other reasons to go.

A one-time well-digger in Spokane, Washington, Gates had been working as a lowly bull cook in a roadhouse near Circle City, an Alaskan mining camp near the Arctic Circle, when he heard about the Klondike strike. He became part owner of Eldorado 13. Most miners dismissed the claim as an unlucky loser, but it soon proved to be fabulously lucrative. Now rich, Swiftwater Bill devoted most of his efforts to gambling and good times. Known for his Prince Albert coat and for always—and proudly— wearing the only starched shirt collar in town, his antics generated a slew of colourful tales. One night, when Gates sat down at a faro table, luck didn't join him: in just one hour he lost gold nuggets worth $7,500. "Things don't seem to be coming my way to-night," he said as he stood up and stretched. "Let the house have a drink at my expense." The teetotaller paid the $112 tab, then lit a cigar worth $1.50 and ambled out of the saloon. Gates was hopelessly smitten with Gussie Lamore, a dancer who'd also been in Circle City. After spotting her in a restaurant eating fried eggs with another man, he bought every fresh egg—for as much as $2 a piece—in Dawson. What happened next depends on who's telling the tale. He may have bestowed them on Lamore to prove his love for her or he may have fried the eggs up and served them to dogs or he may have given them to other dancers. Whatever really happened, the gesture earned him the title of the Knight of the Golden Omelette.

Before leaving town, Lamore agreed to meet him in San Francisco. And it just so happened that he soon had an excuse to go there. The Monte Carlo Dance Hall and Saloon operated out of a tent on Front Street, but owner Jack Smith convinced Gates to invest in a permanent building for the pleasure palace. He then agreed to let his new partner go Outside in search of dancers, booze and furnishings. While Boyle was on his way to Ottawa to sweet-talk politicians, Gates was off to sweet-talk Gussie Lamore. (When he discovered she was already married and had a child, he turned his attention to her sister. To his credit, he had a sense of humour about himself. In April 1900, he attended a performance of a satirical skit called "Stillwater Willie's Wedding Night" at Dawson's Palace Grand theatre and laughed along with everyone else.)

Boyle and Gates were unlikely travel companions. The big and burly Boyle was as steady and disciplined as the small and wiry Gates was flamboyant and unpredictable. One thing they had in common was abstinence from alcohol. Boyle had given it up after an incident in New York. Following the death of a baby daughter and as his marriage was crumbling, he began to drink. According to a story he told Irish relatives, one night he was out on the town with a young boxer when a disagreement with a hansom cab driver led to the pair facing charges of drunk and disorderly conduct, threatening the driver and stealing the cab. While in jail waiting to be bailed out, Boyle said, "It's obvious I can't drink like a gentleman, and since I can't hold my liquor I shall never drink again."

"You'll get so virtuous you'll be giving up smoking next," said his skeptical cellmate.

"A good idea. I'm giving up drinking and while I'm at I'll give up smoking, too." He then gave the boxer a cigar holder that had been a gift from Slavin. "Keep it. I'll have no further use for it." He meant what he said (and later chaired temperance meetings in the Klondike).

Departing from Dawson, they followed the eddies as much as possible as they poled up the Yukon River. Although Swiftwater Bill sometimes boasted of his prowess on the water, his moniker was likely ironic, attained because he wasn't comfortable in boats. On at least one occasion, Boyle had to rescue him from the river. After the first day, there was always a thin layer of ice on their poles, which made them hard to hold. Three days in, ice floes slowed them down dramatically and began damaging the collapsible boat, forcing them to repair the bow three times. Eventually, they abandoned their craft and continued on foot. Each day, they rose at five o'clock, hunted for enough wood to build a fire to cook a breakfast and thaw out their belongings. It was too cold to make bread, so they ate flapjacks made of flour, water, baking powder and salt or, once their baking powder and salt ran out, just flour and water, which made them "as tough as an old rubber boot." Each day, after fighting the ice on the river, with only a frozen flapjack for lunch, they stopped at four o'clock and ate a dinner of flapjacks, bacon grease and smoky tea before sleeping in the snow.

At Carmack's Post, they ran into several other men, including a U.S. Mail carrier, who'd been stranded on their way out. They combined supplies, appointed Boyle captain of the expedition and continued on, snowshoeing in the deep cold along the Dalton Trail, which ran from Fort Selkirk, at the confluence of the Yukon and Pelly rivers, to Haines Mission on the Alaskan coast. "The days were short and cold, the nights longer and colder, and the trail seemed endless," he later said. They reached the mouth of the Chilkat River on November 21; the journey from Dawson to the coast had taken fifty-eight days.

While they waited in Juneau for a steamer called the *City of Seattle*, they relayed their story to a reporter. Gates, who had a round face, a short beard and a dark complexion, was dressed in a fur coat, peaked fur cap, fringed buckskin breeches, fur leggings, moccasins and "a red cravat of bargain-counter style, but the best that could be had in Dawson, and it cost him $4.50, second hand at that." Wearing a pea-sized diamond on the cravat and two bigger ones on his left hand, he carried sixty pounds of gold nuggets, worth $12,500, in his buckskin sack. Boyle expected his companion to "'blow' it all."

In Seattle, several of the men who'd made it out along the Dalton Trail celebrated at a restaurant called Maison Tortoni. The belated American Thanksgiving dinner was also a chance to thank Boyle. "He was the life of the party, his extraordinary strength being of great service to his companions in more than one difficulty," reported the *Post-Intelligencer*. "At one time he forded a river waist deep, carrying over, one at a time, the men and their packs." No doubt that was an exaggeration, but Swiftwater Bill and the others did give their captain a gold watch and chain at the dinner. The inscription read: "Presented to Mr. J.W. Boyle in token of the expedition from Dawson City, N.W.T., to Chilkat, Alaska, and in token of their appreciation of his most excellent management thereof." The legend was growing.

- EIGHT -

"Weldy Young is a great piece of stuff"

"**H**ey, kid, want to see the game?" On his way to a football match in Montreal in 1897, Weldy Young spotted a boy on the street.

"Sure do." The star back with the Ottawa Football Club had read his mind.

"Come on, I'll take you in."

Learning that the thirteen-year-old liked hockey, Young said, "Right. I'll be here with the Ottawa team next winter. How'd you like to be the stick boy?"

Lester Patrick had started playing hockey after his family moved to Montreal a few years earlier. His father had taken him to see Winnipeg's Victorias seize the Stanley Cup from the local Vics at the Victoria Rink in 1896. But serving as stick boy for the Ottawas really ignited his love of the game. That winter he began playing hockey seriously and he was good at it. Starting out in the working-class Pointe-Saint-Charles neighbourhood, the family moved seven times. Each street had its own boys' hockey team. Eventually, he played against a kid named Art Ross in wealthy Westmount. The two jocks were soon scalping tickets to senior league games, getting as much as a buck for thirty-five-cent tickets. Before long, fans would pay up to see them play. (Patrick would win the Stanley Cup six times as a player, coach and general manager; Ross would win it five times. Both would also be instrumental in the sport's development in the first half of the twentieth century.) Patrick would later acknowledge Young's role in launching his life in the game. "It just goes to show what a thoughtful act will do for a boy," he said. "Maybe I'd have got into hockey some other way but that gesture by Young set me on my way."

The Ottawa cover point had, as his kindness to that kid on a street corner showed, a generous side. He handed out thirty or forty turkeys to the city's less fortunate citizens one Christmas Eve. He once offered to furnish "the best hat that can be bought in Ottawa" as a prize for a reporters' cycling race. Young Bros. watchmaking and jewellery business had expanded into the sales and service of bikes, and Weldy was now working with his brothers, so this may have been as much about promotion as philanthropy. Regardless, he was an affable and gregarious man with many friends and an active social life.

Weldy and Robert Young were two of the charter members of the Thirteen Club, which was dedicated to "downing dark, drear and shackling superstition." The group, which formed at the Ottawa Amateur Athletic Club with thirteen members, were avid cyclists. On weekends, they'd do one-hundred-mile rides. In the winter, they played exhibition hockey games and held bowling matches and other competitions with rival clubs. But mostly they enjoyed doing things that were supposedly unlucky: they booked room thirteen in hotels; they walked under ladders; they bought lottery tickets with the number thirteen, or a multiple of it, on them; and, naturally, they always sat thirteen at the table for dinner. So while some hockey people held superstitions, Young didn't indulge in them.

As big-hearted and convivial as he was off the ice, Young could be a terror on it. He took many penalties, often five-minute ones, and played a style that led to many injuries—to his opponents and himself. Young was an early prototype of the hockeyists who follow the game's code of playing through injuries. In January 1895, a week after a crosscheck broke two of his ribs in a game against the Vics, he played the MHC. In the first half, he scored a goal and collided with Billy Barlow so violently it left the Montrealer unconscious. In the second half, an opponent jumped on his back and brought him down. Young retaliated with his stick, earning a ten-minute penalty. After he'd served it, he took such a hard hit that he lay unconscious on the ice and had to be carried to the dressing room. That was an injury he couldn't play through and he didn't return to the game.

His involvement in sports went beyond being a gifted and rugged athlete. He joined the hockey club's management committee while still a teenager, and later became team captain; served as a league vice-president; and was respected as a referee in hockey—as well in football and lacrosse—because he had "a thorough knowledge of the game and a reputation for squareness." While Young was a sportsman any city would be proud to call one of its own, he wasn't sure he wanted to call Ottawa home forever. After the 1896 hockey season, he left to go gold mining in British Columbia. At a late-March goodbye dinner at Gorman's Restaurant, Harvey Pulford and other teammates and friends honoured the cover point with speeches, songs and recitations. They also presented Young with a purse containing $110 in gold, an odd gift for someone on his way to mine the precious metal.

By mid-November, when the Ottawas had their annual pre-season meeting, he still wasn't back and his father told the club there was no guarantee he'd return. Still, his teammates were hopeful enough to make him one of three candidates to be captain, the position he'd held the two previous seasons, though goalie Fred Chittick won the vote. In early December, Young was again at Gorman's as the guest of honour during another evening of song and speeches. He'd lost weight out west, but was ready to play, though he might not have been prepared for all the off-ice drama. A few days after he returned, three newly elected officers of the executive, including vice-president Chauncey Kirby, resigned amid club squabbling. Kirby, whose brother Halder helped form the original OHC, was a small, crafty forward who wouldn't back down from bigger men. He'd joined the senior team in 1891 and had been at the 1892 banquet where Lord Kilcoursie read Lord Stanley's letter and sung "The Hockey Men." The verse about Kirby went:

> Well, first there's Chauncey Kirby,
> He's worth his weight in gold,
> For though he is not very big
> He's very, very bold.

So bold, in fact, that he refused to play that season. Young assumed the vice-presidential duties. Unhappy with the way the club had treated Kirby and George Murphy, two loyal members, P.D. Ross wrote in his diary, "Notified Young was done with Ottawa Hockey Club." Then at a meeting, the executive read a letter from the trustee announcing his resignation as honorary president.

Ross's displeasure with the club didn't stop him from asking Young to ref the 1896 Stanley Cup game in Winnipeg, which led to a rumour the Ottawa player would move to the Prairie city. "It is said that Mr. Young will not return east after the match but will permanently reside in Winnipeg," reported the *Free Press*. "He is an expert engraver and overtures have been made to remain here. Should he decide to do so his decision would be received with great pleasure by the sport loving public. He would be a valuable acquisition to one of the big hockey clubs." While he might have considered staying out west, he returned home and resumed his usual brand of hockey. In the first match of the season, the

Citizen reported, he "showed that he had not forgotten how to play, filling his position in the most creditable manner." The Ottawas finished with a winning record again. But they ended up tied for second in the AHAC, behind the Montreal Victorias, who were in the midst of an impressive Stanley Cup run.

Although Young's club was still waiting for a chance to engrave its name on the trophy, Ottawa was now a real hockey town. Even the newspapers had teams. "If there is blood on the moon or any other unusual astronomical disturbances to-morrow night, the natives need not become unduly alarmed. There will be a hockey match at Rideau rink, and if some part of nature's machinery does not get a very severe wrenching the participants will be very greatly disappointed. The opposing forces will be the employees of the *Free Press* and *Journal*, and it goes without saying that all the other games of the season will be thrown in the shade by this," according to a March 1897 *Journal* story under the headline "Hockey, Well Yes." Ross was his paper's star point. "The game will be called at ten o'clock and a competent staff of physicians will be in attendance. The ambulances have been ordered for eleven o'clock."

Though distinguished, Young's tenure with the OHC wasn't without its own controversy. He created a lot of dissension in the fall of 1897 when he briefly left the team for what he thought would be a better opportunity. In the late nineteenth century, amateurism still ruled in hockey, at least officially. But where sports had once supposedly been about character-building and camaraderie, they were increasingly about winning. The lure of championship trophies such as the Stanley Cup spurred competition, which encouraged building the best teams possible. These awards held special appeal to the civic pride of towns and cities as well as the egos of wealthy men. And if winning a championship took money—to attract stars from other towns and to give players more time to practise and become more skilled—then so be it.

Money was no problem for Joseph Emm Seagram. Born in 1841 and orphaned as teenager, he worked his way up from bookkeeper to manager at a couple of mills before moving to one that used its surplus grain to distill whisky. Over time, he bought out the partners behind the enterprise and by 1883, he was the sole owner of the Joseph Seagram Flour Mill and Distillery Company. He focused on booze, and by the 1890s, it was selling well in Canada and the United States. He'd bought a half-share of a racehorse when he was just nineteen. But now, as a rich man, Seagram was free to pursue the sport of kings with vigour. He entered a horse in the Queen's Plate for the first time in 1889, but went on to dominate the race, winning it fifteen times, including eight consecutive victories between 1891 and 1898. Joe Boyle's father was the trainer for the last two victories in that streak.

The whisky baron, whose sons played hockey, wanted a Stanley Cup. He may also have been prescient enough to see the game as a good way to promote his products. In early November 1897, he sent a representative to Ottawa to recruit talent. "Mr. Seagram, the well-known distiller and horseman, it is said is willing to put up the necessary to give Waterloo the best hockey team in the country," reported the *Journal*. The targets included rover Harry Westwick and leading scorer Alf Smith. A week later, Joe Seagram Jr. made a foray to the nation's capital to interview Westwick, Smith and Charles Spittal. That wasn't his only trip. Everyone knew why he was coming to town, but no one knew who would leave.

Once all the wooing was over, Westwick and Young, two of Ottawa's best players, surprised their teammates by accepting offers of day jobs to go with spots on Seagram's Waterloo team. They hopped on a 10:35 p.m. westbound CPR train on December 8. Eight days later, they bolted, taking a train to Toronto. The jobs Seagram had promised weren't permanent and the players weren't sticking around for anything less. Although the *Globe* suggested Young might play for a Toronto team, he went home, arriving a few weeks before the galling experience of watching another Ottawa team challenge for the Cup.

The rules Ross came up with in 1893 reveal that he foresaw some growth in the game, but not this much, this fast. New leagues had spread the sport across the country, but also created confusion and conflict, and that meant new hassles for the trustees. Even in their hometown. The Capital Athletic Association, launched in 1895 as a competitor to the OAAA, wanted its own hockey team. A year later, it had one. Not lacking ambition, the Capitals immediately applied to join the AHAC. The Ottawas didn't want another team stealing its players, its limelight or, especially, its paying fans, and the other member clubs weren't supportive, either.

Rebuffed, the Capitals formed the Central Canada Hockey Association with Brockville and Cornwall for 1896–97. Before the season was even over—with all three clubs still tied—the league wrote the trustees about a challenge. Ross and Sweetland's worst fears were coming true: if every province had several leagues, determining a provincial champion eligible to compete for the Cup would be a nightmare. In the mid-1890s, they had asked the AHAC to take over administration of the Cup, but the league refused. And as the *Ottawa Citizen* noted in early 1897, the trustees had no way out of their jobs: "They have nobody to resign to in this country and they don't feel like writing Lord Derby to tell him they can't be bothered looking after the cup."

With no other challenges that year, they allowed the CCHA winner to face Montreal's Victorias early the following winter since it was already mid-March. "The trustees beg respectfully to add however, that they may not hold this acceptance as precedent for the future," the reply stated. "Hitherto they have not had to consider what is meant by 'recognized hockey associations,' having had challenges only from provincial organizations." Approving the challenge was not the trustees' best decision. The Capitals won the CCHA championship and in December played the first match of the series with the Vics before an unenthusiastic crowd of just 600. The home team embarrassed the challengers 15-2. It was also a financial disaster for the Caps: since most of the people who watched the game at the Victoria Rink were season ticket holders, the visitor's quarter share of the gate amounted to not much at all. Thinking better of a second match, the team decided, "It would not be in the best interest of hockey generally to continue the present contest."

While Young's defection didn't last long, the resentment of some of his teammates did. Having not taken the job or any money from Seagram, he escaped repercussions from the Canadian Amateur Athletic Association. And if the OHA didn't like Young's flirtation with Waterloo, it didn't matter because of Ottawa's acrimonious departure from the organization in 1894. So in late December, Pulford, the captain that season, included his long-time defence partner when selecting a squad to face a touring Winnipeg club in an exhibition match. That choice was so contentious that other Ottawa players demanded a meeting. No one questioned Young's talent, of course. His loyalty was another matter. Worse, Young had accepted a position on a subcommittee the day after meeting Joe Seagram Jr. Not only was he disloyal, some teammates charged, he was dishonest. Not wanting to play with someone they couldn't trust, they insisted the executive committee revoke Pulford's decision, but the motion didn't pass. Unhappy with the vote, club president S. Maynard Rogers immediately wrote a letter of resignation and walked out of the meeting.

Chauncey Kirby was particularly upset. After a year away following his departure from the executive, he'd planned to return to the club. Now he threatened to retire for good rather than play with Young. Kirby wasn't the only player the team lost that year. Alf Smith joined the Capitals and the CAAA had suspended Westwick because of his involvement with the Capitals lacrosse team, which was caught up in a professionalism scandal. Westwick had been a spare man with that club and hadn't taken money so he won reinstatement after missing only three OHC games. But the turmoil continued. At a February game against the Vics, fans were surprised when Alex Cope, of the intermediate Aberdeens, was between the flags, as tending the goal was sometimes called. Many in the crowd wondered aloud, what is the matter with Chittick? The veteran goalie had walked out because he was upset about not receiving free front-row tickets to the match, as Young and Pulford had. Ottawa lost 9-5.

Young's performance that night showed off both sides of his game. He was strong on defence, lifted effectively and rushed the puck well. But he also let his temper get the best of him. Upon hearing "an unparliamentary remark by a fresh young supporter of the Vics," he jumped into the stands and bulled his way through the Rideau Rink crowd to, depending on the newspaper, seek an apology or strike the disrespectful loudmouth. Other fans scurried to the scene and Young didn't get away unscathed because the miscreant had several friends who roughed up the cover point before he could return to the ice. The *Citizen* called it "a disgusting scrap." Young's frustration might have had something to do with his club's fortunes at the time. Cope was one of five teammates to play their first game at the senior level that year; the others included a fifteen-year-old kid named Davie Gilmour. The Ottawas had been among the best clubs in the country for several years, but they'd still never held the Cup. And now, as they began to struggle while going through a rebuild, the trophy seemed further away. That season they won just two of eight league games and finished last.

At least Young's rugby football team, which became known as

the Rough Riders that year, fared much better in 1898. Pulford and a talented teenager named Frank McGee were also on the squad, which won the Canadian Dominion Football Championship for the first time. Young was a big part of that success. "Weldy Young is a great piece of stuff," the *Journal* noted. "He has been a prominent figure in senior athletics for fourteen years and is putting up better football this year than he ever did." He had trouble staying healthy, though. In a game against the Toronto Argos that was full of "plucky and effective" tackling, he broke his nose. And about twelve minutes into the championship game in late November, a play ended with several players in a heap. When the others got up, Young stayed down. After he came to, he tried to keep playing but was too groggy. He went to the dressing room, where he fainted. The doctors believed he'd "suffered an attack of concussion of the brain." The *Globe* reported that "the worst was feared," before adding, "He is now progressing favourably."

Sure enough, within a few weeks, he was back with the hockey club. Kirby returned after his second season away and the team elected him captain. Young survived his teammates' bitterness and the two veterans patched up their differences. But there were other changes. Pulford missed the season due to an injury and Westwick rejoined the Waterloo team and stayed this time. Although Ottawa again debuted some new faces, including goalie John "Bouse" Hutton and brothers Bruce and William Hodgson "Hod" Stuart, it was a more successful year. Young continued his fine play, with his customary side of orneriness. In a mid-January game, he received a ten-minute penalty for punching a Quebec player, though both the *Journal* and the *Citizen* thought that punishment was too severe. He also provided veteran leadership. One day after a late January practice, the club had some fun honouring his longevity. The trainer made a show of leading the naked player before his teammates. Then, while pouring a bucket of water on the veteran, Bob Shillington, coach of both the Rough Riders and the hockey seven, proclaimed, "I christen thee Pa Young."

Despite the ribbing, Young was only twenty-seven and still an excellent cover point. He proved it two nights later against the Vics. "Of the Ottawa team, Young was unquestionably the star. His work at times was phenomenal," according to the *Citizen*. "He repeatedly went up the ice through the Montreal crowd with apparent ease. 'Chalk' was up to all Howard and Horsfall's tricks, and the two speedy Montreal forwards were fooled many a time. Every Montrealer laid for Young, and gave him as much dirt as possible. He was tripped, struck over the legs, bodychecked and knocked about generally, but Chalk always came up serenely, and was in the game until his shoulder was dislocated." Ottawa lost but Young served notice that he was still a force on the ice. No one imagined this was his last season with the club.

- NINE -

*"In the front ranks of our
most substantial citizens"*

After surviving their trek Outside in the autumn of 1897, Joe Boyle and Swiftwater Bill Gates went to San Francisco. Joining the pair was an Indigenous guide known as Indian Charlie, who'd been travelling with them since Carmack's Post. The newspapers were fascinated by all three. When they visited the racetrack, one reporter claimed Boyle showed off a nugget "nearly as large as a football," though Gates was more likely to do something like that, if he even had a nugget that size. Then Boyle was off to Woodstock to visit his family for Christmas, where he found a message inviting him to Washington. Concerned about the danger of starvation in the Klondike, the U.S. War Department wanted him to command a relief effort using Norwegian reindeer to transport food to the North. Realizing the plan wasn't feasible, he turned down the request. Early in the new year, he made it to Ottawa. He wanted to lobby politicians, especially Clifford Sifton, for approval of his idea of leasing a large chunk of land along the Klondike River in order to bring in dredges. Understanding the significance of the Russell House to official Ottawa, Boyle checked in there.

Sifton was the powerful minister of the interior and superintendent general of Indian Affairs in Wilfrid Laurier's Liberal government, which had been elected in 1896. A lawyer by training, and still in his mid-thirties when he joined cabinet, he was energetic and ambitious. The talented, though often controversial, politician soon developed a reputation as "the Young Napoleon." His primary role under Laurier was spurring a huge wave of immigration to open up the west. But the administration of the North-West Territories was among his other duties. While Boyle was scraping his way out of the North, the minister was on his way to the Klondike. He and a large party of officials, Mounted Police, staff and one hundred dogs arrived at Skagway on October 8. Sifton went up the Chilkoot and made it as far as Lake Bennett before returning via the White Pass, so he never made it to Dawson. But he saw enough to believe in the need for an all-Canadian route to the goldfields.

The challenge of the passes was only part of it—he wanted to supply the Klondike from domestic sources. He proposed building a railway from Telegraph Creek, on the Stikine River in northern B.C., to Teslin Lake in the Yukon. From there, travellers could reach the Klondike by water. The line would be 150 miles long and, wanting it completed by September 1, Sifton contracted a company with experience in rapid railway construction. His bill passed in the House of Commons, but the Conservative-dominated Senate killed it. He then pushed Laurier to negotiate a Canadian port in Lynn Canal; for a time, the talks seemed promising but, in the end, the U.S. government refused. Meanwhile, having already imposed a ten percent royalty on all gold finds, he installed government administration and boosted police in the Yukon. Miners hated the tax, especially the Americans who made up the majority of the Klondike's population. But at least Canada allowed foreigners to mine its gold; most countries didn't. Sifton also considered applications for mining concessions.

In December, Paddy Slavin filed an application to lease an eight-mile section of land along the Klondike River with the gold commissioner in Dawson. Then he joined Boyle in Ottawa before Parliament reopened in early February. Government approval, if they could get it, was one thing. The money they required was another. By March, ads ran in Montreal's *Gazette* offering shares in the Yukon-Klondike Co-operative Mining Company and an expedition led by Boyle and Slavin, "Famed for their success in prospecting and on the trail." The idea was to take shareholders to Dawson, leaving Vancouver in late March, and put them to work under the direction of experienced miners. The company had an option on a claim on Meadow Creek. The project never happened. They also thought they had the financial backing of James J. Guerin, a Montreal doctor and a minister without portfolio in the Legislative Assembly of Quebec. But by April that deal had also fallen through.

Although Boyle wasn't about to give up, he also realized that dealing with politicians and financial backers was frustrating and far from fast. Eventually, he took the train to Vancouver and snagged a spot on one of the many overcrowded ships bound for Alaska. This time, he climbed the Chilkoot Pass, registering at the North West Mounted Police checkpoint on July 1.

The border between Alaska and Canada in the region had long been under dispute. In February 1898, Sifton addressed the issue with a bold move designed to prevent the Americans from pushing the contested territory all the way to Lake Lindeman. The NWMP, which had maintained a post inland at Tagish Lake, set up customs stations at the summits of the Chilkoot and the White Pass and armed them with Maxim machine guns.

Superintendent Samuel Benfield Steele was the lead Mountie for the Upper Yukon River district, including the summits. Big and burly with a barrel chest and broad shoulders, he had blue eyes, a walrus moustache and impressively erect posture. At fifteen, he joined a militia during the Fenian Raids. In 1873, the twenty-four-year-old was the third man sworn into the NWMP—at the rank of sergeant-major. In the early 1880s, he was the force's main man on the Prairies during the building of the CPR. Long before he came to the Yukon, he'd earned a reputation for fearlessness and for making people fear him. His time in the North did nothing to diminish that reputation. Steele's demeanour was gruff, his mindset was military and his conviction that he knew best was unshakable.

While Klondicitis compelled dreamers to drop everything and take off for the Yukon, the problem was getting there. Stampeders could choose from several options, ranging from the unreasonable to the impractical. The overland Edmonton Route meant travelling a punishing 1,500 miles while choosing a path along a jumble of ill-kept trails. One journalist called it "a species of treason." Despite Sifton's efforts, no attractive all-Canadian route ever emerged. Even the supposedly cushy all-water route proved hopeless for the first wave of gold seekers. Sailing up the North American coast took so long that none of the boats that left in the summer of 1897 reached St. Michael and the Yukon River in time for passengers to switch to river steamers and make it south to Dawson before freeze-up. Only a few dozen people who took this "rich man's route" made it to the Klondike in 1897 and they had to work hard to do so, finishing the trip on land.

By far the most popular way to go was over the Coast Mountains from Skagway and Dyea, so ships, invariably crammed far beyond capacity, soon swarmed Alaska's Lynn Canal. Despite its early promise, the White Pass proved to be no better than the Chilkoot. Though the latter was almost 1,000 feet higher, and much steeper, it had the advantage of being direct. The White Pass could accommodate pack animals, which made moving supplies easier, but it was longer, muddier and had its own challenging sections, including mountains, canyons, cliffs, boulders, bogs and rivers. Unlike the Chilkoot, though, it wasn't passable in the winter, which caused Skagway's population to explode as people who hadn't left in time waited for spring. Notorious gangster Soapy Smith treated everyone who came through town as another mark.

If they escaped Smith unscathed, stampeders still had to contend with Steele, who made them pay customs on all the supplies they brought in from the United States. Although he had no legal authority to do so, he decreed that everyone who entered the Yukon had to bring 1,150 pounds of food, roughly the equivalent of three pounds a day for a year. The typical shopping list included coffee, condensed milk, flour, cornmeal, salt, sugar, oatmeal, lard, bacon, dried potatoes, beans, dried fruit and chocolate. People also needed soap, candles and matches and gear such as a tent, cooking utensils and prospecting and carpentry tools. Steele's requirements, which the NWMP strictly enforced, meant each person's kit weighed about a ton.

Shuttling their supplies in five-mile stages, with an average of sixty-five pounds on their backs at a time, stampeders took about ninety days to travel the forty-five miles from Skagway to Lake Bennett on the White Pass. They could reduce that time by pulling larger loads on sleds or relying on horses, mules and oxen. But many had no wilderness experience or familiarity with the animals and worked them to death. "Rain fell in torrents for several weeks, making the trails knee deep in mud," according to Steele. "Oats and hay became scarce, horses and mules to the number of 3,000 died from ill-usage and starvation, choking the trail with their carcasses, and many men became discouraged and returned home." The White Pass became known as the Dead Horse Trail.

Maybe climbing the Chilkoot, which was just thirty-three miles, didn't seem so bad after all. Still, fifty pounds was about all most people could carry up that incline, which was thirty-five degrees at its steepest. That meant about forty trips. They could also hire help, but the packers, many of them Tlingit and other local Indigenous people or stampeders who'd run out of money, raised prices to meet the demand, so that was expensive. *Harper's Illustrated Weekly* sent Tappan Adney, a New York journalist who was also an outdoorsman and adventurer, to cover the Gold Rush. In his 1900 book *The Klondike Stampede*, he called both routes "confessedly so hard" and reported, "One man, who had been upon both, expressed himself thus: 'Whichever way you go, you will wish you had gone the other.'" That may explain why Boyle chose the Chilkoot the second time.

From the summit, White Pass travellers continued on to Lake Bennett. The Chilkoot led to Lake Lindeman, but many on that route kept trudging on to Lake Bennett to avoid the gnarly, boulder-filled canyon between the two bodies of water. Wherever they started, they had to cut spruce and fir trees to build boats capable of staying afloat in the swift-moving Yukon River. The 560-mile route to Dawson included two notoriously treacherous sections—Miles Canyon, a deep, narrow gorge with unclimbable granite walls on both sides, and the White Horse Rapids—as well as less dangerous, but still tricky, whitewater at the Five Finger and Rink rapids. Not everyone made it through the frothy and freezing cold water unscathed. A few drowned, others needed to be rescued and plenty lost their kits.

Steele came up with his own solution. "There are many of your countrymen who have said that the Mounted Police make the laws as they go along, and I am going to do so now for your own good," he announced before setting out his new edicts. Every boat, canoe and scow had to be registered, with the number painted on. The Mounted Police would record the names and next of kin of all aboard and ensure that every vessel was seaworthy enough to make it down the river. Boaters also had to pay experienced pilots $5 to safely run the crafts through Miles Canyon and White Horse Rapids. As authoritarian as they were, Steele's rules undoubtedly saved lives.

The majority of the estimated 100,000 stampeders who'd set out for the Klondike never made it. Most of the men and women who headed north in the summer of 1897 left too late to make it all the way down the Yukon River before freeze-up, if they even made it into Canada. An aspiring young writer named Jack London spent the winter in a cabin on the Stewart River, where he developed scurvy. Even Major James Walsh, the newly appointed commissioner of the Yukon, which was to split from the North-West Territories to become its own territory in June 1898, didn't make it to Dawson. After going up the Chilkoot with Clifford Sifton and his party, Walsh had to wait until May in Little Salmon, an Indigenous winter camp at the confluence of the Big Salmon and Yukon rivers. Many people turned back and plenty died from various calamities or diseases, including falls from cliffs, drowning, exposure, pneumonia, influenza, meningitis, gangrene, starvation and scurvy. Some took their own lives.

For those who made it, the sense of accomplishment was often mixed with disillusionment. If they reached Dawson in the fall of 1897, they found a town with so little food that residents were fleeing. If they arrived early enough the next spring, they saw people getting around town in canoes because the Yukon River flooded on May 28, sinking Dawson five feet underwater. The water subsided by June 5, leaving mud rivers where streets had been. Gold seekers who'd spent the winter in Bennett and elsewhere in the Upper Yukon began showing up June 8. They found housing hard to come by and services limited. And then there was a typhoid outbreak.

Worse, many dreamers had set out believing that at the end of their journey—which for many proved to be far harder and longer and, frankly, more ridiculous than they ever could have imagined—a fortune awaited them. Instead, they'd made it to a gold rush where most of the land was already staked. By the end of August 1896, claim-staking was complete along Bonanza

Creek, the new name for Rabbit after the discovery. Nearby creeks such as Eldorado—which flowed into Bonanza and ended up being the richest creek in the world—Hunker and Gold Bottom weren't far behind. Some newcomers had enough money to buy claims; others earned good wages working for claim holders. Most had no mining experience and though they'd fanaticized about gleaming nuggets just waiting to be plucked from creek bottoms, or at least easily panned, most of what they sought was buried deep in gravel in alluvial, or placer, deposits.

Extracting it was gruelling, hazardous and miserable work. The job first required melting the permafrost with fire or, later, steam. The fires made the river valleys thick with black smoke, giving an apocalyptic look to what had been pristine wilderness. Once they'd melted a layer of permafrost, miners scraped away the earth and rock with picks and shovels before lighting another fire to melt some more. Eventually, they'd dig a shaft down to a layer of frozen gravel that, if they were lucky, contained gold. The miners hoisted this paydirt to the surface. There, they'd run water through it in a sluice box, a narrow wooden chute with riffles at the bottom to catch the gold, which is nineteen times heavier than water, while allowing the gravel, which is only four times heavier than water, to wash out. The Yukon climate presented a problem, though. Miners had to sink their shafts in the winter to avoid flooding from surface water, but they couldn't sluice in the winter because there was no running water. So they piled the paydirt beside the shaft until the spring, when they could set up the sluice box in a stream.

Still, the dreamers kept coming. At the peak of the Gold Rush, two summers after the original discovery, the Klondike was home to an estimated 30,000 people, with about 18,000 in Dawson City, most living in tents or quickly assembled shacks. Although a lot of the stampeders hailed from the West Coast, many came from all over North America and, indeed, the world. People from forty countries briefly created the largest city west of Winnipeg and north of Seattle, a place some people called "the Paris of the North" or "the San Francisco of the North."

By the time Boyle returned early that summer, Dawson was a much different place from the one he'd left the previous fall. But unlike many of the newcomers, he knew what he was doing and had a plan. Although he made another trip to Ottawa later that summer, he didn't stay away long and mostly set about building a Klondike business empire with Slavin while waiting for a decision from the politicians. Boyle also briefly worked as a bouncer at the Monte Carlo. He definitely had the physique for it. And if nothing else, the job offered him a revealing vantage from which to watch the Gold Rush zaniness. According to legend, Dawson was a wild frontier community full of saloons, gambling dens and brothels—and unchecked crime. The myth was first created by southern journalists writing shamelessly exaggerated stories for newspapers and magazines and later solidified by the popularity of literature such as "The Shooting of Dan McGrew," Robert Service's 1907 poem about a barroom gunfight. (Service lived in Whitehorse when he wrote it and had yet to even visit Dawson, though he moved there in 1908, shortly after it was published.)

Dawson was never quite as riotous as the storytellers would have it. For a brief time, the city possessed a boisterous boomtown energy and was home to many characters, some buoyed by new wealth. While drinking, gambling and prostitution were popular pastimes, that was hardly a surprise given that a huge chunk of the population was young, single men. But it was not a particularly violent place and handguns were banned. And if the bars and brothels were full, so were the Klondike's many churches. Although the Mounted Police—or "the Boys," as Yukoners called them—kept busy with non-violent crimes, from dog-stealing to fraud, saloon shootings weren't a big problem.

When Steele arrived in September, the departure of the dreamers was already well underway. Most returned home with far more tales of adventure than nuggets of gold. In fact, many never did any mining and most of those who did found little or none of the precious metal. Some had stayed only a few days, as if just making it to the Klondike had satisfied whatever itch had sent them North in the first place. But plenty remained and more kept arriving, though in smaller numbers.

The subarctic wasn't for everyone. While Dawson was increasingly adding the trappings of a city in the south, it was, according to Steele when he first saw the place, "far from attractive in any way." The Klondike was also painfully remote and the climate was harsh. Mosquitoes and blackflies could be a curse in an otherwise stunning summer. And winter was depressingly dark and could be dangerously cold. The daylight shrank to a little over four hours and, on average, the nighttime temperatures sank into the minus-twenties. Some residents adjusted by finding outdoor recreation. During Steele's first winter in town, he saw people playing hockey and a few, mostly Norwegians, skiing.

Still, the homely town on a swamp did have its charms. For one thing, northern skies are always a marvel, with long, long hours of lovely twilight, fascinating cloud formations scudding overhead and magical performances of the aurora borealis in the fall and winter.

Boyle and Slavin began acquiring mining claims their first summer in the Klondike. By the winter of 1899, they had enough to provide work for forty men. They also operated the Arctic Sawmill, strategically located on the Klondike River, close to several of the gold-producing creeks. Providing firewood as well as lumber for buildings and sluice boxes proved lucrative. In the spring of 1899, the NWMP arrested Boyle and Slavin for operating on the Lord's Day. But the pair escaped punishment because

Steele deemed the work necessary due to the high demand for wood to build sluice boxes.

Later that spring, when the partners split, Boyle took full control of their business interests, including sawmills, timber stands and logging camps as well as mining properties. He was still working on bringing in a dredge, but Boyle was already rich and had established an enviable reputation in town. In September, the *Dawson Daily News* fawned over him: "Although from the splendid results accomplished it is evident that Mr. Boyle has worked hard and incessantly, his work has had no ill effects, for there is no finer specimen of physical manhood in the world today—his magnificent physique, great strength and happy, sympathetic nature, coupled with a total abstinence from liquor or tobacco make him an ideal character for this rigorous climate."

Aside from his business acumen, he was respected for helping make Dawson a better place. When Front Street became impassable for horse teams in the fall of 1898, he led the effort to lay a slab road, completing the job in one day. He served on the Board of Trade's Legislation and Municipal Affairs Committee; advocated a special tax to support St. Mary's Hospital; raised $1,741 at a benefit for the indigent poor fund in the winter of 1899; and hosted an annual picnic for Dawson's children. Boyle was, according to the *Klondike Nugget*, "in the front ranks of our most substantial citizens."

All that esteem didn't mean he had no critics or rivals, especially after the federal government finally granted him a hydraulic mining lease in November 1900, creating the Boyle Concession. From the early days, he had an erratic relationship with Arthur Newton Christian Treadgold. A clever, smooth-talking Englishman who claimed to be a descendent of Sir Isaac Newton, he'd heard about Klondike gold at a party early in 1897. His source, a Torontonian going to school in England, was the sister-in-law of Charles Constantine, the NWMP inspector in the Yukon at the time. Although Treadgold possessed two degrees from Oxford, and held a teaching job at a prestigious school, he headed to Canada in January 1898. Before he left, he secured assignments to write about the Gold Rush and the Canadian West from the Manchester *Guardian* and London's *Mining Journal*. He used his status as special correspondent for the publications to meet influential people such as Sifton.

Boyle and Treadgold both stayed at the Russell House early in 1898. Though they had decidedly different personalities, the two enjoyed each other's company and spent many hours discussing gold mining and the Klondike. The Englishman made it to Dawson by early summer. Like everyone else who arrived then, he was too late to stake a claim but was full of ideas. He worked for wages, making some money and gathering information as he plotted his next moves. After just one summer in the Yukon, he produced a book confidently titled *An English Expert on the Klondike*. But it soon became clear that he was more concerned with mining than writing. Small but thickset, he was wily, alert and tenacious. He observed that many miners worked a claim quickly and crudely and then abandoned it, leaving gold behind in the tailings. Hydraulic mining, which used high-pressure water to melt the permafrost and push the gravel into sluice boxes, was a better approach. But the creeks didn't have enough water so he wanted Sifton to grant him a Klondike River concession giving him access to all he needed. At some point, Treadgold also imagined big dredges, or stole the idea from Boyle. Over the next decade and a half, the two men would sometimes work together and sometimes be bitter adversaries in the goldfields.

Boyle was the more popular of the two in town. He was already a respected member of the community, a philanthropist and a civic-minded man. Charming, gregarious and an entertaining storyteller, he could be modest about himself. But deep down, he was a promoter—of pass-the-hat concerts, boxing matches, mining projects—so he knew how to sell and his powers of exaggeration were acute. Although no expert at hockey, he was a leading sportsman in the Klondike and would play a central off-ice role in Dawson City's Stanley Cup challenge.

- TEN -

"When professionalism begins,
true sports ends"

E ven before construction was complete, the new building going up at the Montreal corner of St. Catherine Street and Wood Avenue in the fall of 1898 revealed so much about the state of hockey at the end of the century. The Victoria Skating Rink, the Duluth Avenue Rink and the Crystal Rink were no longer big enough for all the paying fans. Realizing that owning a building made more sense than taking a share of the gate in someone else's, some MAAA members, including the amateur association's president, created the Montreal Arena Company. They sold 7,000 shares at $5 each. The investors weren't worried about stylish architecture. The structure, constructed of wood and clad with red brick, had a utilitarian exterior with three arched entrances at the front. The word "arena" appeared above the middle arch.

Even that name was significant, though not because, as the *Montreal Star* suggested, "it conjures up visions of the fights of gladiators, the struggles of the early Christians against wild beasts." All previous curling and skating venues, indoor or out, had been called rinks. Indeed, press accounts often redundantly referred to "the Arena rink." Also known as the Montreal Arena or the Westmount Arena, it wasn't just bigger than what came before. While it hosted a variety of events, from concerts to flower shows to movie screenings, it was the first building developed especially for hockey, which is to say, it was the first one designed for hockey spectators.

Steel trusses held the pitched roof over a natural ice surface that was 200 feet by eighty-five feet (the dimensions of today's National Hockey League rinks). The rounded corners were one innovation; another was the four-foot-high wooden fence that enclosed the Arena's ice. Caroming the puck off these boards became an effective tactic. So did bodychecking opponents into them, leading to more aggressive play. But the Arena's benefits to spectators were even greater. It featured private boxes close to the ice, and the tiered seating, which rose from ice level to the second floor, offered an unobstructed view to 4,000 fans. There was also ample standing room on the promenade around the top row of seats. To keep chilly patrons comfortable, the building offered a heated dressing room for women and rented blankets for a dime in the auditorium. The Victoria Rifles band provided entertainment during waits and there was "a well conducted refreshment room, where people can compare notes during the intermissions."

Not that many years earlier, rink owners, who faced taxes, insurance, maintenance and other costs, had been reluctant to rent their ice to hockey teams. Charging skaters was a better way to make money. Once owners realized fans were willing to pay to watch matches, especially when the best players competed, they became promoters, offering teams a share of the gate. The growing number of popular teams and paying spectators, and the hunt for more profit, created the need for venues such as the Arena.

The men with the buildings were hardly the only ones getting rich. The railways, which had made competition between towns practical, also profited: trains didn't just transport the players, they also encouraged fans to see their favourite teams play away games. Soon they regularly ran newspaper ads for reduced-fare jaunts on special trains. As early as February 1891, before a match with Montreal at the Crystal Rink, both the Canadian Pacific Railway and the Canada Atlantic Railway offered $2.50 excursion rates to Ottawa fans. The team was taking the CPR and encouraged fans to do the same. Three years later, Montreal negotiated a $2 rate to Ottawa by guaranteeing 200 supporters would take advantage of the deal.

These excursions were also popular with small-town fans. Essentially party trains, they were thick with cigar smoke and rambunctious passengers passing around bottles and flasks. Once the steam locomotive reached its destination, the train crew often joined the rowdy march to the rink to watch the game. According to Scott Young in *100 Years of Dropping the Puck: A History of the OHA*, "They'd make their bets, shout their cheers, the home folks would shout and sing back, and then there'd be the action—while the train puffed quietly at rest in the station ready for the homebound run's exuberant noise or grumpy silence, depending on the score."

That some railroads also owned telegraph companies, which promoted the sport by offering the early "broadcasts" of games, was a clever, if originally unexpected, bit of corporate synergy. Newspapers also reaped rewards. Fans followed the sport by buying papers, which devoted more, and more prominent, space to hockey coverage. Along with increased circulation revenue, publishers sold their sports pages to advertisers as men's pages. The popularity of marquee teams spurred more people to play the game, which boosted equipment sales. That was good for big retailers, including Eaton's, Simpson's and Woodward's, as well as local stores, and companies such as skate-maker Starr Manufacturing of Dartmouth, Nova Scotia, which also handled the sale of Mi'kmaq sticks, but called them Mic-Mac. In 1897, A.G. Spalding & Company, the American sporting goods manufacturer, promoted the game—and its products—by publishing a manual called the *1898 Ice Hockey and Ice Polo Guide and Playing*

Rules. Two years later, it published a Canadian version. Retailers and manufacturers also advertised in newspapers.

Even amateur athletic clubs and associations made money. The MAAA, for example, removed a ban on charging admission from its constitution in 1886. When Montreal clubs played in the Victoria, Crystal and Duluth rinks, they received half the ticket revenue. The move to the Arena meant getting forty percent of a much larger gate. Some league and team officers received three-figure honoraria, but under amateur rules the guys battling it out on the ice never saw any of the money. The entire situation was so hypocritical that it was ludicrous: hockey was now a profitable industry—for everyone except the players, who were, after all, the essential element in the whole enterprise.

The Ontario Hockey Association wouldn't have it any other way. Amateur wasn't in the league's name, but it was a bedrock tenet. Perhaps the founders left the word out because it was too obvious to include. Since its formation in 1890, the OHA had grown rapidly in size and influence as urbanization and trains made wider competition possible. So many towns wanted franchises the organization added a junior series, initially with no age limit, for the 1892–93 season and an intermediate series three years later. The problem for all adherents of amateurism was that as athletic competitions became spectator sports, they joined the entertainment industry. Baseball had a professional league five years before the creation of the National League in 1876, which led to pro teams in Canada. Boxing had an uncomfortable mix of professionals and amateurs. Champion rower Ned Hanlan, the first Canadian to hold a world title, became a pro in the 1870s. And by the 1890s, money was moving into the home-grown sport of lacrosse.

As the century came to a close, open pay-for-play had yet to invade hockey. But it operated by stealth. Sometimes that meant slipping five or ten bucks into players' boots. Sometimes out-of-town ringers played under the names of local men. Sometimes teams used inducements such as jobs to get around the rules, as Joseph Seagram's Waterloo team did with Weldy Young. The OHA worried the cheating hurt hockey's image, but there wasn't much evidence that was the case. True, the popularity of gambling made the possibility of fixing games a legitimate concern, but other than that, the sport's growth suggested the league didn't have much to be distressed about.

From the adoption of the OHA constitution, the executive committee, dominated by Torontonians, had complete control. Although the league held an annual meeting, there was no real pretext of democratic decision-making. During the December 1897 annual meeting, held in a parlour at the Queen's Hotel, the executive escalated its fight against professionalism with draconian new rules. One amendment at the meeting was a thirty-day residency requirement to discourage ringers. Whatever its supposed goal, this rule helped the teams in Toronto, since it was by far the biggest city and had the most local talent.

Outgoing OHA president James McFadden, who believed the existing measures to control professionalism weren't forceful enough, introduced another amendment: "When the status of any individual is questioned, the burden of proving his innocence shall rest with the accused, inasmuch as the real and true facts of the case must lie within his own personal knowledge, and, consequently, he should be in a position, if unjustly accused or suspected, to prove his innocence to the satisfaction of the Executive."

Surprisingly, McFadden's proposal wasn't that controversial. A few delegates, including representatives of the Berlin and Waterloo clubs, argued the existing rules were enough and expressed concern that the amendment was too arbitrary and contrary to law. But when it came to a vote, support for presuming those accused of professionalism guilty until proven innocent was almost unanimous. And rather than criticize the move, Toronto's newspapers applauded. "The association is to be congratulated," declared the *Evening Star*. "Professionalism is not in itself a crime. But professionalism, masked and cloaked in an assumed amateurism, is a crime against morals." Noting the difficulty of proving such an offence, the paper added, "The machinery of law is not available, and amateur athletic organizations are quite justified in making a law of their own and forcing the accused to prove his own innocence."

New powers rarely go unexercised for long and the OHA executive waited only a few weeks. Berlin (later renamed Kitchener) had won the inaugural championship of the intermediate series in 1897. In its first game the next season, the team faced arch-rival Waterloo. Fan interest for the early January match was intense. More than 2,000 spectators squeezed into the rink; many others were disappointed. Arthur Farrell, who'd left the Montreal Shamrocks for a year, played for Berlin while Joe and Ed Seagram, the distiller's sons, suited up for Waterloo. The spirited game was filled with penalties, injuries and goals.

When it ended, Berlin had won 6-4. George Rumpel, the proprietor of the Berlin Felt Boot Company and the city's new mayor, was delighted. His good mood may have been more than civic pride; if the rumour was true, he'd just won a large bet on the match. He marched into the dressing room and handed a $10 gold coin to each of the seven players. Rewarding team members with watches and rings was common, especially after a championship victory. The MAAA gave the Montreal Hockey Club gold rings in 1893 for being six-time league champions and gold watches for repeating as Stanley Cup champs the next year. The Winnipeg Victorias received gold watches for winning the trophy in 1896. To amateurism fetishists, these gifts counted as mere souvenirs. Gold coins were different: they were spendable.

The OHA pounced. During a three-and-a-half-hour meeting at the upscale National Club in Toronto, the executive considered affidavits from the mayor and the players and subjected Farrell and team manager Oscar Rumpel, the mayor's son, to a tough cross-examination. Berlin fought the allegation. The mayor's affidavit said the coins were for purchasing souvenirs; some of the players claimed they'd planned to turn the coins into watch fobs. The OHA executive was having none of it. The league expelled the team and declared all seven players professionals. But defeating the scourge wasn't as simple as making an example of one club. Worse, teams realized the league's strict approach represented a good way to overturn losses. Protests proliferated.

In the 1898 playoffs, Waterloo protested that a Kingston player had competed under an assumed name. The OHA suspended Montrealer Charlie Liffiton and rescheduled the match. In the other semi-final, Waubaushene unsuccessfully protested that one of the umpires had favoured Listowel. Immediately after losing the final 10-4 to Waterloo, Listowel protested that point Joseph "Grindy" Forrester had competed in a skating race with cash on the line. League president Alexis Martin, who'd been such a dismal referee the first time the two Victorias played for the Stanley Cup in 1896, expelled Waterloo. After the decision, the two clubs continued to argue in the press. Forrester denied ever skating for money and stated: "I have been wrongfully used by the O.H.A., as, in my opinion, and I think it is British law, that a person is always innocent until proven guilty, and if any court would rule on the case after going over all the evidence and affidavits I would not have the least fear of the result." His team argued that its opponent had confused Forrester with his brother, allegedly also known as "Grindy," and claimed that Listowel's captain had raced for $15 in Berlin the previous year. None of the sniping changed anything and Listowel kept the intermediate championship.

The year had been a messy one for the OHA, but at the annual meeting in December, the executive congratulated itself on how well it had handled everything. A subcommittee's report declared there was comparatively little professionalism in the league, though it regretted that clubs were not more help in fighting the menace. Too often, teams waited until they'd lost a match before saying anything about their opponent's corruption. Still, for all the rule-bending and protests and disputes, the sport continued to boom in the province. In 1896, twenty-seven teams played in two OHA series; two years later, fifty-four teams competed in three series.

The highlight of the meeting was John Ross Robertson's donation of a championship trophy. It didn't matter that senior teams had competed for the Cosby Cup since the OHA's first season. Now, they would play for the J. Ross Robertson Silver Challenge Trophy. The delegates were so chuffed at the gift that they unanimously made the benefactor a lifetime member. Although Robertson resisted the pressure to accept the position of honorary president, the meeting marks the beginning of his eventful relationship with the sport.

Robertson is a complicated villain in hockey's history. Growing up wealthy, he attended Upper Canada College, an exclusive boys' school modelled on British ones. He'd been the founder of the school paper, the captain of the cricket club and, he claimed, "the presiding genius of a 'shinny club.'" In 1876, after years working as a journalist, including covering the Riel Rebellion for the *Globe*, he launched the *Evening Telegram*. An immediate success, the newspaper was especially popular with working-class, conservative Protestants who loved all things British. In 1896, he ran for Parliament in the Toronto East riding but sat in the House of Commons as an Independent Conservative as Wilfrid Laurier's Liberals formed the government. According to Stephen J. Harper in *A Great Game: The Forgotten Leafs and the Rise of Professional Hockey*, Robertson was "an ardent British imperialist who distrusted the involvement of the United Kingdom in Canada's affairs; an antiracist, antislavery advocate who regularly employed racial slurs and railed against French Canadians and the Catholic Church; a staunch Tory who consistently opposed the Conservative Party; a strict disciplinarian who indulged his children to their ruin; a figure popular and respected, yet authoritarian and controversial."

His connection to the OHA was initially through his son. John Sinclair Robertson, better known as Cully, was on the league's eleven-man executive and became a vice-president in 1898. While abroad during the summer, father and son were on London's Regent Street, where Lord Stanley's aide had ordered the Dominion Hockey Challenge Cup. Cully suggested his father buy a trophy for the OHA. Robertson's trophy was far more ostentatious than Stanley's punch bowl. According to the *Telegram*, it "was made by Her Majesty's jewellers and silversmith, London, England, out of the purest Canadian silver. It is lined with Canadian gold, and richly decorated with bas relief of lions, masks, fells, etc., which stand out from the piece in high relief. The most striking feature of this original cup is the three leopard handles, which are beautifully modelled and chased. Its weight is 130 ounces. It is thirteen inches in diameter and ten in height, and stands on a handsome ebonized plinth, six inches in height, with six silver Hogarth-shields for inscribing the winners' names."

At the 1898 annual meeting, Robertson delivered both the trophy and a revealing speech that checked off some of the greatest hits of Victorian dogma. Evoking Muscular Christianity, he said, "A manly nation is always fond of manly sports. If we want our boys to be strong, vigorous and self-reliant we must encourage athletics." Expressing the era's ethnocentric view of the world, he argued, "the winners in the great struggle in life are those who, descendants of the great Anglo-Saxon race, to which it is our pride to belong, have also been successful in sporting competitions." And, of course, he glorified amateurism: "Sports should be pursued for its own sake," he declared, "for when professionalism begins, true sports ends."

- ELEVEN -

"Gentlemen, I am trying to do my best"

Dan Bain was, as usual, the best player on the ice. And the first Stanley Cup game in the new Arena—a February 1899 rematch between the two great teams named after the Queen—provided the paying customers with plenty of drama to compare notes over in the building's refreshment room. In the first half, Bain set up right winger Tony Gingras to put Winnipeg's Victorias up one. Ten minutes into the second half, he rushed at Mike Grant as the Montreal Victorias' cover point was executing a lift. The puck struck the westerner over the eye and knocked him unconscious. When Bain came to, the doctor wouldn't let him continue. Jack Armytage stepped in for him. Now the coach, he'd been the captain who'd led Winnipeg to Cup victory in 1896, but he'd retired after losing the trophy in the December rematch that year. Bain, who'd also played in those games, was his worthy successor.

Born in 1874 in Belleville, Ontario, Donald Bain, who usually went by Dan or Danny, was six when his family moved west. Like many of the game's early stars, he was an excellent all-round athlete, having also won titles in gymnastics, cycling, trapshooting, roller skating and figure skating. He was a great scorer and gifted playmaker with a muscular build who combined speed, grace and toughness. Losing him to injury was a blow to the Bisons and Montreal's Vics scored twice in the last minute to win 2-1.

Fortunately for Bain's team, and hockey fans, the two clubs had agreed to a best-of-three series this time. After losing and winning the Cup in 1896, the eastern Vics defended the trophy the next year by humiliating the Ottawa Capitals. With no challenge in 1898, Montreal fans had waited three years between serious Stanley Cup matches on home ice. The new Arena's increased capacity would definitely not go to waste. On the first night, the boxes and reserved seats were packed, and though a few more people might have squeezed into the standing room area, it was the largest crowd that had ever seen a Cup game. Meanwhile, in Winnipeg's new Auditorium, hundreds of fans on skates and in the seats followed the entertaining tilt via telegraph bulletins.

Bain missed the second game on Saturday and the team feared he'd never play again. But the diminished star power didn't dampen interest in the match. By noon on Friday, fans had snapped up all the reserved seats. On Saturday, the demand for standing room was so great that hundreds of people couldn't get in. The mild weather made the ice soft at the beginning of the match and pools of water formed by the end. For all its spectator-focused features, the Arena still had natural ice. According to a CPR telegraph bulletin at the start of the game, slower ice favoured the Montrealers. Russell "Dubbie" Bowie, who'd go on to be a prolific scorer, was a rare young player on the team's roster of aging stars. Led by Grant, the Vics were Canada's best and most prestigious hockey team. Although the club hadn't been the first to get its name on the Cup, it had kept the honour longer than anyone else. Aside from ten and half months in 1896 when the other Vics were the champions, the team had held the trophy since 1895. Travelling in Canada and the United States for exhibition games more than other squads had increased their fame.

Whichever seven it helped, the soft ice meant the hockey wasn't as electrifying as it had been in the first match. The *Montreal Star* called it "almost dull, at time listless, oftentimes degenerating into mere shinny." The home side was up 3-2 with thirteen minutes left in the second half when Bob McDougall slashed Gingras across the knee. Referee J.A. Findlay, a Montrealer who'd officiated a Cup match before and was respected for his knowledge and fairness, assessed a two-minute penalty. Gingras limped to the dressing room, followed by his outraged teammates. The doctor declared the player done for the night. Findlay briefly came in to check on the injury and then McDougall appeared. "I made a vicious swipe," he said. "I lost my temper and am very sorry for it." The Winnipeggers thanked him and accepted his apology. But that wasn't the end of the matter.

Referees policed fourteen skaters and were supposed to enjoy absolute authority. But they often struggled to stave off havoc. Players and teams regularly challenged calls; skated off the ice and refused to return; and issued protests. That the sport's rules were still being settled added to the challenge. With no set lengths for penalties, a ref could send a player "to the fence" or "to the side" for thirty seconds or the whole game or anything in between. He also managed the timekeepers and appointed the umpires, who stood on a platform ten feet behind the goal and waved a flag when someone scored. Teams often demanded a new umpire when they were incensed by a call.

Early goals were utilitarian: two four-foot posts, down from the original six-foot ones, jammed into the ice or sitting on pods six feet apart. Although there were often flags on the posts, there was no crossbar. So umpires didn't just have to decide if pucks had crossed the unmarked line between the posts, they also sometimes had to decide if shots were below the imaginary crossbar. Pucks that high weren't common, but determining which side of a post a shot fired from a sharp angle had passed wasn't always easy. Disagreements over whether the puck went in or not were frequent. While referees and umpires worried about abuse from angry fans and players, rink owners fretted that delays scared away the patrons.

Although he often refereed matches, and regularly received praise for his work, Weldy Young was one of the irate players during a late February 1898 game between the Ottawas and the Quebecs. The ice was soft and slushy, so the hockey was slow and unimpressive. With the score tied 4-4, the umpire signalled a Quebec goal. Everyone else in Rideau Rink was sure the shot had been well wide. The umpire was James Davidson, president of the Ottawa Capitals and a city alderman (and later mayor). Furious, Young skated up to him and pointed his stick at the path the puck had made through the slush several inches wide of the post. That, he insisted, proved it hadn't gone in. Davidson, who later claimed that Young had jabbed him with his stick, jumped at the player, grabbing him by the throat. The cover point responded with a punch, which brought a crowd of people, including two or three cops, onto the ice and led to a skirmish between players and fans. Since the police weren't much help in calming everyone down, it fell to Ottawa captain Harvey Pulford to break up the donnybrook.

There had to be a better way. And, of course, there was: netting. William Abraham Hewitt—known as W.A., Bill or Billy—told the story this way: he and Francis Nelson had been worried about the inadequacy of the goals until Nelson travelled to Australia and saw fishermen with large nets. The Toronto *Globe* sports editor returned to Canada with two of them, which he sent to Montreal, where his friend was sports editor of the *Herald*. Hewitt arranged for the netting to go on the goal posts before an 1899 game between the Victorias and the Shamrocks. Rival papers ridiculed the idea, but the experiment was a success. "The nets caught and held the puck," Hewitt later wrote in his memoir, "and also preserved the skins of the goal umpires and the dignity of the referee." The more plausible explanation is that hockey simply copied other sports, including lacrosse and ice polo, that already used nets. One account has it that Quebec City goaltender Frank Stocking presented a design that included netting hung from a crossbar at the 1899 annual meeting of the Canadian Amateur Hockey League, successor to the AHAC, and in December of that year, the loop mandated the new goals. Soon, nets and crossbars were standard equipment in rinks across the country, though the design went through many iterations over the following years. Needless to say, nets did not put an end to all arguments over whether a puck went in or not (even slow-motion video with freeze-frame capability, shot from several angles, doesn't do that). But it helped reduce them, making the job of umpires a little less vexing and the job of referee slightly simpler.

Though he never officiated a Cup game, the most renowned early ref was Fred Waghorne. Known as Wag, he'd emigrated from England, where he'd been an avid rugby player, and quickly took to hockey and lacrosse. By 1898, he was reffing hockey matches and would go on to handle, by his estimate, 2,400 games over five decades. Many refs were also players, but Waghorne dedicated himself to officiating. He wasn't a big man, but he was so respected he kept even the most contentious games under control. That didn't mean he didn't suffer some inadvertent physical abuse during faceoffs. Originally, refs placed the puck on the ice, then moved the blades of the two centres' sticks against it before stepping back and yelling, "Play!" Inevitably, some centres didn't wait until the ref was safely out of the way before swiping at the puck, often hitting toes, ankles and shins.

This practice lasted until Waghorne came up with what now seems an obvious solution. Fed up with all the bruises he'd received during a game in southwestern Ontario, he told the two centremen, "That's it. Rules or no rules, I'm not going to take any more of that punishment. From now on I'm going to stand and drop the puck between your sticks. Get ready." The players and even the fans liked it. The leagues added it to their rules.

Wag made perhaps his craftiest ruling during a game in Belleville: he disallowed a goal because the two-piece puck had split apart after hitting the post and only one half went in the net. "The rule book says that a puck is one-inch thick," he explained later. "That piece of rubber that went into the goal was only half an inch thick, so it couldn't qualify as a puck. And if it wasn't a puck, it certainly couldn't have been a goal." Two-piece pucks soon gave way to one-piece ones.

Even Waghorne had trouble with fans. The dimly lit rinks made some spectators braver and as if catcalls weren't enough, they sometimes threw objects—including a surprising number of empty whisky flasks—at him. He had to stop one game eleven times to clean the debris off the ice. Usually, there was no point in seeking help from the local cop, who was likely a hardcore fan of the home team. Fortunately, many rinks had back exits, allowing refs to escape unharmed, though it also helped to know a route to the train station using backstreets.

For all the fussing and fighting over refs, the controversies didn't hurt hockey's credibility. To the fans, such incidents were just part of what was so entertaining about the sport and provided more fodder for debate in the bars and kitchens and living rooms of the nation. Still, because it happened during a Stanley Cup match, the Findlay furor at the Arena was not a shining moment for the game.

The day before the first game of the Vics versus Vics series, Findlay and team representatives met in Montreal's Windsor Hotel. The ref assured them that if any player deliberately struck an opponent with intent to do bodily harm, he'd throw him out of the game. Now in the Arena, McDougall admitted his slash was deliberate, so, Winnipeg argued, he should be gone. When Findlay refused to change his original ruling, goalie George Merritt complained that his team couldn't get any justice because the ref had been unfair all along.

"Captain Armytage, have you been satisfied with me until now?" asked Findlay.

"Yes," he responded.

"Then your men have no right to talk as they do."

Finally, a rattled Findlay had had enough. "Gentlemen, I am trying to do my best. If I have made a mistake, I am sorry for it but cannot change my decision," he told the players. "As you are not satisfied with me, I will retire at once from the ice and have nothing more to do with the game." With that, he left the rink.

Montreal suggested continuing with a different ref, but Winnipeg insisted only the trustees could select the official. As the delay dragged on, the spectators grew restless. They passed along rumours and made as much noise as they could by stomping their feet and chanting. In the corridors, fans asked, "Where is the referee?" And others answered, "He has gone crazy." When Arena management announced that Findlay had gone home and the game would have to be postponed, the fans reacted with loud chorus of "No" and sustained jeering. The chastened authorities reacted by saying they'd get him back.

About twenty minutes later, Findlay returned. It was almost 11 p.m., and while some fans had given up and left, most had waited impatiently for an hour. A lively bunch in the north end of the building sang "We Won't Go Home Till Morning," which lightened the mood a bit. Findlay gave Winnipeg fifteen minutes to get on the ice. Even if the team had been willing to play, it was too late. The players were already in street clothes; some had left the building. Findlay put his skates back on and waited on the ice. Once the fifteen minutes were up, he awarded the unfinished game to Montreal. "It should have been the greatest hockey match on record," noted the *Gazette*, "but instead of that it degenerated into one of the worst tangled-up fizzles in the history of the game." If the Montreal paper was disappointed, Winnipeg's *Tribune* was disgusted: "The easterners are welcome to the cup, which this year carries with it the slugging as well as the hockey championship."

Neither of the trustees had attended the game. Ross had watched Ottawa beat the MHC at Dey's Rink. The next evening, he went to the train station to meet with Findlay and then, according to this diary, "To Russell, where talk with Sheriff Sweetland, re Stanley Cup fiasco." For a man whose job included writing newspaper editorials, Ross seemed to go out of his way not to editorialize in his personal journal. He didn't reveal his inner thoughts, make snarky comments or dish on anyone. Calling it a fiasco was as close to opinion as he came.

Of course, it was a fiasco. The largest crowd to ever watch a Cup match had seen it dissolve into chaos. The western Vics wanted a do-over. The eastern ones suggested they'd walk away from the trophy rather play again. That left Ross and Sweetland with an uncomfortable choice, until Winnipeg issued a statement on Monday indicating that even if the trustees overturned the ref's decision, the team would be unable to play due to the injuries to its two best men. This effectively freed the trustees from making a ruling that might have turned a bad day for the Cup into a lingering crisis. They'd have lucked out, if only they'd stayed quiet. But they took the curious last line of the club's statement—"We only ask you, in view of the state of affairs, to leave the situation as it was before we came to Montreal"—as a request to invalidate all bets on the game. Ross and Sweetland met again at noon on Monday and that evening the *Journal* ran their response: "The view of the trustees is this: Their business is to arrange playing conditions for the cup when people want to play for it. The trustees have nothing to do with betting and want nothing to do with it . . . The betting men can get out of their own troubles."

Already upset about how the game ended, Prairie fans were now livid. The trustees always seemed to back the referees when teams complained—before or after matches. And now they were suggesting the Vics were merely concerned about gambling. "The statement, coming as it did, officially from the men who are the trustees of the Stanley trophy, has occasioned the greatest indignation in this city, and it is felt that insult has been added to the already brutal treatment accorded the Winnipeggers," huffed the *Free Press*. "The net result of the most unsportsmanlike action of the Montreal men has been to make Winnipeggers feel proud that in the west, at least, the morale of the sport has not reached so low an ebb that 'victory at any cost' is made the governing principle of the game." Despite the paper's righteous umbrage, the Vics returned to Montreal the next year for another challenge.

- TWELVE -

"It is remarkable how I have
turned against milk at that price"

Come September, Dawson City sat at the bottom of a golden bowl. Starting on the flood plain on the east side of the Yukon River just north of the Klondike River, the town climbed a bit up the side of a large rounded hill called the Midnight Dome. Fall comes early in the subarctic and the birch and aspen trees produced a gorgeous, if short-lived, display of colour in the river valley. Above, the autumn buckbrush gave the bowl a purplish crimson trim. Overlooking the community, which sprawled to Klondike City to the south and West Dawson on the other side of the Yukon, was Moosehide Slide, a giant scar on the hillside at the north end of town. According to legend, cannibals often bothered the Hän Hwëch'in who stayed at Tr'ochëk. One time, to get a better view of their enemies, they snuck away and climbed to the top of the hill, where they found a tree of mythic proportions. Knowing it was a gift to solve a problem, they rolled the tree down the hill, wiping out the cannibals and causing a rockslide that left behind the unusual geological feature, which looks like a moose skin stretched for tanning.

The Slide and the golden vegetation greeted Weldy Young as his steamer came around a bend in the river before the unlikely town of Dawson revealed itself to him in September 1899. Few people who saw that view ever forgot it. The boat passed Klondike City on its starboard side, sailed through the clearer water of the Klondike River spilling into the brown, silted water of the Yukon before reaching Young's new home.

Although he'd grown up in Ottawa, the star athlete had already moved away twice. While neither his mining stint in B.C. nor his ill-fated move to Joseph Seagram's Waterloo team was permanent, both demonstrated his wanderlust. So his friends and teammates shouldn't have been too shocked that he was Yukon-bound in August of 1899. Still, the abrupt departure might have caught them off guard. "Weldy got the offer of a good thing there, which meant immediate acceptance," the *Citizen* reported, "and he left by train yesterday afternoon." There was no time for elaborate goodbye dinners before he took off with a man named Houston, who was an associate of Alex McDonald. "Big Alex" was a Nova Scotian who'd made an early Gold Rush fortune, but unlike some other instant millionaires in the Klondike— Swiftwater Bill Gates, for example—he didn't have much interest in spending his fortune recklessly. Or at all, really. He didn't drink, dress fancily or even talk much. Instead, he collected more claims and other businesses. Young's "good thing" was to manage his supply ships on the Yukon.

The journey was much easier and shorter than the one stampeders faced in 1897 and 1898. Rather than climbing one of the dreaded passes, Young took a scenic ride on the new White Pass & Yukon Route Railway, which began running between Skagway and Bennett in July. From there, the WP&YR's fleet of sternwheelers meant the Klondike was just a pleasant two-day boat ride away with a tramway saving passengers and freight from danger at Miles Canyon and the White Horse Rapids. "The scenery along the route was very beautiful, the banks of the river well-wooded with a luxuriant growth of fir, spruce and birch," wrote Steele of his trip from Bennett to Dawson in

September 1898. "The cut banks were many and thickly covered with swallow's nests, built against the clay."

Dawson wasn't a boomtown anymore, but it was no longer a glorified tent city, either. In fact, most of the tents were gone, replaced by cabins, and two big fires earlier in the year had forced the town to rebuild much of its downtown core. The place had transformed itself into a northern metropolis that looked to have staying power with a surprising number of substantial buildings, including several large warehouses, and many shops with colourful awnings. When Young arrived, the town had forty restaurants and cafes, twelve hotels, ten dentists, seven jewellers, six sawmills, five dairies, four churches, three theatres, two breweries and one gymnasium. There were also four social clubs and four fraternal societies. The Yukon Order of Pioneers and the Arctic Brotherhood were specific to the North; the Elks and the Fraternal Order of Eagles came from Outside. The place was increasingly like any other conventional western city. And, of course, September brought that gorgeous display of golden flora.

Young's first month in the Klondike was Sam Steele's last. The Mountie's successful supervision of the great influx of stampeders earned him a promotion to lieutenant colonel and command of the NWMP in the Yukon and British Columbia. Arriving in Dawson in early September 1898, Steele found it "full of loose characters who had come into the country to prey upon the respectable but, as a rule, simple and unsuspicious miners, and I dealt with them with the utmost severity." Quickly deciding that neither the jail nor his force was big enough, Steele ordered the construction of thirty-four additional cells and put in a requisition for more men. Then the punctilious cop, dressed in his scarlet serge, made his presence felt with daily walks around town and regular forays into the Klondike Valley.

He forced all establishments that served liquor to buy licences, ordered monthly medical examinations for prostitutes and insisted that all businesses, including saloons, close on Sundays. One of those more-British-than-the-British types from Ontario, he was a resolute adherent of Victorian ideology and a proud defender of Queen and Empire. After an actor slagged the monarchy, "he was given the opportunity to say he would sin no more or take his ticket for the outside," Steele later recounted. "This had the desired effect." A blue ticket was the NWMP's order to leave the territory and never return. Not even the Americans or other nationalities in Dawson held his extreme Britishness against him. Each night, a gaggle of citizens showed up at the police station to jaw with him until well past midnight.

His influence went beyond law enforcement. His men ensured the collection of Clifford Sifton's much-despised ten percent mining levy; served as escorts for the transfer of gold; and delivered the mail to and from the Alaskan coast in the winter. The cost of caring for the sick was high, especially with the typhoid outbreak as well as cases of malaria and dysentery. So he recommended the creation of a board of health and then became its chairman. "It was now quite clear that the Klondyke was no place for any but those with the most powerful and sound constitutions," he wrote in his memoir. "No finer men could be found in any country than those of the rush of 1897–8, but large numbers of them succumbed to the climate and the great hardships attendant on residence in the Yukon." While his men checked health hazards such as drains and latrines, he created a fund for the hospitals and raised thousands of dollars by increasing the fines for the less serious crimes handled by the police court, including public drunkenness, firearms offences and cardsharping. A fine was a much preferable punishment than a sentence to work in the government woodpile. With his new jail cells, his blue tickets, his big fines and his dreaded woodpile, Steele maintained peace and order in Dawson. Good government wasn't so easy.

Sifton was a master of political patronage, and corruption flourished among many of the officials he appointed. In Ottawa, the opposition Conservatives howled unsuccessfully for an investigation; in Dawson, Steele did what he could to limit the sleaze. He challenged appointments and contracts to Sifton cronies and refused to let them take over collection of the gold royalty from his men. That Steele had married the daughter of a Conservative MP—and was believed to be a Conservative himself—may not have helped his cause with the Liberals. By the end of the summer of 1899, the minister had had enough and ordered his transfer out of the Klondike.

The citizenry was furious. "They cannot understand why an officer who has given such universal satisfaction would be relieved of such an important command just at the time when he had restored order out of chaos and who has the entire confidence of all classes, irrespective of nationality," noted the *Dawson Daily News*. "Indeed, those were not wanting who remarked that it was because Col. Steele is too good, too just, too upright and honourable as a man and an officer to suit the powers that be." The *Klondike Nugget* was blunter, blaming "the nefarious schemes of the Sifton gang of political pirates."

Joe Boyle chaired a meeting in the Criterion Theatre that approved sending a message to Ottawa to convey the town's dissatisfaction with the decision. When the government refused to reconsider, he helped collect donations of gold to thank the policeman for his service. As Dawson's benevolent dictator, the Lion of the North could be a bully, but he was as popular as he was feared. When he boarded a boat bound for Whitehorse on September 26, thousands of people from town and the creeks went down to the waterfront to cheer and wave hats and handkerchiefs as the steamer chugged upstream and out of sight.

The obvious problem with the "good thing" that had lured Young to the Yukon was that winter was coming, which meant a halt to boat traffic. But before that even happened, he and Houston parted ways. So Young needed a new job and quickly found one as a bookkeeper at the *Yukon Sun*. The Gold Rush had spurred not just a race for claims, but also a competition to be the Klondike's first newspaper. A salesman for a struggling Seattle printing company, Eugene Allen was a slender, sharp-faced redhead in his late twenties with outsized nervous energy. He was itching for adventure and a chance to get rich. One morning in July 1897, he stood among a mob of people at Schwabacher's Dock and watched men laden with gold file down a gangplank, a row of Wells Fargo guards on either side. He turned to colleague Zach Hickman and said, "Let's get started."

After sailing to Skagway—"the boiling pot of hell," according to Allen—early in 1898, he and his younger brother George, as well as Hickman and his cousin, started to tackle the White Pass on February 18. Ten days later, as they humped a printing press and one ton of paper along with food and other supplies, they learned that George Swinehart had left the *Mining Record* in Juneau with the same idea. The Seattle men tried to move faster, but eventually realized they needed a new plan. Leaving the others behind to wait until the Yukon River opened, Allen went ahead by dogsled.

At the end of an eventful, sometimes perilous, journey on the ice and, from Lake Leberge, on a raft and then a boat called the *Black Maria*, he reached Dawson on May 17. He was all but broke but made about $100 in gold dust for a day of shovelling gravel into a sluice box on a friend's Bonanza Creek claim. To ensure his newspaper was first, he typed up Vol. 1 No. 1 of the *Klondike Nugget*, which included an interview with new Yukon commissioner James Walsh. He posted it on a bulletin board he'd built in the centre of town on May 27. More editions, including coverage of the big flood, appeared on the board in the following days.

Stuck in Caribou Crossing on Lake Bennett, Swinehart published one issue of the *Caribou Sun* on May 16 before continuing on to Dawson. While Allen was still waiting for his printing press, Swinehart arrived with a small one that he used until a larger one came upriver from St. Michael. The first issue of the *Yukon Midnight Sun* hit the streets on June 11. Allen was unimpressed, dismissing it in his diary as "nothing but a government propaganda sheet." Five days later, the *Nugget* printed a proper edition on its press. A lively newspaper war ensued. Outside news was dated and not always entirely reliable as staff fought over old newspapers carried in by new arrivals or interviewed newcomers. But events in the goldfields and the doings of people in town offered plenty to write about. The *Nugget* particularly enjoyed chronicling Swiftwater Bill's exploits. Politics gave them lots to argue about, though neither paper liked the Canadian bureaucracy or Sifton's gold tax, even if the *Nugget* was far more vociferous about it that the *Sun*.

When the *Dawson Daily News* launched in July 1899 with the slogan "The News When It Is News," it was much more like a big-city paper than its competitors in coverage, format and quality. The completion of the telegraph line to Dawson the month Young arrived made Outside news, including Britain's war in South Africa, much more timely and plentiful. But in the fall, Gene Allen sold the still-profitable *Nugget* to his brother for $1. George continued publishing the paper with no less piss and vinegar. The most sensational publication in town also featured the Klondike's best-known journalist, a man everyone called Stroller. Working for the *Skagway News* in the early days of the Gold Rush, Elmer John White regularly covered Soapy Smith until the gangster's death in a shootout in the summer of 1898. The next year, White moved to Dawson. In an era when bylines weren't common, he wrote "Stroller's Column," which often included tales about local characters, especially those who frequented the dance halls, gambling dens and saloons. Like the *Nugget*, the *News* maintained a pro-American editorial stance, including regularly attacking local officials and regulations. The weekly *Sun*, now owned by Thomas O'Brien, was Canadian. Henry Woodside, the editor since April 1899, was born in Ontario and had lived for many years in Manitoba. He was such a patriotic British subject that he left Dawson for several months in 1900 to fight in the Boer War. His strident pro-Canadian positions frequently led to accusations of anti-Americanism.

While Young worked on the business side at the *Sun*, he'd arranged to be a special correspondent for the *Citizen* before he left Ottawa. Sometimes his updates took the form of letters to the paper; other times, letters he'd written to his parents made it into print. "We have all had a mistaken idea of this country," he wrote to his mother a few weeks after he'd arrived. "In the first place, instead of coming to a country where one has to rough it from the start, you are accorded splendid accommodation while traveling and met on every hand with signs of civilization almost as marked as those which have surrounded us at home." He went on to praise the NWMP, especially the recently departed Steele. He pointed out that while miners wore clothing that befit their jobs, the people who worked in town—the lawyers and doctors and government people—dressed no differently than people back home.

Despite his rosy description, Dawson wasn't Ottawa, and not just because, as he noted, there were no brownstone mansions, paved streets or parlour-car trains. As a cheechako, the local term for newcomer, Young was learning that the town's remoteness meant there were some things he couldn't get or were too expensive, even though the cost of food had lately been falling. With fresh cow's milk going for fifty cents a glass, Young admitted, "It is remarkable how I have turned against milk at that price." By late November, he was desperately missing fresh vegetables and bemoaning the cost of beef: $1.25 a pound.

Still, he was enjoying himself. He lived in a house with fourteen other young men, including his brother Bob. The guys spent many enjoyable evenings playing music together, though his description of how women made money in the dance halls suggests he also patronized those establishments. "Sharp at twelve o'clock the show is over, and the promiscuous dancing, in which the audience may participate, begins. There are usually lots of girls present, who earn their living in divers ways. You ask one of the girls to dance. And, by the same token, the orchestra is as good as we have at home. Immediately after the dance you must adjourn to the bar, where you pay $1.50 for a drink for two. The house gets $1 and the girl fifty cents per dance, and it is a case of 'Next,' as soon as you have parted yourself from your money."

He copped to only one regret. Dawson had received its first snowfall, about four inches, a few days before Young wrote his October letter, and although he'd bought a fur-lined pea-coat cheaply, he realized it was a mistake not to have taken his racoon coat.

On his first trip to the Yukon in 1887, William Ogilvie correctly predicted significant gold deposits. Originally from the Ottawa area, he mapped large areas of Canada—including parts of the Prairies, the Yukon River and the border with Alaska—during his prolific career. In January 1897, he surveyed Ladue's townsite, laid out the streets in a grid and named it after his former boss, George Mercer Dawson, who'd become the director of the Geological Survey of Canada. Five months later, Ogilvie sat on a log on a bank of the Yukon River and, using his camera box for a desk, wrote a letter explaining that he'd "made a survey of all the lands applied for or near Dawson, surveyed nearly 100 claims on the Bonanza and Eldorado Creeks; got nearly all, if not all, the disputes on those creeks, and they were many, settled quietly and without trouble; and, most important, educated the miners pretty well in the requirements of the mining laws."

Yukon gold made Ogilvie famous; family made him uncle to Clifford Sifton's wife. In July 1898, the interior minister named the fifty-three-year-old surveyor the new territorial commissioner, replacing James Walsh. During his military career, Walsh had served as a negotiator between the U.S. Army and Sitting Bull, who was in exile in Canada. In 1873, he joined the just-created NWMP and quickly rose to inspector. Later he went into the coal business in Winnipeg, where he befriended Sifton. Despite the impressive résumé, Walsh gained a reputation for chicanery within two months of making it to Dawson. Sifton's appointment of Ogilvie was more political than practical. "Few men have deserved celebrity more and courted it less," the *Globe* said of the new commissioner, adding, "He had the great opportunity to possess himself of great wealth, yet he came out of the Yukon country as he had gone into it, poor in pocket though rich in reputation."

The Liberal paper claimed Ogilvie was well-equipped for the position, but in truth he lacked any relevant administrative experience. Fortunately, he made a valuable ally even before he arrived in town. Steele and Ogilvie travelled down the Yukon River together in September. Somehow, the straitlaced cop and the gregarious surveyor hit it off. "He was a perfect mimic, and his yarns would have filled a large book," Steele later wrote. "He was indeed a delightful companion, a true friend and an upright, self-denying officer of the government."

The Walsh controversy wasn't the only one Ogilvie had to contend with. Another swirled around gold commissioner Thomas Fawcett. Even for a capable administrator, handling the crush and chaos of a gold rush would have been challenging. But Fawcett, who preferred leading the choir at the Presbyterian church to his job, managed to combine arrogance and incompetence. It didn't help that his staff was overworked and underpaid or that miners were a difficult and querulous bunch. Beyond perhaps understandable confusion, though, the office made suspicious—possibly corrupt—decisions on the approval and rejection of claims.

On the creeks and in the saloons, griping about Fawcett was already widespread when Gene Allen first made it to Dawson. With so many disputes over claims, the gold office closed a large section of Dominion Creek to do a proper survey. In addition, it deemed only claims registered by November 15, 1897, valid. Allen's first typewriter-written edition included an item headlined "The Dominion Muddle." Wanting the *Nugget* to be the friend of the miner and a crusading paper, he decided the removal of Fawcett would be its first crusade and gathered his staff. "We're going to change things at the Gold Commissioner's office," he told them. "This fellow Fawcett doesn't belong there. We'll expose all this dirty work. The only thing we want is to be sure of every fact—then let him have it!"

By July, the muddle was a full-on scandal. The gold office reopened the creek to staking, but insiders, including people connected to Walsh, had the jump on everyone else. The headlines over the next few months escalated: "The Gold Commissioner Exposed" in July, "Colossal Moral Turpitude" in August, "Fawcett's Scheme" in September, "Get Him Out" in October and, finally, in November, "Goodbye Fawcett."

A new gold commissioner, Edmund C. Senkler, was on his way to Dawson. Fawcett sued for libel over the "Colossal Moral Turpitude" article, which accused him of committing criminal acts for the benefit of his friends. The paper withdrew the charges, but he refused to drop the suit. Although Ogilvie created a Royal Commission to investigate Klondike corruption, it didn't prove terribly illuminating, in part because many witnesses had already left town. But in a February 1899 letter to Sifton, the commissioner made it clear he had no great respect for the *Nugget*. Referring to its coverage as "inflammatory and seditious," he said, "it appears these people have never had any newspaper experience heretofore and have not learned that many of the stories they hear are simply emanations of frenzied individuals who imagine they have lost a fortune because they cannot get the claim they wish or some similar idea." Regardless, the Fawcett crusade endeared the *Nugget* to many miners, which was good for business. And the accusations of corruption against government officials wouldn't end there.

Yet by September, when Steele left and Young arrived, the Klondike no longer seemed so unruly or exotic. True, mail to and from the Outside could still take weeks, or as much two months in the spring and fall. Sometimes it disappeared altogether. And the telephone system operated only within town and a few creek communities. But the Skagway-to-Dawson telegraph line, built in just 133 days, meant the speedy delivery of messages and news, connecting the Klondike to the rest of the world. The White Pass & Yukon Route Railway and steamship service also reduced the sense of isolation by making the journey to and from Dawson shorter and simpler. Of course, many of the disillusioned, as well as a few of the newly rich, took advantage of that and went south. But gold fever is an intoxicating obsession and not easy to cure. Plenty of people didn't go home, even if they didn't stay in the Klondike. During the winter of 1899–1900, just as Young was settling in, as many as 8,000 Dawsonites joined the rush to Nome, Alaska, upon hearing of a strike there. Another couple of thousand headed to Fairbanks. New gold dreams weren't the only reason they left; many, especially the Americans, hated Canada's restrictive mining laws and Sifton's ten percent royalty.

Unlike Forty Mile after the Klondike discovery, though, Dawson didn't become a ghost town. For one thing, too many people had sunk too much money into the place. By September 1899, the top three businesses—the North American Trading and Transportation Company, the Alaska Exploration Company and the Alaska Commercial Company—had invested $5 million. Besides, as the capital city of the new Yukon territory, Dawson was the beneficiary of numerous civil service jobs and, soon, a government building binge. Ogilvie had previously estimated gold mining would provide work for 2,000 people and keep the economy humming for two decades. Even in 1900, as the population was falling, he expected it to settle at between 10,000 and 12,000. The federal government bought into his optimism, but it also wanted to exert its sovereignty in the region, especially since most Americans considered the Klondike part of Alaska. The town's economy didn't diversify much beyond servicing miners and government jobs, but Dawson stayed alive.

- THIRTEEN -

*"Happy, contented faces are
everywhere to be seen"*

The Yukon River ice finally moved at 4:45 a.m. on May 8, 1900. As word spread, Klondike residents alerted their neighbours with "shouts of gladness and incessant firing of guns and pistols." Spring breakup was a major event. For one thing, it was sometimes loud and dramatic as massive hunks of ice cracked and crunched and crashed into each other. For another, there was always the danger of a repeat of the flood of 1898. Most of all, it meant the heaps of garbage that had accumulated on the ice during the winter would disappear downriver, boat traffic was coming soon and summer wasn't far off. Dawsonites began betting on the timing of the breakup in 1898 (the tradition continues today with a popular charity contest). Despite the early hour, hundreds of people gathered along the banks. They didn't hear much loud cracking, just some grinding as a massive ice floe slowly moved away. It gathered speed before splintering into large chunks downriver, jamming just above the Indigenous community of Moosehide.

Although the water rose four feet by noon, it didn't flood the town. The next day, the river flowed and residents waited for a jam at Five Finger Rapids to break because the *Flora*, one of two steamers waiting there, carried a large shipment of mail from Outside. Having endured his first Yukon winter, Young graduated from being a cheechako to a sourdough. The general definition is a veteran of the territory; the more specific definition is someone who'd stayed long enough to see the river freeze-up in the fall and breakup in the spring. To Klondikers, the social distinction between cheechakos and sourdoughs was significant.

As the *Citizen*'s special correspondent, Young offered a glimpse of how Dawsonites lived and worked; details of his own life there; coverage of the exodus to Nome and a large fire in January; gossip about former Ottawa residents; and a surprising amount of political opinion. Although he worked for the government organ in town, he was no fan of Clifford Sifton or the country's mining regulations. Inevitably, he also talked about sports. Yukoners had played shinny as early as 1884 and eighteen people showed up to the first meeting of the Dawson Hockey Club in the fall of 1898. In one match that winter, the team defeated the Ottawa Dawsonites 5-2; in another, it lost by the same score to the Canadian Permanent Force Hockey Club. A proper league was the next step. In a missive dated the first day of the new century, Young reported, "An effort is being made here to have hockey, but playing in the open with the mercury frozen in the glass does not present any great attractions for yours truly."

He did warm to the community, though. By May, he was on the sports committee planning the celebration for the Queen's birthday; was secretary of a campaign to raise funds for sufferers of a catastrophic fire in Hull and Ottawa and on a subcommittee charged with arranging an evening of entertainment in one of the theatres; and joined the Dawson Militia, a volunteer group that drilled twice a week. He clearly enjoyed the onset of spring weather. "Happy, contented faces are everywhere to be seen," he wrote. "Miners after their long, tedious winter of hardships and privations are once more in town with heavily-laden 'pokes' full of 'the precious,' business has improved by leaps and bounds, navigation has opened up, the banks are open from 7 a.m. until 10 p.m. to receive the output of the various creeks, concert halls, gambling and drinking saloons are more than active, and the finest climatic conditions to be found under the British flag at present prevail." He marvelled at the "never-ending daylight," for though the sun set around 11 p.m. at that time of year, darkness never came, just a twilight bright enough to require heavy blinds for sleeping.

Though he didn't mention it in his letters, Young also made an unusual appearance in court. Lawsuits involving the newspapers—sometimes between the newspapers—were common. In April 1900, the *Sun* accused gold office employee Joseph Clarke of taking bribes and swindling friends from his hometown of Brockville, Ontario, to finance a mining project. When Clarke sued editor Henry Woodside, Young took the stand as the paper's bookkeeper. "Weldon C. Young was a very reluctant witness and was not sure of anything connected with the management of the paper," reported the *News*. "He had not read the articles, the cause of the libel suit; he was not sure what position Henry J. Woodside occupied; he just paid him off at the end of every month for services rendered. When Weldon C. Young finished his testimony the Court could not determine whether there was such a position as editor on the paper." The judge ruled in Clarke's favour.

In July, Young and other local sportsmen began exploring the idea of creating a Dawson Athletic Club. He was bullish on its prospects, writing, "Dawson will soon have an up-to-date athletic association: at present the roll shows a membership of four hundred, and a clubhouse is sure to be built, together with an athletic grounds, skating and curling rinks, etc." The *News* reported that "over 300" people had indicated interest. While he may have embellished the numbers, he wasn't wrong about the clubhouse, just premature.

Despite Young's reluctance about playing outdoors in the deep freeze, he did suit up with the Dawson Hockey Club. The *Sun* reported, "The town boys will hold a meeting at an early date, and if the predictions of Mr. W. C. Young may be accepted, they will place a formidable team in the field to contest the honors with the N.W.M.P. and bankers. The air will soon be rife with challenges and big talk on the part of the would-be champions." That summer, he warned *Citizen* readers the team was preparing a Stanley Cup challenge—and that Outsiders shouldn't "hold us too cheaply." Later that year, he reported that he would play for the Civil Service squad in what he expected to be a seven-team Dawson Hockey League. A local jewellery firm had created a trophy valued at $250 that would go to the champions, who would then issue a challenge for the national honour. To Dawsonites, this seemed a perfectly reasonable plan.

Henry Woodside lost his job because of hockey. At least, that was the excuse. Early in 1901, Edgar Mizner, the local manager of the Alaska Commercial Company, pulled his advertising from the paper. The ACC dominated retailing in the Yukon, so publisher Thomas O'Brien had no choice but to ask for the journalist's resignation. "With this issue we terminate our connection with the *Yukon Sun* as editor," Woodside wrote in a brief "Editorial Announcement" in the February 9 issue. "We have no apologies to offer or regrets to express for our course, which has to the best of our ability, been in the higher interests of Yukon and Canada. To our readers and friends we wish a goodly share of that prosperity which we predict for this young and growing territory and its ambitious capital, the most northerly city in the British empire."

Two days later, he wrote a letter to the *Vancouver World*, which the *News* reprinted. It presented a lengthy self-defence in the third person. After noting that the editors of Dawson's American-owned papers could say whatever they wanted about the country they operated in, a Canadian editor who took a "straight-forward patriotic course" faced accusations of anti-Americanism and "must be removed on some pretext no matter how trivial it may be." The trivial pretext, according to Woodside, was his coverage of hockey. When O'Brien asked Mizner why he was pulling his ads, the explanation was, "First, when his hockey team, on which he had spent a $1000, had beaten the civil service team (by a fluke) the editor had not praised the team. Second, the editor had given credit to some players from a rival company's team who had helped his men win (the other papers did the same after the match). Third, the editor had put a slight on Americans here."

After watching Canadians play hockey in the winter of 1898–99, the ACC wanted to form an American team. When it defeated a "third-rate" squad—"by accident," to Woodside's way of thinking—the company put photographs of the victors in its shop windows, declaring them "Champions of Dawson." These pictures disappeared after bad losses in the next two games. The next winter, in an effort to improve, the company recruited a couple of Canadians—only to lose its first game 12-0 to the Civil Service. In January, the ACC, now with an all-Canadian lineup, managed to beat the Civils, who were missing Young.

Instead of praising the victors, the *Sun* attributed the upset to two Canadian ringers from the Alaska Exploration Company, which was involved in mining, real estate and transportation. Woodside's attitude toward U.S. players was an early example of Canadian chauvinism against hockeyists from other countries. In his letter, the former editor accused the ACC of less-than-gentlemanly play and refusing a rematch challenge from the Civils. "Individually, the A.C. players in the majority of instances are very good fellows, but as a team they seem to become imbued with an unsportsmanlike spirit," wrote Woodside. He claimed this was the reason the league collapsed, though it reorganized in mid-February with four teams: the Civil Service, the Police, the ACC and another retailer, McLennan, McFeely & Co., which ran ads in the *News* for skates ("All Sizes") and sticks ("Come early and avoid the rush").

That Mizner used hockey coverage as the excuse in his dispute with Woodside was indicative of how much the game already meant in town. Regardless, the editor was gone. Although the *Sun* claimed its circulation rose due to a less antagonistic attitude toward the Americans in town, O'Brien soon sold the paper. Frederick Tennyson Congdon, a lawyer from Annapolis, Nova Scotia, had come to the Yukon to be the legal advisor to the territorial commissioner in March. He soon quit to join a Dawson law firm and started building a political machine, including buying control of the *Sun* and turning it into a daily.

By then, Young had already left the paper and landed a job with the help of the gold commissioner. A goalkeeper for the Civil Service hockey team, Edmund Senkler had played hockey and football for Osgoode Hall in the early 1890s. He'd been a forward on the Legalites when they lost the OHA Championship to Young and the Ottawa Hockey Club in 1892. So when Senkler faced accusations of corruption in 1900, Young responded by forcefully defending him in the *Citizen*. "To those of us who had the pleasure of knowing him on the outside the idea that he is a grafter is absurd," he wrote. "Can it not be possible that he is being made to bear the onus of blame for the rottenness of those who have gone before him? And echo answers, yes—a thousand times, yes."

When mining activity picked up at Clear Creek, a tributary of the Stewart River, Senkler recommended Young for the job of mining recorder and inspector of mines there. "I have known him for a great many years, and can vouch for his honesty, and know him to be capable," he wrote to Ogilvie in December. The next month, the commissioner approved the appointment.

Mining recorders registered, and often went out to check, staked claims. Young's salary was $125 a month plus living expenses. He stayed and worked in a one-room office, and after his first winter, he asked for a dog team to make getting around easier. Prospectors regularly dropped in without food or money and he fed them out of his own pocket. While Senkler didn't want to encourage this practice, he realized it was sometimes unavoidable and recommended reimbursement in those cases. Now working for the government, Young had softened his opinions about its competence. In a letter to his father, he said much had changed for the better, including Sifton's reduction of the gold royalty—which many miners had avoided paying by smuggling gold out of the territory anyway—and the introduction of new mining laws that Young believed were "practicable and just." Unfortunately, a job that far out of town meant less hockey.

When Young updated the folks back home in the summer of 1900, he made Dawson seem downright cosmopolitan. "Just a few lines from the 'frozen north' where the midday heat is intense, where steamboat arrivals are an hourly occurrence, where at present market garden stuff, fresh fruit and beautiful flowers are much in evidence, where the lady folk are clad in the most bewitching muslins, gee-gaws and accompanying frills, and where even the well-known dress of duck trousers with the blue coat are worn by many of Dawson's gay cavaliers," he began, perhaps hoping to assure everyone that he wasn't much missing the comforts of the south. And he may not have been.

After Steele civilized the inhabitants, Ogilvie had set about improving the infrastructure. When Governor General Minto and Lady Minto made an official visit in August 1900, Dawson was ready to show itself off, though many Americans in town referred to the viceroy as "Governor Minto" and assumed he was coming to hear their grievances and tales of hard luck. His Excellency arrived at a prosperous community with electric power; electric street lamps; telephone service; drainage ditches to reduce flooding; proper sewers and a clean water supply to lower the chances of another typhoid outbreak; fire brigades; buggies and bicycles on five miles of graded streets, including macadamized ones in the business district; and twelve miles of wooden sidewalks. With six lumber mills running, frame buildings of two or three storeys had begun to replace the log cabins in the core.

His hosts hoped the governor general would be impressed with the modern city they'd built deep in the Yukon wilderness. Instead, he was appalled by the territory's corrupt governance and unimpressed with Ogilvie. Only the NWMP met the viceroy's standards. He made it clear who he blamed: "My verdict is,—criminal administration by the Min. of the Interior."

Though Sifton indulged in political patronage, there was no evidence he'd done anything illegal. He micromanaged the administration of the Klondike as much as possible, given the distance, a habit that Ogilvie bristled at, so he was well aware of the problems there. He'd instructed the commissioner to do whatever was necessary to clean up the gold office and the post office. But he also insisted on exercising his powers of appointment. After Ogilvie hired some Conservatives, Sifton responded by telling him, "under our system of Government we cannot appoint our opponents to office, and while you are an Administrator under a party Government you will have to be guided by this rule." Needless to say, patronage made reform harder.

The Klondike situation was only one point of friction between the interior minister and the governor general, and Sifton wasn't afraid to use the *Manitoba Morning Free Press*, the paper he'd secretly bought, to attack Minto. Some of the viceroy's distaste seemed rooted in classism. He thought Canada needed "a leisured class with a stake in the country" and considered Ogilvie "weak, and vacillating, and does not even possess any social weight." Minto should have stayed out of it, but he tried unsuccessfully to convince Laurier to get rid of Sifton.

Although Ogilvie survived Minto's visit, he proved underwhelming as commissioner, especially the political aspects of the position. As accusations of corruption continued to dog government officials, the *Nugget*, which had originally welcomed Ogilvie as an improvement over Walsh, turned on him. Worse, Sifton finally lost patience with him. Ogilvie was indecisive and inconsistent and had a habit of ignoring the minister's edicts. Believing that the commissioner should hold himself aloof and above, Sifton didn't like that Ogilvie hung out with regular people in Dawson. Similarly, as much as Sam Steele liked and respected the commissioner, the Mountie had been privately less impressed with his old friend's partying.

In October 1900, the territory finally held elections for two positions on the Yukon Council. It had been an entirely appointed body because the federal government was reluctant to allow self-government in a volatile region dominated by Americans. When both of the candidates favoured by the Liberals—including *Sun* owner Tom O'Brien—lost the election, Sifton blamed Ogilvie for not finessing a result more to his liking. Early in 1901, the minister allowed him to resign "for health reasons." Though Ogilvie was devastated, Steele believed his friend had never enjoyed the job anyway. "The commissioner's years in the Klondyke, while holding his high office," he wrote, "were one long nightmare."

Unlike his predecessor, Ogilvie departed with his reputation intact, though his forecast for the Klondike's future didn't fare as well. Even though Dawson now boasted amenities that were at least the equal of similar-sized cities in the rest of the country, the population had fallen to 9,142, according to the first official census. That was already below his prediction and it showed no signs of holding steady. Still, the old surveyor could take pride in leaving the Klondike a better place.

As did many other Canadians, some Yukoners liked to gather in saloons to shoot the shit, and the Klondike offered no shortage of venues. Tellingly, a bar was one of the first buildings erected in Dawson City. After Joseph Ladue staked the townsite in September 1896, he opened a sawmill and a saloon. "There was a little whiskey in the place and a good deal of water," according to Ogilvie in May 1897, "but the boys, for the sake of old times, were willing to pay fifty cents a glass for the mixture." By the summer of 1898, more than twenty drinking establishments operated in rudimentary structures of canvas or reassembled logs, making a good time the Klondike's second-largest industry. The larger ones offered gambling and stages for everything from vaudeville acts to prize fights to, starting in 1899, motion pictures. Before long, out on the creeks, roadhouses and even a general store or two served the miners who were too busy working claims to go into Dawson.

In the beginning, the booze was neither cheap nor good— the whisky was "the most pernicious kind of poison" and the champagne was really just soda water mixed with alcohol and "champagne essence"—but that did little to dampen sales. The drinks improved once transportation improved and bringing in commercial alcohol from the south became easier. The shrinking population, new liquor regulations and a police crackdown on crooked gambling and other infractions had calmed the scene a bit (and, really, the truly wild times had lasted only for that one summer of 1898). But by the time Young arrived, there were still plenty of spots to drink, including at the bars in hotels such as the Dominion, the Northern and the Fairview.

Inevitably, a few old-timers would have told tales about the peak of the Gold Rush. With characters like Swiftwater Bill to work with, they'd need no embellishment to entertain a table, though that doesn't mean they refrained from exaggeration. There would also have been plenty of gabbing about present-day mining: gossiping about what claims were doing well, speculating about other creeks that might be promising and grumbling about the hydraulic concessions Clifford Sifton was granting. And, of course, people would have talked about the weather:

bitterly cold during the short days and long nights of winter and then, after the muddy spring, glorious, though buggy and dusty, during the endless days of summer.

They also debated more substantive subjects. The Klondike was not full of illiterate miners. After all, it supported three newspapers and two libraries. The Standard Circulation Library served those willing to pay a membership fee. The Free Library, with 900 books, was public. Both were soon also lending reading material in the surrounding creek communities. And all the Gold Rush memoirs and diaries that soon surfaced suggest some people were writing as well as reading. The local newspapers regularly published poetry from locals and a few scribblers sold short stories to Outside publications. Active political organizations held debates as well as public meetings where "miners vented their spleens, often to the wild delight of packed houses."

Many barroom babblers would also have boasted about their sporting prowess. In the summer of 1901, town sportsmen ordered twelve dozen lacrosse sticks from the Lally Lacrosse Company of Cornwall, Ontario. Exhibition matches had also given way to organized curling and baseball. (Soon, the town would add leagues for association football, indoor baseball and other sports.) And, of course, there was hockey.

Given this scenario, it's not hard to imagine a bunch of guys—Young among them—egging each other on about a Stanley Cup challenge over drinks. Similar plans emerged in other communities, but this being Dawson, what might have been just idle chatter didn't stay that way despite the ridiculously long odds of pulling off such a feat. Or perhaps that's overthinking it and the truth was as simple as Young having carried his Cup aspirations with him to the Klondike, unable to leave his close calls with the trophy behind when he left Ottawa. Regardless, support for the idea that had first surfaced in 1900 had only grown stronger by the next summer. But even before Young reached the Yukon, hockey had begun changing.

- FOURTEEN -

*"The other half rose as one man and
broke into prolonged and frantic cheers"*

Winnipeggers no doubt thought it a small measure of justice that less than two weeks after the western Vics lost their 1899 challenge in what became known as the Great Hockey Fizzle, the eastern Vics lost their league championship. With it went the Stanley Cup. The Shamrocks were the new champs. Affiliated with the Shamrock Amateur Athletic Association, they were Montreal's Irish Catholic team; the Vics and the MHC represented the city's wealthy and powerful Scottish and English Protestant communities. But unlike the working-class Shamrocks lacrosse team, the hockey seven were mostly middle-class and included several McGill grads. After taking over the old Crystals franchise and joining the AHAC in 1894, the Shamrocks had losing seasons until they joined the new Canadian Amateur Hockey League.

The CAHL owed its existence to the Ottawa Capitals. Despite their humiliation at the hands of the Vics in 1897, the Caps wouldn't go away. They applied to the AHAC again that winter, but the most the league was prepared to offer was a spot in the intermediate series. When they made a third attempt in December 1898, things got messy. A member of the OHC executive told the *Citizen*: "The city has not enough first-class players to form two first-class teams and with the Caps and ourselves dividing these men between us, neither of us would have a strong enough team to hold our own against the Montreal aggregation."

The application was destined for defeat until the intermediate teams passed a resolution to change the voting rules and then outvoted the senior teams to let the Capitals in. The Ottawas, the Vics, the MHC and Quebec City walked out of the meeting. Four days later, those teams met to form their own league. The Capitals settled for the OHA's senior series and the Shamrocks, who'd supported their AHAC bid, had no choice but to join the new loop. That worked out just fine because they not only had their first winning season, they finished first. Which meant the Cup was theirs.

With the ascent of the Shamrocks came the rise of scientific hockey. At least that's what the players called it, though there wasn't much science involved. Strategic hockey would have been a more accurate name, but "scientific" was a popular buzzword at the time, especially in the business world, as factories sought to be more efficient. Still, Arthur Farrell's loose use of the term in *Hockey: Canada's Royal Winter Sport* did recognize how the game was evolving. After Weldy Young helped start the trend of cover points rushing the puck, instead of simply lobbing it down the ice, others copied the tactic. One of the best was Mike Grant, who'd joined Montreal's Vics in 1894. Meanwhile, forwards developed their passing skills. The game was more about teamwork and less about spontaneous individual feats.

Scientific hockey took that even further. The Shamrocks focused on attacking and defending as a unit and maintaining puck possession with good combination work, strong stickhandling and conscientious positional play. They believed the unselfishness of the combination play was crucial to successful hockey and that passing the puck to a teammate in a better position was less tiring than trying to score with an individual effort. "The fancy play, the grand stand play, is a waste of energy, childish, worthless," according to Farrell, who noted the point of the game was to score goals.

The mastermind behind the club's structured approach was Harry Trihey. The Shamrocks' best player, he was a centre who handled the puck deftly and had a great shot. During the 1899 season, he scored nineteen goals in seven games, including ten in one match against Quebec. His wingers were Farrell and Fred Scanlan, creating a forward line that excelled at passing the puck. As captain, Trihey led the team in offensive drills and stressed positional play. He wanted both members of the defence pair to be part of the offence and cover points to be good stickhandlers. Meanwhile, rovers, usually the fastest skaters, competed all over the ice. But not idly or without purpose—they went wherever they were needed most. When the defence was struggling or out of position, the rover helped out. "He should be the busiest man on the team," Trihey explained, "because, as a forward, he must attack, and follow up every attack on his opponents' goals; he should also be the particular player to return to help his own defence against every rush by his adversaries." Increasingly, though, rovers didn't lag behind the attacking centre and wingers. "The prettiest spectacle afforded by a good hockey match, is the rush down the ice, four abreast, of the forwards," Farrell wrote. "This play to a man of sporting instincts, verges on the beautiful."

Scientific or not, hockey was now faster, more skilled and more engaging, which was great for fans and encouraged more people, from more backgrounds, to take up the game.

The Eurekas were likely the best hockey club down east at the turn of the century. They just never had a chance to prove it because they were Black. The Halifax team was the class of the Coloured Hockey League of the Maritimes, which also included teams from

Africville, Dartmouth, Amherst and Truro. The games were popular with white fans; in fact, crowds sometimes swelled to 1,200 people, three or four times the typical attendance for white teams. No wonder: the players were fast, talented and tenacious and the matches featured big hits and fights as well as dazzling skating and creative playmaking. Eurekas cover point Eddie Martin may have been the originator of the slapshot, and the league, which lasted until 1930, was the first to let goaltenders go down to make saves. But the Eurekas couldn't even play the Crescents, Halifax's white champions, let alone vie for the Stanley Cup. (Segregation persisted for decades. The National Hockey League's colour barrier remained unbroken until 1958, when Willie O'Ree played for the Boston Bruins.) So in 1900, the Crescents became the first Maritime team to challenge for the Cup.

A year earlier, the Shamrocks had embarked on an eastern exhibition tour in between first winning the trophy and defending it against Queen's two weeks later. The Crescents tied the Shamrocks in the first game and lost the second by a respectable 4-2 score, giving them confidence that they could compete against the country's best. But the Shamrocks were even better the next season, winning eight of its nine league matches, often running up the score, and then turning away the Winnipeg Vics in mid-February in a thrilling best-of-three Cup series before raucous over-capacity crowds at the Arena. After all that excitement, Montreal fans and papers had little interest in a challenge from some unknown Nova Scotians and the crowds were disappointing. So was the hockey. The Shamrocks dispatched the Crescents 10-2 and 11-0 in a two-game, total-goal series. (No other East Coast team challenged for the Cup until 1907, when the New Glasgow Hockey Club lost to the Montreal Wanderers, and despite two subsequent attempts, no Maritime team would ever win the trophy.)

Westerners kept coming, though, and the Vics tried again at the end of January 1901. Dan Bain and his teammates won the first match. Two nights later, they went back to the packed

Arena hoping to finish the Shamrocks off. The play was fast and rough. "Most of the boys seemed to the think that it was better to give than receive," noted the *Gazette*, "and did their best to follow out that doctrine." With the score tied at one after regulation, the teams went into overtime. Seven minutes in, the fans who listened to the Great North Western telegraph bulletins in jammed hotel lobbies heard: "Shamrock takes it up. Scrimmage on the Winnipeg goal. Flett brings it down. Offside. Face. Goes outside the post. Grant takes it up. Dan shoots. Game for Winnipeg. Bain put it in. It was a beauty."

The Winnipeg captain was the Cup's first overtime hero. "The enthusiastic outburst which greeted his performance is beyond the power of the pen to describe," claimed the *Free Press*, though the next sentence aptly captured the scene and, the gender pronoun notwithstanding, showed how fans always react to big goals: "Half the people in the rink sat motionless with the word disappointment written all over their countenances; the other half rose as one man and broke into prolonged and frantic cheers." Hundreds swarmed the ice, put the Vics on their shoulders and carried them to the dressing room. Afterwards, Bain sent a telegram to Winnipeg: "At last we have landed the cup. We will certainly have a good time. Boys are all O.K. and am feeling fine myself.—Dan."

The 1901 matches marked another development in favour of more skill. Winnipeg point Rod Flett and cover point Magnus Flett rarely resorted to the long lift to relieve pressure from the Shamrocks. After the second game, the *Tribune* declared the tactic's days over: "It does no good and simply wearies the team for nothing." Sure enough, within a few years, lifting would be all but gone from the sport.

While the quality of play improved, the game had other problems. P.D. Ross's *Journal* argued that the growing number of lengthy stoppages in play reduced the spectators' enjoyment. The piece appeared a few days after a league match between the

Ottawas and the Vics that featured several long delays due to injuries and broken skates. Instead of ending by 10:30, the match dragged on until 11:30 on one of the coldest nights of the season. For fans, this meant "three hours of shivering, stamping their feet, clapping their hands, and, incidentally, of thinking strong thoughts and expressing strong opinions about the way matters were going on." Substitutions weren't practical because visiting teams brought as few players as possible to reduce travel costs. So the paper proposed that when a player had to temporarily leave a match due to injury, broken skates or torn apparel, the other team should take a man off until the first man was ready to return. The *Journal* also wanted fines or forfeiture for teams that didn't hit the ice within a short grace period of the advertised start time.

The *Gazette* was worked up about something else. Many Cup challenges were carry-over series as a league champion from one season took on the Cup holder early the next. When Winnipeg's Vics met the Shamrocks again in January 1901, it didn't matter that the Montrealers were now past their prime and headed to a third-place finish in the CAHL. "It is like playing up against a dead man . . . The Stanley Cup practically represents the champions of a year ago," the paper said. "Far better hockey may be played, and has been played, in the regular scheduled matches, but the interest hangs to the name of the cup." The argument came from a losing city's paper, but it was true.

These were quibbles. Hockey's bigger problem, though the press didn't cover it, was that it remained stubbornly middle-class and hostile to professionalism. Farrell, the son of a city alderman and retailer, revealed the snobbery central to amateurism by contending in his book that mastering the game took so much time it kept the "the ruder, undesirable element" out. That, he claimed, was good because "the social standing and the 'bon hommie' of its players" were part of what made hockey so great. Along with classism, there was more than a little moralism at work here as he argued for stamping out professionalism because "when a young man sees his way clear to earn a livelihood at sports, he will seldom fail to throw away on them the most valuable time of his life, by neglecting the duties that his age demands."

That was a losing argument. The Flett brothers were two of three Indigenous members of the Vics; Tony Gingras, one of the best stickhandlers in the game, was the other. Although hockey was popular in many First Nations communities, Indigenous players remained a rarity in the senior leagues. And no team would have even considered recruiting a member of the Eurekas. So there was a long way to go, but the inclusion of Métis players on the Vics was an indication of how the game was slowly expanding beyond its elitist roots. And another ethnic group was about to enter the game and influence it in a big way.

Montreal's English community had never shown much interest in spreading hockey to outsiders and seemed content to let the Québécois devote their energies to snowshoeing and lacrosse. Similarly, in the nation's capital, which was one-third francophone, the OHC had had only one French-Canadian player. That was Albert Morel, an early goalie on the team. Eventually, though, Irish and French Catholics in Montreal began playing together on college squads. Le National Hockey Club, formed in 1895, and the Montagnard, founded in 1898, took on anglophone teams.

While only one-tenth of Montreal hockey players were francophone by 1900, the city's three founding peoples—the French, the English and the Irish—were now finally part of the game at the senior level. "In one way we expect sports to mirror the social arrangement of their society. But sports are a hammer as much as a mirror, breaking social conventions as they invent them . . . Hockey reflected the social order of late-19th century Montreal, but it disturbed that order too, in healthy and invigorating ways," writes Adam Gopnik in *Winter: Five Windows on the Season*. A few pages later he explains why: "If for no other reason than that the tribal urge to defeat the enemy in surrogate warfare is stronger even than ordinary social bigotry."

When several Irish-Catholic members of the Shamrocks, including Farrell, retired after the 1901 season, French Catholics Louis Hurtubise and Louis Viau were among their replacements on the roster. And Le National was a founding franchise in the Federal Amateur Hockey League in 1903, before moving to the CAHL after one year. Hockey's popularity among Montreal's francophones led to the launch of le Club athlétique Canadien for the 1909-10 season. That team would go on to win the Stanley Cup more often than any other. And French Canadians—including Edouard "Newsy" Lalonde, Maurice "The Rocket" Richard, Guy Lafleur, Raymond Bourque, Mario Lemieux, Patrick Roy and Martin Brodeur—would be some of the sport's greatest of all time.

The success was feeding on itself. As more—and more diverse—people took it up, the better the hockey became, which attracted more fans and more players. And so on. The game flourished.

Four rinks dotted the Yukon River in the winter of 1901. The Civil Service played near the bank on one with a wooden fence around it and wooden benches for the players. But when the river water level dropped, the shore-side ice could be four feet higher than the other side. The Northern Commercial Company operated one called the Villa Lion and the Standard Oil Company maintained one at the foot of George Street that Dawsonites called the Tin Can, or Oilcan, Rink. The Mammoth was in the middle of the river and had canvas walls and tents for dressing rooms. Although exposure to the cold, wind and snow meant all these venues had their flaws, the town enthusiastically supported men's and women's hockey. No one doubted the Klondike could compete with the best teams in the east. Just how much "scientific hockey" had made the sport more polished and entertaining was lost on the local players, isolated as they were in the subarctic.

Despite Young's August 1900 letter home that claimed a challenge was in the works, there's no indication anyone followed through until the next June, when this letter went out to trustees: "On behalf of the Civil Service Hockey Club of Dawson, hockey champions of the Yukon Territory, we hereby challenge the Victoria Hockey Club of Winnipeg, the present holders of the Stanley Cup, to a series of matches for the championship of Canada," wrote G.T. Kirkson, the team's president, and C. Shannon, its honorary secretary. "We would be pleased if you would officially notify the Winnipeg club of our challenge. Owing to our isolated position, we would deem it a favor if you would act for us in this matter, and let us know as soon as possible the dates set for the games. We would suggest the latter part of January 1902, as a suitable season, as the winter trails in this country would by that time be in good condition for travel."

After recapturing the Cup in 1901, the Vics faced no challengers that winter. Ottawa won the CAHL, but after a gruelling season, decided against a challenge that would require a trip to Manitoba. Berlin of the Western Ontario Hockey Association reportedly wanted to play for the Cup, but few hockey people took it seriously. As Woodstock's *Sentinel-Review* put it: "They couldn't beat a drum." So Ross and Sweetland were open to legitimate challenges.

Although Dawson's Civil Service team wasn't part of a provincial association, the Cup's final rule provided a loophole: "9. In case a senior league is ever formed representing the best hockey irrespective of local associations, the trustees may give its winning club the right to challenge for the cup, and if successful to hold thereafter subject to new championship regulations." But the Civils hadn't won a recognized senior league; they'd won a four-team loop in a small northern town with a population that had fallen to a little over 9,000 people. The trustees had no way of knowing if Dawson's league represented "the best hockey," though they surely suspected it didn't. Seeing the Montreal Vics embarrass the Ottawa Capitals and the Shamrocks shellack the Crescents should have given Ross and Sweetland pause.

Regardless, they forwarded the challenge to Winnipeg and the *Toronto Daily Star* reported that the trustees had "every hope of being able to arrange a match at a date satisfactory to the star team of Dawson City." Vics captain Dan Bain said he hoped the Yukoners would come. "He was sure they would be given a good time, as the Victorias would appreciate their coming so far to play a game of hockey," the *Tribune* reported. "He did not think, however, that they would stand much of a show of winning from the Victorias."

In October, Dawson lawyer William McKay stopped in the Prairie city on his way to Ottawa. Confirming the challenge was a serious one, he claimed the Klondike had an excellent team led by Young and Lionel Bennett, a talented centre. McKay also said local hockey enthusiasts were willing to put up the money for the trip. But in mid-December, the *Journal* reported that while the trustees had asked the Civil Service team about suitable dates, they never heard back, suggesting the Yukoners had decided against going that winter. Or maybe the letter never completed its journey.

But it's also possible that the trustees had quietly discouraged the team. Perhaps Ross, Sweetland and Bain appeared accommodating in public out of courtesy but were privately reluctant to entertain a challenge from a team they considered inferior. The *Vancouver Daily News* said out loud what many hockey people were thinking. After dismissing Young as too old, the paper predicted, "It will no doubt be an enjoyable trip, and the Dawson boys can loosen themselves of their nuggets, but no Dawson team can lift that cup unless all the Vics drop dead."

- FIFTEEN -

*"But it is the way of the north
to decide and to act"*

Thomas William Fuller came to Dawson in the middle of 1899 to remake the city. He'd grown up in Ottawa and worked for his father, also named Thomas, who was the Chief Dominion Architect. But as the government's resident architect in the Klondike, charged with designing and supervising the construction of federal buildings, he established his own reputation. Since Dawson was just a few years old, he had much to do and all the territorial officials swamping him with requests for repairs or renovations to their homes didn't help. Two months after he arrived, he wrote to David Ewart, his father's successor as Chief Dominion Architect: "I must say Mr. Ewart, I have never worked so hard in my life." His toil wasn't for naught. During his two and a half years in the Yukon, Fuller was responsible for the design and construction of six significant public buildings. All of them reflected the city's confidence about its future.

The Government Telegraph Office was his first project. Then he went to work on the Post Office, which was two storeys with a three-storey octagonal tower. He followed that with the Territorial Court House, the Central Public School, the Territorial Administration Building and the Commissioner's

Residence. Although construction of the latter two didn't begin until early July 1901, both opened before the year was out. Sixty civil servants moved into the imposing two-and-a-half-storey neoclassical Administration Building, which cost an estimated $120,000. The Commissioner's Residence, a large three-storey neoclassical house with a generous wraparound veranda and ornate trim, cost more than $40,000, with another $7,000 for the elegant furnishings.

Fuller's buildings were primarily wood because it was the most readily available material and, compared to stone and brick, was less susceptible to damage from shifting with the freezing and thawing of the top layer of permafrost. (Nevertheless, these were all substantial, well-constructed structures; all but the school, which burned down in 1957, still stand today.) Settling due to the permafrost also made the use of lath and plaster impractical, so Fuller imported fir and cedar from British Columbia and had it oiled, shellacked and varnished to finish the interiors. The Administration Building was the largest and most ambitious of his Dawson buildings, but the Commissioner's Residence was the grandest and would soon host many swanky social events for the town's elite.

The Gold Rush had upended a lot of Victorian biases. Class, gender and even race didn't mean much to people who'd made the trek to the Klondike and could tough it out in the subarctic. Poor people became fabulously wealthy in an instant. Swiftwater Bill Gates, for one; failed California fruit farmer Clarence Berry, who'd been tending bar in Forty Mile, for another. Originally, the class distinction that mattered the most was between cheechakos and sourdoughs. Women were some of the Klondike's best entrepreneurs. Belinda Mulrooney, originally from Ireland, made her fortune with numerous business ventures. She climbed the Chilkoot Trail armed with women's clothing to sell once she arrived in Dawson in June 1897. Then she ran a successful restaurant; became a property developer selling cabins for thousands of dollars; and, in August of that year, began operating a popular roadhouse called the Grand Forks Hotel with a busy bar and dining room at the confluence of the Bonanza and Eldorado creeks. She made even more money from the shares in gold claims she amassed, often in return for grubstaking miners. Then she built the Fairview Hotel, perhaps the finest in Dawson. After it opened in July 1898, miners in from the creeks stayed on the third floor; the tonier crowd kept to the second; and a saloon and high-end restaurant did booming business on the main floor. Although there were only ninety-nine Black people among the 30,000 residents during the Gold Rush summer, the Klondike was already welcoming Black boxers at a time when most of the rest of North America didn't.

Over time, though, Southern snootiness invaded Dawson and class consciousness increased, especially as a more sedate lifestyle took over. The population remained highly transient, but as more people left than arrived, the excess waned. Although drinking, gambling and prostitution didn't go away completely, they faced stricter restrictions. In 1900, Major Zachary Taylor Wood, Sam Steele's protege, took command of the NWMP after the force recalled Aylesworth Bowen Perry to Regina. The great-grandson of former U.S. President Zachary Taylor continued his mentor's efforts to civilize the place. That was now a much easier job. Many of the criminals Steele hadn't already chased out of town moved on to more promising locales.

While the undesirables departed, or were absorbed into the civilized community, families stayed. Middle-class values began to dominate. The dance halls and gambling dens were now less the centre of the town's social life than fraternal organizations, clubs and operatic societies. Some of these associations had been around since the Gold Rush, but they now took on more prominence. Citizens also formed groups such as the Women's Vigilance Committee and a branch of the Women's Christian Temperance Union to fight sin. The timing was right for Clifford

Sifton to pressure Wood to be more aggressive. Naturally, the interior minister's motives were political: he didn't want stories of Klondike vice to become an issue in the 1900 federal election.

Prohibitionists in Dawson and in the rest of Canada pressured Sifton to eliminate alcohol from the Yukon. But liquor was the territory's second-biggest source of revenue and the issuing of permits was a valuable cog in the Liberal patronage machine. So instead of banning booze, the territory tightened the rules, even making it illegal for women to drink in saloons and theatres. The NWMP also cracked down on gambling until it was completely illegal by the end of 1902. Although Steele had been appalled by the prostitution in Dawson, he'd been pragmatic enough to not even try to eliminate the trade altogether. Instead, he had controlled it with the monthly medical inspections and other tactics. But Wood had orders to adopt a tougher approach, and the Yukon Council pushed out the Third Avenue sex workers. They moved across the river to Klondike City, which was commonly known as Lousetown.

The first commissioner to live in the new Residence was James Hamilton Ross, who replaced William Ogilvie in March 1901. Effective and popular, he improved the civil service, was a better delegator than his predecessors and spearheaded a much-needed road-building spree to connect all the gold-producing creeks. The city incorporated and gained its own municipal government, with a mayor and six aldermen, in 1902. While gold still dominated the economy, Dawson was now also a government town. The private sector was still a major presence, though, having built close to fifty large, corrugated-iron warehouses and operating the power, telephone and other utilities, among other businesses.

The Klondike continued to support three papers, but the *Daily News* was still the most sophisticated publication. Following trends set by big-city dailies, it added features such as a women's page, a fashion column and increased sports coverage. It also responded to the new moralism in town by launching a campaign against prostitution. But the dominant issue for the newspapers was the mining concessions. While the Dawson papers often viciously disagreed with each other, all three sided with the individual prospectors and placer miners over the companies that held the concessions, though the pro-government *Sun* was less outraged than the *News* and the *Nugget*. Still, these mining industry developments were inevitable and, like the new public buildings, further evidence that the Klondike was growing up.

Clement Bancroft Burns arrived in June 1902 to serve as the territorial secretary. He soon realized that despite all of T.W. Fuller's impressive new government buildings, the town was still missing something. Burns invited nine leading residents, including Joe Boyle, to the gold commissioner's office in the Administration Building. Before their meeting was over they'd agreed to create the Dawson Amateur Athletic Association and build a clubhouse. The idea had been around since at least 1900, as Weldy Young had noted in one of his letters home, but since nothing had ever come of it, people in town were understandably skeptical.

That Burns was an unknown cheechako didn't help. "At the beginning Mr. Burns received no encouragement whatever, money was tight and the scheme was pronounced chimerical, but he hammered away at his hobby," the *Nugget* noted later. He and the other founders scrounged up dozens of shareholders, including local sportsmen such as Young, Sheriff Eilbeck and his son Jack, "to carry on the business of an athletic association for the promotion of purely amateur sports in all branches; also to conduct and carry on a general club house in conjunction with such association, combining reading, writing and dining rooms; also to combine skating and curling rinks, and all other sports and games." At $100 a share, the association initially raised

$20,000, then more than doubled the amount of stock when the enterprise proved more expensive than originally estimated.

Construction of the massive building at the northwest corner of Fifth Avenue and Queen Street began in September of 1902. Within two weeks, the roof was on and though there was still plenty of work to do on the interior, a *Nugget* editorial crowed: "Prosaic easterners would scarcely be able to realize the possibility of an undertaking of such great magnitude completed in so brief a period. But it is the way of the north to decide and to act."

The building was far enough along in early October that shareholders were able to meet in the reception room to elect a board of governors. After celebrating Burns for his accomplishment, William McKay, who chaired the meeting, cited Boyle for his hard work on the building committee and helping draft the club's constitution. Boyle went on to serve on the board and chair both the Gymnasium and Sports Committee and the Light and Heat Committee.

The D-Three-A formally opened November 24. "The social life of the Klondike is likely to be entirely revolutionized this winter by the opening of the splendid building of the Amateur Athletic Association," wrote Stroller White in the *Nugget*. "It comprises all the leading society of the city, and possesses all the facilities in its own building for both large and small parties." The first bash was a large one. Ignoring the blizzard outside, hundreds of people showed up to celebrate the opening. From 8 to 10 p.m., skaters packed the rink as the twelve-piece Mounted Police Orchestra played, while spectators filled the sides and the balcony. At 10 p.m., the party moved upstairs and crammed into the large second-floor gymnasium with its twenty-foot ceiling. Guests did what they could to find enough space to dance as the band swung until 1 a.m.

The 20,000-square-foot complex, which was two storeys with a pair of three-storey towers, quickly became the social and athletic hub of the town. The large reception room, which featured russet leather tête-à-tête chairs and circular divans, was a popular spot for large meetings, while the parlours were good for smaller gatherings and card games. There was a reading room; a room where "ladies" could "assemble and leave their wraps"; a buffet bar; a billiards room; a Turkish bath; and shower and tub rooms. The building also hosted musical and literary events; Boyle performed a piano solo at a concert in February 1903.

For the sporting set, there were bowling alleys; handball courts; the large gymnasium; and a running track around the second floor. In the summer, the big attraction was the natatorium. Lined with sheet iron, the swimming pool was eighty feet by thirty-five feet with an average depth of seven feet. The steam-heating system that kept the building warm during the cold months maintained the pool's water at a comfortable temperature during the summer. In the winter, the building had two curling sheets and a skating rink, which was 160 feet long and seventy-five feet wide. There were heated dressing rooms for the players and lots of space for spectators. Eventually, the club would add a theatre and bill itself as "The Amusement Centre of the Klondike Metropolis."

The gymnasium provided a new permanent home for boxing. Fights had been popular in the Klondike since the Gold Rush, in part because of the presence of Boyle and Frank Slavin. Boyle promoted boxing matches, refereed bouts and even entered the ring himself. Other early promoters in town included Tex Rickard, who would later buy and rebuild New York's Madison Square Garden and launch the New York Rangers, and Arizona Charlie Meadows, a veteran of Wild West shows who built Dawson's Palace Grand Theatre in 1899 (a rebuilt version still stands today). Once or twice a week, the Palace Grand—normally home to plays and concerts—hosted "glove contests" in which local challengers from the creeks unwisely went into the ring with Boyle, Salvin, local champ Nick Burley or an imported pugilist. There were also bouts between professional prize fighters from Outside, which were better exhibitions of the sweet science. While the Monte Carlo, the Tivoli Theatre and the Orpheum also hosted bouts, the DAAA provided fight fans with a set-up that impressed even the faraway *Baltimore Sun*: "Just imagine an amphitheatre seating nearly 5,000 people, with a 241 foot stakeless ring in the center, padded floor and the whole affair brilliantly illuminated by electric light, then you will have an idea why the Dawson City sports can claim the premier boxing club of the world."

Several athletic groups became affiliated with the DAAA. One was the Dawson Curling Club, which had originally formed in October 1900 with forty-five charter members. During that first winter, the curlers competed in a wood-frame building with canvas walls on a slough behind the police barracks. That ice kept heaving and cracking, so the next year the club rented a Front Street warehouse. The two sheets in the new DAAA clubhouse allowed the club to expand its membership and reduce the dues.

The skating rink, which was also used for pleasure skating and fancy-dress carnivals, boosted enthusiasm for hockey in Dawson. Even the town's children were caught up in the excitement for the game. In September 1902, the public school had a record enrolment of 233 students. In November, eighty of them signed a petition to Zachary Wood, who was serving as the acting commissioner of the Yukon following James Ross's election to Parliament. Noting that they were the "future voters and officials of the Yukon territory," the kids asked that the fire department flood a portion of the schoolyard to make a rink and promised to do their best to keep it clear of snow. Within a week, Wood and Mayor Henry Macaulay sent a constable and two prisoners to stake out a rink in front of the school. The prisoners used picks and shovels to level the ground and create an embankment around the rink. Then the fire department handled the flooding, though it took a while before the youngsters were happy with the quality of the ice.

The rink in the DAAA was much better than that, but it still didn't eliminate postponed games when the temperature sank too low outside. And it had its quirks. The ice surface sat over the swimming pool, which led to some uneven freezing and a bulge in the middle. While that didn't exactly make for the ideal hockey conditions, and no spectator would ever mistake it for Montreal's Arena, it was still the only indoor rink west of Winnipeg.

A lively rivalry between the town's lawyers and doctors—the Jawbones and the Sawbones—was popular with fans and a source of fun for the newspapers. "The M.D.'s are talking of playing Dr. Randy McLennan," reported the *Sun* before one game, in reference to the former member of the Queen's University club, "but the jurists have applied for an injunction to prevent this being carried out." One thousand people showed up to watch the match and the gate was about $275. Their next game attracted 700 fans.

Another crowd-pleaser was a so-called fat men's match between "Bell's Babies" and "Cowan's Lilliputians." All the players weighed at least 215 pounds. The papers delighted in covering the game with as much fat-shaming humour as possible: "It was a lead-pipe cinch that at least fifty pounds of delicately tinted, quivering, pink flesh was dissipated . . . ," reported the *Nugget*. "Perspire? No, indeed, it was plain, vulgar sweat and it rolled off in bucketsful . . . " The 219-pound Boyle scored a goal and was the speediest skater of the bunch. According to the *Sun*, "He pranced around like Og, king of Bashan, looking for white elephants to devour." The merchants, the surveyors and various companies also put together squads for exhibition games while two women's teams, called the Maids and the Matrons, competed against each other.

Since Young was still living and working out of town, making it into Dawson only occasionally, he couldn't play hockey regularly. But there was never any doubt that if the Civil Service team headed east for a Cup challenge, he'd be on it. And the idea wouldn't die. In September 1902, the *Vancouver Province* reported that Dawson might send a team to Montreal to vie for the trophy, noting, "The trip would cost $10,000, but that wouldn't worry the people in the land of the midnight sun."

- SIXTEEN -

"The disguises of the professional are
as many and varied as the pebbles on a beach"

Two blasts of the whistle would ignite a frenzy of ecstasy. A third one would lead only to dismay. The big whistle was at the Front Street powerhouse of the Toronto Railway Company, which operated the city's electric streetcars. The simple, high-decibel code would communicate the results of the big games taking place on the Prairies in the winter of 1902. So while many fans gathered outside telegraph and newspaper offices to follow the play via the telegram bulletins, others stayed home but left a window open and kept an ear cocked. Stanley Cup fever had finally reached Ontario's largest city.

A large crowd, including John Ross Robertson, assembled at Union Station to cheer the Toronto Wellingtons before they boarded a train to Winnipeg. OHA champs two years in a row, the Iron Dukes—the team's name was a tribute to the Duke of Wellington—were to take on the Victorias in a best-of-three carry-over challenge.

Although the Ontario league was the country's largest, none of its teams had yet won the Cup. No Toronto team had even challenged for it, though George McKay, the captain of the Wellingtons, had been on the Queen's team that lost the

1895 bid. So it was no surprise that the snobbery regarding the quality of hockey played anywhere but the CAHL and Winnipeg still reigned. Many fans outside Toronto—and a few in it—didn't consider the Wellingtons serious challengers; some even doubted the Iron Dukes would score a goal against the champs.

The Vics had moved from the old McIntyre Rink to the Auditorium Rink for the 1898-99 season. With a capacity of at least 4,000, the wood building, which had cost $20,000 to erect, offered fan amenities such as a coat check and a ladies' room. The ice surface was 200 feet by eighty-five feet, the same as Montreal's Arena. The Wellingtons played out of the Caledonian Rink, also known as the Mutual Street Rink, which was much smaller. That was one disadvantage. Worse, playable ice was not common in Toronto until late December and an unusually mild January had afforded the team little chance to practise. The Vics were sure to be in better condition. Weak challengers often meant smaller crowds in Montreal, but Winnipeggers and former Torontonians in the city filled the Auditorium for the first game. And while the Wellingtons were clearly the underdogs, their fans back in Ontario hoped that after at least two of the three games the powerhouse whistle would blow only twice.

When the first match was over, they were sad to hear a third toot. Winnipeg had won 5-3. But Toronto had put a scare into the Vics. The Iron Dukes had outplayed them in the first half, even taking a 2-1 lead. In the second half, though, the Cup holders showed why the trophy was theirs. The *Globe* didn't miss the opportunity to crow about the respectable play of the Toronto team. "The fiction that Winnipeg and Montreal had a monopoly of really first-class hockey was thoroughly exploded on Tuesday night, the very first occasion on which it was on trial," the paper declared. "It had no other foundation than the 'say-so' of some young gentlemen who write for the newspapers in those places. Having seen no other hockey than their own they came to the conclusion that there was no other, and succeeded, to a large extent, in bringing their readers to the same opinion."

True, the Wellingtons had surprised a lot of people in the Prairie city with their performance—not enough to make anyone in Winnipeg worry about losing the Cup, but impressed nonetheless. While disappointed, Toronto fans were proud of their team and now had faith the second game would yield a favourable ending. Around midnight, just for a few seconds as they held their breath after twice hearing the big whistle, they must have been in a fleeting state of anxious delight. Alas, a third blast soon followed.

The papers responded with a weird mix of defensiveness and braggadocio. "It has now been proved, it is hoped, to the satisfaction of those hockey nabobs in Montreal and Ottawa that just as fast and clever men play the game in Toronto and other places, affiliated with the Ontario Hockey Association, as in any association in the Dominion," Robertson's *Evening Telegram* thundered. "One gratifying result of the two contests is the blow that has been struck at the false prophets, the men who tumbled over each other in an eagerness to bet the Victorias would double the Wellingtons' score or that the Iron Dukes would not be able to tally."

Despite those smug words and the better-than-expected showing by the team, the games were more evidence that Ontario hockey still wasn't as good, as fast or as physical as in the neighbouring provinces. Toronto manager William Lamont allowed that the Wellingtons would benefit from the education they'd received at the hands of the Vics and even the players admitted the better club won. "We were fairly beaten," McKay said. "We played as hard as we ever played in our lives, but the checking and bodying was much harder than we were accustomed to. It was fierce."

The players had the injuries to prove his point. When the team arrived home, Charles "Chummy" Hill had a cut eye,

Frank McLaren was limping and McKay's arm was in a sling. George Chadwick was in bad shape and would be diagnosed with scarlet fever the next day, though he could hardly blame that on rough play from the Vics. The train was seven hours late, so the crowd wasn't as big as it might have been, but the banged-up team received an enthusiastic greeting from fans and dignitaries at Union Station and later that night at Shea's Theatre. Torontonians, and their newspapers, were convinced that the city was now part of hockey's elite. Of course, what they needed to prove it, and silence the critics for good, was a Stanley Cup win.

When the OHA held its annual meeting that December, the J. Ross Robertson Silver Challenge Trophy held a prominent place at the front of the room. Unfortunately for Toronto fans, this was the honour Robertson cared about more than the Stanley Cup. A year after donating the trophy that bore his name, he'd ascended to the OHA presidency by acclamation "amid uproarious cheers" from the delegates at the annual meeting in December 1899. In his acceptance speech, he attributed the organization's growth to its commitment to pure amateurism and uttered a line that managed to refer to the Boer War, channel Lord Wellington and celebrate his Victorian attitude toward manhood and honour. Instead of apologizing for Canada's winters, he said, "We should be proud of them because they had served to develop the young men who are now in South Africa playing Britain's game of war."

A physically imposing man with a big head, a jowly face and prodigious eyebrows over his deep-set eyes, Robertson had a personality to match. The OHA had never had a member of its executive with his standing in Toronto, his connections or his wealth, and while it already had a formidable record of fighting professionalism with ruthless discipline, the publisher soon became known as the "Iron Fist" as he banned a string of teams and players. After his first year in power, he used his address at the annual meeting to give a long, slightly unhinged diatribe against professionals. "Our creed is to encourage the amateur and discourage the professional sport. The former has the first place in our list of friends," he said. "The latter is our enemy. He prates and preaches, but he never practices." Contending unconvincingly that he didn't have a problem with professionals as long as they kept to themselves and stayed away from amateurs, he complained about how onerous it was for the executive to root out the scofflaws. "The disguises of the professional are as many and varied as the pebbles on a beach. He is a past master in the art of deception. His heart is as full of guile as an egg is of meat. His schemes are so novel that they would stagger a politician."

Robertson's speeches did little to end the cheating. As London defeated Stratford 6-1 in an intermediate series match in mid-January of 1901, a fan noticed that the player who claimed to be Campbell Lindsay wasn't local man Campbell Lindsay. He was Frank Winn from Montreal. Stratford also contended that neither William "Riley" Hern nor Ernie Lang met the league's residency requirements. London responded with several affidavits, including one from Lindsay, attesting to the team's innocence. But when pressed, Lindsay admitted he hadn't played and had made the false declaration to help London out. The league also determined that Hern had previously played for pay. The OHA expelled the club and its officers and declared all the players professionals, even those, such as point Harry Peel, who knew nothing of the deception. It also handed the false affidavits over to the Crown and threatened to press perjury charges. The *Globe* cheered: "Fortunately for the good reputation of Canadian pastimes, this monstrous rascality has been promptly detected, exposed and punished."

The OHA executives spent much of their meetings dealing with protests. Many concerned professionals or players who didn't meet the residency requirements or, in the junior series, overage players. But teams also complained about violence as well as the referees, umpires and timekeepers. Orillia wanted a loss overturned because the rink in Coldwater didn't have goal nets. Even as the league tossed clubs, more wanted in. The growth, and the Wellingtons' respectable performance against the Vics, suggested the association was healthier than ever.

And yet, Robertson was making a Cup victory more remote. Sure, he'd welcome the glory of an OHA team winning the trophy, but his enthusiasm was muted. In fact, he rarely mentioned that silver bowl. He used his annual addresses for promising to smite professionals rather than vowing to win the Stanley Cup. The trophy with his name on it meant more to him. "It is a pleasure to see that one of our teams, the winner of the senior championship—the Robertson Challenge Cup—proposes to try its fortunes with the champion team of the Dominion in Winnipeg," he said in his 1901 annual address. "I am sure the good wishes of this association will follow the senior champions." The morning after the Iron Dukes lost the first game of the series, Robertson sent a message to the team's manager: "Everybody is delighted with your showing. Keep on. Win or lose, you are a credit to the city and the O.H.A." Those words might have displayed sportsmanship but they were free of the passion for the Cup that gripped Toronto fans.

Worse, even though Robertson published a populist paper favoured by the city's working classes, his hatred of creeping professionalism just helped ensure Ontario hockey remained a sport dominated by people with the means to play it for free and, when teams could get away with it, people paid on the sly. The problem for leagues was the more successful the game became, the harder it was to keep the players amateur. Predictably, efforts to do so just pushed them south of the border. Indeed, the most influential player in the development of professional hockey in the United States had spent time in the OHA's doghouse.

Born and raised in Berlin, Ontario, John Liddell Macdonald "Jack" Gibson was his hometown team's seventeen-year-old cover point when the OHA expelled the club in 1898. After reinstatement by the league at the end of the season, Gibson fielded offers from several other clubs, including Toronto Varsity, but decided to play for Berlin's Young Men's Christian Association team until going to the Detroit College of Medicine to study dentistry. He played hockey at school, but also returned home to help Berlin win the new Western Ontario Hockey Association title. He scored three times in the championship game, leading appreciative fans to hoist him on their shoulders and parade him off the ice.

During his college career, he played an exhibition game in Michigan's Upper Peninsula, where a copper mining boom was creating several wealthy resource towns. After graduating in 1900, Gibson settled in Houghton, a town full of miners and lumbermen on the south side of Portage Lake. It was part of Houghton County, which was home to 100,000 people, twenty newspapers, seven theatres, two opera houses and a streetcar line connecting three towns. At first, Gibson focused on building his dental practice and didn't give much thought to hockey. But he'd kept a scrapbook of newspaper clippings. One day, a young reporter with the local *Daily Mining Gazette* saw it in Gibson's office and decided to write about the dentist's athletic accomplishments. The coverage led to the formation of the Portage Lakes Hockey Club, which played in an Upper Peninsula league with games in the Palace Ice Rink in nearby Hancock.

A big man, Gibson could rush and score and dish out clean but punishing bodychecks. He led his team to the championship in 1901 and again the next year. Then a group of Houghton businessmen headed by James R. Dee built a bigger arena called the Amphidrome. Gibson—now nicknamed "Doc"—took advantage of a good eye for talent to rebuild the team with an all-Canadian roster. That season, he captained the seven to an undefeated record, including a 1-0 victory over the Pittsburgh Bankers in a game to decide the unofficial championship of the United States.

The Bankers were part of the semi-professional Western Pennsylvania Hockey League, which operated out of Duquesne Gardens in Pittsburgh (spelled Pittsburg at the time). The Gardens held 4,000 spectators and was home to one of the country's two artificial rinks. Fans in the largely working-class city liked this new game better than ice polo, which had been popular.

Good local players were scarce, so teams imported Canadians, including several who'd run afoul of the OHA. Hern and Peel, from the banned London club, joined the Pittsburgh Keystones. Peel raved about the experience. The hockey, the rink and the treatment were all excellent. "We have in the league some of the fastest in the East," he wrote in a letter to a friend, "but myself and the rest of our boys are staying with them." And, of course, there was the money. "They make no bones whatever about paying men," said a player whose team gave him $25 a week and set him up with a job for another $15 a week. "I had a room in a lawyer's office, where I used to sit and write letters to myself."

Hockey had spread to several states, including Michigan, Pennsylvania and New York. Though the country had its supporters of amateurism, most Americans weren't hampered by British hang-ups about it, so the debate wasn't as intense as in Canada. A professional league was inevitable. And Gibson would help make it happen sooner than Robertson and the OHA feared.

- SEVENTEEN -

"You can have everything in Winnipeg except the Stanley Cup"

Referees, again. By now, P.D. Ross expected wrangling over officials for Stanley Cup games. But resorting to drawing lots must have seemed a bit much. A month after the Victorias beat the Iron Dukes, the trustee received another Cup challenge and wired Winnipeg. The next day Ross recorded in his diary simply, "Declined Ottawa challenge for Stanley Cup." The reason: the Vics weren't convinced the OHC would repeat as league champs. They were right. The MHC clinched the title that night with a win over the eastern Vics. At a meeting the following Saturday afternoon the team agreed to go for the Cup. The next morning, club executive Charles Chitty met with Ross in Ottawa to deliver word of the challenge and suggest March 13, 15 and, if necessary, 17 as the dates, meaning the series would start in less than two weeks. "The Montreal boys are bound to have that cup," Chitty said afterwards. "The trip is a big undertaking on short notice, as well as a very expensive one. No doubt the gate receipts will help a lot, but we do not care anyway, we will go if we have to beggar ourselves."

Ross approved the challenge and asked Winnipeg to wire the names of three referees to the eastern team. The MHC declined all three, even though two of them—Harry Trihey and Arthur Farrell of the Shamrocks—were Montrealers. The third was William Macfarlane of the Winnipeg Hockey Club, who'd pleased both sides when he reffed the Vics-Wellingtons series. The Winged Wheelers feared he wouldn't be strict enough on rough play and too many of their players would end up in the hospital. After Montreal proposed three names, Vics president Jack Armytage wired the trustee to say that none were acceptable because no one in the Prairie city knew them. He added that his club had accepted local refs for challenges in Montreal and if the MHC wasn't prepared to do that in Winnipeg, it should at least agree to a ref both sides knew.

Sensing a stalemate was likely, the trustee had already asked the Wellingtons for suitable candidates. To MHC president Harry Shaw, the idea that a Torontonian could handle the job "was preposterous, because the Ontario men did not know sufficient about the kind of game that is to be played." Equally unimpressed, the Vics suggested flipping a coin or drawing lots to choose either Macfarlane or Shamrock Percy Quinn. The Montrealers agreed. On March 7, Armytage received a telegram from Ross: "Trustees draw lots between Quinn and Macfarlane in presence of W. Mackenzie, Ottawa correspondent of the Winnipeg *Free Press*, and D. Ranage, Ottawa correspondent of the Montreal *Star*. Macfarlane was chosen. Trustees hereby appoint him referee." But Macfarlane initially refused to take the job because of the MHC's comments. Ross then considered appointing Roy Schooley of Toronto, which appalled both teams. In the end, Macfarlane agreed to do it and the first match would go ahead on March 13.

The MHC planned to go as a party of thirteen: seven players, three spare men, trainer Paul Lefebvre, club secretary W.C. DeWitt and Shaw. Not everyone was comfortable with that. From the days of the Montreal Winter Carnival to its second Cup win, the club had enjoyed unparalleled success. But a run of underwhelming seasons began after thirteen players and executives sat for what became known as the "hoodoo" photo in 1894. Shaw, who was in that photograph, believed the curse was now over. "When we won the Stanley Cup that time, we had our picture taken, and there were thirteen in the crowd. That, superstitious people would say, hoodooed us," he said. "The fact is we were in hard luck till one of that crowd died." Not everyone was so confident the hex was no longer in effect. One suggestion was to expand the party to fourteen to avoid the unlucky number. But the problem solved itself when Ronald Elliott, one of the three spares, was unable to go and his replacement, Billy Bellingham, a cover point on the intermediate team, couldn't leave until a few days after the other players.

Now one of the MAAA's affiliated clubs, the MHC headed west a week after issuing the challenge. Between 300 and 400 people, many of them association members, went down to the CPR station in a snowstorm to see the team depart in its own well-appointed Canadian Palace sleeper car. At each stop, the players ran sprints on the station platform before getting rubdowns from the trainer. On March 11, 800 people, including members of the Vics and the Winnipeg Hockey Club, met the train at the CPR depot and gave the Montrealers an exuberant cheer. Hacks then carried the players to the Clarendon Hotel.

Over at the Auditorium Rink, as temperatures in the city climbed as high as sixty-three degrees, workers tried to salvage the ice. They soaked up water with blankets and then wrung them out, filling no fewer than twenty large tubs. Management cancelled public skating but allowed the MHC to practise. The Vics were full of smiles, snickers and confidence the first time they saw the diminutive Montrealers on the ice. Dickie Boon, the young captain, weighed just 125 pounds or so. Even in an era when most players tipped the scales at between 145 and 180 pounds, he was small, especially for a cover point, who tended to be bigger men. But he was fast and smart. Offensively, the team relied on its speed, strong stickhandling and short passes; defensively, it preferred to play the puck, not the man.

The veteran Vics were older, bigger and more physical, but less fit. Several of the players had been around since the infamous 1899 challenge against the Shamrocks, though Winnipeg left winger Fred Scanlan had played for Montreal in that series. Centre Dan Bain had been with the team since the Cup victory in 1896, while rover Charlie Johnstone had played in the December match that year. They certainly had experience.

The temperature reached fifty-three degrees on March 13. While some observers thought soft ice would favour the slower Bisons, the Montrealers argued they had more experience with such conditions. At least the more than 2,000 disappointed fans who'd failed to get in after jostling for a chance at fifty-cent standing room tickets hadn't had to worry about the cold. The high prices ticket hawkers charged were another matter: a man from St. Paul, Minnesota, paid $50 for a pair of reserved seats. Unfortunately, the hockey wasn't the finest because the ice surface was more liquid than solid. "There was a general impression prevalent that somewhere beneath the broad lake which formed the arena there was ice, but no person present could pose as an eyewitness of this fact," noted Montreal's *Daily Herald*. The poor conditions made passing, rushing and staying dry difficult. "It was a common thing to see four men at one time sliding on their stomachs for a distance of 15 yards over the water-covered ice," according to the *Star*. "It was desperately tricky work, but the play never stopped." With goals hard to come by, the home team won 1-0.

The close score ramped up the anticipation for the second match as the weather turned wintery. The high on the Ides of March was minus-fourteen degrees and the city was in the grips of a forty-eight-hour blizzard. Although some snow made it through a few broken windows, the ice conditions were ideal. Undeterred by the storm, 4,500 fans packed into the rink only to see the worst defeat the Vics had ever suffered, as Montreal dominated 5-0. Somehow even more people squeezed into the Auditorium for the deciding match as the temperature fell further and "never did a more enthusiastic audience assemble in Winnipeg to witness a hockey match," according to the *Tribune*. Just about all of them donned team colours—hometown fans were decked out in red and black, while the MHC fans who'd travelled west for the series and the ex-Montrealers who lived in Winnipeg wore blue and white.

The visitors scored twice in the first seven minutes and then held on as the momentum swung. When the Bisons put one past MHC goalie Billy Nicholson in the second half, the Great North Western Telegraph Company's bulletins announced: "Vics score. Bain put in the shot. Montreal 2, Vics 1. Crowd crazy; it's awful, the noise." But Nicholson stopped everything else. The papers agreed that the game was a classic, probably the fastest and most exciting in Winnipeg history and, according to the *Star*, "one of the hardest fought battles on ice ever seen in this city, or, possibly, anywhere."

Other big city newspapers covered the series, but naturally the excitement was greatest in Winnipeg and Montreal. "Canadian hockey may now claim at least equal honors with lacrosse as the national game of the Dominion. Indeed, its devotees are probably far more numerous," said a *Tribune* editorial before the first game, adding that while hockey enjoyed "universal allegiance," lacrosse was one of several popular summer games. "And what contests in any other sport command the interest of the whole community as do the Stanley Cup matches?"

In Montreal, the MAAA gymnasium was packed for all three games, with up to 600 people smoking, singing songs and listening to the telegraph updates. Thousands of others followed the play by gathering around bulletin boards outside the *Star* head office at the corner of St. Catherine and Peel and the Pointe-Saint-Charles branch office. After the third game, the fans "divided up into battalions, and paraded the streets, literally singing the praises of their heroes, till a very early hour this morning."

During the series, the *Star*'s sports editor Peter Spanjaardt dubbed the team the Little Men of Iron. His coverage of the first game noted, "They are plucky little men of steel." And the headline on his report of the second game was "Montreal's Little Men of Iron Won." The story noted, "The heavy bodying of the Winnipegs was a waste of energy, for if the little men of iron from the East were thrown off their feet against the fence they were down only a second, and before the spectators could look they were up and carrying the puck merrily toward the Vics' citadel." No Winnipeg paper used the name, though the *Tribune* did call the team the "Lionmen of Iron" two days after the series. But it stuck in Montreal.

Carriages bearing banners that proclaimed "Our Little Men of Iron" and "Champions of the World" waited at Windsor Station. Ignoring the hacks, fans picked up the players as they stepped off the Atlantic Express at 8:25 p.m. and carried them to the MAAA gymnasium on their shoulders. The band leading the way played "The Conquering Hero." Club executives flaunted three prizes: the Stanley Cup; the CAHL's championship trophy, which the team had picked up when their train stopped in Ottawa; and a sign from a jewellery store in the Prairie city that had warned the challengers: "You can have everything in Winnipeg except the Stanley cup."

The route to the association clubhouse on Mansfield Street was packed. Estimates ranged from seven thousand to thirty thousand people. The temperature hit fifty degrees that day, with a good amount of rain, so many stood ankle-deep in springtime mud. With not enough police to control the unprecedented crowd, the procession took nearly forty-five minutes to travel a few blocks and most fans struggled to get even a glimpse of their heroes. At the clubhouse, delighted members and guests listened to speeches by dignitaries, gave three cheers for the vanquished opponents and sang "God Save the King." A Montreal team held the Cup once again and if the citizens of Canada's largest city had ever taken the trophy for granted, they didn't anymore.

For most of the Cup's first decade, three Montreal sevens— the MHC, the Victorias and the Shamrocks—held the trophy. Other cities had tried, of course: Kingston, twice; two clubs from Ottawa; Toronto; and Halifax. But only Winnipeg had been able to break the stranglehold, holding the honour for most of 1896 and again from 1901 to 1902. Two days after the Bisons lost to the Winged Wheelers, the *Free Press* declared, "Winnipeg hockeyists, be they Victorias, Winnipegs or some other combination, will never give up trying for possession of the silver mug, and it is bound to come back here again."

The Vics soon tried again with a carry-over challenge in February 1903. Bain had retired and the team included three new faces. After a humiliating 8-1 loss in the first match, the Bisons were determined to rebound in the second game. The contest began at 8:35 on Saturday night but suffered several delays due to injuries and a broken skate before going into overtime tied 2-2. At 11:52 p.m., Westmount police informed rink management that the mayor had decreed there would be no hockey in his town on a Sunday. Not even Lord Stanley's cup was exempt from the Lord's Day laws. Eight minutes later, the Arena's big gong sounded twice. As the cops stood guard, the players reluctantly filed off the ice. Twenty-seven minutes of overtime had settled nothing. Even without a winner, the crowd had watched two skilful teams play nearly an hour and a half of hard, fast, "rattlingly good" hockey— more than enough excitement for the money.

The teams were less satisfied. Referee Percy Quinn made no call on whether the match was a tie or an unfinished game. This had never happened in Cup history and no one was quite sure what to do. Unbeaten after two games in defence of the Cup, the Montrealers argued they should keep it. Winnipeg disagreed. Quinn decided to refer the matter to the trustees. On Sunday afternoon, Abe Code, president of the Vics' league, and MHC president Charles Chitty joined Quinn on the train to Ottawa. They met with Ross and Sweetland at the Russell House that evening and decided to continue the match on Monday. If the Little Men of Iron scored, they'd keep the Cup and there'd be no need for a third game. If the Bisons scored, the two teams would take a ten-minute break and then play the third and final match of the series. Code was happy; Chitty respected the trustees' decision.

The problem, everyone soon realized, was that the plan would crush ticket sales. "The deciding game might last two seconds or two hours," the *Gazette* pointed out, "and people hate to give up dollars for two seconds' entertainment." Arena management offered to let the second game go ahead without a crowd at no charge, but the teams declined. Instead, they agreed to flip the order of the first proposal and play the third game as scheduled. If Montreal won, it would keep the Cup; if Winnipeg won, the two teams would complete the second game that night. Since the trustees' policy was to get involved only when teams disagreed, they gave their approval. But this solution didn't last, either. The new one was the most obvious and potentially the most profitable option: play the third match and then, if necessary, schedule a fourth.

Meanwhile, animosity flared between the teams. Montreal kicked Winnipeg's manager out of its dressing room and there were reports the Vics had refused the MHC's hospitality. The ill will may have contributed to Boon's outburst. He was still upset Ross had approved the mid-season challenge, which put the players' health at risk, potentially jeopardizing their chances of repeating as league champs. As much as Montreal fans and newspapers valued the Stanley Cup, the senior teams in the city still considered the CAHL title an even greater honour. If the MHC kept the trophy, he threatened to recommend the executive committee return it to the trustees. Under a "Poor Dickey" headline, the *Tribune* claimed that Boon believed Ross "has not properly administered his trust, and that the cup has been a detriment, instead of a benefit to the game."

When Winnipeg won the third match 4-2, setting up an unprecedented fourth contest, the CAHL was unhappy. It had already wanted to put an end to mid-season challenges, and now instead of two or three games, there would be a fourth. Worse, it would be on Wednesday, potentially depressing ticket sales for Saturday's league game. Trihey, now CAHL president, polled the member teams to see if they had any objections to Montreal playing a fourth game. Ottawa wired back: "None whatever." The other clubs were fine with it, too. But Quinn refused to ref another game because both teams had criticized his work. Chauncey Kirby took over as referee and Montreal ended the series with a 4-1 victory. Afterwards, Boon went to the Winnipeg dressing room to shake hands, putting an end to any hard feelings between the clubs. But the *Free Press* had not forgotten his threat to send the trophy to Ross and Sweetland: "It is now up to Dicky Boon to return the pewter to the trustees. If the cup is going to be so much trouble for the eastern clubs, guess we'll have to bring it west and keep it in Winnipeg." But there was no more talk of Montreal relinquishing what it had fought so hard to win.

Despite the flurry of controversies, the four games generated a record gate of $15,000. The Vics went home with $3,000, but the Cup stayed in Montreal. For a few more weeks anyway.

Early in January, as the Vics had prepared to face the Little Men of Iron, several other teams began talking about issuing challenges. The Iron Dukes wanted another crack at the trophy if they kept the OHA title. Out west, senior hockey had split into two loops. The Vics and the Winnipeg Rowing Club formed the new Western Canada Hockey League, leaving the Manitoba and North West Hockey League to the Winnipeg Shamrocks, Brandon, Portage La Prairie and the Rat Portage Thistles. As the Rowing Club considered a challenge, two representatives of the Thistles met with the trustees in Ottawa. Ross made it clear the teams needed to determine a provincial champ. In addition, all challenges had to wait until the CAHL season ended on February 28. But it was already clear the Little Men of Iron, who'd lost Charlie Liffiton to the professional Pittsburgh Bankers after one game, would not retain the Cup.

Who would take the trophy remained uncertain when the Victorias and the Ottawas tied atop the standings. Rover Russell Bowie led the Vics, scoring twenty-two times in seven games. The OHC had bolstered its lineup with centre Frank McGee, who scored fourteen in six. The tie made a playoff necessary, further delaying any Cup matches—and increasing the uncertainty about ice conditions. Ross wanted the league to settle on a champion quickly to allow for three Cup contests the week of March 9. He proposed giving the Wellingtons one match, and the Thistles, since they had the longer and more expensive journey, a two-game, total-goal series.

CAHL secretary Fred McRobie read the trustee's letter at a league meeting. But McRobie, who'd won the Cup with Montreal's Vics in 1899, was also that club's president and wanted to give Bowie's injured foot as much time as possible to heal. Declaring that the Vics would refuse any playoff games before March 7, he argued the CAHL should give no consideration to what the trustees wanted and that the Cup was interfering with the league's affairs. When the other teams voted in favour of a two-game, total-goal series on March 5 and 7, McRobie said the Vics would default, giving the Ottawas both the CAHL championship and the Stanley Cup. But OHC president Percy Butler relented and agreed to matches on March 7 and 10. The meeting finally adjourned at 2:30 in the morning.

A two-week wait for a new champion made more than one challenge all but impossible. Ross's solution was to make the Wellingtons face the MHC. If the Little Men of Iron won, they'd cede the Cup to the winner of the Ottawa-Vics series. If the Wellingtons prevailed, or the Winged Wheelers refused to defend it, the trophy would go to Toronto, where the rarity of playable ice in mid-March almost assured there could be no more challenges until the next season. Ross probably counted on the Little Men of Iron beating the Iron Dukes, but it was a risk.

No one liked this idea. "Under such circumstances, it would be absurd to speak of the Stanley cup as being the emblem of the national championship," declared Winnipeg's *Tribune*. "It will become a meaningless piece of metal, the holding of which confers no distinction. That would be a great pity." The situation was one more mess for the Cup and the trustees. Fortunately, the Wellingtons, depleted by injuries and departures, and uninterested in playing the MHC for the honour, dropped their challenge. That left only the Thistles.

Ottawa and the Vics played their first match at the Arena on Saturday night. The watery ice and the tight checking kept offence to a minimum and the score was 1-1 when the gong sounded just a minute before midnight, when the city of Westmount would have ended the match. Because the clubs were playing a two-game, total goal series, there was no controversy. The OHC would have been fine with a tie in the away game, except Harry "Rat" Westwick broke his leg.

He'd joined Ottawa's senior team in 1895 as a goalie but soon moved up to rover. He briefly left with Weldy Young to play for Joseph Seagram's team in 1898. Unlike Young, he went back to Waterloo the next year. Upon his return to Ottawa, he played for the Capitals and eventually rejoined the OHC. A wiry 130 pounds, he was the smallest man on the team. Originally, an

Ottawa fan had compared him to a rat as a compliment because of the way he darted and scurried around the ice. But in 1896, the *Quebec Chronicle* called Young a thug and Westwick a "miserable, insignificant rat."

Despite that nickname, he was a gentleman on and off the ice who was well-known for his competitive but clean and sportsmanlike play. An excellent athlete, he was a fast, shifty skater, a good passer and a prolific scorer. "Time and again he shot down the ice like a lightning flash athwart an inky black cloud," according to a 1903 *Journal* game report. He was also plenty tough. He'd married the sister of former teammate William "Peg" Duval in February, but because of his job at a book bindery and the team's schedule, he hadn't had time for a honeymoon. So the trip to Montreal to play the Vics was to serve as one. Unfortunately, Bert Strachan viciously slashed the newlywed's right leg just above the ankle. As Westwick skated off the ice, a bone was sticking out through the skin. In the dressing room, Halder Kirby, the co-founder of the OHC and now its doctor, set the bone. Then the injured player asked to be carried to the stands so he could watch the rest of the game beside his new wife.

Ottawa would have to win the second game without him. The tobacco smoke was thick in Dey's Rink, as usual, while a thin layer of water covered the ice so that as the players dashed around, they occasionally splashed Lord Minto and his entourage, who were enjoying Ottawa's dominant performance. When the game ended 8-0, fans poured onto the ice to celebrate the new champions before taking their revelry to the city's streets. After a decade of trying, Lord Stanley's favourite team finally held his cup. And though it wasn't part of the OHA, an Ontario team had finally won the honour.

The passing of the Cup from the MHC to the Ottawas marked the end of an era. During the trophy's first decade, hockey's popularity had increased dramatically in breadth and depth to the point that its standing in Canada was well beyond what

Stanley and the trustees, or anyone else, could have imagined. Lord Minto may not have liked what he saw of the administration when he visited the Klondike in 1900, but he liked the hockey he saw in Ottawa. He was another Briton who became an enthusiastic fan while serving as Canada's governor general. When he attended the OHC's 1903 season opener, the crowd represented a broad cross-section of society. "The fashionable set mixed with those not in such fortunate circumstances," according to the *Journal*, "the rich sat alongside of the poor and over it all was wafted the smile of vice-royalty."

After overcoming some early indifference, the trophy quickly became the Canadian grail. While 25,315 spectators attended the eleven regular season games at the Arena that season, the four Cup matches between the western Vics and the MHC attracted 17,866 paying customers to the building. Close to 5,000 more attended the tie with Ottawa. Disputes over referees and other squabbles, as well as minor scandals such as the way the 1899 Vics versus Vics series ended, were inevitable and hadn't turned off the fans. Hockey was full of honourable and skilled athletes, most of whom played for the love of the game, and to many people, the Little Men of Iron were the epitome of that amateur ideal. The previous ten years had been excellent for the sport. But as the Cup's second decade began, increasing violence and a fight over professionalism loomed, threatening that largely blissful early success.

- EIGHTEEN -

"The game was a stemwinder
from start to finish"

Under Sam Steele, Bowen Perry and Zachary Wood, the NWMP gave many undesirables blue tickets out of the Klondike. The declining economic prospects, the clampdowns on gambling and prostitution and the gold strike in Nome reduced their number further but didn't eliminate them entirely. Edward Labelle, a career criminal, and Peter Fournier, an alcoholic drifter, met in Dawson and cooked up a way to make some easy money. They travelled to Whitehorse in June 1902 and hung around the WP&YR station until they found their marks: three prospectors—Léon Bouthillette, Guy Joseph Beaudoin and Alphonse Constantine—headed to the Klondike. Using assumed names, Labelle and Fournier befriended the trio and offered to take them in a small boat for five bucks each, considerably less than a $40 steamer voyage. But on an island near where the Stewart River flows into the Yukon, the pair shot their passengers, took their money and a few pawnable possessions, then weighed down the bodies with stones and threw them in the river.

After the NWMP received a report of a dead man in the water near Stewart River, a postmortem revealed four bullet wounds to the skull. A cheap key chain the killers had neglected to steal had "Leon Bouthillette, P.Q." stamped on it. Beaudoin's body appeared a few days later. Labelle and Fournier had planned and carried out their plot so carelessly that the cops had more than enough clues to easily identify the culprits. Arresting Fournier was simple enough: even after Bouthillette's body turned up, he hung around the Yukon and conspicuously spent a $100 bill in a gambling den. Nabbing Labelle wasn't so easy. Reputedly a one-time leader of an international opium-dealing gang, he'd once escaped custody by jumping out of a moving train in Michigan while in handcuffs. Now he was on the lam again. A detective chased him for more than a month across several western states in a dramatic hunt before finally collaring him in a Nevada work camp. The brutal and premeditated crime horrified and unsettled the increasingly staid Klondike. Labelle had been the "mastermind" of the foolish scheme, but Crown prosecutor Fred Congdon had an easy time convicting both men of murder.

On the morning of January 20, 1903, Sheriff Robert James Eilbeck led the men from their cells to a scaffold that had been erected in a corner of the quadrangle of the NWMP barracks. Despite the intense cold, about one hundred people, including policemen, reporters and a few invited guests, watched. After the condemned men said a few last words, admitting they deserved to die, they were fitted with black hoods and nooses were placed and adjusted on their necks. The masked executioner was an "amateur" with "iron nerves" the sheriff had selected from at least seven people who applied. At 7:45 a.m., Eilbeck signaled with a wave of his hand to pull the lever. The trap door opened. Labelle and Fournier dropped and dangled.

Unlike an American sheriff, a Canadian one was not a criminal chaser, but a court employee. Hangings were one of his responsibilities. Labelle and Fournier were the sixth and seventh men to die this way under Eilbeck's watch. The others included Alexander King, who was hanged in October 1900 for the murder of Herbert Davenport, and George O'Brien, who got the rope in 1901 for ambushing and killing three men. Even at a time when capital punishment was common and popular with the public, many people would not have found it an easy job. But then Eilbeck, who was tall, moustachioed and stern-looking, was not an easy man. At a Christmas Day banquet hosted by Zachary Wood in 1900, Eilbeck responded to a toast to government officials, by saying, "It is to be regretted that all of the American residents of Dawson are of the 'Soapy Smith' kind." Among the gentlemen in the room was American Edgar Mizner, who didn't appreciate the comparison to the late Skagway crime boss. He leapt to his feet and said, "Am I to be insulted?" before storming out of the hall. That may have been the extent of the disagreement, but one report had it that Mizner smashed his glass before leaving, another that he threw wine in the sheriff's face. Whatever happened, Eilbeck's job and his role as a leading sportsman meant the incident didn't hurt his standing in town.

Born in Newcastle, Canada West, in 1850, he moved to Kingston in 1871 to work as a Dominion Telegraph Company operator. A good baseball player—he could hit, run and catch well—he helped introduce the game to the Limestone City. He claimed to have played against Albert Spalding, a major leaguer in the 1870s who popularized the baseball glove; became the president and part owner of the Chicago White Stockings; wrote the first set of official baseball rules; and co-founded the A. G. Spalding sporting goods company. As captain of Kingston St. Lawrence, sometimes known as the Brown Stockings, Eilbeck led one of the best teams in the province during the 1870s. By 1876, when the club joined the Canadian Baseball Association for the inaugural season of the sport's first league in the country, the lineup included five Americans pros. In the 1880s, Eilbeck captained the local rowing team, played cricket and became a baseball manager, taking the helm of Kingston's new Eastern

International League franchise in 1888. He also served as a local alderman and was active in the Liberal Party.

The widower went west in the early 1890s to mine in Helena, Montana, and prospect in the Yellowhead Pass area. After he returned to Kingston, he used his Liberal connections to land a job as the secretary of the Penitentiary Investigation Committee, before being named the first sheriff of Dawson. He arrived in the Klondike in January 1900 and quickly become a prominent figure in town. He remarried in 1902 and his wife was a social leader who hosted at homes that made the papers.

Nepotism being no big concern at the time, John Milton Eilbeck, known as Jack, became a deputy sheriff. Father and son were also major sports promoters and fierce competitors, especially when it came to baseball. The *Whitehorse Daily Star* dubbed Jack Eilbeck "the greatest baseball crank in the Yukon." With all the Americans in Dawson, the sport was a popular pastime. In the summer, the season was short but the days were long, allowing games to continue until midnight around the solstice. Players took it seriously and could get aggressive and sometimes even unruly. During a 1903 game between the Idyle Hour and the Civil Service, Ben "Eldorado" Smith came home a little too hard for Lionel Bennett's liking. The two men threw punches, drawing in other players, before some nearby constables put an end to the dust-up. In the winter, the games moved indoors to the Arctic Brotherhood Hall. Teams competed eight a side and the "diamond" had two bases—first and third—and home plate.

Baseball wasn't the only sport in town, and with the opening of the Dawson Amateur Athletic Association, hockey increased in popularity. A stocky cover point, Jack Eilbeck was an avid player. He'd be a catalyst for Dawson's Stanley Cup challenge.

Construction of the DAAA was almost finished early in October of 1902 when local sportsmen met in the Administration Building to create the Yukon Hockey League. A few days later, the Civil Service team gathered in the gold commissioner's courtroom to plan for the upcoming season. A couple of nights later, the Athletics, a DAAA team, formed in the new clubhouse. They were joined by the Police, a NWMP and Dawson Rifles entry, and the City Eagles, a squad sponsored by the Fraternal Order of Eagles. The four teams agreed to play nine games, with a trophy going to the champions at the end of the season.

If past success was any indication, the Civil Service were the favourites. Weldy Young wasn't the only accomplished player in the Klondike. Rover Donald Randolph "Randy" McLennan was a strong skater with Cup experience. Born in 1870 in the Eastern Ontario village of Williamstown, not far from Cornwall, he graduated from McGill in 1892 and then, at Queen's, studied medicine, played football and was on the hockey team that lost the first official Cup challenge. After joining the Gold Rush, the well-respected McLennan worked as a doctor, a miner and a mining recorder. Centre Lionel Bennett had played in the Maritimes before moving to the Klondike. Norman Watt, from Aylmer, Quebec, across the Ottawa River from the nation's capital, had worked in the gold commissioner's office since 1900, moving up from janitor to keeper of records. On the ice, the 140-pound left winger was fast and feisty. Gold commissioner Edmund Senkler was the goaltender.

The only question was if they'd all be in Dawson. Bennett had just returned from Forty Mile, where he'd been the mining recorder, and was to spend the winter in the gold office. McLennan was the assistant mining recorder at Stewart River, but a transfer to Dawson was in the works. Although Young was still the mining recorder at Clear Creek, the club hoped he'd be able to make it in for games. With so much roster uncertainty, the Civils recruited George Kennedy, who'd previously played with the Polars and the City Eagles. An Indigenous man from Selkirk, Manitoba, he'd played in Winnipeg and Rat Portage and was known for his ability to fire the puck. His nickname was "Sureshot." The team added Jack Eilbeck to fill in for Young when it became clear he was just too far away. One trip into town with a dog team the previous April had taken two days and included a twenty-hour stretch of continuous travel. "The blizzard I ran into my first day out was something of a corker," Young said when he finally made it. The wind had turned his face bronze and his eyes bloodshot. Although not all his trips to Dawson took that long, trying to play hockey regularly just wasn't practical. But while in town in early January, Young helped the Police team to an unexpected tie with the stronger Eagles.

Despite their dominance—probably because of their dominance—the Civils weren't fan favourites; in fact, by midseason, many spectators in the DAAA cheered for any team playing against the men in the red and black sweaters. At the end of February, the Civils were undefeated as they hit the ice for their ninth game of the season. The crowd of 400 was solidly behind the Athletics, who'd strengthened their squad by adding some members of the Police team, which had dropped out of the league. "The game was a stemwinder from start to finish and for the first time this season, the Civil Service realized they were up against the real thing," reported the *Nugget*. The players avoided getting too cute with their plays. "'Old Hoss' McLennan is a past master in juggling with the puck and under ordinary conditions and with the average knight of the stick he can play with him as a cat would with a mouse, but he cut that all out Saturday night and sawed wood as assiduously as though the championship of Canada had been at stake."

The match should have marked the end of the season and been a mere formality in terms of the standings, since the Civil Service had already clinched the championship. Except the promised trophy never materialized. Worse, after the last-place Police team amalgamated with the Athletics, the schedule increased to twelve games. The Civils threatened to play no more that season. Even if they lost the last three matches of the revised schedule, they'd still win the championship. "We do not consider we have had a fair deal at all this winter," said Bennett, the team's captain. Within days, the players reconsidered, but once the City Eagles dropped out, the season ended. Although the Civils hadn't lost all winter, Reynolds Morton of the NWMP wasn't convinced they were invincible. He challenged the champions to play a picked squad of his choosing. Joe Boyle was willing to put up a trophy for the winner of a best-of-five series and Sheriff Eilbeck wanted to bet $1,000 on his son's team. The series would have thrilled local fans, but it never happened. No matter, the club was working on something bigger.

Early in March, the sheriff and his wife hosted a dinner for the Civil Service players at their home. Following a round of toasts, they headed over to the Auditorium Theatre to see *The Pirates of Penzance*. At the conclusion of the show, the players performed their team yell from their two reserved boxes and the company responded from behind the curtain with "For They Are Jolly Good Fellows." But the evening may have been more than just a celebratory dinner and a night at the opera. A few days later, the team announced a three-month tour of the east that would include playing for the Stanley Cup. The *Sun* was enthusiastic about the idea, confident it would be profitable and declaring, "It will be easy for the Civil Service boys to make the trip and lift the cup next year."

The team would take seven starters, three subs and a manager. Speculation about who would go began immediately. The forwards—McLennan, Bennett, Watt and Kennedy—were a given, as was Weldy Young at cover point. The players wanted "Dad" Eilbeck to accompany them as manager, but if his son also went, that would leave the sheriff's department in the lurch.

The plan was to leave in mid-December, giving the players several weeks of practice before departing if the ice in Dawson was playable by early November. That was a luxury their Outside opponents wouldn't have. The team planned to travel east from Vancouver or Seattle on a route through St. Paul, Minneapolis, Chicago, New York, Boston, Quebec City, Montreal, Ottawa, Toronto and Winnipeg before heading home. Barnstorming tours—which provided competition, adventure and money—were common at the time. Boyle and Frank Slavin had been on a boxing tour when they heard about the Gold Rush. And McLennan had been part of the Queen's hockey team that played matches in Pittsburgh, Baltimore and Washington in late December 1895 and early January 1896.

The Civils were more worried about the cost of transportation than the quality of the competition they'd face. Jack Eilbeck wrote the Pullman Car Company about renting a sleeping car. He also wrote a friend at the New York Central Railway Company. "The replies are satisfactory," reported the *Daily News.* "They show that the trip will not cost the barrel of money many people expected." For about $500 per man, they could travel for three months on their schedule in a private car with a cook, porter and waiter. The cost would be lower if some supporters came along. Eilbeck also sent letters to teams across the country in an effort to arrange matches. Several expressed interest but preferred to face an all-star team.

For whoever went, the tour would be a vacation Outside, which most of the players hadn't had since making it to the Yukon; a chance to promote the Klondike, which had lost prominence since the Gold Rush; a profit-making venture, or at least a way to break even; an opportunity to show easterners just how good Dawson hockey was; and, of course, a chance to achieve the ultimate goal: win the Stanley Cup.

By the summer of 1903, a certain urban maturity had settled in. Dawson's business section was three streets deep, the civil service hummed in the government buildings and construction was underway on a Carnegie Library. Crime was down; gambling hadn't completely disappeared, but it was illegal; and open prostitution had moved to Klondike City. That didn't mean all the fun had left town. There were still saloons, hotels and restaurants, and the receptions at the Commissioner's Residence even gave the place a hint of sophistication. July saw a record number of marriages and births in the Yukon, but a new gold rush in Alaska's Tanana region threatened to lure more people away. Between the dominance of the *Daily News* and the stagnating economy, the *Klondike Nugget*, which had won the race to be Dawson's first paper in May 1898, could no longer keep going. George Allen sold the business his brother had started to the Record Publishing Company. Two days after the *Nugget*'s last issue, the *Dawson Record* debuted.

The big front-page news in August was the Commission to Inquire into the Treadgold and Other Concessions of the Yukon, better known as the Britton Commission, which was holding hearings into the concessions Sifton had granted Arthur Treadgold, Joe Boyle and others. Treadgold's was the most controversial lease (and the government would cancel it in 1904). The coverage was a good reminder that despite the big-city trappings, Dawson was still at heart a glorified mining camp. But one visitor noticed a difference. In other camps, people all had the same look—the men hunted, the women scared—but Dawson was different. "Here every man throws out his chest and says, 'I am it,' and the women wear enough jewelry to buy out a couple of trusts," one visitor wrote in the *Record*. Another noted, "The men and women of the Yukon have given the greatest exhibition in the civilized world of persistency, endurance and stout heartedness."

One thing that wasn't different from other mining towns, or anywhere else, was greed. Since the early days of the Gold Rush, accusations of corruption had been an occupational hazard for civil servants. Sometimes these charges were legitimate; sometimes the problem was really just incompetence; sometimes the complaints arose from miners' misunderstandings, frustrations or sour grapes. In November 1902, Young joined the list of the accused when three miners said he'd defrauded them of claims. The most serious charge came from David Barton Lowery, who contended that the mining recorder had demanded a half interest in a claim before registering it.

Young mushed into Dawson in January to swear an affidavit denying the charges. The next month, Clifford Sifton ordered the suspension of Young and his colleague Tom Hinton pending an investigation. Criminal charges were a possibility. Dawson's newspapers often led campaigns against corrupt officials, but not this time. Both men were popular in the Klondike. "While the government is to be commended for its prompt action in the premises," noted the *Sun*, "the many Yukon friends of 'Tom' and 'Weldy' will consider them not guilty of any wrongdoing until the same has been proven."

In March, Young submitted several sworn statements and a letter from miners attesting that he'd always treated them fairly and acted in a professional manner. Thomas Spraitzer, one of the owners of the discovery claim on Clear Creek, went further. His affidavit stated that he'd often heard Lowery malign the mining recorder's character and "from what I know of Lowery, he would stop at nothing to defame Young and would make any statement that would tend to bring discredit on Young."

The charges hung over him for months. Finally, at the end of August, a board of three officials—Senkler; Fred Congdon, now the commissioner of the territory; and inspector of federal offices W.W. Cory—assembled in the Administration Building to consider the case. They didn't take long to decide the charges were groundless and the accused deserved an honourable acquittal and reinstatement plus two months' back pay. But Young didn't return to government work. Instead, after a three-week leave of absence, he wrote a letter of resignation to Congdon. Under a "Citizen Weldy Young" headline, the *Dawson Record* reported that Young didn't want to "remain in a position where, if accused of wrongdoing, he is wholly deprived of the means of self-vindication." Instead, he bought a couple of claims on Lower Dominion and launched a mining operation with sixteen men and a forty-horsepower boiler.

Now that he was "a free and untrammelled subject of King Edward," as the *Record* put it, he was also available to take part in any hockey tour. In October, Eilbeck went Outside but without any teammates; instead, he left for a vacation. But that didn't mean anyone had given up on a Cup challenge. The CAHL annual meeting at Montreal's Windsor Hotel in December included the reading of a letter from the secretary of the Yukon Territory Hockey Club regarding the arrangement of matches with eastern teams. Two weeks later, Toronto's *Globe* asked, "Who Would Go to Dawson?" and suggested that while the Klondikers didn't seem to have a strong team, they were sure to fill arenas wherever they played. "Just imagine if they should win the Stanley Cup and away off home with it, though!" the paper continued. "It would be a long time before any team would get the nerve to challenge for it and take a couple of months off to play the game." This was not the first, or the last, time someone—both in the south and in the Yukon—made this point. Of course, it was all hypothetical until a Klondike team won the Cup. To do that now, Dawson would need to beat the new champions, the team Young had left behind in 1899.

- NINETEEN -

"For a minute or so I stood spellbound"

Less than three decades after James Creighton organized the first indoor match, hockey welcomed its first true superstar. Generational players sell sports to new fans and strengthen bonds with old ones. For a game suffering growing pains, the timing couldn't have been better, and if hockey had a marketing department, it couldn't have conjured a more saleable hero than Francis Clarence McGee. The scion of an illustrious and influential family, he was a clean-cut man with blond hair, blue eyes and fine features, and a dapper dresser on and off the ice. "His hair was as perfectly parted as though he had just stepped out of a tonsorial parlor; his spotless white pants were creased to a knife-like edge; his boots had been polished; his skates glistened under the glare of the arc lamps," raved a Calgary sporting editor, "and his complexion—that was what magnetized my attention—seemed as pink as a child's. For a minute or so I stood spellbound." Once the match started, the westerner watched McGee play: "I saw him seize the puck at center, skate in with the speed of a prairie cyclone and shoot. I saw him backcheck, dodge here and there, flash from side to side; stickhandle his way through a knot of struggling players, slap the puck into the open net and go down in a heap as he did so."

Adding to the mystique, his uncle had been the most eloquent of Canada's Fathers of Confederation. During Ireland's Potato Famine, Thomas D'Arcy McGee was a leader of the Irish independence movement. Rather than face arrest for treason, he escaped to America, where he worked as a journalist, publishing a series of newspapers in Philadelphia, New York and Boston and writing several books. Never afraid to change his mind, he renounced his revolutionary ideals and advocated peaceful reform in Ireland. Meanwhile, he argued in favour of nationalist revolutions in Europe, better treatment for Roman Catholics in the U.S. and the American takeover of Canada. After becoming disillusioned with his adoptive country, he moved to Montreal in 1857. Quickly turning against American annexation, he became a powerful supporter of a Canadian nation within the British Empire. By the end of the year, he ran for political office and won, serving as a member of George Brown's Reform Party until he defected to John A. Macdonald's Conservatives and became a cabinet minister.

Although his idea of a separate province for Indigenous peoples never came to be, he was a close and invaluable ally of the prime minister, helping to sell Confederation, especially in the Maritimes, with his sparkling tongue. That tongue also made him enemies. He'd denounced the Fenians, criticizing the Irish nationalists' tactics and objectives, even though they were similar to the ones he'd subscribed to in his youth. One night after a late session in the House of Commons, less than a year after Canada became a Dominion, a Fenian sympathizer assassinated him outside his Ottawa rooming house.

Before his 1868 death, McGee had made the decision to leave politics and Macdonald had agreed to give him a civil service job that would offer him more time to write poetry and history books. So perhaps it was fitting that in 1882, his youngest brother, John Joseph McGee, became Clerk of the Privy Council, the top civil servant in the country. He and his wife had two daughters and five sons, including Frank, who would grow up to excel at lacrosse, football and, especially, hockey. While he was still at Ottawa College, the *Journal* wrote: "F. McGee of College forward line showed himself to be a coming man. He is an excellent stick handler and a fine skater." After he joined the Aberdeens in 1899, the *Journal* declared, "Frank McGee is as good a forward as there is in the city." Since his day job was as a CPR timekeeper, he was also on the company team, which competed in the Canadian Railway League. "Frank McGee was the best dodger and stickhandler on the ice," the *Journal* reported in 1900. "He played a wonderful individual game."

Only an injury kept him from the senior ranks. After a puck struck him above the eye in 1899, he received several stitches and returned to the match. The next year, another puck hit him above the eye while he was playing for the CPR squad in an exhibition game to raise money for the Canadian Patriotic Fund, a charity that supported soldiers' families during the Boer War. This time he didn't return. And his career was in jeopardy. Despite his colourful, posthumously bestowed moniker, "One-Eyed" Frank McGee, he did not lose an eye, though he did suffer a significant loss of vision. Continuing to play risked further damage or, worse, something happening to the other eye. But hockey is a hard game to quit.

Excitement over hockey's newest phenom spread before his debut in January 1903. "Frank McGee is out practicing with the Ottawa Hockey club and the fans in the Capital are proportionately pleased," reported Winnipeg's *Tribune* a few days before the OHC hosted the Montreal Hockey Club in the third match of the season. "Frank gave promise of proving one of the best in the business, but two years ago he had the misfortune to suffer an injury to one of his eyes, which distracted a good deal from his ability on the ice. He is, however, still a swift and dangerous forward." McGee scored twice and showed that nothing distracted from his ability on the ice. "He invariably got the better of the face-off and was always on the puck," noted the *Tribune*, which called him the star of the evening. But it took more than one promising player to crush the Cup champs 7-1. When Dickie Boon skated over to Alf Smith and asked what he'd done to make the team so good, the coach replied, "Wait till you see them at the end of the season."

Boon had good reason to be surprised, especially given the exodus to the United States. At the CAHL annual meeting, league president Harry Trihey had noted the loss of so many players to the Western Pennsylvania Hockey League. The departures hit the OHC hard. Even though the growing civil service meant easily accessible day jobs at home, several local boys headed south. Arthur Sixsmith left the Ottawas to play for and manage the Pittsburgh Victorias in 1902. The next fall, he recruited his brother Garnet and three OHC players: captain "Peg" Duval; Bruce Stuart, who'd scored nine goals the previous season; and Harold "Chic" Henry. The first thing Smith needed to do was rebuild Ottawa's roster.

Unlike McGee, Smith grew up in a working-class family. But like his young star, he excelled at sports. He quarterbacked the Ottawa College football team to the Canadian championship, won national lacrosse titles with the Capitals and joined the OHC in 1895 as a forward. He was talented, tough and could be mean as hell. But he developed a reputation as a lazy player who was reluctant to backcheck or dig for the puck in the corners. After three years, he jumped to the Capitals hockey team, but then lost his amateur status because he'd taken an end-of-season bonus from the lacrosse Capitals. Unable to play, he coached the hockey Capitals in 1900, the year they joined the OHA. The next year he coached the Ottawas to the CAHL championship. But he missed playing and spent the 1902 season with the Pittsburgh Athletic Club in return for a salary and a job. Now back coaching the OHC again, Smith was fortunate the team still had an excellent veteran core to provide leadership. Harry Westwick remained one of the game's best rovers. Harvey Pulford was still dishing out heavy checks at point. In net, Bouse Hutton, who'd played his first two games with Ottawa during Young's last season, had a "cool head and quick eye" and smiled when he saw pucks coming at him. Charles "Baldy" Spittal, who'd first played for the team in 1897 but was often relegated to spare, was also back. To fill out the roster, Smith raided the intermediate Aberdeens Hockey Club, bringing in cover point Art Moore and three brothers at forward. Dave "Davie" Gilmour, who'd played one game with the team as a fifteen-year-old during the tumultuous 1898 season and two more in 1902, and wingers Hamilton "Billy" Gilmour and Sutherland "Suddie" Gilmour. The in-season addition of McGee completed the squad of local men who took pride in representing their hometown. The club could easily afford the loss when Spittal became the sixth man from Ottawa on the Pittsburgh Victorias in February.

With depth, no obvious weaknesses and an enviable mix of experience and youth, the OHC was the top team in town. Top hockey team, that is, because Ottawa had become a leading sports city, with lacrosse's Capitals and football's Rough Riders winning national titles around the turn of the century. Many of the best jocks were able to stay in top condition by playing lacrosse in the summer, football in the fall and hockey in the winter. Pulford, Hutton and McGee won football championships with the Rough Riders. Pulford was also Eastern Canada's boxing champ from 1896 to 1898; excelled in rowing and canoeing, winning several national titles; and played lacrosse with the Capitals for five years. Westwick and Hutton won several lacrosse championships, including the first Minto Cup, another viceregal donation, in 1901. (Minto's successor, Lord Grey, completed the hat trick with a football trophy in 1909. Then, in 2006, Governor General Adrienne Clarkson donated the Clarkson Cup for the championship in women's hockey.)

Aside from a good eye for talent, Smith was a clever coach and a good mentor and teacher. At practices, he donned his skates and worked with the players to develop their skills. Of course, great players make good coaches and McGee's performance in his first game was just a small preview of what was to come. Three weeks later, in a rematch with the Vics at the Arena, the OHC prevailed 7-6 on the strength of five goals, including the winner, from McGee. He finished the season with fourteen goals in six games. He added three more as Ottawa took the playoff series with the Vics to win the CAHL championship and, for the first time, the Stanley Cup.

The Ottawas didn't have much time to savour their long-awaited triumph. Two days later, they defended the Cup against the Rat Portage Thistles. Formerly the site of a Hudson's Bay Company trading post, Rat Portage was an Ontario town on Lake of the Woods near the Manitoba border. By the early 1900s, its population had swelled to more than 5,000 and its resource economy boomed because of the lumber mills, the gold mines and the railroad. Weldy Young and Jack Eilbeck might have seen Ross's willingness to approve a challenge from a town even smaller than Dawson as a promising sign, but at least the trustee had an idea of the quality of the league Rat Portage played in.

The Thistles made it east just in time to get to Dey's Rink before the start of the second game of the CAHL showdown. Watching Ottawa demolish the Vics 8-0, the challengers must have been impressed by the new champs' firepower, though they remained unfazed, at least publicly. "That McGee is a wonder and we are more afraid of him than of any of your other forwards," said goalkeeper Fred Dulmage. "But you may rest assured that

Ottawa will never run up 8 goals on us." He wasn't lying: the final score was 6-2.

The bad news for the hometown team and the Dey brothers was that the Cup wasn't as lucrative for them as it had been in Montreal. In 1896, Ted and Billy Dey had opened the second Dey's Skating Rink on Gladstone. Located at the south end of town but accessible by Ottawa Electric Railway streetcar, it replaced the rink the family had operated from 1884 until 1895, when it came down to make way for a Canada Atlantic Railway depot. Unlike the first rink, they built the new one to serve both hockey players and pleasure skaters—the ice surface was 200 by eighty-one feet—but Montreal's Arena, and the idea of designing a venue that catered to spectators, was still a couple of years away.

After close to 5,000 spectators paid $2 to watch Ottawa and the Vics at the Arena, fans packed Dey's as the OHC clinched the championship. The *Journal* estimated the attendance at 3,000, though the seating capacity was only 1,622, plus standing room for a few hundred more. "Every corner of Dey's rink was crowded," reported the paper. "The aisles were crammed and the boys hung from the beams about the side." But once the Ottawas finally took possession of the Cup, only 1,500 fans were willing to pay to see their team defend it for the first time. True, there were reasons. Montreal was a much bigger city; the Thistles were unknown and from a small northern town too far away for Special Excursion trains full of fans; and it was almost spring. Still, the crowd was nowhere near a sellout. Ross's *Journal* expressed its disappointment: "A hockey team cannot be run on wind and unless the public patronize the game there is not much encouragement for the players and executive to go on and bring honours to the city."

Ottawa won the second match 4-2, to keep the trophy for the summer. In four Cup contests over eight days, the three Gilmour brothers—"a sort of family compact," according to the *Journal*— scored twelve goals, even though Suddie missed the last game.

McGee scored seven on his own. "He is almost blind in one eye," said the *Journal.* "But sees perhaps quicker with the one good one than any other player in the business sees with the two." Even his brilliance didn't fill the stands, as only 1,000 fans showed up to the second match against the Thistles. The gate for the two contests was just $1,500, with the rink and the two teams each taking a third of that. Unfortunately, the trip had cost the challengers $1,300. At least their hosts treated them to a post-series banquet at the Russell House.

That summer, a railway construction crew discovered silver near Cobalt, Ontario, and set off a massive silver rush. Bob Shillington, a pharmacist who owned a successful Ottawa drug store, was an early investor in the region. A gregarious guy who liked hanging around athletes, he was an executive with football's Rough Riders, the lacrosse Capitals and the OHC. As manager of the Ottawas, he was thrilled with the team's success. Wanting to show his appreciation, he used his Cobalt connections to obtain silver nuggets for the players. When he handed them out, one of them said, "We ought to call ourselves the Silver Seven."

Around this time, the Ottawas began receiving more than silver souvenirs. The OHC wasn't the only club doing this, but its new dominance made it the subject of sly digs in the press. Increasingly, teams had little choice but to compensate players because so many good ones were going to Pittsburgh. So clubs did reward them, but secretly, which was making a mockery of amateurism. While most fans didn't like the hypocrisy, they were also unhappy when stars left for the States. More and more of the growing number of fans, who were increasingly influential in the game, didn't really care about the amateur status of the players as long as the hockey was good and their side won. Nor did most care about some effete pissing match between amateurism and professionalism. The top players were now more often than not young men with low-paying jobs and little or no family money. The fans expected them to train to stay fit even as their teams practised more and played more matches, many requiring out-of-town travel. The elitists defending amateurism wanted them to do all this—essentially devote much of their lives to the game—without any compensation, even as everyone else involved in the sport made money. "Shamateurism" was the inevitable result of this impasse and it might have damaged the game's reputation if the sport didn't have such a crowd-pleasing new star to provide a distraction from the controversies.

McGee quickly established himself as a complete player: a fast skater, a crafty stickhandler, a gifted playmaker and, because of his great shot, a prolific goal scorer. Although he stood just five feet, six inches high and weighed 160 pounds, he was strong, with a thick, muscled body that was perfect for the winter sport. Lester Patrick thought he "had an almost animal rhythm," and McGee's teammates called him "Cresceus"—after a horse that had won the harness racing championship—because of his power and speed. He was best known for his finesse, but after the Ottawas first won the Cup, the *Journal* declared, "When Frank checks he checks to win." Not every hit was clean, though. A year earlier, when he was still with the Aberdeens, the paper said cheekily, "F. McGee is a very aggressive player, in fact just a little too much so and in consequence he generally decorates the side of the rink about half the time." He was highly competitive and quickly earned a reputation as a big-game player. And he played many big games.

His pressed uniform might suggest too much earnestness, but he had a sense of humour. As one delightful—though perhaps apocryphal—story goes, Lord Minto invited the OHC to Rideau Hall for a celebratory dinner after a Cup victory. To McGee, this was no big deal. Having grown up in the Sandy Hill neighbourhood, he was accustomed to the rules and rituals of Ottawa society. But some of his teammates felt a little out of their element. McGee reassured them that they'd have nothing to worry about if they just followed his lead. The finger bowls must have baffled some of the players so when McGee picked his up and began slurping from it, they did, too. And according to the *Dictionary of Canadian Biography*, "It is said that the governor general too decided it was appropriate to drink from his finger bowl."

If McGee had played a century later, he'd have been a promotional dream for the game: a dynamic player who was handsome and always presentable; was intelligent and cultured; bore a prestigious name; was a bit of a character; and, best of all, had a reputation as a winner. But hockey wasn't about celebrity back then. The telegraph bulletins didn't include colour commentary with details about the athletes' lives. There were no television interviews with sweaty players, no all-sports broadcasters covering all manner of minutiae, no gushy internet fan sites and no rumours on social media. Newspapers covered games, sometimes extensively, but they didn't run long profiles of players and didn't even interview that many of them. Teams might have public personalities, players not so much. Ottawa fans didn't need to know a lot about McGee's personal life to adore him, and coverage of his on-ice accomplishments in newspapers across the country made him a national sensation.

He wasn't the only great player during the first decade of the 1900s. Russell Bowie, for example, scored 234 goals in eighty games with the Vics, even notching ten in one match. But while superstars make the players around them better, they also need talented teammates to win championships. McGee had those in Ottawa and he ensured his place in the history of the game by helping create hockey's most impressive early dynasty. Newspapers rarely called the team the Silver Seven, though they occasionally referred to them as the Senators; the Capitals, even though there was another team called that in town; and the Barber-Poles, because the players wore red, white and black striped sweaters. Whatever the handle, the club was as versatile as it was skilful; it excelled on hard, fast ice with short, accurate passes or on soft, slow ice by using long lifts. McGee and the Ottawas were capable of playing clean, finesse-filled games, and sometimes did, but they were more than happy to match big, tough opponents hit for hit or even beat up smaller, less physical teams. They won a lot.

· TWENTY ·

*"If it continues we will have to
wire home for more men"*

The worst violence of the end-of-December match happened behind the play, so most people in the rink missed the mayhem. The Winnipeg Rowing Club was in Ottawa for a Cup challenge when rover Joe Hall delivered a vicious bodycheck to Alf Smith, who, having won reinstatement as an amateur, was back at right wing with the home team. Then, as the puck and the other players moved down the ice, Smith retaliated by cracking his stick over Hall's head. Referee Harry Trihey penalized neither man, though they both received stitches: five for Hall and four for Smith. Both finished the game with bandages covering their scalp wounds. Not all of Hall's teammates were so fortunate. Right wing Clint Bennest crashed into the fence and broke his thumb while left wing Billy Bawlf sprained his back after a hard check from Harvey Pulford. Winnipeg point Percy Brown slashed Frank McGee in the head, but after some doctoring, the Ottawa centre dashed the length of the ice and fired a shot and Harry Westwick knocked in the rebound. McGee later added a third goal, as his team won 9-1 in the first game of the Stanley Cup series between the two teams. Although Trihey called many penalties, he still faced complaints he was too lenient. Most of the players ended up well bruised and battered. "All I can say is that it was about the dirtiest match in which I have ever participated," said Billy Breen, the visitors' speedy centre and captain. "If it continues we will have to wire home for more men."

The OHC hadn't softened its rugged style over the summer of 1903. "It was one of the bloodiest battles ever fought on Ottawa ice and one or two more like it will just about kill hockey here," said the *Citizen*, admitting the hometown team was the worst offender. "There is no necessity for the players slashing each other over the head and a departure from good hockey will have its effect on the attendance." The Ottawas couldn't afford that, especially since they'd just moved to the Aberdeen Pavilion because, as Cup champs, they expected bigger crowds than Dey's Rink could accommodate.

Erected six years earlier as an architectural hall for the Central Canada Exhibition, the Pavilion had an ornate exterior that included a dome, towers at the corners, a curved roof, pressed metal cladding and lots of windows to let the light in. The steel frame meant no interior columns, leaving a massive uninterrupted space more than big enough for a rink. The Central Canada Exhibition Association wasn't offering as generous financial terms as the Dey brothers, but the club was keen and city council, including Alderman P.D. Ross, approved the deal. The OHC contributed $500 for renovations to give the place a capacity of 4,000, plus amenities such as new dressing rooms. In some ways, the Pavilion offered a good set-up for spectators, but it was cold and draughty and fans complained that the walk from Bank Street was long and dark.

Despite the disappointing attendance for the Rat Portage series at the end of the 1903 season, the Ottawas hoped for better crowds for the carry-over series against the Rowing Club. But once again, the challengers were unknowns and the first match drew only 2,500 spectators. The lopsided score prompted a *Journal* headline that read: "The Stanley Cup Likely to Stay in Ottawa." That take was premature. The banged-up Breen was back for game two on New Year's Day and his Oarsmen rebounded to win 6-2 in a much less violent tilt. Some fans, possibly those who'd lost wagers, claimed the fix was in to ensure revenue from a third match. The Winnipeg papers dismissed that notion, attributing the turnaround to better performances from both the Rowing Club and the ref. "Last night's match merely shows what a referee can do," proclaimed the *Free Press*. "In the first game Trihey allowed anything to go. In the last game he forced both teams to play hockey—and Winnipeg won." The close third match was filled with hard, but largely clean, body-checking, and Ottawa won 2-0 to keep the Cup.

Successfully defending the trophy had been a good way to start the new season, and beating the westerners suggested the only serious threat would come from the CAHL. But in February, following a dispute over an unfinished match with the Victorias, the undefeated Ottawas shocked the hockey world with their mid-season resignation from the league. The failure to start games on time had been a problem for years and led to much stern talk from league officials as well as disgruntled editorials in newspapers. Five thousand spectators were in the Arena before the advertised start time of eight thirty. They waited ninety minutes—"an attempt being made to keep them in good humour by a discordant band"—before the Ottawas, not appearing in too much of a rush, finally showed. The players claimed their equipment trunk had been mislaid and arrived on a later train. Several injuries and a broken skate created further delays. Here, the Vics were at fault: due to the late start, the referee suggested that in the event of injury, the other side would take a man off. Ottawa agreed; Montreal did not. McGee's three goals had his team up 4-1 with sixteen minutes to go when the midnight curfew put an end to play—and the start of the squabbling. The Vics wanted a do-over; the Ottawas did not.

As league president, Trihey convened a special meeting at the Windsor Hotel after a Saturday match between Quebec and the Montreal Hockey Club. Before the session began, OHC representative John Dickson warned Trihey: "If the league compels the teams to play the match over, the Ottawa Hockey Club will resign from the C.A.H.L. I would rather sacrifice the Ottawa Club than depart from a principle." The men within earshot thought he was bluffing. When it came time to vote on making the teams replay the game on February 24, Dickson reiterated his ultimatum: "Now, gentlemen, before voting, understand Ottawa's position in the matter. If ordered to play the match again, we will refuse to do so and will resign from the league." The motion passed, with only Trihey's Shamrocks siding with Ottawa. Even as the others continued to discuss the matter, Dickson wrote a letter to OHC president Halder Kirby explaining what had happened.

On Monday morning, club executives met at the Russell House. They believed the unfair and unsportsmanlike treatment stemmed from a grudge the other teams nursed because Ottawa held the Cup. True to his accommodating nature, Bob Shillington wanted to play nice with the league, but the other executives didn't want to back down. Their only concern was the Cup. Before making a final decision, Kirby, Dickson and Shillington visited Ross in his office at the *Journal*. The trustee assured them that even if his former team left their league, it would keep the Cup until a challenger took it away. He had a precedent to work with: the Vics kept the trophy after leaving the AHAC for the new CAHL in 1898, though that had not been a mid-season departure. Reassured, the executive committee voted unanimously to quit the league. Dickson wired Trihey. The *Journal* put the news on the front page that evening.

After the vote, a club deputation went to Parliament Hill's East Block, where William Foran was the secretary of the Board of Civil Service Examiners. The former president of the upstart

Ottawa Capitals was also now the president of the upstart Federal Amateur Hockey League. After unsuccessfully applying to join the CAHL, the Capitals, Cornwall and Montreal's Le National launched the new league late in 1903, though including amateur in the name was a dubious choice. Dickie Boon and several other Little Men of Iron, once again wanting more autonomy from the MAAA, along with a couple of Vics, created a fourth franchise called the Wanderers. While simply spending the rest of the winter competing against Cup challengers was an option, the OHC hoped to join the Federal League. Foran told the club's representatives he'd support their application.

Ottawa's decision gave the telegraph and telephone lines a workout and led to many hastily arranged meetings as hockey people tried to divine what it meant for the two leagues and the Cup. Rumours that the Shamrocks would follow Ottawa to the new league proved untrue. Some rivals from the old loop argued that since the Cup was to be held by champions of recognized leagues, and Ottawa was no longer part of one, the CAHL should take possession of the trophy until the end of the season, when the team that came first would get it. But Ross quickly squashed that line of thinking. On Wednesday, Foran took Ottawa's formal application to the FAHL with him on a train to Montreal. That evening, league representatives convened at the Savoy Hotel. Foran called the proceedings to order, read a letter from the OHC and held the vote. Satisfied, he adjourned the meeting, which had lasted just ten minutes.

Even though it was too late to play any league matches that season, Ottawa turned down an offer of $1,500 for exhibition games in Winnipeg. Instead, the club planned to keep busy defending the Cup, though it did beat the Capitals 18-1 in an exhibition tilt. As part of its Federal League application, the team agreed to accept a challenge from the undefeated Wanderers. But the trustees still had to approve it and they were a bit swamped.

For Ross and Sweetland, managing all the challenges had long been an onerous responsibility. Keeping everyone happy had proven impossible, especially with the proliferation of new leagues. Late in 1903, Ross devised a plan to pass the management of the trophy to a committee of the presidents of the leading associations in Quebec, Ontario and Manitoba. For the idea to work, though, the CAHL would need to adopt a system that invited the previous year's champion intermediate team into the senior series, with the last place squad dropping down. Ross believed giving control to the three associations would discourage the creation of new leagues in those provinces. In December, he drafted a letter detailing the proposal to Trihey. But the next day, before he could mail it, the Federal League formed, "which altered the whole situation," Ross said, "so the letter went into the waste basket." Two months later, the Cup reached peak challenge.

Whatever regrets Ross had about his role as a trustee, he still loved hockey. The Rideau Rebels reformed in December 1903 and, now in his mid-forties, he played Wednesday nights with them. In mid-February, he helped the married men defeat the single men 6-3 at Rideau Rink. It must have been a welcome distraction from his official duties. The day before, the *Journal* reported the CAHL clubs intended to issue a challenge as soon as their season was over. Still upset with Ross over his ruling that Ottawa could keep the Cup, they thought their challenge should take precedence. They even threatened to take the whole matter to Frederick Stanley, now the Earl of Derby.

The next day in the *Gazette*, CAHL secretary Fred McRobie called that story a canard. In fact, he'd sent Ross a letter indicating that once the season ended, the league champions would defend the Cup and ask the trustee to forward information about the pending challenges. In his response, Ross reiterated that he and Sweetland recognized Ottawa as the Cup holders. "Under ordinary circumstances the trustees have followed the practice of regarding the cup as a league matter, rather than a club one," he admitted, but noted that these were not ordinary circumstances and cited the previous case of the Vics switching leagues. "The trustees, therefore, in 1898 used, as they do now, the discretion which Lord Stanley's deed of gift stipulated, that 'the cup shall be held or awarded by the trustees as they think right, their decision being absolute.'"

By this point, challenges had come in from Ontario, Manitoba and the Federal League. While Ottawa had no league games to interfere with scheduling matches, winter wasn't going to last much longer. The trustees approved the OHA challenge. Expecting the various leagues to determine one challenger per province per year, Ross and Sweetland wanted the Manitoba champions to play each other first. That meant the Rowing Club would likely face Brandon. As for the FAHL challenge, which would see the Wanderers get the series Ottawa had promised when it joined the new league, the trustees put off their decision.

Other clubs also wanted the Cup. Queen's University, of the Canadian Intercollegiate Athletic Union, issued a challenge. And despite being turned down three years earlier, Berlin tried again. Over five years in the Western Ontario Hockey Association, the team had amassed a dominating record of fifty-five wins, seven losses and three ties. Many of Berlin's goals came from centre Oliver Seibert, one of the first players to master the wrist shot, but Toronto's *Telegram* dismissed the club as "tin-foil champions" of a "fence corner league." When it first reported the challenge, the *Globe* had added, "Berlin may have a team that could beat anything in Canada, yet will not be recognized by the Stanley Cup trustees." The Amherst Ramblers, who'd won the Nova Scotia Amateur Hockey League, issued the season's sixth challenge, but it was too late to even consider.

The good news for the besieged trustees was the Quebec situation settled itself, though not to everyone's satisfaction.

Once the OHC quit the CAHL, most hockey people expected the Vics to win the league. But the Quebecs surprised them. It helped that their January visit to Ottawa had been cancelled due to a snowstorm. That game and the return match, scheduled for after the champs' departure, became wins by default. The Vics, on the other hand, had faced the Ottawas twice, losing both times. After winning their first title, the Quebecs wired the trustees with a bold message: "As champions of the Canadian Amateur Hockey League, we are prepared to defend the Stanley Cup." They followed up with a letter explaining their position: "The Ottawas won the Stanley Cup by winning the championship of the C.A.H.L. And we, as champions of the same league, do not intend to challenge for the cup, which we consider we have won." Unswayed, the trustees announced the Wanderers would take on the winner of the series between the Ottawas and the Toronto Marlboros.

John Ross Robertson delivered another revealing speech at his league's 1903 annual meeting. "The Ontario Hockey Association is a patriotic organization, not in name exactly, but in nature most assuredly. A force we stand for is fair play in sport, and sport is one of the elements in the work of building up the character of a young nation," he said, making it clear he believed his moral crusade against professionals was a battle to save all that was good and right in the Dominion. "We have tried to live up to the ideals which are part of our birthright as Canadian sons of the greatest of countries, and as British citizens of the grandest of empires." At the end of the Saturday morning session, the delegates moved up to the tenth floor of the Temple Building for a luncheon that featured just two toasts. To the King. And to the league president.

Although Robertson was a control freak, he needed loyal allies. Francis Nelson, sports editor of the *Globe*, first joined the

OHA executive in 1899 and later ascended to first vice-president. *Toronto Daily Star* sports editor Bill Hewitt (father of Foster, the future broadcaster) became OHA secretary in 1903. No one accused these newsmen of a conflict of interest, because sports journalists being involved in organizations they covered seemed normal at the time. Hewitt had been unsure about running for league secretary until *Star* publisher and editor Joseph Atkinson told him, "Mr. Hewitt, if you can get enough votes, you take it."

With authority over the sports pages of three major Toronto dailies, the triumvirate gave the OHA a powerful public relations department. While that didn't mean all the league's problems went away, it assured fawning coverage. "The association convened in the morning and business was conducted in the most admirable systematic manner," the *Globe* swooned after the 1900 annual meeting. "There was a lot of very important work on hand, but it was despatched in such prompt and thorough style as to bring from the delegates the declaration that in no other organizations in their experience was there any chance for comparison."

Both the *Globe* and the *Star* also regularly heaped over-the-top praise on Robertson, even though he published a rival paper. The conservative *Tely* didn't just compete with the *Globe* and *Star* for readers and advertisers. The *Globe* was a Liberal organ and the *Star*, launched by striking printers and writers from the *Toronto News*, operated on progressive principles under "Holy Joe" Atkinson. But the executive met in the *Telegram*'s building and, as secretary, Hewitt had frequent informal meetings with Robertson there. Despite his initial reluctance to welcome Nelson and Hewitt to his offices, the OHA president had found kindred spirits in the fight against professionalism.

The three papers were also of one mind when it came to the way the Ottawas played hockey, as became clear when the Toronto Marlborough Athletic Club challenged for the Cup. Succeeding the aging Wellingtons, who'd disbanded just before the season started, as the OHA's best seven, the Marlboros inherited a nickname from the former champs. Named after the Duke of Marlborough, the young club became known as the Little Dukes or just the Dukes. The star was Tom Phillips. Originally from Rat Portage, the twenty-one-year-old rover had moved to Montreal the previous season to study at McGill and joined the MHC, replacing Charlie Liffiton, who'd left for the Pittsburgh Bankers after one game. Phillips helped the Little Men of Iron defend the Cup in the four-game series against Winnipeg. Now going to school in Toronto, he was eligible to play for the Marlboros. An effortless skater with a good shot, he also enjoyed an abundance of stamina and competitive spirit.

In the opening game of the Ottawa series, the challengers took a 3-1 lead in the first half, but the champs stormed back in the second half to win 6-3. Under Robertson's rule, the OHA played a tamer version of the sport and most of the Little Dukes were small even by Ontario standards, though Phillips was a notable exception. The *Journal* conceded that Toronto "played vigorous, brainy hockey and swept the Ottawas off their feet" in the first half, but the challengers began to wilt under energetic checking. "It was not that the play was any rougher than is usual and expected in eastern hockey, but it was something new to the Marlboros, who alleged that they were never before treated in such an unladylike manner." Even Montreal's *Gazette* thought, "The game was comparatively free from roughness, and only three men were ruled off."

Toronto saw things differently. Robertson's *Telegram* said, "Marlboros can play hockey but when it comes to actual warfare trained soldiers like the Ottawas appear to have the best of it." In the *Globe*, Nelson claimed the Marlboros would have won had the game been strictly hockey instead of the "hammering and jamming" they received. "The style of hockey played by Ottawa seems to be the only one known here," he grumbled, "and people consider it quite proper and legitimate for a team to endeavour to incapacitate their opponents, rather than excel them in skill and speed." Under a "Slugged and Bodied into Submission" headline, Hewitt's *Star* maintained that the Marlboros had been beaten, but not at hockey: "They were unaccustomed to the style of game that permits downright brutality, cross checking in the face and neck, tripping, hacking, slashing over the head, and boarding an opponent with the intent to do bodily harm."

According to a popular conspiracy theory, the disparity in play between the first and second halves was due to a dastardly half-time deed: Ottawa management, alarmed at the visitors' speed, salted the ice to soften it and slow down the Marlboros. Later, in his memoir, Hewitt would write, "Whether or not that trickery occurred was for long a subject for debate; and even though I was the O.H.A. representative at game, I was never able to prove it."

Since the Pavilion was only two-thirds full for the first game, another rumour suggested Ottawa would throw the second match to set up a third one on Saturday night, which would produce a larger gate. The second game made it clear the champs weren't going to take a fall and didn't need to cheat to slow down an opponent. A less aggressive affair, before 2,500 fans, the match was even more decisive. Ottawa won 11-2, with McGee scoring five times. "The Ottawa men did not play roughly on Thursday," admitted the *Telegram*. "They did not need to. They had the Marlboros afraid of their lives after the first night's drubbing."

The *Citizen* praised Phillips—"much too fast a man for the company in which he is travelling"—and twenty-year-old goaltender Eddie Geroux — "one of the slickest in the business for with a less competent man before the nets the score might have been doubled." But it was less impressed with the rest of the team and downright ungracious about some colleagues in the news business. "The squealers from Squealville-on-the-Don raised an awful howl against the alleged brutality of the holders of Lord Stanley's silverware," the paper taunted.

"According to the Toronto press the Ottawa team were guilty of almost every atrocity it was possible to commit with a hockey stick, and these men of standing in O.H.A. circles who wrote the stuff alleged that had the champions played hockey alone the results would have been disastrous for Ottawa. But they got their answer good and hard last night."

After the OHC dealt with the Marlboros, the trustees dealt with the remaining challenges. They set dates for the Wanderers series. They approved Brandon's bid but barred Joe Hall and Clint Bennest because they'd played for the Cup with the Rowing Club earlier in the season. They told Queen's they'd approve the school's challenge if Brandon didn't come east, though with examinations approaching, the students might not be able to play anyway. They denied Berlin of the Western Ontario Hockey Association, which displeased club secretary George Debus. "Candidly speaking, the club management here feels the O.H.A. nabobs have used all their influence to sidetrack the W.O.H.A.," he wrote, noting the *Globe* had reported the challenge, and that the trustees wouldn't accept it, on the same day, which was especially curious given who the paper's sports editor was. "Why should an O.H.A. executive officer be the mouthpiece of the Stanley Cup trustees?" Debus asked them to reconsider. If what appeared in his newspaper was any indication, Ross was unimpressed by the letter: "After receiving this the Cup trustees would be quite justified in taking Berlin for a boys' club, and very young boys at that." Ross and Sweetland did not change their minds.

Early in March, the Ottawas took the 4 p.m. train to Montreal as the CPR provided special buffet service for the players and their fans. One of the rewards of holding the Cup was home-ice advantage. But the OHC agreed to play the first game of the series in Montreal. Because: money. The Wanderers were a good draw in their home city and the Arena had a bigger capacity than the Pavilion, where the attendance had been disappointing anyway. The Ottawas and the Marlboros received just $175 each for their first match and only $115 for the second, meaning the Toronto team reaped $200 less than its travel costs. An Arena game was sure to be profitable. As it happened, that afternoon snowslides from the Pavilion's rounded upper roof ripped two holes in a lower part of the roof, sending two thirty-five-foot strips of metal to the seats below. The stands were empty so no one was hurt, but local league games scheduled for that night had to be cancelled.

The more than 5,000 fans at the Arena didn't see hockey at its finest and not just because the ice was so soft. The match was "the dirtiest game two senior teams ever participated in on Arena ice," according to the *Gazette* and "probably the dirtiest that has ever been played for the Stanley Cup," according to the *Journal*. The *Citizen* said it "was sufficiently sanguinary to rank among the war news." After letting too many transgressions go in the first ten minutes, referee Dr. Kearns of the Capitals lost control of the match. By the end, he'd called a record thirty-six infractions. With the exception of the goaltenders, every player received at least one penalty. Still, the *Journal* thought Kearns was too lax. "There were men laid out on both sides who had to be taken to the dressing rooms for repairs, and when the match was over four or five men were on deck with bandages around their heads." The match had started at 8:40 p.m. but all the injury delays meant regulation time ended at 12:40 a.m. The score was five all. Given their wounds and the late hour, neither club wanted to continue and agreed to call the game a tie.

Later, though, the Wanderers claimed captain Billy Strachan had offered to keep going, but that Alf Smith, who was acting captain in Pulford's absence, had refused so the match should be considered "not played." Smith and Kearns denied Strachan had proposed any such thing. Harry DeWitt, the Wanderers' representative who travelled to Ottawa to discuss the matter with

Ross, admitted it wasn't true but still pushed to restart the best-two-out-of-three series with a new referee and the first game, or possibly the second, in Montreal. The Wanderers argued that the two teams were playing for the Federal League championship as well as the Stanley Cup so the matches should be in both cities. Perhaps figuring that home ice against a tough opponent was now more important than more money, the Ottawas rejected the proposal. Ross backed them. After declaring the first game a tie, the trustee offered a choice: the trophy would go to which-ever side scored the most goals in the next two matches or the clubs could play one "sudden death" game. Either way, Ross set a deadline of March 7 to determine a winner. At 2 p.m. on the day of the second match, James Strachan, Wanderers president and Billy's brother, phoned Shillington with a last-ditch proposal: the Wanderers would head up to Ottawa that afternoon if the Arena could host the third game. Shillington rejected this idea "with scorn." The Wanderers stayed in Montreal; the Ottawas kept the Cup.

Once the Wanderers abandoned their challenge, the battered champions nursed their injures and turned their attention to the next opponent. The Brandon Wheat Cities, including Bennest, along with some supporters, came east in their own sleeping car attached to the transcontinental express and displaying a "Wheat City Hockey Team" banner. The players arrived with enough time to fit in a couple of practices and attend a luncheon in their honour at the home of Clifford Sifton and his wife, fol-lowed by a drive around the city. The riding the interior minister represented included Brandon.

As the weather turned colder, promising good ice for the match, one problem remained: finding a referee. Trihey had declined. "Regret I cannot reconcile my views to your wishes," he wired. "The Stanley Cup decision by the trustees in reference to Quebec compels me to refuse your offer." Brandon was willing to accept any Montrealer of Ottawa's choosing, but the defending champs held out for a local man. In the end, Fred Chittick, the former OHC goaltender, took the job. The other outstanding issue was Bennest. Reasoning that he'd played only part of the first Cup game with the Rowing Club due to injury, his new team hoped Ross and the Ottawas would have a change of heart and let him play. They did not.

In the first game, McGee scored three to lead his team to a 6-3 victory. But the Wheat Cities acquitted themselves well, especially the strong defence pair. Lorne Hannay "was the star and mainstay of the challenging team, and about the best cover point seen here this season." He opened the scoring with one goal and added a second in the losing effort. His partner was someone a few of the Ottawas already knew. Lester Patrick, the kid Weldy Young recruited as a stick boy in Montreal, was now taking on the club he used to serve. The twenty-year-old had started playing point when he joined Brandon because that's where the team had an opening. He was steady on defence and often joined—or led—the rush, making him a bigger part of the offence than points had ever been. But while the Brandon forwards were good skaters and showed good combination work, they weren't great shooters and lacked "either the ability or the desire to go in close on the nets." The westerners played a gritty, hard-checking style, but Chittick was a strict ref and stayed in control so the match was free of unnecessary rough stuff. "It showed that Ottawa can and will play a clean game if the opponent is after square hockey," noted the *Citizen*, which quoted a Brandon executive saying, "That team needn't be dirty to play scientific hockey."

Little did he know the second match would show just how dirty the Ottawas could be. The first half, which was wide open and not overly rough, ended with the home team up 5-3. That left the challengers hopeful going into the second half, which was much rougher. Chittick called many penalties but four unanswered Ottawa goals made the final score 9-3. Even though McGee went off for ten minutes, he still scored twice. Two Brandon players ended up at Ottawa's Protestant hospital for repairs: rover George Smith had five cuts to his head and a split lip; centre John Brodie had several cuts to his head. The *Journal* admitted that in the second half "there was a good deal of unnecessary slashing and Brodie and Smith of the visitors came in for considerable attention from Ottawa players who were very properly sent to the fence for any dirty work the referees caught sight of." Afterwards, Brandon goalie Doug Morrison said Ottawa was the roughest team in hockey and singled out Alf Smith as the worst offender, with fill-in cover point Jim McGee, Frank's older brother, a close second. "We don't mind getting our bumps in scrimmages and when playing the puck," Morrison said, "but we can't stand for these butchers who sneak up behind us and cut us down without provocation or any chance to defend ourselves."

As the season ended, the Ottawas had solidified their reputation as an excellent and dirty team. In four CAHL contests, one exhibition game against their crosstown rivals and eight matches in defence of the Cup, the OHC had lost only once and outscored their opponents 100-39. Still, plenty of teams wanted to face the champs for a chance at the Cup; others, including in Winnipeg and New York, invited them for money-making exhibition games. Nor had Ottawa's handling of all comers in 1904 dissuaded the Yukon hockeyists. But the way Ross and Sweetland turned away so many challenges did not bode well for Weldy Young and the other Klondikers.

- TWENTY-ONE -

*"Athletic sport is worthless if it does not
include manliness and fair play"*

While in Ottawa on business during the summer of 1904, Joe Boyle hand delivered a letter to P.D. Ross. Weldy Young had written it hoping to use his connection with the trustee, whom he'd known for fifteen years, to bolster the case for Dawson's Stanley Cup challenge. The plan to send the Civil Service team had given way to the idea of assembling an all-star team. Another letter, signed by team president J.H. Wagon and honorary secretary Norman Watt, went out to Ross and Sheriff Sweetland on August 24, 1904: "The Klondyke Hockey Club of Dawson, Y. T., hereby challenge the Ottawa Hockey Club, of Ottawa, to a series of games for the Stanley Cup, emblematic of the hockey championship of Canada, said series of games to be played under and in accordance with the regulations governing the trophy in question."

Young's letter to his former OHC teammate was longer and less formal. After saying he was excited by the prospect of visiting his hometown after five years away, he laid it on thick about all the success the city's teams had experienced since he'd left. "It is a most common sight on the main street of Dawson," he noted, "to see a group of well known Ottawa men, with heads close together discussing the chances of the Stanley Cup champions, the Rough Riders, the College team, the Capitals or some other home organization that has placed the city on the topmost rung of athletics in Canada." Attempting to deal with any concerns that he was past his prime, Young said it was "particularly gratifying to see that five of the last winter's unbeaten champions were teammates of my own as far back as '98 and to me it exemplifies beyond doubt the truth of the old adage 'The old dog for the hard roads, etc.,' and holds out for me, I must admit, no little consolation." Young was referring to an Irish proverb—"The old dog for the hard road and leave the pup on the path"—about the advantage of experience in the face of a difficult task.

Travel from Dawson to Ottawa would cost the team, by his estimate, at least $10,000. But the entire community, including Yukon Commissioner Fred Congdon, enthusiastically backed the challenge. The team's preference was to play Ottawa in mid-January, leaving a month to complete a barnstorming tour and still return to the Klondike in March. The exhibition games would generate enough funds to get the players back home. As Cup champs, which they were confident of becoming, they were sure they'd pack 'em in wherever they played.

Figuring Ross would have doubts about his teammates, Young sought to put him at ease. "Speaking of the team itself, I can assure you that they are as likely a bunch as ever happened," he wrote. "True we are badly handicapped by so little competition but unless I miss my guess by a large majority I will produce at the right time as good a forward line as ever went a-hunting for a Stanley Cup." The postscript said Boyle was representing the team in the east and had full authority to arrange dates. The mining promoter's many business trips to Ottawa had made him well known at the Russell House, where the powerful and the connected, including the trustee, hung out.

Ross acknowledged receipt of the challenge on September 9, though Young and his teammates would have to wait to learn if his personal appeal was enough to win approval. Ross had other worries. As a trustee and a man who loved hockey, he was protective of the integrity of not just the trophy, but also of the game. On the surface, the sport looked to be in great shape with more players, more teams, more leagues and more fans. And yet, Ross was smart enough to worry about the future.

From that scuffle after the first indoor game in the Victoria Rink in 1875, violence had been part of hockey. In 1886, Quebec City suffered so many injuries that it had no choice but to forfeit a match to the Montreal Crystals. The team didn't have enough players to continue. The formation of leagues, followed by the arrival of the Cup, increased competition, which stoked belligerent play. But the blame really goes back to the sport's ancestry. Influences such as association football stressed passing while rugby and lacrosse emphasized physical contact. "So hockey—both grim and graceful, brutal as much as balletic—belongs both to the family of association sports, or control sports, and to the rugby family of collision sports," Adam Gopnik writes in *Winter: Five Windows on the Season.* "Its history, in a sense, is the struggle to see which of its two parents will determine its legacy."

That struggle attracts and repels fans. "This game appears to be a most fascinating one & the men get wildly excited about it," Lady Aberdeen, wife of Stanley's successor as governor general, wrote after watching an Ottawa-Montreal game in January 1894. "But there can be no doubt as to its roughness, & if the players get over keen & lose their tempers as they are too apt to do, the possession of the stick & the close proximity to one another gives the occasion for many a nasty hit." She noted that one man played with a badly broken nose and the referee stopped the game twice: after the puck hit a player in the mouth and for an unconscious captain to be carried off the ice. When the latter regained consciousness, he resumed playing. While she didn't think the risk of injury was worth it, she observed, "There are many men & boys here in Ottawa who practically live for hockey. It must be said that it is beautiful to see the perfection of skating that is involved in the playing of the game—the men simply run on the ice as if they were on the ground."

Though she'd caught hockey's compelling combination of grace and savagery, it didn't take her long to sour on the sport completely. She attended another game the next month at the Quebec Winter Carnival and this time the barbarity overwhelmed the beauty. "The more I see of hockey, the less I like it—it presents too fierce a temptation for roughness & unfairness for any average person," she wrote. "I am sure I should murder my opponents if I were to play at such close quarters & with a stick in one's hand." Despite the referee's best efforts, "the number of the hurt & the maimed & the disfigured . . . is distressing."

Lady Aberdeen may have been turned off, and editorial writers may have been outraged, but for some spectators, the rowdiness was part of the attraction. There was more to that than the long-held human fascination with violence. In a society that feared losing its manliness, to play or to watch a tough sport was to show how rugged and manly you were. When Ottawa and the Wanderers battled in 1904, the Arena remained full of paying customers when the vicious game finally ended after midnight. As the *Citizen* noted, "Everybody stayed until the last moment to witness what was about the most hair-raising finish ever seen in a Stanley Cup game."

That some bloodthirsty fans enjoyed the spectacle gave Ross little comfort. He was concerned that "many men and most women" were turned off. He expressed his distress in an unsigned comment headlined "Decadent Hockey" in the *Journal*: "Unless a radical change occurs at once in the conduct of hockey matches, the noble winter sport of Canada must, in at least this part of Canada, sink in the public estimation to the level of pugilism." The trustee itemized some of the problems:

teams hitting the ice up to two hours late; tolerance of delays for injuries and broken skates that could double the game time; and aggresive, unsportsmanlike play. Repeated two- or five-minute penalties were inadequate when the offender "has had a chance to disable an opponent for the match—or season, for that matter." He called for more vigilant refereeing and stiffer penalties, suggesting refs should toss from the match any player who receives a second penalty for rough play. "The finest game in the world to watch, hockey as our Canadian teams can show it, is being made a by-word and a disgrace by the manner in which matches are conducted and foul play tolerated," he argued. "Athletic sport is worthless if it does not include manliness and fair play."

To the advocates of amateurism, increased violence wasn't so much a refereeing problem as an inevitable result of the rise of play-for-pay. "So long as it remains free from the taint of professionalism [hockey] will remain dear to the hearts of all true sportsmen, all good athletes, but as soon as this vice creeps in the knell will sound for its death as a popular pastime," Arthur Farrell wrote in *Hockey: Canada's Royal Winter Sport*. "Because when a monetary consideration depends upon the result of a match in which professionals figure as participants, roughness, brutality, will characterize it, to the disgust of the spectators, whose attendance sustains the interest and provides the sinews of war which keep the game alive." Five years later, after watching the wild 1904 clash between Ottawa and the Wanderers, R.J. Whitlaw, honorary president of the Winnipeg Victorias, stuck to the same talking point. "The spirit of professionalism has crept into the game and there was evinced a 'win or die' determination, which resulted in a game utterly unworthy of the best spirit of honest amateurism," he said, adding that hockey "has deteriorated into a struggle where strength and roughness are great factors in determining superiority. In former matches, the players went on the ice to test their skill, and were satisfied that when defeated the better team had won." That was a tidy bit of revisionist history.

Predictably, John Ross Robertson saw the trend as part of what was being lost as the game moved away from an outdated British conception of sports. And, on this, he wasn't all wrong. Hockey was changing. Along with more openness to people from other classes, the emphasis was increasingly on winning rather than the glory of Victorian ideals such as sportsmanship, character development and physical fitness. But the situation was far more complex than Robertson was willing to admit. Yes, the reigning Cup champions were both dirty and not legitimately amateur. And, yes, violence and professionalism had increased over the years, though correlation is not causation. Players and teams were more competitive: greater speed and skill, larger crowds, the increased public standing of athletes, civic pride and local rivalries and gambling all increased the pressure to win. But amateurs wanted to win just as much as the pros did. Brutality had always been part of the game and there was no evidence that those who competed for money were any dirtier than those in it for the love of the game. Weldy Young, for one, was involved in many violent episodes on the ice and he played for Ottawa before professional hockey was even an option. Still, Robertson and his lieutenants used their newspapers to paint pros as hooligans, especially when reporting any violence in the Western Pennsylvania Hockey League.

The OHA president went so far that he met some resistance from his executive. After the league banned London in 1901, Harry Peel played in the WPHL. Before the 1902–03 season, he admitted taking money as a teenager in Pittsburgh, regretted it and unsuccessfully sought reinstatement as an amateur. When he tried again in December 1903, the executive voted nine to one against him. Robertson's position was that once a professional, always a professional. Executive member A.B. Cox of London disagreed and worked to rally others to his view. In February, with Robertson on a business trip to Europe and Egypt and Francis Nelson serving as chair, the executive voted to reinstate Peel. Nelson and Bill Hewitt were two of the three votes to uphold the expulsion. Nelson immediately submitted his resignation, but the others refused to accept it because only he and the absent Robertson had signing privileges with the league's bank.

Despite his victory, Cox continued the skirmish in the press, a brave move given the other side ran the papers. In a letter to the *Globe*, he noted that Peel had returned from the WPHL before the OHA banned that league's players; the OHA had reinstated men in the past; and "we are dealing with boys playing games, and not with criminals." He added, "To efface from the hockey list every lad who does foolish things is merely to create an ever-increasing body of players, whose only outlet lies in the formation of professional clubs and associations."

He was right about that. Before the 1903–04 season, Doc Gibson, the Michigan dentist and OHA exile, did more recruiting for his Portage Lakes team, largely by raiding Pittsburgh teams. Among the players who joined him were Hod and Bruce Stuart, formerly of the OHC, and goaltender Riley Hern, Peel's teammate on the expelled London club. Hern admitted he made the move because he'd make more money in Houghton. When the team in Sault Ste. Marie, Michigan, began paying players, it put the Algonquin Hockey Club, in Sault Ste. Marie on the Ontario side of the St. Marys River, in an awkward position. Located much closer to Michigan than other OHA teams, the Algonquins had little choice but to play against pros in the Upper Peninsula. Robertson banned them. After Toronto Varsity travelled northwest over the Christmas holidays to take on both Soo teams, the university squad met the same fate. Fortunately, the students hadn't breached Canadian Intercollegiate Athletic Union rules, so they could still compete against other schools.

Now all-professional, Portage Lakes defeated the Pittsburgh Victorias to win the so-called Championship of the United States again. The team was so dominant that it needed better competition. Most Canadian clubs were afraid of the repercussions if they played against professionals, but not the Federal League's Wanderers. The two squads met at the Amphidrome in a two-game series promoted as the World's Championship, even though the Wanderers didn't hold the Stanley Cup and, in fact, had abandoned their challenge to Ottawa earlier that month. Portage Lakes swept the Montrealers 8-4 and 9-2.

Before the year was over, Robertson rescinded Peel's reinstatement and, with an overhauled executive, continued to do his best to make Cox's prediction come true as he held steady on the OHA's prime directive. "I am not trying to dictate," he declared, apparently with a straight face, at the annual meeting. "The members of the association have the question in their own hands. If they propose to keep the O.H.A. free from the taint of professionalism they must adhere to the principle that a man who leaves the amateur and steps into the professional ranks can have no place or habitation with those who play hockey as it is played under the flag of the O.H.A." He banned all senior lacrosse players because the summer sport let amateurs and professionals play together and the Canadian Amateur Athletic Union had declared the Canadian Lacrosse Association professional. Even Fred Waghorne was nearly a victim of this purge. Robertson wanted the ref banned because he'd been field captain of a professional lacrosse team. But the Iron Fist lost that vote after a member of the executive argued, "Mr. President, if we debar Mr. Waghorne, who will referee our final games?" So many top athletes competed in more than one sport that Robertson's new offensive made a lot of great talent ineligible for OHA clubs.

This was great news for the Americans. James Dee had begun promoting the idea of a professional league in 1903 and by the fall of 1904, it was coming together. Originally to be called the American Hockey Association, it became the International Hockey League after the Algonquins joined. The Canadian Sault Ste. Marie team became the first openly professional club in the country. The four other franchises were in Pittsburgh and the Michigan towns of Houghton, Calumet and Sault Ste. Marie. Gibson managed, and played for, Houghton's Portage Lakes club. Late in 1904, the teams were busy building their rosters for the IHL's inaugural season. Canadians jeopardized their amateur status back home and, unless they signed with Pittsburgh, they'd be living in a small, remote town, but they all made a salary and some received jobs. The new league wooed plenty of high-end talent from north of the border. But some OHA stars used the threat of signing with the IHL—whether they'd received an offer or not—to negotiate better deals such as jobs with inflated salaries from their Ontario teams. Robertson's league wasn't as pure as he pretended, though no one was going to get an inkling of that from Toronto's press.

Even as they ranted about amateurs, newspapers helped make professionalism inevitable. From the beginning, they'd been crucial to the growth of hockey, showcasing the game and making heroes out of local teams. Many papers also glorified the Stanley Cup, giving matches for the trophy extensive coverage. Reporters often described these games as the fastest, the best, the most exciting ever played. True, the sport was new and still evolving and the players were becoming more skilful, so matches were getting faster, better and more exciting. But there was obviously a lot of hyperbole at work here. By the late 1890s, newspapers, especially Montreal's *Gazette* and *Star*, increasingly emphasized victory over fair play. "The press became more interested with winning and losing, though it did still make a point to praise the skill level of both clubs," according to sports historian John Barlow. "However, this praising of both clubs had less to do with good sportsmanship than it did with the commercialization of the game and the need to sell tickets, the sport of hockey, and, ultimately, newspapers. Winning became of paramount importance."

When it came to violence, the press played both sides: glamourizing roughness in game reports and condemning it in editorials. Sometimes they covered it with a wink. After a scrap between Weldy Young and Cam Davidson of the Montreal Vics in 1898, the *Gazette* said Young had "more than a wordy discussion with Davidson and there was an exchange of fistic compliments. They did not send long letters to the papers saying pleasant things about each other. They just got their difficulty over quick and then the referee gave a five minutes rest, to discuss the situation. There were a few other little incidents of a like nature which relieved the monotony in a way not to be commended."

Newspapers regularly decried the visiting team's dirty tactics while overlooking the home team's infractions or putting them down to grit and toughness. Or they mocked the other team, especially if it was from Toronto, for its lack of toughness. When it came to the OHC, the non-Ottawa papers revelled in the chance to paint them as savages. Winnipeg's *Tribune* conceded the Ottawas had "earned a horrible reputation" for defeating four challengers in 1904 by what it called "brute force." But the paper put the blame on the referees of the matches, while also casting doubt on their own ink-stained colleagues: "It seems scarcely creditable that so much rough work as has been reported in the press could have actually occurred without some one being killed or permanently disabled." All of this made for good copy, which helped boost circulation.

Oblivious to its own role, the press was content to condemn the professionals or the referees. But one paper had a different take. "Truly, the old cup has been productive of more hard feeling than any other trophy around here," offered the *Gazette's* sporting editor. "It would only be a venial sin if some good-hearted burglar would carry it away in his swag bag, and melt the white metal into serviceable spoons or something of that sort." Calling it "a mischievous trophy," he bemoaned the ill will it had fostered between clubs, "and it will take many a cup to drown the sorrow of insolence." Although he said there was "too much talk of gate," he never mentioned professionalism. Instead, the trophy had eliminated what was enjoyable about hockey. "These clubs may prate about honors and all that tommyrot but the real secret of the strenuous game is the acknowledged drawing power of the trophy. Take that away, and at once the real evil element is removed."

Since the editor's comment appeared in the wake of the ill-fated match between the Ottawas and the Wanderers, the *Journal* reprinted it under a "Case of Sour Grapes" heading. But Ross must have recognized some truth in that criticism. The irony was that Lord Stanley, a member of the British nobility, had donated the Cup to encourage hockey "fairly played under rules generally recognized." But Canadians wanted his bowl so badly that the honour soon fuelled the win-at-all-costs attitude Victorians abhorred. A good-news story might be just what the trophy, and the sport, needed.

In mid-October, Ottawa agreed to face Dawson. Perhaps Young's letter swayed Ross. The trustee obviously knew what a good hockey player the cover point had been for the OHC in the 1890s and respected him enough to appoint him referee of the second Cup match of 1896. Young was also a name familiar to every Ottawa hockey fan, which would help ensure healthy ticket sales. Or perhaps the trustees simply put aside their concerns about the quality of the challengers because they saw a series as good public relations. They may have wanted a distraction from the increasing violence, the shamateurism and the loss of so many good players to the United States. If the rumoured new pro league in Michigan became a reality, even more players were sure to go. Whatever the reason, and despite the skepticism of many eastern hockey people, the trustees and the Ottawas approved the challenge—and gave Weldy Young a chance to finally win the Stanley Cup.

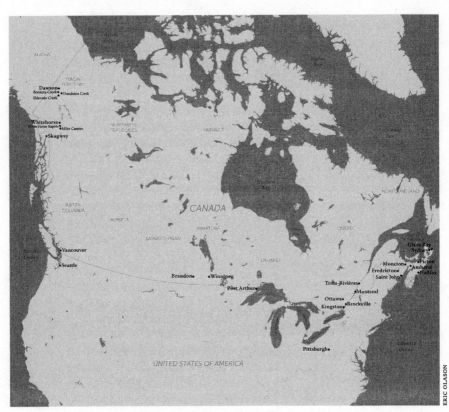

STOPS ON THE KLONDIKERS'S 1905 TOUR.

ERIC OLASON

PART THREE

Part Three

- TWENTY-TWO -

"We have splendid material here for a team"

After five years, Weldy Young was well familiar with the sounds of the Klondike. With the arrival of spring came the gorgeous tinkling of candle ice breaking, the rough grinding of ice chunks along the riverbank during the spring breakup and the joyous burble of water running in ditches as snow melted. At various times, he'd hear the alien-sounding calls of the sandhill cranes migrating overhead as well as the calls of other birds such as ptarmigan, red polls, spruce grouse, ruffled grouse, grosbeaks, canvasback ducks, teals and merganser ducks. All year, the ravens croaked. In summer, the rhythmic rattle of sternwheelers paddling up and down the river and the high-pitched whine of countless mosquitoes were inescapable. In autumn, the wind rustled dried-on-the-branch leaves. Caribou snorted softly and clomped along while moose bugled, broke branches as they burst through underbrush and splashed as they surfaced after diving to eat in the river. Out on the creeks, dredges made a hell of a racket, which was audible for great distances. During a walk in the winter, on a lucky night, he'd have heard the crackling of the northern lights overhead and, if he was in downtown Dawson, the squeaking of the wooden sidewalks below. During the day, neighing horses pulled delivery sleighs. For much of the year, axes thunked against wood and sparks hissed and clicked through the pipes of wood stoves. And, always, the dogs barked and fought and barked. So many dogs.

Even as the sounds he heard remained a reliable constant, Young had seen Dawson change dramatically—and he hadn't even been there for that booming summer of 1898. Vancouver was now a week away with regularly scheduled sternwheelers and the WP&YR Railway to the Alaskan coast. The telegraph made communicating with the Outside easier, though the lines sometimes went down, and in January 1904, the telephone company printed its first directory for its 500 subscribers. Dawson's Carnegie Library opened in August that year.

In the rest of the country, the great Canadian experiment—the creation of a non-American nation out of the northern part of the continent—was going well. The last few decades of the previous century had brought urban growth and increased industrialization as well as social and cultural change. The Victorian era was over, but parts of Canada, especially Ontario, remained terribly British. King Edward VII conferred the title Royal upon the North-West Mounted Police in 1904. But the country was also beginning to forge its own identity separate from the mother country. Some tensions emerged. In 1903, Canada lost an arbitration case over the border with Alaska because the one United Kingdom member of the panel sided with the three Americans. The decision spurred anti-British sentiment.

Meanwhile, Clifford Sifton's immigration drive was well on its way to helping the national population double to seven million within fifteen years. The big push was to settle the wide-open west and north. The Gold Rush had drawn people to the Yukon, at least briefly, but Sifton had the most success attracting people to the Prairies. He especially encouraged immigrants with agricultural backgrounds from similar climates, so many of the newcomers arrived from the Ukraine, Romania and other European countries. Inevitably, this policy was unpopular among some Canadians, who feared their British sensibilities would be swamped by these exotic foreigners. Sifton wanted people to farm, not flock to urban centres, but Prairie cities grew as well. Many newcomers embraced hockey. A *Tribune* editorial before the first game of the 1902 Stanley Cup series between the Montreal Hockey Club and the Winnipeg Victorias said, "Look over the names of some of the boy's teams. You will find Poles, Jews, Russians, Italians, Syrians, Hungarians and Galicians playing side by side with British, French, Scandinavians or native Canadians . . ."

This expansion, as well as more railways, helped make the country prosperous. And optimistic. "As the 19th Century was that of the United States," Prime Minister Wilfrid Laurier declared in a January 1904 speech at the Canadian Club in Ottawa, "so I think the 20th will be filled by Canada." That was a bold—OK, fanciful—prediction, but he knew he'd likely call an election before the year was out. Yet his buoyant outlook genuinely reflected the spirit of the times. In 1903, a couple of bicycle makers named Wilbur and Orville Wright managed to get a plane airborne for twelve seconds, flying above some sand dunes near Kitty Hawk, North Carolina. That same year, Henry Ford started selling his first Model A automobile. He opened a Canadian plant the next year. The bevy of inventions unveiled at the 1904 World's Fair in St. Louis included the X-ray machine, the baby incubator, the electric plug and wall outlet, the electric typewriter and an early version of the fax machine. New York opened a subway and work began on the Panama Canal. Marconi's wireless telegraph was revolutionizing communications.

In some ways, Dawsonites shared that optimism, even as the town suffered its toughest times yet. Although there was still plenty of gold, mining had changed. At the start of the Gold Rush, individual prospectors worked their own claims. Then people amassed more claims and hired wage-earners to handle the moil. Now, corporations and syndicates were taking over. Joe Boyle didn't have a dredge yet, but he was getting closer. Dredges meant fewer mining jobs. When it became clear the previous year's gold strike in Alaska's Tanana Valley was substantial, plenty of miners and labourers went downriver to Fairbanks after spring breakup. Many small merchants soon followed their customers out of town. That led to a shakeout among the newspapers. The *Dawson Record* lasted just three and a half months before being absorbed by the *Yukon Sun* in November 1903. The *Sun* closed the next year after it became clear that all government advertising would go to the *Yukon World*, a new paper sponsored by Fred Congdon, the increasingly controversial territorial commissioner. Long an active member of the community, including serving as a director of the DAAA, he was well liked in town. His appointment was initially popular and his wife made the Commissioner's Residence a social hub. Congdon set about modernizing the Mining Act to help individual miners, but he also built a corrupt and ruthless political machine that rewarded supporters and punished critics. Despite his political patronage, the Liberal *World* was just four pages and the *Daily News*, which was American-owned but edited by a Briton and was politically Conservative, published ad-rich eight-page editions.

While the *News* remained healthy, the departure of small merchants hurt the tax base. With less money coming in, many of the civic amenities that made the unlikely city such a good place to live now seemed too expensive. The Yukon Council had incorporated Dawson in 1901 over the objections of many in the business community, who feared higher taxes. One place to cut costs, companies and property owners argued in 1904, was to get rid of the elected, and paid, city council. They pushed for a plebiscite on the issue, and with the support of Congdon, the Yukon Council agreed. The *News* fought the idea; the *World*, not surprisingly, supported it. Dawson voted on the proposal in

September after a campaign marred by dirty tricks and charges it had been rigged. Local democracy lost. The territory took control of the city. Of course, the cost savings and lower taxes weren't the biggest benefit of the move: without meddlesome citizens to worry about, the wealthy had more power to sway decisions in town. While Dawson continued to maintain an air of a modern, permanent city, losing elected local government was definitely a step backward. The citizens needed some good news. A Stanley Cup victory would boost everyone's spirits.

If anyone had doubts about what sports meant to Yukoners, the 1904 pennant scandal took care of that. In May, several baseball enthusiasts met in the Arctic Brotherhood Hall to organize the Dawson Baseball League. Deputy sheriff Jack Eilbeck became the president despite what happened when he held that position in the previous summer's league. He'd had to deny charges he'd bribed a pitcher to throw a game. The new league bestowed the titular roles of governor and honorary president on Congdon and Sheriff Eilbeck. The season started with four teams: the Arctic Brotherhood's ABs; the NCs, sponsored by the Northern Commercial Company; the Nonpareils, with a roster of "old-time Dawson players"; and the Colts, run by the two Eilbecks, though the son was officially the manager. In response to past problems, the league was to be strictly amateur and players couldn't compete for more than one team. The games were Tuesday and Friday nights and often attracted crowds of between 2,000 and 4,000.

By the end of August, the ABs dropped out of the league, leaving the other teams fighting for the pennant. Following two protested contests, both involving the NCs and the Colts, Eilbeck ignored verbal and written requests for a meeting to deal with the matter. Finally, in early September, the other executives met without him. They deposed him as president and elected NC manager Sam Mangum to the position. "It has been impossible to get Mr. Eilbeck to pay attention to the affairs of the league," the new president explained in a letter. He also charged that his predecessor "has acted so manifestly unfair and arbitrary in his dealings, both with the league and the individual teams, that the change is not only justifiable, but absolutely necessary."

Refusing to recognize the meeting or the change in the executive, Eilbeck declared the season over and the Colts, by virtue of being in first place at the time, the champions. With a week of scheduled games to go, Magnum wanted the Colts to give the previous year's pennant to the league secretary to hold until the season was officially over. The deputy sheriff claimed to have no idea where the flag was, though it would have been hard to misplace given that it was twenty-five feet long and eight feet wide at the base. Sure enough, two days later, he was smiling and pointing at the pennant as it floated in the breeze above the courthouse. After briefly trolling everyone, Eilbeck took it down, but didn't hand it over to the league. The Colts defaulted their remaining games and the NCs won the title. Magnum arranged for a new pennant from A.G. Spalding & Company and one afternoon in mid-September, a flag that read "Champions 1904 Yukon Territory" went up at the Northern Commercial building. Later that day, the old pennant was once again flying above the courthouse. Apparently, just because a league was amateur, and everyone was a gentleman, didn't mean good sportsmanship necessarily prevailed.

Baseball wasn't the only sport in town, of course. Hockey, curling and boxing were especially popular, even if the competition wasn't as childishly ruthless. Klondike sportsmen took hockey particularly seriously—seriously enough to believe they were as good as any players in the country.

As Joe Boyle approached middle age, he was still a physical force, "a huge Irishman with penetrating blue eyes, a round, red face, and a firm jaw." He'd also established himself as a financial force as he continued his efforts to launch his dredging operations. He spent the autumn of 1904 in the east on business. Much of the time, he was in Ottawa, where the thirty-seven-year-old played several games as an inside wing for the Rough Riders. He also assumed the role of manager of a hockey team.

Boyle had no apparent connection to Dawson's Stanley Cup dreams until he delivered Young's letter to P.D. Ross in the summer. But it's not insignificant that once he became involved, an idea mooted in the Klondike since at least 1900 started to come together, even if there were still plenty of snags ahead. In mid-October, Boyle informed everyone back home that he'd won approval for the series. About ten days later, Norman Watt received a letter from the secretary of the Ottawas that included a copy of the letter the club had sent Ross officially accepting the challenge "upon the condition that the Klondike Hockey Club play no other matches, exhibitions or otherwise, with any other club before they play the Stanley Cup series here, and that the series should end not later than January 10th, 1905."

Although some people in Ottawa worried the Yukon's early winters would give Dawson an advantage, the insistence on no exhibition games wasn't to ensure the northerners would arrive unprepared. It was a business decision. Expecting the Klondikers to be popular with fans, the OHC wanted to host them first. The champs also feared if the Yukoners suffered any bad losses to inferior clubs on the way, it would dampen ticket sales. So the challengers' training would be limited to games against other Dawson teams and whatever practice they could fit in after they arrived in Ottawa. But federal politics messed that up. Laurier dissolved Parliament at the end of September to seek a third mandate. The election was slated for November 3. As usual, though, Yukoners would cast their ballots six weeks later. (The territory finally abandoned this practice in 1921.) To ensure the series wrapped up by January 10, the players would have to leave

Dawson without exercising their democratic right on December 16. Or they could cut it close by staying long enough to vote, but that would mean sacrificing any practice time between the end of their trip and the start of the first game.

In late October, Dawson hockeyists wired Boyle to ask him to seek new dates. While he waited for the OHC's reply, the manager talked a big game to the press. In early November, he said the players would head east soon and arrive a few weeks before the series was to start. "His team, he says, will be in the finest possible condition, well seasoned, by the date of the games, though, of course, the long trip will not be without the adverse effects. However, a short rest on arrival will set them all right," the *Gazette* reported. "Mr. Boyle, who is one of the best versed men on sporting topics in the country, is confident that the men from the Far North will give Ottawa a great fight for the coveted trophy."

While he could be modest when talking about himself, Boyle wasn't averse to exaggerations when pursuing his interests. After all, after a career as a boxing promoter, he was now a mining promoter. So he knew how to spin. He said the team had been holding practices since early October. "In fact," he claimed, "the ice on the Yukon River was in good condition in September." This was a ludicrous claim. The river never froze that early; in fact, the last steamer of the year left Dawson on October 22. Skating began earlier on local sloughs and creeks, but most years the earliest anyone could reasonably hope for playable rink ice was the beginning of November. While the DAAA kept teasing the town with promises of an early opening of its rink that fall, by the time Boyle talked to the *Gazette*, the team hadn't even held tryouts.

That didn't mean players weren't getting ready. Lionel Bennett, Norman Watt, Randy McLennan and Weldy Young worked out in the DAAA gym while George Kennedy and Hector Smith skated near the mouth of Bear Creek. Like Kennedy, Smith was an Indigenous man from Selkirk, Manitoba. He hoped to make the team as a spare. Meanwhile, Young in Dawson and Boyle in the east continued to work on setting up the post-series tour of cities in Canada and the United States. Hod Stuart, who'd briefly been Young's teammate on the Ottawas, had just moved to the Calumet Miners of the new International Hockey League following two years on Doc Gibson's Portage Lakes team. Along with playing cover point, Stuart coached and managed Calumet. He'd be pleased to arrange a game with Dawson. Other teams also expressed interest, but getting them to commit to dates wasn't easy. Winnipeg's Victorias, for example, were initially keen, but later wrote Boyle to say they could make no promises until the team made it east. One concern was finding available dates during the busy season. Another was that if the Klondikers played against U.S.-based professional teams such as Calumet and Portage Lakes, the Vics didn't want to jeopardize their amateur status by playing Dawson.

Toward the end of November, Watt received some good news in a letter from Boyle. The OHC executive had agreed to delay the series a few days to allow the players to vote and still fit in a week of practice in Ottawa. "I arranged these dates after consulting sailing dates of coast steamers and determining how long you would need to get here," wrote Boyle. The first game would now be Friday the 13th.

When the DAAA rink opened on the evening of November 14, skaters and spectators packed the place. As always, the indoor ice and the club's other facilities provided an invaluable diversion during Dawson's dark winter months. Skating was a popular pastime with both the easterners in town, many of whom were already comfortable on blades, and those from coastal cities such as Vancouver, Seattle and San Francisco, who were just learning. But this year, the opening also meant the selection of a team to go after the Stanley Cup could begin. The previous Saturday, the hockey team's executive committee held a meeting in the DAAA parlours. On the agenda: create subcommittees and plan for the trip Outside. Four men, including Young and Jack Eilbeck, would recommend the final squad.

Practices in the D-Triple-A ran nightly from seven to eight and were open to the public. Off the ice, according to the *Daily News*, players were doing "gymnastic exercise and hardening themselves in several ways." The team needed seven players and a spare or two, but at least nineteen wanted to go. So at a second meeting, the executive opted to hold four tryout games. "It has been finally decided that the Klondike hockey team will leave Dawson on the 20th of December," Young announced in a telegram. "We will give ourselves eighteen days to make the trip, so that we will arrive in Ottawa on January the ninth. I have been chosen captain. We have splendid material here for a team, and we will play a series of four matches to decide what men shall go."

With all his experience, Young was the obvious choice for captain, and while he couldn't match Boyle as a promoter, he didn't lack enthusiasm. In a letter to his father, he said he now weighed more than 180 pounds, up from his old playing weight of 165, and had never been in better shape or trained so hard. As for his teammates—who had yet to be selected—Young promised the defence "will all be strong, husky fellows with speed as well as weight." And then, as if he had a little Boyle in him, he added this: "Most of the members of the team will be government officials and composed not of men who sit in offices, but men who think nothing of walking from 50 to 100 miles a day for a good many days a week."

For the first formal tryout game on November 25, the fourteen players who'd survived the early cuts split into two teams. Jack Eilbeck was not on either seven. His father had gone Outside a few days earlier and planned to spend the winter in California, so he was responsible for the sheriff duties. McLennan was the captain of the Blues; Young captained the Reds. The match attracted lots of spectators, though the play was not particularly fast or accomplished. Still, Hec Smith made a good impression. "He was in every play from the first blow of the whistle," said the *World*. "He has speed, is a heady player and possesses every attribute of a winner."

By the end of November, they had a team. But one without Lionel Bennett, the best centre in town. He decided to stay behind to be with his wife. In December 1903, she was crossing the street at the corner of Third and Queen when a runaway horse-drawn delivery sleigh, travelling at full speed, hit her and dragged her sixty feet on the hard-packed snow. She managed to hold on to her purse and the other items she was carrying until the rig lurched and she became untangled from it. Initially, she thought she was just shaken up, realizing only after she returned home how serious her injuries were. Nearly a year later, she was still recovering and Bennett didn't feel right leaving her alone for several months.

Smith would fill in at centre with the rest of the Civil Service forwards: rover McLennan, left wing Watt and right wing Kennedy. Behind them, Young would take his familiar spot at cover point with James Kennedy Johnstone at point. Johnstone, who grew up in Ottawa where his father handled accounting for the Post Office Department, joined the North-West Mounted Police in 1900 shortly before his eighteenth birthday. In 1901, when the force was looking for men willing to transfer to the Yukon, he applied. But he hadn't been the most diligent cop, accumulating a string of citations for minor transgressions such as tardiness, absence and damaging government property. Bowen Perry, by then the NWMP commissioner, wrote, "This constable is only 19 years of age, not too strong and has been very careless since he joined. I should not care to send him to the Yukon at present." The next year, though, Johnstone made it to White

Horse Station. After finally transferring to Dawson, he took to the place. In October 1904, half a year before he was due to be discharged from the force, he arranged a furlough to take a job as the night watchman at the post office.

Gold commissioner Edmund Senkler wasn't going east, so Albert Forrest would be the team's goaltender. An apprentice printer at the *Yukon World*, the eighteen-year-old was handsome and fresh-faced, with a crooked part in the middle of his dark hair. In 1897, his father had been working as a foreman at a small gold mine in Grass Valley, a town in the western foothills of California's Sierra Nevada mountains, when he heard about the gold strike in the Yukon. He quickly joined the rush out of San Francisco while his wife, daughter and youngest son, Emil, returned to Trois-Rivières, Quebec, where Albert and oldest son, Paul, were still in school. There, the family would "await the bullion by the sack full as we fully expected to be shipping out to us." While that didn't happen, Forrest père did well enough to return to the east for the winter of 1898-99. When he went back to the Klondike in the spring, he took Paul with him. The rest of the family followed in July 1901, and over the next several years, the Forrest brothers regularly won sporting competitions in town. Paul, a bailiff in the sheriff's office, had also tried out for the All-Klondike team. Albert was the champion speed skater of the Yukon, a star in baseball and basketball, an accomplished long-distance cyclist and the centre on the DAAA hockey team. He'd been between the flags only a few times so he'd need to rely on his natural athleticism, rather than experience, to keep the puck out of the net.

Those who didn't make the cut immediately began talking about forming squads to play for the Cup once the team returned from Ottawa with the championship. They didn't wait that long to issue their first challenge. Jack Eilbeck picked the seven and served as captain. His teammates included Archie Martin, Paul Forrest and, in net, Emil Forrest. The "hockey festival" at the D-Triple-A on December 14 began with a match between two women's teams. The Dawsons wore white sweaters and the Victorias, who won 3-0, wore sweaters that "were of a warm red hue," according to the *Yukon World*, which also noted in a story that reflected the unabashed sexism of the times that "there is something about a sweater which makes a woman look very charming indeed." The paper reported that while a couple of the players "showed very excellent form," others needed more practice. The hockey wasn't much but "there was not a slow moment . . . and the spectators were very sorry when the cow bell that was used in lieu of a whistle rang to show that the game was at an end."

The *World* was more complimentary of the men's game, calling it "one that Dawson need not be ashamed of even if she were a city four times the present size." The seven that would play for the Cup made "some brilliant plays and also an excellent combination that every day's practice makes more perfect." In the second half of the match, Albert and Emil Forrest switched goals so the former could face the better players. The final score was 4-1 for the All-Klondike team.

As the players worked themselves into form with daily practices, Boyle began taking his role as manager more seriously than anyone likely expected. He wasn't just handling administrative details such as dates, accommodation and the post-series tour. Despite his bravado for the press, he knew the long journey would make staying in game shape impossible, and that at 200 feet by eighty-one feet, Dey's Arena was forty feet longer and six feet wider than the DAAA rink. "Bring light training apparatus for use on the steamer and trains," Boyle insisted in his letter to Watt. "Bring at least three sets of pulling machines, Indian clubs and dumbbells." He wanted one player to serve as drill captain and keep track of the workouts; naturally, he expected to see those records when the team arrived in Ottawa. He suggested they take a day off in Winnipeg, where they could go for a long walk and get a good skate in.

Given his experience as a boxing manager, his training advice shouldn't have come as a surprise. But he went further. "I want you all to play hard, fast, clean hockey and if there is dirty work let the other team do it," he wrote, adding that he'd suggested to the OHC management that any man guilty of a deliberate foul should be tossed from the game. "I will look to every man as a matter between himself and myself to keep in his best condition and play his best." He even had rules for their off-ice behaviour. While some of the players on the team were teetotalers, others weren't, so Boyle instructed, "I know many of the boys need no admonition but insist that on leaving Dawson all players cut out liquor and tobacco."

Another concern was money. While Boyle had committed to some financial support, the selected players needed to do some fundraising. Tickets to the well-attended tryout games were fifty cents, with the gate going to help pay for the trip Outside. In addition, Young was on the organizing committee for a big fundraiser at the Arctic Brotherhood Hall. The venue, which opened in 1901, had the largest dance floor in town, as well as a stage and boxes in the gallery so, along with being home to indoor baseball, it hosted banquets, concerts and most of the big social events that mattered in town. (Since 1971, the building has been home to Diamond Tooth Gerties, a gambling hall with Gold Rush–themed entertainment.) Tickets for the hockey dance were a steep $5 for one gentleman and "the ladies that he may bring." But a week before the bash, the organizers cancelled it. The date was too close to another dance sponsored by the Arctic Brotherhood and conflicted with election events; besides, the team executive was confident that supporters had already pledged enough money to finance the trip.

Before leaving, the team named only one spare: Archie Martin of the DAAA Athletics. Originally from Aylmer, Quebec, he'd had a job setting type at the Government Printing Bureau in March 1898 when he read a front-page story about the

Gold Rush in the *Ottawa Journal.* A few days later, he hopped on a westbound train and was soon climbing the Chilkoot Trail. He befriended Boyle and later worked for him. Although he was better known for lacrosse than hockey, he'd be available in case of injury to a teammate and would help take care of business matters for the club.

The selected players made arrangements to leave their homes and jobs for three months. Johnstone's boss at the Department of Public Works was not happy about the request because the new man had already made a couple of other scheduling changes. But his boss's boss, Chief Dominion Architect David Ewart, approved it. The players who worked for Senkler's gold commissioner's office had an easier time of it. Watt, for example, secured a paid leave of absence from December 19 to March 23, though any extension would be unpaid. Only Young had a problem. He'd landed another government job, handling election returns and serving as an enumerator for South Dawson to prepare the voter rolls for the upcoming Yukon Council elections. He realized he wouldn't be finished in time to leave town with the other players. He'd have to complete his work and then try to catch up to his teammates.

- TWENTY-THREE -

"More of the beautiful would be welcome"

At this time of year, just a few days before winter solstice, the Klondike made do with precious few hours of daylight. The Dawson townsite, sitting down on the flats at the bottom of the river valley, received no direct sun at all for more than four weeks. So it was dark when George Kennedy, Hector Smith and Archie Martin left town on foot at seven o'clock in the morning on December 18, 1904. Their itinerary: walk the 330-mile Overland Trail to Whitehorse, ride the WP&YR to Skagway, board a coastal steamer to Vancouver and ride the rails to Ottawa, arriving four days before the first game, allowing some practice time. The players wore parkas and moccasins and carried some food and a few essentials on their backs. They took their skates but no other hockey equipment. Although they'd planned to let a dog team pull their gear, so little snow had fallen that it wasn't possible. The Klondike had received much less of the white stuff than usual that autumn and a warm spell in December, with temperatures above freezing, led to melting. (The common misperception that the players travelled by dogsled may exist because miners often called a long walk a "mush.") Many residents cheered them off that Sunday morning and the *World* noted that the team was going east to "battle for the Stanley Cup and incidentally show some of the old time cracks how the noble game should be played." The Yukoners weren't about to accept the role of underdog; that simply wasn't in their nature.

The mercury read minus five on Monday morning as Randy McLennan, Norman Watt, Jim Johnstone and Albert Forrest climbed on their bikes and rode out of town under clear skies with a north wind behind them. The cyclists hoped to make it to Whitehorse in a week, but that depended on the trail conditions. In stretches with no snow or where previous travellers had packed it down enough, the bikers could make good time. But unpacked snow, or a new dump of it, would require getting off their wheels and pushing. On the day they left, the *Daily News* reported the snow was mere inches deep on the trail. Heavily laden stages sometimes cut through that thin layer, making the sleigh runners drag badly, especially on steep grades. The charming subheading on the story was "More of the Beautiful Would be Welcome."

Travel between Dawson and Whitehorse was much easier when the Yukon River was open. A flotilla of sternwheelers and scows carrying people, food, supplies and the mail shuttled 460 miles between the two towns. This connection to the south meant so much to Dawson that the papers regularly reported arrivals and departures, along with passenger names and the amount of mail coming in. From late October to at least early May, though, the sternwheelers stayed put and travel between Dawson and Whitehorse became more of an adventure.

In the summer of 1902, workers began cutting a twelve-foot right-of-way with axes and cross-saws; graded the ground with horse-drawn plows; built culverts; and reinforced retaining walls with wood. Rather than follow the Yukon River, the Overland Trail took a more direct path, often relying on Indigenous routes. By November 2, it was ready for the first travellers—and, crucially, the mail. For the WP&YR, which had obtained the lucrative government contract to move the post on its steamers in 1901, the Overland Trail made delivering the mail twelve months a year possible. So the WP&YR's Yukon Stage Line was also known as the Royal Mail Service. Meanwhile, the government, which had invested $129,000 in the route, hoped the project would open up more land for farming (this mostly proved to be wishful thinking, though it did generate more mining development). For Dawsonites, the road eliminated the town's winter isolation from civilization. The mail now came even during the freeze-up and breakup of the river, and people could travel to and from the Klondike whenever they wanted.

The trail wended around lakes, up steep climbs and through deep valleys. When the beautiful was deep enough, horse-drawn sleighs travelled the route; when it wasn't, stagecoaches did. The sleighs held up to fourteen passengers and a ton and a half of luggage and supplies; the stages carried twelve passengers and one ton of cargo. The drivers, called skinners, who wore coonskin coats with long red sashes around the waist, had the right of way over independent stages, dog teams, skiers, cyclists and people on foot—the route's only rule of the road. The trail had five sections, each separated by a river crossing: at the Stewart, Pelly, Yukon and Takhini rivers. Before and after the ice was thick enough for ice bridges, expert canoeists transported passengers and cargo across to a coach waiting on the other side. Drifting snow could make the road impassable without a lot of shovelling, and water from a spring could cover the road with ice, making the trip even more treacherous. In spring and fall, travellers might encounter floods, mud, rockslides and washouts. Not every stage completed its journey safely.

The thrice-weekly service increased to daily in March, when more people wanted to be in Dawson to get a head start on business before the sternwheelers, and even more people, returned. The Royal Mail Service employed more than 200 horses and the skinners stopped at posts every twenty or so miles to change teams. A post typically included stables, storehouses, woodpiles, men's and women's outhouses and, a great relief for passengers, a roadhouse. The company advertised a five- to five-and-a-half-day trip, though it could be as long as ten—or, occasionally, as short as three—depending on the weather and road conditions. (Although there were three cars in Dawson by 1901, no automobile drove the Overland Trail until 1912. Joe Boyle and his wife attempted the feat in December of that year, eventually abandoning their twenty-horsepower Flanders and hopping on a sleigh for the remainder of the trip to Whitehorse. Later that month, Yukon Commissioner George Black and a gold company executive made it all the way in a chauffeur-driven, sixty-horsepower Locomobile, a jaunt that took less than thirty-six hours.)

Despite the branding as a "first-class" service, the experience was far from restful. The Yukon Stage Line initially tried standard Concord coaches, but the metal springs couldn't handle the rough terrain and had a tendency to become brittle and snap in the subarctic cold. Instead, the company built its own coaches featuring leather springs, called "thoroughbraces," which meant a much bumpier trip. The sleighs offered a smoother ride on snow. Either way, it was cold. The company provided buffalo robes and, to warm feet, heated bricks or burning coal in metal boxes on the floor. Many travellers resorted to sipping from flasks. In *I Married the Klondike*, Laura Beatrice Berton tells of taking a trip that started at 4 p.m. one Monday in late February. "Off we went into the silent night and into a silent world of white. For five days we would sit in this open sleigh, our noses icicled, our feet warmed by hot bricks and charcoal, while we crossed the Yukon Territory in a wavering diagonal line north. I have never embarked on a stranger journey," recalls Berton (whose son, Pierre, would also write about the Klondike). She borrowed a man's coonskin coat, which was something of a uniform for regulars on the service. "It was not a comfortable trip.

The seats had hardly any backs and we had not been out long before I became unpleasantly aware of my neck. It just wouldn't hold up my wobbling head."

In his summer letter to Ross, Weldy Young said the players would walk from Dawson to Whitehorse in nine days to stay fit. He later explained to his father that by walking they'd avoid stiffening up due to all the bouncing around in a coach. While riding a stage was indeed an endurance test, the team's decision to walk and cycle may have been an attempt to save money. A trip cost $125. For eight players, that would add $1,000 to the travel expenses, though if there'd been enough snow, going by sleigh would have been a little less. Whatever the real reason, the *Daily News* bought the spin about training, noting, "The bicycling and sprinting work on the trail will develop their muscles as well as their breathing capacity."

The day after the cyclists left Dawson, the temperature plunged twenty degrees between noon and 10:30 p.m. and it continued to tumble during the week. The team walked and dog-trotted, or rode, on the zig-zagging and hilly route through forests of white and black spruce trees and leafless aspen, balsam poplars and birch. Each day, the skies would morph from darkness to crepuscular glow to daylight and then back again. One report said those on foot made it forty-six miles down the trail the first day and put another forty-one behind them on the second. But by the third day, blistered feet slowed them down and they covered only thirty-six miles. Another report had it that they started slowly and then picked up the pace, travelling only twenty-three and twenty-six miles the first two days, but averaging forty-five miles by the last three.

Whatever distance they'd covered each day, they had to worry about where to stop at night. The best choice was a roadhouse. These establishments—which ranged from foul tents to charming hotels—played a special role in the development of the Yukon, sprouting in new mining camps, established towns and anywhere people travelled. The Overland Trail had more than twenty of them between Dawson and Whitehorse. The Yukon Stage Line regularly used about fifteen, many of which it owned and managed or leased to responsible operators. These were some of the best roadhouses in the territory. A typical one was in a two-storey, forty-foot-by-twenty-five-foot log building, though some were only one storey. They weren't fancy. But they were well heated with good lighting and offered a place to warm up, rest and eat. Most had good food and decent beds and many operators were renowned for their hospitality; in fact, some roadhouses went by the name of the host rather than the location. Travellers could buy a meal for $1.50 and, if they were stopping for the night, a bed was $1. A private room, if available, went for two bucks or more. Most roadhouses had liquor licences and some had saloons. A shot of Seagram's rye whisky was fifty cents.

If the players didn't make it as far as a roadhouse or were trying to save a couple of bucks, they camped out at a police post. Before they'd left Dawson, Major Zachary Wood of what was now the Royal North-West Mounted Police had offered them the use of the posts along the way as well as the assistance of patrol teams, if they weren't busy. While rudimentary compared to roadhouses, and much smaller, the police accommodations provided some warmth and shelter from the wind. Another option was a tent, though that was not conducive to a good night's sleep. "The temperature was 50 below on the trail and at night we slept in tents or half-way houses on the way," Johnstone later recalled. "When I say we slept I mean we stopped. Some nights we put up in a 12 by 12 tent that already held from 10 to 15 prospectors, and we just sat up."

The lack of snow at the beginning was good news for those on foot, who didn't have to wade through a fresh blanket or worry about sinking deeply into drifts. For the cyclists, it was even better. The 1890s were the Golden Age of Bicycles, and the so-called "safety bicycle," with two wheels the same size and pneumatic rubber tires, had replaced the high-wheeled penny-farthing. Bikes were so popular in the Klondike that some people considered them a nuisance. "I have often to step off the sidewalks to let some bicycle rider past," said Justice Macaulay while fining a man $5 plus costs for riding on a sidewalk in the fall of 1902. "They seem to own the town." Bikes were also common on trails and the frozen Yukon River. Some gold seekers had even left for Nome on two wheels. Still, riding more than forty miles a day down the Overland Trail was a tough slog.

The beautiful did finally begin to fall and eventually those on bikes abandoned their wheels, either because of the snow or mechanical breakdown. On Friday, four days after leaving town, Forrest wired home to say all the cyclists had reached Yukon Crossing, more than halfway down the trail. But passengers on a stagecoach that arrived in Dawson on Sunday night reported they'd seen a cyclist—probably Forrest—on a southbound stage after his bike had broken down. They also said the players were "pretty badly scattered out." They'd passed two of them near Minto, while another had stayed at the Pelly roadhouse the same night they did.

According to one account, some of the players spent Christmas night in a police post during a snowstorm. Two days later, all seven men arrived in Whitehorse, tired but well. Those who had left on foot had been on the trail for ten days and nine nights. The *World* later made the trek sound more like a lark than a grind: "These hardy northerners rolled and tumbled in the snow like kittens at play all along the long journey, stopping occasionally for a snowball battle." They may have thrown a few snowballs at each other, but they had a lot of ground to cover—the walkers averaged thirty-three miles a day—so there wouldn't have been much time to fool around. Given the rough terrain, a good pace was a mile every twenty-five minutes, meaning they walked about fourteen hours during an average day. River crossings added more time.

But travelling in the Yukon, especially in the winter, meant doing just three things: moving, eating and sleeping.

With long distances, short hours of daylight, bitter cold, blistered feet, frostbite and little sleep, the time on the trail wasn't a pleasant experience, even for these rugged Yukoners. And while the team was engaging in a form of cardiovascular training, each day of the expedition was another day off skates.

- TWENTY-FOUR -

*"There will be no further concessions granted the
Klondykers, despite the fact that they came so far"*

The railway station, on the western bank of the Yukon
River, was the most consequential building in town.
Even before it existed. Safe navigation on the waterway began
just downstream from the dangerously turbulent six-mile stretch
that included Miles Canyon and the White Horse Rapids,
so this was the obvious place for a transfer between a railroad
and the river. The government ceded 600 acres along a nearly
two-mile stretch of the river to the WP&YR for a townsite.
The inhabitants of a village that had existed on the eastern bank
since the Gold Rush quickly sensed what this meant and crossed
over. They'd lived mostly in tents, but took some buildings with
them, including the Hotel Savoy, which they dragged over the
frozen river. By the summer of 1900, the new town had two
hotels; several restaurants, including one owned by Fred Trump
(whose grandson would become president of the United States);
a variety of stores; a barbershop; and a bank.

The WP&YR Depot, which opened that fall, sat just steps
from the sternwheelers that, for nearly six months a year, carried
people and cargo downriver to Dawson. The railroad company,
financed by Close Brothers, a London merchant bank, wanted

to call the town Closeleigh. But Yukon Commissioner William Ogilvie nixed that and opted for the name of the former settlement on the east side of the river. As the gateway to the goldfields, Whitehorse boomed around the new train station as shipyards, warehouses and other related businesses sprang up. Despite some nearby copper and gold mining, the town, often called White Horse in the early days, was primarily a transportation hub.

By 1904, the tents had given way to a cluster of frame buildings and log cabins between the river and the low hills not far to the west. The town now had numerous hotels and rooming houses; restaurants, saloons and a dancehall; wooden boardwalks; and about 1,000 year-round residents. In the summer, the population swelled by a few thousand and a steady stream of travellers moved through. While winters were quiet, the hockey players likely ran into a few friends who were either on their way north or headed Outside. Among permanent residents, they knew some local athletes, having competed against them over the years. They also knew Stroller White. Earlier in the year, the popular Klondike columnist had moved south to become editor of the *Whitehorse Daily Star*.

A new but soon-to-be famous resident who'd have meant nothing to them was Robert Service. The Canadian Bank of Commerce had transferred him from Kamloops, British Columbia. He was, by his own admission, a "solitary spirit" and "morose as a malamute." But he socialized, shyly and reluctantly, enough to hear great stories. Some of those tales were fodder for the poems he'd write, with White's encouragement, that were crucial to perpetuating the Gold Rush mystique. (By the time the bank moved Service to Dawson in 1908, he'd already published *Songs of a Sourdough*, which included "The Shooting of Dan McGrew" and "The Cremation of Sam McGee.") After what the Dawson players had endured on the Overland Trail, they'd be forgiven if all they wanted to do in was tuck into a hearty meal, enjoy a good night's sleep and, in the morning, board the train to Skagway. But some local sportsmen had other ideas and "royally entertained" the team.

The most sensible path for a railway between the coast and the Yukon River was through the White Pass, the trail Joe Boyle had taken the first time he travelled to the Klondike in 1897. The British supplied the financing, an American was the chief engineer and a Canadian—Michael Heney, a railroad contractor originally from the Ottawa Valley—oversaw the construction. With terrain that included mountains, gorges, cliffs, glaciers, rivers, lakes and swampland, the project was a daunting challenge, made worse by the climate and the distance from the source of materials such as iron and timber that wouldn't splinter. But "Big Mike" Heney, still in his mid-thirties, was cocky. "Give me enough dynamite and snoose," he said, referring to snuff, "and I'll build a railroad to Hell." Enough of the former turned out to be 450 tons of explosives.

Starting in the late spring of 1898, between 1,000 and 2,000 men a day worked in round-the-clock shifts. A few weeks into construction, many of the labourers rushed off to Atlin, B.C., after hearing of a gold strike there. Fortunately, new recruits were plentiful in Skagway, where many men had run out of money—or lost it in one of Soapy Smith's scams—on their way to the Klondike. The work paid well but was arduous and perilous; in some places, men hung from ropes to do the job. At least thirty-five people died. By July 1899, the first forty-one miles from the Lynn Canal to Lake Bennett were operational. On July 29 the next year, after twenty-six months and $10 million, Samuel H. Graves, president of the White Pass & Yukon Route Company, drove a golden spike at the Yukon village of Caribou Crossing (renamed Carcross in 1904). The aerial tramways on the Chilkoot Trail were no match for the new train, but just to make sure, the WP&YR bought and dismantled them. The original plan was to extend the line to Fort Selkirk, and for years, rumours persisted that the railroad would soon reach Dawson. But it never went beyond Whitehorse. Although the trains didn't start running until after the Gold Rush, they served as a crucial transportation link for the Yukon and parts of Alaska.

The White Pass wasn't as steep as the Chilkoot, but the Baldwin Locomotive steam engines gobbled fuel and water to make it up the 111-mile route that included grades of almost 3.9 percent. At one point, the train climbed nearly 3,000 feet in twenty miles. There were also cliffhanging turns of up to sixteen degrees, as well as bridges, trestles and two tunnels. Narrow-gauge railway technology made the tight turns possible and reduced the cost. The tracks were just three feet apart—standard gauge is four feet, eight-and-a-half inches—and the roadbeds were only ten feet wide. Starting on Broadway, Skagway's main street, WP&YR trains began climbing the Boundary Range of the Coast Mountains. After emerging from a tunnel, they rattled onto a steel cantilever bridge that carried them 216 feet above Dead Horse Gulch, where so many pack animals had perished. Passengers could see the bones from above when there was no snow on the ground. Beyond the summit, trains trundled past the lakes, Miles Canyon and the White Horse Rapids.

The route so many dreamers had taken during the Gold Rush ran through the bush next to, or under, the track. When Robert Service rode the WP&YR two months before the team did, the rain in Skagway turned to snow as soon as the train pulled away from the town. "Far below I could see the old trail of ninety-eight, but I did not dramatize it. It looked tough enough, though. I was glad of the comfort of this funny little train, perhaps the most expensive in the world. Had not my ticket, for about a hundred miles of transportation, cost me twenty-five dollars?" Service wrote later. His initial impression of the scenery, which so many people found captivating, was not favourable. "Stunted pines pricked through the snow, and cruel crags reared over black abysmal lakes. A tough country indeed.

I was glad I had not been one of those grim stalwarts of the Great Stampede."

The Dawson players, a couple of whom had been among those grim stalwarts, now chased a new dream and, having conquered the Overland Trail, they expected the rest of their trip to be cushy. The first-class train was to leave Whitehorse at 9:30 in the morning and arrive in Skagway at 4:30 that afternoon; a second-class train would leave at 7 p.m. and arrive at 4:15 a.m. But now the players faced a new problem: too much of the beautiful. The White Pass had received two feet of snow the day before the players arrived in Whitehorse and it was still falling. Seventeen snowslides on the White Pass blocked the trains and even covered some telegraph poles. Unable to get through to the coast, the players were going to miss their boat. The team sent word to the *Amur*, hoping the steamer would wait. With so few passengers aboard, Captain McCoskrie delayed the ship's departure. After waiting twenty-four hours, the *Amur* pulled out of Skagway—two hours before the team's train pulled in.

As they tasted the salty sea air for the first time in several years, the players checked into the Fifth Avenue Hotel, which promised a first-class experience in its large, three-storey building. Having missed the *Amur*, they were stuck until the next southbound ship sailed. At least the delay was an unexpected chance to work on their conditioning and they took morning dives into the icy Skagway River. But the Alaskan port was not much of a hockey town and the weather was mild, so finding playable ice was a problem. Norman Watt later recounted, "We had about half an hour's practice on a little rink with dimensions of about 40 by 50 feet, half covered with sand and which dulled all our skates."

The great local interest in the team made the players minor celebrities and earned them access to the White Pass Athletic Club and the Elks Lodge. The members of both organizations proved to be excellent hosts and may have provided less healthy diversions. Life in the coastal town was a lot tamer than it had been in the days when the village was bloated with stampeders and Soapy Smith ran it as a criminal enterprise. But there was still lots of fun to be had and some of the players may have enjoyed themselves a little too much. According to legend, one observer claimed, "They were in serious liver training." True or not, the layover didn't improve the team's fitness.

The SS *Dolphin* docked at 11:20 a.m. on December 31. When it left port at 6 p.m., the players were among the roughly thirty passengers aboard the vessel, which had a capacity of several hundred. Among the Dawsonites who celebrated the new year with them was Fred Congdon. When Wilfrid Laurier called the federal election, he also appointed James Ross to the Senate, leaving the Yukon seat in the House of Commons vacant. Congdon resigned as the territory's commissioner to run for the Liberals. He was now on his way to Ottawa, though not as an MP, as he'd hoped. Despite ceaseless and shameless cheerleading by the *World*, he'd lost the vote to Alfred Thompson, a Klondike doctor.

The problem for everyone planning to take the CPR train to the east was that the *Dolphin* was an American ship, owned by the Alaska Steamship Company, and bound for Seattle. So they'd have to take a train up to Vancouver, meaning more lost time for the team. Thick fog cost the steamer thirteen hours. Worse, the choppy water made for an unpleasant voyage and left the players seasick. "The trip down the coast was extremely rough," according to the *Ottawa Journal*, "and all the boys were in such a condition that they cared not whether the ship sunk or not."

For Canada's newspapers, the Yukoners' journey was an irresistible story. After all, it combined the nation's fascination with hockey; the romance of the Klondike Gold Rush and the exotic north; a small, remote community against a powerful eastern city; and the charming— though quite possibly quixotic—quest of some unlikely underdogs who were in the midst of the longest-ever pilgrimage to rescue the now-revered Stanley Cup from the arrogant champions. Shortly after the Ottawa Hockey Club accepted Dawson's challenge, the *Citizen* said, "The spectacle of a team travelling 4,000 miles and at an expense neighbouring around $6000, is something calculated to overawe anyone not aware of the popularity of Canada's great winter game."

So far, though, the papers had nothing to report. On January 4, both the *Citizen* and the *Journal* ran briefs stating that there'd been no word from the challengers since they'd left Dawson. "The boys from the frozen north are probably busy stepping the distance between the gold land and civilization, across the snowy wastes of the north land," suggested the *Citizen*. They were a lot closer than that. The next morning, the players walked off the *Dolphin* in Seattle. If one of them picked up a copy of that day's *Seattle Star* as they waited for the afternoon train to Vancouver, they'd have been amused to read a headline declaring, "'Swiftwater Bill' Wants Another Wife." The story claimed the celebrated Gold Rush character was now striking it rich again in Tanana, but was "weary of his lonely condition."

A crowd of well-wishers saw the team off in Vancouver as it boarded the CPR's Atlantic Express on the afternoon of Friday, January 6. The press was also at the station and the players were happy to report that they were "as hard as nails" after their trek. "They are a sturdy, well knit bunch of athletes," observed the *Vancouver Daily World*, "but they are rather down-cast over the absence of the famous Weldy Young, the cover point of continental fame." All the delays they'd met between Whitehorse and Vancouver hadn't been enough to let their captain catch up to them. No way he was going to make it east in time for the first match. Talk of seeking a postponement surfaced, and not just because of Young. The players had expected to reach Ottawa in eighteen days and they'd already been travelling for twenty. The first game was just a week away. The 2,786-mile train ride they were about to take would consume most of that week and game shape was just a memory for the players.

In the spring of 1903, Jack Eilbeck had looked into renting a Pullman car that would have allowed the touring team to travel and exercise in comfort. Such luxury wasn't part of the Boyle-Young adventure. Fortunately, there weren't many passengers on the train and none were smokers, so the crew gave the players exclusive access to an eight-foot square smoking room to use as a training room. Skipping rope was the primary exercise, but given the tight confines, only one man could work out at a time. So much for the rigorous regimen Boyle had prescribed. And they were so far behind schedule that a layover in Winnipeg wasn't possible. They did have two hours there, though. That was enough time to meet the press. Reporters informed them that some people considered the challenge something of a joke. As acting captain, McLennan spoke for the team. His confidence may have been shaken by Young's absence, or he just may not have had Boyle's or Young's gift for boosterism, but he didn't guarantee the Klondikers would win the Stanley Cup. He simply promised they'd make a good showing and perhaps even surprise easterners.

Pleas for a postponement grew more specific. Dawson wanted the first game delayed until January 16. The *Montreal Star* reported that if Ottawa was unwilling to accommodate the request, Dawson might default the first game and try to take the Cup by winning the second and third matches. The paper cited Watt as the source, though he later denied it. Ottawa manager Bob Shillington said he'd yet to hear from the team directly, though that suggested he'd heard or read the rumours. Regardless, he wasn't willing to consider any delay. Since his club had booked the rink, paid for the advertising, printed the tickets and adjusted the league schedule, he said,

"There will be no further concessions granted the Klondykers, despite the fact that they came so far." The next day, Boyle, who was in Detroit on business, wired to say that while the players wanted a postponement, if one wasn't possible, they'd take the ice Friday night.

But they did strengthen their roster. Lorne Hannay joined them in Manitoba, most likely in Winnipeg, though some accounts say it was in Brandon, his former home. Perhaps because he'd spent most of his career in relative obscurity in a Prairie town with 8,500 people and eight grain elevators, Hannay was an underappreciated star. He'd graduated to the Wheat City's senior seven while still a teenager, and over the next several years never missed a game or even left one early, despite not shying away from the rough stuff and suffering broken fingers and other injuries. A master of long, low forehand lifts, he also excelled at rushing the puck, though he did sometimes get caught up ice and he had a tendency to take a lot of penalties.

Long considered one of the best cover points in the west, he finally attracted the attention of the rest of the country during Brandon's 1904 challenge. Although his team lost, he and his defence partner, Lester Patrick, impressed Ottawa fans. At the start of the 1904-05 season, he left the club he'd once captained to play rover for the Winnipeg Victorias. The position switch wasn't easy. "Lorne Hannay is a good defence man, but he was out of his element on the forward line," the *Free Press* said after a late December match. "As a matter of fact, he acted as a second cover-point nearly all the way through. This gave the Vics a very strong defence . . . but a weak attack." Perhaps he regretted the move (though he returned to the Winnipeg seven the next year), or the opportunity for an adventure enticed him, but after just two games with the Vics, he jumped to the Klondikers.

Dawson also recruited Dave Fairbairn, a Portage la Prairie winger, who would follow the team in a day or two. The intention was for him to be a spare during the Cup series, then play in the tour. But Hannay was clearly a ringer, someone who definitely improved the roster. Which wasn't exactly the best sportsmanship. Some accounts suggest he'd previously lived in the Yukon, and that may have been the rationale Boyle or the players used as justification, but it probably wasn't true. Still, if the Klondikers were to have a hope against the Ottawas, they needed more talent, especially with Young still not with them.

At least he'd finally left Dawson. Enough snow had fallen on the Overland Trail for sleighs to run, and he arranged to ride in a private one by serving as majordomo to George Pulham, the superintendent of the winter mail service. He left in such a hurry that he didn't even sign the voting lists he'd enumerated; they'd have to be redone by someone else. After arriving in Whitehorse on January 9 and taking the train to Skagway the next day, he boarded the *Amur* at 8 p.m. as his teammates' train chugged closer and closer to Ottawa. At stops along the way, fans turned out to cheer the team on. They may have been saluting the remarkable journey. Or they may have been hoping this was the seven that could finally wrest the Cup from the Ottawas. Probably both.

In the dozen years since Lord Stanley's donation made it to Canada, the railway had helped spread hockey throughout the Dominion. Now a train was carrying the latest challengers from the country's far northwest back to the trophy's birthplace.

- TWENTY-FIVE -

*"The men from the Klondike
put up a plucky game"*

After checking into the Russell House, the Dawson players still had much to do. Needing hockey equipment, they went to Ketchum & Company, the sporting goods store at the corner of Bank and Sparks streets that promised "everything but ice for clubs and individuals." Along with the necessary gear, including sticks, gloves and shin guards, the players picked up the uniforms they'd ordered after the Ottawas had accepted their challenge. If nothing else, they'd look sharp in black sweaters with gold trim at the collar and wrists, white trousers and black stockings. Then they limbered up with a light skate at Dey's Rink. It must have been a great relief when they finally climbed into bed and enjoyed a good night's sleep, the first in many days without the rumble of the train, in Ottawa's finest hotel. Though they'd finished their long mush from Dawson to Whitehorse two weeks earlier, one player said he walked forty miles in his dreams.

The next morning, curious local scribes and fans waited at Dey's for the Klondikers to show. (Just as the OHC wasn't the Silver Seven at the time, the Dawson team became the Nuggets only in lore.) The visitors who took to the ice for a proper practice must have disappointed anyone expecting grizzled and unkempt prospectors. Most of the players had spent at least some time mining, though none had struck it rich, but all of them were clean-shaven, save for McLennan, who sported a droopy handlebar moustache. Despite their tame appearance, they were a rugged-looking lot and a good-sized squad. At 190 pounds, Jimmy Johnstone was the largest, with Sureshot Kennedy not far behind at 180. While Norman Watt was only 140 pounds, he played much bigger. But what local hockey enthusiasts wanted to know was if the team had any skill.

Since Hannay had recently competed in two matches with the western Vics, he looked the best, but his new teammates didn't disappoint the railbirds. "Among the spectators at the practice the impression was strong that though the Dawsonites are not likely to walk off with the Ottawas, cup and all," reported the *Journal*, "they will put up a stiff argument." Joe Boyle arrived from Detroit at 11 a.m. and went straight to the rink to greet the team and watch the practice. Afterwards, the players, still in their gear, posed for a team photo with him outside Dey's because it was too dark inside. They all wore stern expressions, as if they were trying to look as intimidating as possible. That evening, Boyle and McLennan met with OHC executives and agreed on Harlow Stiles, a referee from Cornwall.

While the Klondikers went to the OAAC clubhouse, where they became honorary members and enjoyed watching some boxing, the Ottawas held their usual Thursday night practice. The club had returned to Dey's Rink for the 1905 season because the Aberdeen Pavilion hadn't attracted the hoped-for huge crowds, and the Dey brothers wooed their high-profile tenant back with expanded capacity and more generous financial arrangements. But a planned return to the Canadian Amateur Hockey League fell apart when the executives refused to admit the Wanderers because they didn't consider them amateurs. Veterans Alf Smith and Harry Westwick were back with the club, but Harvey Pulford, whose wife had died during childbirth, had yet to return. Angus "Bones" Allen filled in for him at point. Gone permanently was Bouse Hutton, who'd been such a dominant goaltender for the team. He gave up hockey to play professional lacrosse in Brantford, Ontario. Dave Finnie—whose brother Oswald was the chief clerk in Dawson's gold commissioner's office—replaced Hutton, keeping the Ottawas strong in goal. The three Gilmour brothers were all but gone. Davie Gilmour hadn't returned after the 1903 season. Suddie Gilmour left town to look after his lumber interests in Quebec in 1904. And Billy Gilmour was now studying at McGill, where he was captain of the school's hockey team, though he would play for Ottawa late in the season.

Another loss was Jim McGee. The twenty-five-year-old captain of the Rough Riders football team had been a reliable and enthusiastic spare for the hockey seven. But while out for a ride in May, he fell off his horse and suffered a severe concussion. Five days later, he was dead. Having lost his brother, Frank McGee felt pressure from his family to retire and ensure he didn't damage his good eye. But he kept playing. So, despite some turnover, the team's core was intact and the champs were still determined to defend the Cup. Not that they were taking anything for granted. Before the series started, the Ottawas threatened to protest if Hannay played, because he wasn't from the Yukon and had been on the Brandon team that challenged for Cup the previous March. The *Montreal Star* suggested this decision was simply a matter of principle rather than a protective move in case the unthinkable happened and Dawson won.

Many people—including old friends as well as fans who remembered his OHC days—were disappointed that Weldy Young hadn't arrived with his teammates. But the Klondikers were popular in town. It wasn't just that Dawson had travelled twice as far as any other Cup hopeful, it was what the team had to go through to make it. As Albert Forrest had wired back home,

"Enormous interest is shown in our trip throughout the whole country, and big excitement in Ottawa." The fascination with the team made for powerful marketing and had led to a rush when tickets went on sale Wednesday morning. Naturally, enthusiasm was also high back in the Yukon. Paul Forrest was already assembling a team—with Jack Eilbeck at cover point and himself at left wing—to challenge the new champions when they returned to the Klondike. "The team that Brother Paul has in mind is superior on avoirdupois and would thump against the present cup aspirants like a stone wall," said the *Daily News*, which also reported the match in Ottawa was "the all-consuming theme" in town. As game time approached, Dawsonites gathered at Thomas Fuller's Telegraph Office to follow the game through the play-by-play bulletins.

Ottawans had a well-established habit of not showing up in great numbers for matches against unheralded opponents. That wasn't a problem on this night, though. Fans filled every seat and space in the standing room area was hard to come by well before the crowd cheered Earl Grey as he stepped on the ice at 8:45 p.m. P.D. Ross, who was running as a Conservative for a seat in the Ontario legislature, was one of the local dignitaries who escorted the governor general. Only recently arrived in Canada, Albert Grey, like his predecessors, had quickly become a hockey fan. After he attended the Ottawa-Wanderers match the previous week, the *Citizen* reported, "His Excellency and the Government house party were among the most liberal of the spectators in their applause of the carnival of grit and skill." But this was different: this was a Stanley Cup game. He said a few words to the players, including congratulating the Yukoners for their stout-heartedness, then shook hands with the referee and team captains, Alf Smith and Randy McLennan. Both sides responded with three rousing cheers for His Excellency. From the edge of the rink, well clear of any swinging sticks, Grey faced the puck by blowing a whistle and the game was on.

After pushing the puck through Hector Smith's legs, Westwick passed it to the Ottawa captain, who shot from the side and Forrest made his first save. McLennan rushed and passed to Watt, who shot wide. Allen lifted it out of the Ottawa end, but Hannay, playing despite Ottawa's objections, and McLennan brought it in again and set up Hector Smith for a shot. Alf Smith and Westwick moved down the ice with it until Hannay intercepted a pass. Soon, McGee had his first chance but couldn't beat Forrest. Early indications were that Dawson could compete with Ottawa.

Neither team made much effort at a clean game. Along with heavy bodychecks into the fence, there was lots of tripping, slashing and cross-checking, much of it uncalled by Stiles. Before long, the crowd at Dey's received an introduction to Watt's boisterous style when he and Alf Smith collided. The result for the little winger was a cut on his head and an inflamed temper. He retaliated by throwing punches, most of which Smith was able to duck. Stiles sent them both to the side for ten minutes. After a long lift from Hannay, which Allen stopped, McGee took a shot that went high. McLennan and Kennedy came down the ice with the puck, but Finnie denied the rover's bid. Ten minutes into the match, it was still a scoreless tie. Then Westwick and McGee worked their way through their opponents until McGee fired one that Forrest couldn't stop.

The next penalty went to Kennedy for tripping Fred White, who'd graduated from the intermediate Aberdeens to replace Suddie Gilmour at left wing. After Forrest stopped Westwick, Johnstone carried the puck down to Ottawa's end, where Allen blocked him. Once all three penalized players returned, McGee set up Alf Smith for another goal. Then, with Moore off to the side, Dawson was able to apply some pressure, but couldn't solve Finnie. At the other end, Forrest stymied a couple of pretty plays from the hometown seven, which earned him applause from the crowd. After Hector Smith had a chance, Alf Smith dashed down the ice. Edged away from the goal by Johnstone, he passed to White, who passed to Westwick, who beat Forrest. But just twenty seconds later, McLennan finally scored. The Dawson tally suggested a comeback was possible if the challengers could get the next goal. Watt and Alf Smith had another run-in, but it didn't lead to in any penalties, and there was no more scoring before time ran out on the first half.

The second half started with the points and cover points trading long lifts. But it quickly became clear the Klondikers lacked the necessary conditioning and were now too tired to compete with the champions. Less than two minutes into the half, Alf Smith scored. Two and a half minutes later, he did it again. A minute after that, Westwick put one in. The most violent episode of the match occurred with the score 6-1 and the game out of reach for Dawson. Watt tripped Moore; Moore cross-checked Watt in the face, sending him to the ice; Watt picked himself up, approached Moore from behind and delivered a two-handed smash to his head. Stiles assessed penalties to both players. "He's off for two minutes; what's his name?" the ref asked. "Moore? Is that Moore? Make it three minutes." The Ottawa player needed four stitches before returning to the match. Stiles gave Watt fifteen minutes.

More penalties followed. Johnstone went for tripping and Hannay moved back to point. McGee also took a tripping penalty. Then Forrest slashed White, who'd crowded the teenager after a shot. That forced Hannay to fill in as goaltender. The Klondikers were already a man short when McGee came back. That led to two goals from White in fifty seconds before Forrest returned. Six minutes later, Alf Smith scored his fourth of the game. Dawson managed to add one more to its total: after his long exile, Watt fired a shot that Finnie stopped, but Kennedy batted in the rebound. Although the final score was 9-2, the fans had been unusually supportive of the visiting team and especially appreciated the work of Forrest and Hannay.

The wooden platform in the rafters at the south end of the renovated Dey's Rink served as a newspapermen's den. But during the first game of the season—Ottawa's 9-3 defeat of the Wanderers—reporters found the seats too low. A carpenter solved the problem before the Dawson series. The scribes were also pleased that rink staff kept anyone without credentials from the press stand. Not all of them were as happy with what they saw on the ice, though. John Ross Robertson's *Telegram*, which was regularly dismissive of any hockey played outside of Toronto, or at least the OHA, stayed true to form and called the match "a keen disappointment." Using a theatre analogy, the *Tely* observed, "It was in every sense of the word a 'first night' performance, with an all-star cast up against a lot of burlesquers." Even the *Whitehorse Daily Star* was snarky: "The Dawson hockey team covered itself all over with glory when it scored even two goals against nine in the first game for the Stanley cup at Ottawa. They are a fine lot of boys but when it comes to playing for cups, a granite tea or coffee cup would be more in their line."

Some newspapers were more generous. "During the first twenty minutes of play," noted the *Globe*, "the challenging team made a remarkably fine showing against the champions, but after that they gradually faded away and were never seriously in the running." Praising Dawson's defence, it expected a better performance in game two. The *Gazette* thought Dawson "fought well and died hard" and, with reference to Ottawa's string of successful defences of the Cup, added, "Many a hockey team considered first class in their own stamping ground have met the same fate . . . and in defeat they are not disgraced."

The papers agreed Forrest was "a marvel" and "a sensation" and the defence—Johnstone at point and, especially, Hannay at cover—was strong. But while the forwards, notably Hector Smith and Watt, had some speed, their combination work was lacking and they took too many shots, many of them wide, from too far out instead of working their way closer to the goal.

Perhaps doing its best to pump up fan interest in the second contest—or to downplay any doubts about the trustees' decision to approve the challenge—Ross's *Journal* was even more magnanimous than the out-of-town press. It pointed out that the Klondikers were unfamiliar with the rounded corners and the larger rink. "Their play was marked at times by a true combination that gives promise of a much better game Monday night, for the men will be better rested, after three days more quiet." The paper liked the play of Forrest, Hannay and Johnstone, who intercepted many passes and made several good rushes. McLennan was the hardest worker, but his stick-handling wasn't good enough and Alf Smith took the puck from him many times. Watt, who'd spent nearly half the game on the side, "was a snappy, aggressive player, fast and tricky, but too short-tempered."

Although Ross made no mention of the series in his diary, he likely wrote the *Journal* editorial entitled "A Bit of Canadian Pluck." It noted the fan reaction and argued Dawson's loss was understandable and expected given the journey, suggesting the players would need at least two weeks to prepare for such elevated competition. But the larger point was about the value of the series in the vast Dominion. "Sport has become one great medium of inter-communication," the editorial argued. "Communities, distances apart, are brought into touch by their athletic representatives, prejudices are levelled and good-feeling engendered."

If Ross took a high-minded approach and saw the series in a broader context, Boyle followed an already well-established custom for losing teams. He blamed the referee. In a report the *Daily News* ran at the top of its front page, the manager complained that Stiles "was not fast enough on his skates nor with his eyes," which allowed several offside Ottawa goals to stand. Forrest contended that six tallies were offside. Back in Dawson, the prevailing sentiment was that the OHC had handed the challengers a raw deal by not allowing them more time to recover from the trip, get back in game shape and allow Hannay time to adjust to his new teammates. Jack Eilbeck had a particularly cynical take. "A visitor has no more show to gain decisions in hockey in a Stanley cup match than a visitor has to win a decision in a prize fight in 'Frisco when against a local 'Frisco man," according to the *News*. "He says it must be a clean knockout for the challengers to win."

The Klondikers were still surprisingly confident. "The score no criterion of game," Kennedy said in a letter to Eilbeck. "If I do say it myself, we played them to a standstill the first twenty minutes, but lack of condition soon told. Then they had us going." Boyle had similar thoughts. "The consensus of opinion among those who witnessed the game is that our boys made the best showing in the first half, and that the lack of condition, due to the effects of the long trip is what told in the second," he wrote, adding, "We have a good chance to win the cup."

Later, in the Bijou Hotel bar, a popular establishment also known as Cassidy's Saloon or just Sam Cassidy's, Alf Smith overheard Boyle badmouth Frank McGee. The centre had scored only once and even the *Journal* said he hadn't worked that hard. Still, it was unwise for Dawson's manager to denigrate the superstar in public, especially since there was already some animosity between the two men stemming from an Ottawa Rowing Club incident. Versions of what exactly he said vary, but it was something along the lines of: "This McGee doesn't seem to be any great scorer." Although Boyle's indiscretion may not have been the first example of "bulletin-board material" in hockey, it remains one of the most regrettable.

- TWENTY-SIX -

*"Dawson never had the chance of a bun
in the hands of a hungry small boy"*

Weldy Young was aboard the *Amur* when the CPR steamer reached Vancouver in the wee hours of the morning on Saturday. He sent his teammates a telegram to say he was now in the south and asked them to seek a postponement of the second and third matches of the series. If Ottawa agreed, he'd leave Sunday; if not, he planned to stay for a short visit with friends. Later, when a reporter caught up with him, Young was happy to talk about the previous night's game, even though he hadn't seen it. "The fact that the team was able to score even two goals under the circumstances was a good showing," he said. Those circumstances included his absence. "The members of the team are accustomed to have me play behind them on the defence line, besides receiving directions from me as their coach." He added brashly, "If the remaining games are postponed until I get there, I think the result may be different."

Back in Ottawa, his teammates felt the sting of the loss and the caress of another good night's sleep. They held two good practices at Dey's and, that night, Randy McLennan wired Young: "Be sure and take to-morrow's train for Ottawa. Remaining matches postponed until you arrive." Since this was obviously untrue, he may have been tricking the cover point into rushing east so he wouldn't miss any of the exhibition tour. Young left Vancouver, though he stopped in Moose Jaw for a visit with his brother Fred. On Monday, the *Citizen* reported the team "showed remarkably good form," in its practices and, perhaps hoping to ensure another sellout, said, "If Dawson can hold the pace they set during the first twenty minutes on Friday night, the Stanley cup series may not end tonight. It will be a fine game anyhow and well worth seeing." After another practice that morning, Joe Boyle was predictably upbeat. "The boys are improving rapidly and they will show it tonight," he said. "Even their flesh seems different after the wholesome, comfortable sleep."

Injured in the first match, McLennan was unavailable for the second. Dave Fairbairn, who'd left Portage La Prairie on Friday, arrived in time for Monday night's match and filled in as rover. Lorne Hannay took over as captain. While Dawson lost a player, Ottawa grew stronger with the return of Harvey Pulford. Another change involved the referee. That Harlow Stiles had failed to distinguish himself in the first game wasn't just Boyle's assessment. "He allowed some rather large off-sides to go," said the *Journal*, "and blew the whistle for many others that were hardly noticeable." And while he called many penalties, he missed plenty. The more experienced Ernie Butterworth of Ottawa agreed to ref the second game.

Later that day, the Dawsonites received bad news unrelated to hockey. In yet another indication of the Klondike's shrinking economy, thirty government employees had lost their jobs as part of a purge in the Administration Building. McLennan and Watt were among the victims. Still, there was a game to play and both teams were pumped. Once again, the rumour spread that the home team might not try so hard in the second game and allow the visitors to win, setting up a third well-attended night. But in the champs' dressing room, captain Alf Smith said,

"There'll be no let-up. We're out to win." Boyle was just as confident, or pretended to be: "We've got the team and will show the Ottawas the real thing tonight."

If the result of the first match dampened the enthusiasm of the fans, it wasn't by much. Dey's was again crowded for the second game, with every reserved seat filled and a crush in the standing room area. Earl Grey, along with his wife Countess Grey and a Government House entourage, occupied the ice-level viceregal box. Initially, everyone was enthusiastic and, again, the challengers' start wasn't too bad, with the defence breaking up many attacks and Hannay leading rushes into the opposing end. But if they were in better form now, it didn't matter, because Ottawa's combination work was devastating.

Four and a half minutes in, Frank McGee passed to Fred White, who passed to Alf Smith who passed to Harry Westwick, who scored. The Rat did it again less than four minutes later. Slightly more than ten minutes into the game, after Albert Forrest made a save with his hip, Fairbairn, George Kennedy and Hector Smith took the puck down to the other end with some strong passing and Dawson's little centre beat Finnie. That made the score 2-1, keeping the Klondikers in the game and earning appreciative cheers from the crowd. But ninety seconds later, Westwick scored again with Hector Smith serving a penalty. A minute after that, McGee put one in, but Butterworth disallowed it because the play was offside.

Strong work by Hannay and Jimmy Johnstone kept Ottawa from scoring for the next six minutes, but they could hold off McGee only so long, and he finally scored one that counted. Ten seconds later, Westwick notched his fourth goal and twenty seconds after that, McGee struck again. With the score 8-1, Dawson's Smith set up Kennedy, who managed to get the puck past Finnie, only to have Butterworth rule it offside. By the time the teams headed to their dressing rooms at the half, Westwick and McGee had four goals apiece and Ottawa was up 10-1.

Unfortunately, Dawson still had to play another thirty minutes. When it came to bodychecking, the Klondikers could compete with the Ottawas, but in all other facets of the game, they were no match for the champs. Just thirty seconds into the second half, McGee put one in. White scored four minutes after that. Five and a half minutes later, McGee put on a clinic: he racked up eight consecutive goals in eight minutes. Ottawa wasn't finished, adding three more from Alf Smith, McGee and Westwick. Then, with a minute to go, the challengers made a late push and Kennedy set up Hector Smith, who notched his second. The final score was Ottawa 23, Dawson 2. A third match would not be necessary.

Blowouts usually incited a steady stream of spectators to walk out long before the match was over. Not this time. Almost all the fans stayed to the end. Some were mesmerized by McGee; others wanted to see how bad the farce would get. A few even egged on the Ottawas, chanting, "Make it larger. Score. Score." The Rat's five-goal game was impressive, but McGee tallied fourteen, setting a record that no one would ever come close to matching in a Stanley Cup game.

Somehow, the papers praised Forrest—"But for him Ottawa's figures might have been doubled," according to the *Citizen*— but most didn't report, let alone celebrate, McGee's remarkable performance. Hockey was a team sport and individual heroics often didn't make headlines. One exception was Montreal's *Star*, though it offered only muted plaudits: "It was a game in which Frank McGee, probably the best centre player in Canada, cut loose and he scored goal after goal just as soon as he wanted to go in and do so." But other than the *Journal*'s recap of the play and the *Citizen*'s scoring summary, McGee didn't make either Ottawa paper. History would be far more admiring of his singular accomplishment.

As he had after the first match, Boyle wired his take to the *Daily News*, which again published it at the top of page one. He admitted the score, then added, "Nevertheless, it was a good game." He noted the loss of McLennan—"and Randy's place in the team cannot be filled, as you know"—and said the players were exhausted from the long journey and Friday night's fast tilt. "The game tonight is regarded by all as a wonderful exhibition of play of a team in perfect condition against a team unfit to play."

Few shared Boyle's sanguine view of the match as a wonderful exhibition. "Dawson never had the chance of a bun in the hands of a hungry small boy," said the *Citizen*, which called the challengers barely above the calibre of the local city league teams. "In absolute point of fact, the champions made the nugget-hunters look like a lot of tyros, innocents, a gang of school-boys who had never seen a puck in their lives," sneered the *Herald*, suggesting that only "a merciful Providence" kept the score from being far worse. "Ottawa simply skated away from them at the whistle," reported the *Globe*, "and continued to pile up the goals with a merciless monotonous regularity which was farcical in the extreme." The *Telegram* was equally dismissive: "For though it is said in all kindness, never has such a consignment of hockey junk come over the metals of the C.P.R. as the latest aspirants for world's championship honors."

Even if the Klondikers had arrived in the east in time to practise for weeks, they'd still have struggled with not just the quality of their opponents but the more sophisticated style of play. The Ottawas used the rink's round corners to carom the puck effectively and they rarely relied on lifts. "They pass the puck," Watt pointed out later. "If necessary they will see-saw twenty times in going ten feet. Short, quick back and forth work toward the goal is their style. This was a new one for us to solve."

Although the Cup champions turned out to be far better and more "scientific" than the Klondikers had expected, the players were understandably still disappointed with the outcome. They'd travelled 3,500 miles by land plus more than 1,000 miles by sea and it had all ended in humiliation. That didn't mean they were about to dispense with the tradition of celebrating with the home team afterwards. On Tuesday night, the Ottawas hosted a banquet at the Russell House that attracted not just the usual sportsmen but also politicians, including Fred Congdon. Once dinner was finished, the cigars and coffee came out, as did more wine, and the toasts began.

Boyle responded to one to the Dawson team by entertaining the assembled guests with a no doubt embellished account of the history of Klondike hockey and the DAAA. He earned vigorous applause for declaring that he hoped no team, save Dawson, would ever take the Cup from Ottawa. Later, he rose again to pander a little more: "The Ottawa Hockey Club, no matter what Montreal or Toronto may say, plays hockey and does not hold the cup by hook or crook, but by playing the game." The warm speeches from the players on the two teams suggested some had socialized together over the previous week and created solid friendships. They filled the Cup with champagne and passed it around the room repeatedly.

None of this would have been of much interest to anyone outside of Ottawa, except that OHC executive John Dickson made news. He attacked the Canadian Amateur Athletic Union for declaring so many players outside Montreal professionals while ignoring similar transgressions by athletes in the organization's home city. The CAAU had even formed a committee to investigate Alf Smith and was planning to create a blacklist of all current and former professional hockey players. "I resigned from the board six months ago because it was composed of men who were just as guilty of professionalization as any of those whom they condemned," he said, calling on all sportsmen to fight the CAAU's actions. If it didn't become more reasonable and stop forcing young athletes—he cited Arthur Sixsmith and Charlie Liffiton as examples—to flee to the United States, then a new association would be necessary. Other speakers, including Boyle and Senator Robert Watson, backed Dickson. Watson hailed from Portage la Prairie, where the hockey team had just had two of its players declared professionals by the CAAU, though the Manitoba Hockey Association passed a resolution making them amateurs again. He went so far as to utter a largely unspoken truth: "I dare say that there are not ten per cent of the young men in senior sport in Canada who are not in some way or other receiving remuneration for their services—it is impossible for them to live otherwise."

What didn't make the newspapers was what happened after the banquet. The party became quite boisterous, and when some Ottawa players left with the Cup, one of them—some accounts finger Harvey Pulford for this—had the brilliant idea that he could dropkick the trophy over the Rideau Canal. Egged on by his teammates, he booted the Cup and it landed on the frozen waterway. Then they all carried on their merry way, leaving the prize on the ice. In the sober light of day, a player returned to the scene of the crime and retrieved the trophy.

Well, that's the legend. A more likely, though less dramatic, version of the story is that while walking home along Canal Street, the players took a shortcut that required climbing over a fence. The man carrying the Cup tossed it in the snow on the other side before going over. Then they all carried on their merry way, leaving the prize behind until the player who wanted to show the trophy to his mother suddenly realized he was no longer carrying it. When they all went back for it, Alf Smith playfully kicked at it as if it were a soccer ball. As the tale grew in the retellings, the players' irritated denials made no difference. "I guess it's got to be a good story," Westwick said years later, "and nobody will believe it didn't happen anyway." Indeed, the Rideau Canal incident became one of the most cherished of Stanley Cup fables.

- TWENTY-SEVEN -

"The boys are not returning with the Stanley Cup"

Joe Boyle oozed confidence before and during the series. That suited both his personality and his role as team manager. According to one theory, though, he knew all along the Klondikers weren't good enough and saw the Cup games as promotion for the barnstorming tour. Boyle asked Frank Ahearn, a local hockey player (and later owner of the Senators and a member of Parliament), to suggest to some of the Ottawas that they avoid running up the score. Ahearn, unaware of the bad blood between Boyle and Frank McGee, passed the message along to the star centre. So much for that idea.

After Monday's discouraging loss, Boyle cancelled Thursday's game against Queen's. He realized the players needed a rest more than a match against Randy McLennan's alma mater. Along with rest, they needed to be better. The good news was that Weldy Young was on his way. And according to one account, Boyle also tried to recruit Fred Taylor, the young star who would soon earn the nickname Cyclone. He was sitting out the season after a dispute with the OHA, but turned down the chance to buttress the Dawson roster. While the players stayed in Ottawa, Fred Congdon took care of them and showed those who were new to the city around. Somehow, the university seven never received the message about the cancellation and the players were miffed when Dawson didn't arrive. The no-show cost the students $100 in expenses, which didn't improve their mood.

On Friday morning, the Klondikers took the train to Montreal. They had a practice and hung out with local sportsmen but didn't play a match. While many teams across Canada, from the interior of British Columbia to Cape Breton Island, wanted to host the Dawson seven, Boyle had yet to confirm a game in the country's largest city. Back in November, the Montreal Amateur Athletic Association had considered the team's request for a match and left the matter in the hands of Harry Shaw, president of the hockey club. After the executive met again in December, the minutes read: "Letter read from Mr. Boyle Manager of the Klondike Hockey Team re playing Exhibition Games during their visit to Eastern Canada. Sec'y instructed to reply 'no dates.'"

Money was also an issue. A proposed tilt with the Wanderers fell apart because, according to Boyle, the Arena wanted to keep two-thirds of the gate. "We are not on a money-making tour," he claimed, which wasn't exactly true, given the players hoped to make enough to fund their return to Dawson. "But neither are we out here to make any fortunes for the Arena or any other rink management. We won't play any games that give more than one-third to any rink." Dawson still wanted to face the Wanderers if suitable arrangements could be made in Montreal or Ottawa. "Don't let anyone think we are afraid to meet any team on ice," said Boyle. "We are not. We simply want fair play." The coolly indignant management of the Montreal Arena Company responded in the press that it had offered the teams forty percent of the gate, the same as for Cup matches, while paying all expenses.

On Saturday, the Klondikers headed to Amherst and the first game of their Maritime tour. After the Ramblers' 1904 challenge had been too late for the trustees to approve, everyone expected them to try again before this season ended. As champions of the Nova Scotia Amateur Hockey League, they'd be a good test for Dawson. While Young hadn't joined the team in Montreal, as planned, he wasn't far behind. He was in Ottawa, where "friends thronged the family residence to see him," according to the *Journal*, which described him as "looking hale and hearty and somewhat stouter than he was when he went north." The *Citizen* said, "his arm was kept working like a pump handle during milking hour." He left Sunday, expecting to be in Amherst by game time.

Excitement had been building in northeastern Nova Scotia for weeks, and not even the disastrous results of the Cup matches scared fans away. Up to 3,000 crammed Aberdeen Rink to watch the celebrity visitors take on the hometown team. Young's train was late so he didn't play, but Randy McLennan had recovered and Dave Fairbairn subbed in for a sick Norman Watt. The Ramblers won 4-2 in "one of the hardest fought games of hockey ever played on Amherst ice." At least the Klondikers had showed they could compete with Outside teams. Following a turkey dinner with the host club and a night's rest, the players moved on to Halifax for a match against the local Wanderers. Despite being up 2-0 at the half, Dawson lost 3-2. A Vancouver *Province* headline mocked, "All-Klondike Team is Bumping into Things on its Tour." A decent crowd of 1,500 had watched, which prompted this *Yukon World* headline: "Hockey Boys Are Making Money, But Not Winning." The next night, the team thumped a Halifax all-star squad 11-2. At the banquet afterwards, Boyle was feeling magnanimous. He declared that he'd pay the expenses for any team willing to travel to the Yukon and play for the Dawson Cup, emblematic of the territorial championship.

In Cape Breton, the first game was a loss to the Sidney Victorias, which left Boyle frustrated. "The Victorias were bound to win, and with the assistance of the referee they succeeded. They slashed like wood choppers and broke seven of their own sticks hitting at the Dawson boys," he claimed in a telegram. "It was by far the worst treatment I ever saw given any hockey team in any place." After another loss and a win in Cape Breton, they won in Pictou, then lost a rematch with Amherst before going to New Brunswick. Following a 4-1 defeat in Moncton, it was Albert Forrest's turn to blame the ref. "The game was a deliberate steal," he complained. "The Klondikers were repeatedly driven back by sticks and two goals scored by us were not allowed." Still, the young goalie was cheerful about the trip and pleased with East Coast hospitality, noting that the players "are made guests of all the clubs and athletics association wherever they visit and are invited to all social functions."

The team won its last three games in New Brunswick. They'd played twelve games in twelve days in the Maritime provinces and won half of them. Several attracted sizeable crowds, but high ticket prices depressed sales in some towns. Only 200 fans paid fifty cents to watch Dawson win in Glace Bay. After 550 people saw the visitors beat the Fredericton Trojans, the *Daily Gleaner* said, "Had the admission charged been 25 cents instead of 35 and 50 cents there would have been fully 1500 people present."

The first of two Quebec games was in Trois-Rivières. Although the players were exhausted, this was Forrest's hometown. In a letter he wrote before the match, George Kennedy told Jack Eilbeck the trip was "a success, although we should not have lost a game." He also noted, "Mr. Boyle is handling matters very satisfactorily." Kennedy was enjoying the experience and had a lot of sightseeing news to share, but there wasn't the time or the space. He ended with: "As I am writing this letter I can look out the window and see the mighty St. Lawrence. Thank God it is not the Yukon this time of the year." That night, Dawson fell 7-2 to Trois-Rivières in an acrimonious match. Young served several penalties and later refused the host club's hospitality. From there, they went to Montreal and checked into the Windsor Hotel. Despite the losses and his refereeing complaints, Boyle wasn't discouraged. "If we have as good material next year as we had this year, we will bring another hockey team east from Dawson," he said. His plan was for the players to come five or six weeks earlier to get comfortable with the different conditions, which had been a handicap. "In fact, the team is not playing in its real form even now. However, we don't complain. We have had a fine trip, and have been very well treated."

He'd finally arranged a Montreal game. Dawson would take on Montagnard, one of the city's francophone clubs, in the Montreal Stadium. The team had joined the Federal League that season, following the departure of Le National to the CAHL, but had yet to win a game. By this point, the Klondikers were banged up. They'd already lost Hector Smith for the remainder of the tour after a knee injury in Saint John. Now Kennedy was hurt, too. He'd written to Eilbeck that despite breaking a tooth in half, he was the only player save for Forrest to dress for every game. But that night in Trois-Rivières, he injured his knee. Without its leading scorer in the lineup, Dawson lost 2-1 to Montagnard (though for some reason the Klondikers continued to claim this game was a 2-2 tie).

Two days later, Federal League president William Foran announced that Young would referee a game between Ottawa and the Wanderers. This was no ordinary match. While the season wasn't quite over yet, the two teams were tied atop the league standings and the winner was all but assured of winning the league championship, which came with the Stanley Cup. So while it wasn't an official Cup match, it had the feeling of one and the Arena was crammed. The Wanderers weren't happy Young would ref, but there was nothing they could do short of forfeiting.

Bolstered by the return of Billy Gilmour, Ottawa won 4-2. Apparently forgetting when the same teams fought for the Cup a year earlier, the *Gazette* proclaimed the "saturnalia of savage butchery" the dirtiest match the Arena had ever seen. Young called twenty penalties. The *Journal* deemed him "equal to the task," reporting, "His penalties were severe, and frequent. At one time he had five men on the rowdy bench." Montrealers didn't see it that way. "Judging from the mingled applause and disapproval with which 'Weldy' Young's decisions were greeted, and the opinions expressed to the writer, many laid the blame to the former Ottawan," said the *Gazette*. "Yet that is not quite fair, for it must be said that Young issued sharp punishment and issued his penalties with good judgement in the face of a difficult task." The *Herald* wasn't so forgiving, arguing that "the Ottawas and Weldy Young defeated the Wanderers."

Young escaped the brouhaha when he and his teammates moved on to Ontario, though it was no kinder than Quebec had been. Queen's, perhaps motivated by the earlier snubbing, crushed them 15-5 and Brockville trounced them 8-2. After going on a three-game run in New Brunswick, the Klondikers lost four straight. They needed a break. The players rode the train up to Ottawa and checked into the Russell House, where they rested and recovered from their various injuries.

Late in February, while the Dawson team was still at the Russell, the Alexandria Crescents travelled to the nearby eastern Ontario village of Maxville for a Friday night match against their long-time rivals. Attendance was a few hundred, including about eighty who had taken the train from Alexandria to cheer on their boys. The ice on the small outdoor rink was soft, the crowd was rowdy and the play was rough. About halfway through, Alcide Laurin rushed the puck up the ice until he ran into Allan Loney. The former was Alexandria's twenty-four-year-old rover and captain, who was known to be high-tempered; the latter was Maxville's nineteen-year-old point, a much bigger man and one who had a reputation for dirty play. After losing the puck, Laurin broke his stick in two with a slash across Loney's legs. The hostilities escalated. Loney, now with a broken nose and perhaps a little dazed from taking a punch, swung his stick at his opponent's toque-covered head. Laurin crumpled to the ice. He didn't move. His brother Leo skated over to attack the culprit with a brutal slash.

An inquest the next day learned that Laurin had died of a fractured skull. The indentation above his left ear was two inches long and a half an inch wide, just the kind of wound a hockey stick might make. But the parade of witnesses couldn't agree on whose fault it was or even the sequence of events that preceded the fatal blow: who'd slashed whom, who'd punched whom and which brother had broken Loney's nose. Local fans were convinced their man had acted in self-defence or had slipped after his skate caught in the ice. Visiting fans were certain it was deliberate and unprovoked. On Monday morning, 1,000 people showed up to the funeral, the largest Alexandria had ever seen.

The same day, Ottawa's *Evening Journal* devoted the top of its front page to the incident. On one side of the report was a formal photo of Laurin; on the other was an illustration of Loney, looking boyish, clean-cut and studious. The headline was "The Killing of Alcide Laurin in a Hockey Match at Maxville." After police laid murder charges—causing the *Journal* to devote more than half its front page to the story—it became a matter for the courts. Even as hockey players became more skilled, the game seemed to be growing more violent, not less. Laurin's was one of three deaths on the ice that year. But, for the first time, a player had to face a jury. And a guilty verdict would mean the gallows for Loney.

As the country awaited the trial, the other big issue roiling the sport affected the Klondikers' tour. So far, the only Ontario games had been against Queen's and Brockville, neither of which were part of the OHA. Boyle had negotiated with several other teams, including Berlin, Brantford, Cornwall, London and Woodstock, and, of course, he wanted matches in Toronto, for the publicity and the revenue. But the OHA contended that Dawson had squandered its amateur status with the barnstorming tour. On March 1, Boyle responded to Toronto mudslinging with this telegram: "We will play either the Marlboros or St. George hockey teams, or both of them, on any ice they select, and will give them all of the gate receipts, and guarantee them that the same shall amount to not less than one hundred dollars." Neither club took him up on the offer.

A week later, the Klondikers headed to the States. But after already losing Hector Smith to injury, the team went down two more players. Young decided to stay in Ottawa instead of continuing with the tour and returning to the Yukon. Watt also left the team. To replace them, Boyle recruited William Lannon, Brockville's right wing. Archie Martin, who was supposed to be the team's spare, never played. His role with the club remains a mystery. While the *Journal* and *Citizen* initially listed him among the players who arrived in Ottawa in mid-January, they didn't mention him again. He might have filled a strictly administrative role for the team. But one theory is that he never left the Yukon. In *The Trail Less Traveled*, Don Reddick speculates that Martin may have injured himself on the Overland Trail, or given up before leaving Whitehorse, or never even left Dawson and the local papers were in on a ruse designed to give the team a chance to add a ringer to play under his name. Whatever happened to him, the team now had almost as many players from the Outside as from the Yukon.

After unsuccessfully applying to the CAAU for permission to play against the professional IHL teams, the Klondikers had just three American games, going two and one against the amateur Pittsburgh Athletic Club. Back in Canada, the team beat Port Arthur, lost to the Winnipeg Victorias and defeated Brandon before a large crowd on bad ice in what Forrest considered the roughest game of the tour. The arrival of spring and the end of playable ice meant the cancellation of late-March games in Regina, Calgary, and Rossland and Nelson in B.C. The final record of the tour was ten wins and twelve losses.

Forrest, McLennan, Kennedy and Johnstone headed home. In Vancouver, McLennan told a reporter, "Well, we did not bring the cup back with us, but we firmly intend to have another try for the trophy next winter." By the time the quartet arrived in Whitehorse on the WP&YR on April 5, Watt had joined them. "The boys are not returning with the Stanley Cup, but they are taking home with them a more extensive knowledge of Canada than they ever before possessed for the reason that their itinerary covered practically the whole of the Dominion, embracing in the neighborhood of 13,000 miles of travel," observed the *Daily Star*. "The boys are also taking home with them pleasant recollections of the treatment accorded them at various cities visited." Forrest made it back to Dawson first after starting out on a bike, abandoning it north of the Pelly River and walking the rest of the way. Most of the snow was gone from the Overland Trail, except on the north sides of hills. After just one week, averaging almost fifty miles a day, he arrived in town wearing a Dunlap derby hat. Johnstone and Kennedy followed on foot, while McLennan and Watt rode a stagecoach.

The Yukon climate provided ice for one more game. Jack Eilbeck's Colts challenged the touring team but lost 9-0. For the Klondikers, it was a small, perhaps insignificant triumph at the end of their great adventure. They'd dreamed they'd win the Stanley Cup and then storm across the continent taking on all comers. While it hadn't worked out as well as they'd hoped, Canadians would remember their challenge long after they'd forgotten most successful ones.

In late March, as the Yukoners made their way home, Loney pleaded not guilty to the reduced charge of manslaughter. The story stayed on the front pages and some papers played up the ethnic differences: Loney was English and Protestant; Laurin was French and Catholic. Not that they needed to—a death in a hockey match provided more than enough to transfix the country. The high-profile case was one more opportunity to debate violence in the sport. As always, some saw it as just part of the manliness of hockey. Others feared it would be the game's undoing, but they couldn't agree on who to blame. The suspects included the often rowdy and occasionally bloodthirsty fans; the newspapers, which denounced and glamourized violence; the referees, who weren't strict enough; the hockey associations, which did little to stop rough play, perhaps because it helped sell tickets; and, of course, professionalization, even though Maxville and Alexandria were both amateur teams. "Not only is the prisoner at the bar on trial," Crown attorney F.J. French said in his opening remarks, "but the game of hockey itself is on trial."

The judge's charge to the jurors encouraged a guilty verdict, but after deliberating for four hours, they found Loney not guilty. They had harsh words for the sport, though. "We cannot too strongly condemn the growing tendency of introducing brutal methods and rough-house tactics into the games of lacrosse and hockey," the jury wrote. "We believe that unless these growing tendencies can be effectively and permanently eliminated from these games they should be prohibited by legislation and put on a par with bullfights and cocking mains." Nothing changed, though, as violence remained part of hockey and the source of never-ending debate. The battle over professionalism, on the other hand, didn't last much longer.

One evening in May, the council chambers of Ottawa City Hall was crowded as citizens celebrated their favourite hockey team. The Cup champs had faced another challenger after the Klondikers. Despite failing in 1903, and losing $800 on the trip, Rat Portage tried again, taking the first game 9-3. But the OHC won the next two matches to keep the trophy for another summer. At city hall, Sheriff Sweetland presented the players with engraved watches and lockets as well as team photos. He praised not only the Ottawas but also P.D. Ross, who was unable to attend. "He has been most active in the administration of affairs in connection with the cup, and I must say too that he has at all times administered these affairs in the most sportsmanlike manner, though the task was not always an easy one." The two men were colleagues, so the tribute was no surprise, but that didn't mean it wasn't well deserved. Lord Stanley's appointment of the newspaper publisher as a trustee had been good for the Cup and the game.

Not every decision Ross made was the right one, of course. And he inevitably faced criticism, especially from teams he ruled against. But his love of hockey and his desire to protect it were never in doubt. He was also pragmatic and willing to adapt. He understood that even if pay-for-play were easy to police, the situation was far from as simple as zealots like John Ross Robertson made it seem. Some players wanted to remain amateurs. But plenty didn't. And many teams just wanted to win and were quite willing to do whatever it took to improve their chances. This was especially true in resource towns, according to sports historian Bruce Kidd, "where interest in sports was high, professionalism was felt necessary to gain a competitive edge, and there were few members of the middle class to oppose it." But big city teams also wanted to win and the crowds that filled their rinks gave them lots of money.

Ross's attitude toward professionalism had evolved. "To tell the plain truth, I feel rather bewildered about the conditions in our athletic sports. I don't know where we are at, nor where we can get to," his own paper quoted him saying in late 1905. He expressed sympathy for the men who ran the leagues. "They all would prefer simon pure amateur sport. And none of them know how to get it, neither do I." The solution, he came to believe, was to accept the inevitable, as long as teams were transparent about which players were professionals and which were amateurs. "I don't see what else can be done—nor do I see much use in those of us who are not called upon to make any of the sacrifice hollering at the fellows who make the sacrifice and want pay for it."

That same month, the Eastern Canada Amateur Hockey Association formed with the Montreal Hockey Club, the Shamrocks, the Victorias and Quebec from the Canadian Amateur Hockey League and the Ottawa Hockey Club and the Wanderers from the Federal League. The new loop allowed just the kind of semi-professionalism Ross imagined: teams could have professionals on their rosters if they were open about it.

This helped put an end to the International Hockey League, which folded in 1907, after just three years. Too much of its talent went home for higher-paid gigs that came with a chance to win the Cup. Although the league hadn't stuck around long, it played a significant role in early hockey history. From 1907 to 1916, every Cup-winning team included at least one player who'd been in the IHL. Thirteen skaters, two goalies and one referee from the league later made it into the Hockey Hall of Fame. They included Doc Gibson, "Cyclone" Taylor, "Newsy" Lalonde, Joe Hall, Riley Hern and Hod and Bruce Stuart. In 1908, the MHC and the Victorias, the two ECAHA teams that had remained strictly amateur, left the league, which then dropped amateur from its name. That same year, Sir H. Montagu Allan donated a trophy—the Allan Cup—for Canada's amateur champions.

Robertson, who apparently didn't mind being on the wrong side of history, wasn't about to give up. Over six years, he'd presided over a period of great growth in Ontario hockey and was responsible for some important innovations, including the delayed penalty. Officially, he stepped down as president in 1905, but he stayed in control as one-third of a powerful subcommittee unofficially known as the Three White Czars. In 1906, Robertson and his sidekicks continued their holy war, barring OHA teams from playing squads from leagues that allowed pros. That meant no more Cup challenges, an unpopular edict with many teams and fans. They wanted the Cup. But no OHA team ever won it and no Toronto team captured it until the professional Blueshirts in 1914. That was two decades after Stanley had donated the bowl, one year after it ceased being a challenge trophy and just three years before the Seattle Metropolitans became the first, but not the last, American team to win it.

As Canada escaped the Victorian era and entered the promising new century, a different country was emerging. Although Clifford Sifton resigned as interior minister in 1905 over a schools bill, the settlement of the west, especially by immigrants from places other than the United Kingdom, was already a success. The Prairies were filling up, Manitoba was thriving and the government carved Alberta and Saskatchewan out of the North-West Territories to make them provinces. The country was slowly becoming more diverse and while some of it remained very, very British, Canada was culturally no longer just a colonial copy of Mother England. That showed in the nation's sports, as always a powerful reflection of society. With more people from other classes and backgrounds taking part, the games people played changed. America's baseball was far more popular than Britain's cricket. Rugby morphed into Canadian football, which was similar to American football. Most popular of all, though, were the homegrown, decidedly ungenteel, sports of lacrosse and hockey. But it went beyond mere games. Hockey brought Canadians together and loosened the British empire's grip on the country's culture. This helped begin the forging of a separate and original national identity.

On the ice, the Klondikers' challenge was a debacle, but neither the sport nor the Cup suffered. The eagerness of the Yukoners to make such an audacious journey, and the public's response to the whole escapade, revealed just how deeply Canadians had fallen in love with hockey. And how quickly. Stanley's unremarkable silver bowl—"like any other trophy, I suppose," as he put it—had been a powerful endorsement, and technology such as the train and the telegraph had helped spread the game from Cape Breton to Dawson City. Most of all, though, it was the unlikely mix of finesse and ferocity at high speed that really struck people. In the dozen years since the trustees first awarded the Stanley Cup, a niche regional sport with a small fan base had captivated the country. Hockey was now the national pastime.

- EPILOGUE -

A year after the Dawson challenge, Weldy Young returned to mining, this time in northern Ontario. In 1910, he managed the Haileybury Comets in the new National Hockey Association. The league also initially included three Montreal teams—the Wanderers, the Shamrocks and a new club called the Canadiens—as well as Renfrew, Cobalt and Ottawa. Since Ottawa, now known as the Senators, held the Cup again, winning the league meant also taking the trophy. In an effort to do just that, Young reportedly paid $4,000 to sign Art Ross, Lester Patrick's childhood friend. But Haileybury lasted only one season in the NHA. The next year, the team returned to the Timiskaming Professional Hockey League and Young kept hoping to issue a challenge. That never happened, but his mining career proved long and successful. In one early deal, he bought a northern Ontario claim for $125 and then sold it for $300,000. Later, in Toronto, he was president of Young-Davidson Mines, a prolific gold producer. He retired in Collingwood, Ontario, and died there in 1944.

Joe Boyle finally got his dredge. With the backing of Detroit-based Rothschilds financial interests, his Canadian Number One began operating at the mouth of Bear Creek in 1905. It earned back its $200,000 cost in two months. (Three bigger dredges followed, including Number Four, which operated from 1912 to 1959 and is now a National Historic Site and open to the public.) He was a demanding boss, but despite his success and his stature as a commanding figure in the Klondike, everyone still called him Joe. In 1916, he sponsored the Yukon Motor Machine Gun Battery, a regiment of more than fifty men, and headed to Europe. He became a war hero known as the Saviour of Romania and, many people believe, the beloved paramour of that country's Queen Marie. He never returned to the Yukon and died in London in 1923. His whole life, including his Klondike years, would make for a fanciful adventure novel.

Frank McGee also went to war after somehow convincing a military doctor that he could see well enough out of both eyes to pass the physical. He didn't make it home, dying in Courcelette, France, on September 16, 1916. In 1945, he was among the first class of inductees to the Hockey Hall of Fame.

By the time he died in 1949, P.D. Ross was a legend of Canadian journalism. He was a founder of the Canadian Press and served as president of the Canadian Daily Newspapers Association. He stayed on as president of the *Journal*, and continued to write for it, until the last year of his life. He remained a Stanley Cup trustee until his death, though that was long after the National Hockey League assumed full control of the trophy. Ross made it into the Hockey Hall of Fame in 1976.

Although Young never fulfilled his dream of winning the Cup, he did leave his mark on it. After defending the trophy in mid-season challenges from Queen's and Smith Falls in 1906, Ottawa's reign as Dominion champions came to an end. The first season of the Eastern Canada Amateur Hockey Association ended with the OHC and the Wanderers tied, setting up a March playoff for the league title and the Cup. The Wanderers walloped the Ottawas 9-1 in the first match of a two-game, total-goal series. That seemed an insurmountable deficit, but the *Citizen* warned, "Montreal may count its chickens whenever it likes but there is a huge amount of money in Ottawa that says the silverware will stay in the Capital and that a lead of eight goals or nine or perhaps ten does not necessarily spell defeat to Canada's greatest sporting centre." Sure enough, Ottawa burst out to a 9-1 lead in the second game. But Lester Patrick, the former stick boy, crushed the team's hopes when he scored two late goals and the game ended 9-3. The Wanderers took the series 12-10.

Ottawa had a final banquet to bid farewell to the Cup—and vowed to win it back. That was a laudable ambition, but once McGee announced his retirement it was going to be tougher to achieve. Although he was only twenty-three, he worried about damaging his second eye in the increasingly violent sport and he wanted to devote his energies to his new full-time government job with the Interior Department. His career had been short but explosive. Aside from his regular season heroics, he'd scored sixty-three goals in just twenty-two Cup games.

After the banquet, Ottawa packed up the bowl and sent it to Montreal, where the Wanderers held a celebratory luncheon. When the new champs opened the box, they were shocked to see the dilapidated condition of the Cup. It was dented and scratched, with the silver plate scraped off in several places. The Wanderers took the trophy to Henry Birks and Sons, the Montreal jeweller, and wrote the trustees requesting permission to return it to a presentable state.

The Cup wasn't just banged up. Several people—including Ottawa players, politicians and others—had crudely carved their names, nicknames or initials into it. P.D. Ross was there. So was Thomas Stanley Westwick, the baby son of Harry Westwick and maybe the first child to be named after the trophy. And, underneath Lord Stanley of Preston's crest, scratched with a penknife, was the name Weldy Young.

- ACKNOWLEDGEMENTS -

Getting to write a book about two of my passions—hockey and the Yukon—is another in a long list of "I can't help if I'm lucky" events in my life. But my good fortune was only possible with the help of a lot of people who deserve thanks and recognition.

The idea started over lunch with Janie Yoon. At first, she liked it more than I did. Good idea or not, I couldn't have written this book without the help of grants from the Canada Council for the Arts, the Ontario Arts Council and the Access Copyright Foundation. In addition, the chance to spend three weeks at the Al Purdy A-Frame Residency was a fabulous treat and a welcome opportunity to focus on writing.

While I did my residency at the Berton House Writers' Retreat in Dawson City before the idea for this book had even struck me, my time there helped enormously. In addition, several Klondike friends helped with local knowledge. They include Greg Hakonson, Glenda Bolt, Meg Walker and Karen McKay.

I visited a lot of archives over the last few years, some more than once. These include the Klondike History Library and Archives at the Dawson City Museum; the Yukon Archives in Whitehorse; the

Library and Archives Canada in Ottawa; the Woodstock Public Library, home of the Joe Boyle Collection; the National Collection in Montreal's Grande Bibliothèque; the Whyte Museum of the Canadian Rockies in Banff; the Collingwood Public Library; the Hockey Hall of Fame Resource Centre in Toronto; and the Toronto Reference Library. The staff at all of them were invariably helpful, but I'd especially like to thank Angharad Wenz and Alex Somerville in Dawson. Thanks also to Rhiannon Russell, who helped with additional research at the Yukon Archives when I couldn't get there (and who took me hiking on the Overland Trail).

Other friends helped in other much-appreciated ways. Haley Cullingham commissioned a piece for *Hazlitt* and Ziya Jones arranged for *Reader's Digest* to run an excerpt. Thanks also to Steve Watt for legal advice, Rob Turner for nautical knowledge and Susan Orlean for a favour.

Chris Goldie, Dave Paterson and Matthew Church took on the unenviable task of reading the first draft. Their insight and advice were invaluable and reminded me how smart they are. Special thanks to Lynn Cunningham, my friend and mentor, who worked her magic on a late line edit that made a huge difference.

Thanks to everyone at ECW Press, including editorial co-ordinator Shannon Parr, copy editor Kathryn Hayward and co-publisher David Caron. I'm especially indebted and thankful to my editor, Michael Holmes. His enthusiasm for this book surprised even me, and he always gave me good advice.

A special thanks to my mother, who bought me so many hockey magazines and books when I was a boy. They nurtured my love of the game, and left me wanting to know more about the Dawson City team that once challenged for the Stanley Cup.

And, finally, thanks to Carmen, whose love, support and patience remain unwavering.

TIM FALCONER

TORONTO, MARCH 2021

- SELECTED
BIBLIOGRAPHY -

Adams, Trevor J. *Long Shots: The Curious Story of the Four Maritime Teams That Played for the Stanley Cup.* Halifax: Nimbus Publishing, 2012.

Adney, Tappan. *The Klondike Stampede.* Vancouver: UBC Press, 1994. (Original edition: New York: Harper & Brothers Publishers, 1900.)

Backhouse, Frances. *Children of the Klondike.* Vancouver: Whitecap Books, 2010.

Bankson, Russell A. *The Klondike Nugget.* Caldwell, Idaho: The Caxton Printers, 1935.

Barzun, Jacques. *God's Country and Mine: A Declaration of Love Spiced with a Few Harsh Words.* Boston: Little, Brown, 1954.

Berton, Laura Beatrice. *I Married the Klondike.* Toronto: McClelland & Stewart, 1954 and 1961.

Berton, Pierre. *Klondike: The Last Great Gold Rush 1896–1899.* Toronto: McClelland & Stewart, revised edition, 1972. (Original edition: Toronto: McClelland & Stewart, 1958.)

Berton, Pierre. *Prisoners of the North.* Toronto: Anchor Canada, 2005.

Bumsted, J.M. *Dictionary of Manitoba Biography.* Winnipeg: University of Manitoba Press, 1999.

The Canadian Journal of Lady Aberdeen 1893–1898. Edited by John T. Saywell. Toronto: The Champlain Society, 1960.

Coast to Coast: Hockey in Canada to the Second World War. Edited by John Chi-Kit Wong. Toronto: University of Toronto Press, 2009.

Coates, Ken S. and Morrison, William R. *Land of the Midnight Sun: A History of the Yukon.* Montreal: McGill-Queen's University Press, 2005.

Coates, Ken S. and Morrison, William R. *Strange Things Done: Murder in Yukon History.* Montreal: McGill-Queen's University Press, 2014.

Cole, Stephen. *The Canadian Hockey Atlas.* Toronto: Doubleday Canada, 2006.

Coleman, Charles L. *The Trail of the Stanley Cup*, Volume 1: 1893–1926. National Hockey League, 1966.

Cosentino, Frank. *The Renfrew Millionaires: The Valley Boys of Winter 1910.* Renfrew, Ont.: The General Store Publishing House, 1990.

Dafoe, John W. *Clifford Sifton in Relation to His Times.* Toronto: The Macmillan Company of Canada, 1931.

Diamond, Dan; Duplacey, James; Dinger, Ralph; Kuperman, Igor; and Zweig, Eric. *Total Hockey: The Official Encyclopedia of the National Hockey League.* Kingston, N.Y.: Total Sports, 1998.

Diamond, Dan; Duplacey, James; Dinger, Ralph; Kuperman Igor; and Zweig, Eric. *Total Hockey: The Official Encyclopedia of the National Hockey League.* 2d ed. Kingston, N.Y.: Total Sports, 2000.

Duffy, John. *Fight of Our Lives: Elections, Leadership and the Making of Canada.* Toronto: HarperCollins, 2002.

Duncan, Jennifer. *Frontier Spirit: The Brave Women of the Klondike.* Toronto: Doubleday Canada, 2003.

Farrell, Arthur. *Hockey: Canada's Royal Winter Game.* Montreal: C.R. Corneil, 1899.

Firth, John. *Yukon Sport: An Illustrated Encyclopedia.* Vancouver: Figure 1 Publishing, 2014.

Fitsell, J. W. (Bill). *Hockey's Captains, Colonels and Kings.* Erin, Ont.: Boston Mills Press, 1987.

Frayne, Trent. *The Queen's Plate.* Toronto: McClelland & Stewart, 1959.

Gidén, Carl; Houda, Patrick; and Martel, Jean-Patrice. *On the Origin of Hockey.* Stockholm and Chambly: Hockey Origin Publishing, 2014.

Gopnik, Adam. *Winter: Five Windows on the Season.* Toronto: House of Anansi Press, 2011.

Gray, Charlotte. *Gold Diggers: Striking It Rich in the Klondike.* Toronto: HarperCollins, 2010.

Gwyn, Sandra. *The Private Capital: Ambition and Love in the Age of Macdonald and Laurier.* Toronto: McClelland & Stewart, 1984.

Hall, D.J. *Clifford Sifton: Volume I: The Young Napoleon, 1861–1900.* Vancouver: UBC Press, 1981.

Hall, D.J. *Clifford Sifton: Volume II: The Lonely Eminence, 1901–1929.* Vancouver: UBC Press, 1985.

Harper, Stephen J. *A Great Game: The Forgotten Leafs & the Rise of Professional Hockey.* Toronto: Simon & Schuster Canada, 2013.

Haskell, William B. *Two Years in the Klondike and Alaskan Gold-Fields 1896–1898.* Fairbanks, Ak.: University of Alaska Press, 1998. (Original edition: Hartford, Conn.: Hartford Pub. Co., 1898.)

Hewitt, W. A. *Down the Stretch: Recollections of a Pioneer Sportsman and Journalist.* Toronto: The Ryerson Press, 1958.

The Hockey Book: The Great Hockey Stories of All Time, Told by the Men Who Know the Game Best. Edited by Bill Roche. Toronto: McClelland & Stewart, 1953.

Hockey Hall of Fame Book of Goalies: Profiles, Memorabilia, Essays and Stats. Edited by Steve Cameron. Richmond Hill, Ont.: Firefly Books, 2014.

Humber, William. *Diamonds of the North: A Concise History of Baseball in Canada.* Oxford: Oxford University Press, 1995.

Jenish, D'Arcy. *The Stanley Cup: One Hundred Years of Hockey at Its Best.* Toronto: McClelland & Stewart, 1992.

Kidd, Bruce. *The Struggle for Canadian Sport.* Toronto: University of Toronto Press, 1996.

Kitchen, Paul. *Win, Tie, or Wrangle: The Inside Story of the Old Ottawa Senators 1883–1935.* Bowmanville, Ont.: Penumbra Press, 2008.

Lynch, Charles. *Up from the Ashes: The Rideau Club Story.* Ottawa: University of Ottawa Press, 1990.

Macdonald, Ian and O'Keefe, Betty. *The Klondike's "Dear Little Nugget."* Salt Spring Island, B.C.: Horsdal & Schubart Publishers Ltd., 1996.

McCreery, Christopher. *Savoir Faire, Savoir Vivre: Rideau Club 1865–2015.* Toronto: Dundurn, 2014.

McGoogan, Ken. *Celtic Lightning: How the Scots and the Irish Created a Canadian Nation.* Toronto: HarperCollins, 2015.

McKinley, Michael. *Etched in Ice: A Tribute to Hockey's Defining Moments.* Vancouver: Greystone Books, 1998.

McKinley, Michael. *Putting a Roof on Winter: Hockey's Rise from Sport to Spectacle.* Vancouver: Greystone Books, 2000.

McKinley, Michael. *Hockey: A People's History.* Updated ed. Toronto: McClelland & Stewart, 2009.

Metcalfe, Alan. *Canada Learns to Play: The Emergence of Organized Sport, 1807–1914.* Toronto: McClelland & Stewart, 1987.

Morrow, Don and Wamsley, Kevin B. *Sport in Canada: A History.* Oxford: Oxford University Press, 2005.

Neufeld, David and Habiluk, Patrick. *Make it Pay! Gold Dredge #4.* Missoula, Mt.: Pictorial Histories Publishing Co., 1994.

Ogilvie, William. *Early Days on the Yukon and the Story of Its Gold Finds.* Ottawa: Thorburn and Abbott, 1913.

Porsild, Charlene. *Gamblers and Dreamers: Women, Men, and Community in the Klondike.* Vancouver: UBC Press, 1998.

Proteau, Adam. *Fighting the Good Fight: Why On-Ice Violence Is Killing Hockey.* Hoboken, N.J.: Wiley, 2011.

Purdy, Al. *Rooms for Rent in the Outer Planets: Selected Poems 1962–1996.* Madeira Park, B.C.: Harbour Publishing, 1996.

Reddick, Don. *The Trail Less Traveled: The Yukon's Dawson City-to-Ottawa Stanley Cup Reenactment.* Norwood, Mass.: Nauset Sound Publishing Company, 2010.

Riding on the Roar of the Crowd: A Hockey Anthology. Edited by David Gowdy. Toronto: Macmillan of Canada, 1989.

Rodney, William. *Joe Boyle: King of the Klondike.* Toronto: McGraw-Hill Ryerson, 1974.

Ross, J. Andrew. *Joining the Clubs: The Business of the National Hockey League to 1945.* Syracuse, N.Y.: Syracuse University Press, 2015.

Ross, Philip Dansken. *Retrospects of a Newspaper Person.* Oxford: Oxford University Press, 1931.

Roxborough, Henry. *The Stanley Cup Story.* Toronto: The Ryerson Press, 1964.

Sauerwein, Stan. *Klondike Joe Boyle.* Canmore, Alta.: Altitude Publishing Canada, 2003.

Scanlan, Lawrence, *Grace Under Fire: The State of Our Sweet and Savage Game,* Penguin, 2002.

Service, Robert. *Ploughman of the Moon: An Adventure into Memory.* Project Gutenberg Canada ebook #733.

Shea, Kevin and Wilson, John Jason. *Lord Stanley: The Man Behind the Cup.* Bolton, Ont.: H.B. Fenn, 2006.

Shubert, Howard. *Architecture on Ice: A History of the Hockey Arena.* Montreal: McGill-Queen's University Press, 2016.

Smith, I. Norman. *The Journal Men: P.D. Ross, E. Norman Smith and Grattan O'Leary of The Ottawa Journal: Three Great Canadian Newspapermen and the Tradition They Created.* Toronto: McClelland & Stewart, 1974.

Smith, Stephen. *Puckstruck: Distracted, Delighted and Distressed by Canada's Hockey Obsession.* Vancouver: Greystone Books, 2014.

Steele, Samuel B. *Forty Years in Canada: Reminiscences of the Great North-West with Some Account of His Service in South Africa.* Toronto: McGraw-Hill Ryerson, 1972 reissue.

Taylor, Leonard W. *The Sourdough and the Queen: The Many Lives of Klondike Joe Boyle.* London, U.K.: Methuen Publishing, 1983.

Treadgold, A.N.C. *An English Expert on the Klondike.* Toronto: George N. Morang and Company, 1899.

Vaughan, Garth. *The Puck Starts Here: The Origin of Canada's Great Winter Game Ice Hockey.* Fredericton, N.B.: Goose Lane Editions, 1996.

Whitehead, Eric. *The Patricks: Hockey's Royal Family.* Toronto: Doubleday Canada, 1980.

Woods, Shirley E. Jr. *Ottawa: The Capital of Canada.* Toronto: Doubleday Canada, 1980.

Wong, John Chi-Kit. *Lords of the Rinks: The Emergence of the National Hockey League, 1875–1936.* Toronto: University of Toronto Press, 2005.

Young, Scott. *100 Years of Dropping the Puck: A History of the OHA.* Toronto: McClelland & Stewart, 1989.

Zweig, Eric. *Stanley Cup: 120 Years of Hockey Supremacy.* Richmond Hill, Ont.: Firefly Books, 2012.

LIST OF ABBREVIATIONS

AHAC	Amateur Hockey Association of Canada
CAAA	Canadian Amateur Athletic Association
CAAU	Canadian Amateur Athletic Union
CAHL	Canadian Amateur Hockey League
CCHA	Central Canada Hockey Association
CPR	Canadian Pacific Railway
DAAA	Dawson Amateur Athletic Association
ECAHA	Eastern Canada Amateur Hockey Association
FAHL	Federal Amateur Hockey League
IHL	International Hockey League
MAAA	Montreal Amateur Athletic Association
MHC	Montreal Hockey Club
NWMP	North-West Mounted Police
OAAA	Ottawa Amateur Athletic Association
OAAC	Ottawa Amateur Athletic Club
OHA	Ontario Hockey Association
OHC	Ottawa Hockey Club
WOHA	Western Ontario Hockey Association
WPHL	Western Pennsylvania Hockey League
WP&YR	White Pass & Yukon Route

- ENDNOTES -

PROLOGUE

- Departure: *Dawson Daily News*, Dec. 19, 1904.
- Hannay: *Winnipeg Daily Tribune* (hereafter *Tribune*), Jan. 13, 1905.
- No exhibition games: Kitchen, *Win, Tie, or Wrangle*, 142.
- No joke: *The* (Montreal) *Gazette* (hereafter *Gazette*), Jan. 11, 1905.
- Cheering fans: *Ottawa Journal* (hereafter *Journal*), Jan. 10, 1905.
- "greatest interest": *Ottawa Citizen* (hereafter *Citizen*), Jan. 12, 1905.
- Arrival: *Citizen*, Jan. 12, 1905; *Journal*, Jan. 12, 1905.
- "a right hearty reception": *Citizen*, Jan. 12, 1905
- 2,500 fans: *Gazette*, Jan. 14, 1905.

ONE

- Banquet: *Journal*, Mar. 19, 1892; *Citizen*, Mar. 19, 1892; *Ottawa Free Times*, Mar. 19, 1892; *Journal*, Mar. 18, 1892; *Citizen*, Mar. 18, 1892.
- Stanley: Shea and Wilson, Lord Stanley, 53-58; *The Globe* (hereafter *Globe*), Sept. 11, 1888.
- "commanding" and "good looking": *The New York Times*, Jun. 10, 1888.
- "trousers were too short"; Paul Kitchen, "Rebels in Name Only," Society for International Hockey Research's *The Hockey Research Journal*, 2012–13.
- Stanley's letter: *Journal*, Mar. 19, 1892.
- "The Hockey Men": *Journal*, Dec. 13, 1909.
- Colville played with Stanley's sons: *Citizen*, Feb. 20, 1889.
- Stanley Cup description: Shea and Wilson, *Lord Stanley*, 372; Hockey Hall of Fame website, hhof.com.

- "like any other trophy": Kent Russell, "Lord Stanley's Grail," Grantland .com, Jun. 17, 2011.
- Sweetland: *Journal,* May 6, 1907; *Citizen,* May 6, 1907.
- "more to cultural identity": Shea and Wilson, *Lord Stanley,* 50.
- Hockey, young men and war: Shea and Wilson, *Lord Stanley,* 92.
- "release that strong liquor": "Fury on Ice," *Holiday Magazine,* 1954.
- "this combination of ballet and murder": Purdy, "Hockey Players," in *Rooms for Rent in the Outer Planets: Selected Poems 1962–1996,* 23–26.
- "heart and mind of America": Barzun, *God's Country and Mine.*
- "break the news gently": *Citizen,* Aug. 18, 1900.

TWO

- "It's a great day for hockey" is a phrase made famous by Bob Johnson, who among other accomplishments coached the Pittsburgh Penguins to the Stanley Cup in 1991.
- Mar. 3, 1875 weather: Environment and Climate Change Canada's Historical Climate Data site, climate.weather.gc.ca.
- "endeavour to keep ourselves": quoted in Cole, *The Canadian Hockey Atlas,* 372.
- Creighton: Shea and Wilson, *Lord Stanley,* 353–354; McKinley, *Putting a Roof on Winter,* 4–18; *Tribune,* Jun. 28, 1930.
- Roots in hurling: J.W. (Bill) Fitsell, "The Halifax Rules," *The Hockey Research Journal,* 2001.
- Victoria Skating Rink: Shubert, *Architecture on Ice,* 29–31, 48; Morrow and Wamsley, *Sport in Canada,* 58; Metcalfe, *Canada Learns to Play,* 135.
- 202 by 80: Michel Vigneault, "Montreal's Hockey Tradition," *The Hockey Research Journal,* 1993.
- Skates and sticks: Vaughan, *The Puck Starts Here,* 116–129 and 108–113; Diamond et al., *Total Hockey,* 5.
- Rum barrel plug: Cole, *The Canadian Hockey Atlas,* 372.
- "fears have been expressed": *Gazette,* Mar. 3, 1875.
- *Gazette* first used "puck" in 1876: Earl Zuckerman, "McGill University: The Missing Link to the Birthplace of Hockey," in *Total Hockey,* 2nd ed., 17.
- Shakespeare: *Gazette,* Sept. 18, 1943.
- "an interesting game": *Montreal Star,* Mar. 4, 1875.
- "well contested affair": Quoted in *Gazette,* Sept. 18, 1943.
- "adjourned well satisfied": *Montreal Star,* Mar. 4, 1875.
- Scuffle after first game: Kitchen, *Win, Tie, or Wrangle,* 3.
- "unfortunate disagreement arose": Quoted in Gidén et al., *On the Origin of Hockey,* 21–23.
- "disgraceful sight": *Weekly British Whig,* Mar. 11, 1875.
- "Captain Creighton": Quoted in *Gazette,* Sept. 18, 1943.

- Victorias seeking rules: Farrell, *Hockey*, 28–29.
- MAAA: Montreal Amateur Athletic Association, "Souvenir Booklet of the Opening of the New MAAA Club House, 1905," MG 28 I 351 Volume 5, File 3, Library and Archives Canada (hereafter LAC); Morrow and Wamsley, *Sport in Canada*, 64.
- Montreal Winter Carnival: Morrow and Wamsley, *Sport in Canada*, 65; *Gazette*, Jan. 27, 1883; *Montreal Star*, Jan. 27, 1883.
- Jack Kerr anecdote: *Journal*, Dec. 13, 1909; Kitchen, *Win, Tie, or Wrangle*, 13.
- "slightly interfered with": Farrell, *Hockey*, 29.
- First OHC contest: *Citizen*, Mar. 6, 1883.
- 1886 Rules: *Gazette*, Jan. 8, 1886.
- "surging, swaying mass": *Gazette*, Feb. 5, 1889.
- Electric lights: Shubert, *Architecture on Ice*, 61.
- "grows in popular favour": Farrell, *Hockey*, 15.

THREE

- Graham anecdote: Ross, *Retrospects of Newspaper Person*, 1–3.
- Metropolitan Club: Ross, *Joining the Clubs*, 14.
- "best game": Ross Collection, LAC, Ross diary (hereafter Ross diary), Jan. 23, 1879.
- Benedicts: *Gazette*, Jan. 15, 1879.
- Umpire: Ross diary, Jan. 15, 1879.
- McGill game: Ross diary, Mar. 6, 1879.
- Philip Simpson Ross: *Journal*, Feb. 2, 1907; *Montreal Herald* (hereafter *Herald*), Feb. 4, 1907; *The Financial Post*, Apr. 28, 1984; Ross Collection, LAC, letter dated Jan. 1, 1879.
- "something like a fortune": "A Private in the Ranks," *Herald*, Feb. 4, 1907.
- "warmest wish": Ross Collection, LAC, letter dated Sept. 30, 1880.
- *Mail* and *News*: Ross, *Retrospects of a Newspaper Person*, 4–5; Jamie Bradburn, "Historicist: The News of Toronto," Torontoist.com, Jun. 9, 2012; Jamie Bradburn, "Historicist: Delivering the Mail," Torontoist.com, Nov. 22, 2014.
- Grogg: Ross, *Retrospects of a Newspaper Person*, 263–265; "Inside a Newspaper," *St. Catherine Standard*, Feb. 23, 1933.
- Macdonald: Ross Collection, LAC, draft of "I Remember" for CBC Radio in 1937.
- Celebrities, boxing: *Journal*, Dec. 10, 1935.
- "deep blue": "Montreal Carnival," *Mail*, Jan. 23, 1883.
- "finest and fastest": "Montreal Carnival," *Mail*, Jan. 26, 1883.
- Oarsman: *Journal*, Jul. 6, 1949; *Journal*, Jul. 7, 1949.
- Fencing club: Ross diary, Jan. 3, 1884.
- Sporting paper: Ross diary, Nov. 16, 1884.

- Coin toss: Ross, *Retrospects of a Newspaper Person*, 24–25.
- Herald editorship: Ross diary, Sept. 27 and Sept. 28, 1884.
- Buying *Journal*: Ross, *Retrospects of a Newspaper Person*, 32–37; Smith, *The Journal Men*, 16–19.
- Insurance policy: Paul Kitchen, "P.D. Ross: How He Came to be a Stanley Cup Trustee," *The Hockey Research Journal*, 2006.
- "4,000 cents": Ross, *Retrospects of a Newspaper Person*, 32.
- "salt creek": Ross, *Retrospects of a Newspaper Person*, 35.
- "Never better": Ross diary, Jan. 1, 1894.
- "unattractive town": *Journal*, Dec. 10, 1935.
- Rideau Hall: Ross diary, Feb. 3, 1888.
- "valuable acquisition": "Editorial Notes," *Citizen*, Jan. 5, 1887.
- OAAA building: Ross diary, Oct. 29, 1889.
- OAAC opening: "The Athletic Building," *Citizen*, Nov. 21, 1889.
- Bicycle club: Ross diary, Mar. 2, 1888.
- Toboggan club: Ross diary, Jan. 7, 1889.
- Skate to Buckingham: *Journal*, Jul. 12, 1949.
- "gorgeous skate": Ross diary, Nov. 21, 1888.
- Rideau Skating and Curling Club: *Journal*, Oct. 13, 1888; *Citizen*, Dec. 26, 1888; *Citizen*, Jan. 8, 1889; Kitchen, *Win, Tie, or Wrangle*, 39–40.
- Rejuvenated OHC: Ross diary, Jan. 26, 1889.
- "skate themselves dizzy": Coleman, *The Trail of the Stanley Cup*, 5–6.
- "hot shot": *Journal*, Mar. 12, 1889
- Humble Votary letter: *Journal*, Feb. 4, 1889.

FOUR

- Ottawa: Gwyn, *The Private Capital*, 35–44; Woods, *Ottawa*, 134–136.
- Russell House: Gwyn, *The Private Capital*, 43–44, 261–263, 396–399.
- Rideau Club: Lynch, *Up from the Ashes*, 41–65; McCreery, *Savoir Faire, Savoir Vivre*, 1–40; Woods, *Ottawa*, 134–135, 211.
- Ottawa Club: McCreery, *Savoir Faire, Savoir Vivre*, 22.
- Rideau v. Ottawa: *Citizen*, Feb. 15, 1889.
- Lady Isobel: *Gazette*, Mar. 9, 1889.
- Rebels tour: *Citizen*, Feb. 10, 1890; Harper, *A Great Game*, 10–13; Paul Kitchen, "Rebels in Name Only," *The Hockey Research Journal*, 2012–13.
- "rougher methods": *Citizen*, Feb. 10, 1890.
- "greatly to be regretted": Quoted in Harper, *A Great Game*, 13.
- "conspicuous": *Citizen*, Feb. 10, 1890.
- Arthur Stanley: Shea and Wilson, *Lord Stanley*, 360–362.
- Kingston: Captain James T. Sutherland, "A Flashback to 1885–86," in Roche, *The Hockey Book*, 1; Hewitt, *Down the Stretch*, 178.
- Queen's Hotel meeting: *Globe*, Nov. 28, 1890; Young, *100 Years of Dropping*

the Puck, 7–15; Shea and Wilson, *Lord Stanley*, 363–364.

- Ottawa City league: *Gazette*, Nov. 28, 1890.
- General sources for evolution of sports in Canada include Kidd, *The Struggle for Canadian Sport*; Metcalfe, *Canada Learns to Play*; and Morrow and Wamsley, *Sport in Canada*.
- Montreal Curling Club: History of the Royal Montreal Curling Club, club website, royalmontrealcurling.ca.
- Upper class pursuits: Kidd, *The Struggle for Canadian Sport*, 15.
- British attitude to amateurism: Kidd, *The Struggle for Canadian Sport*, 27; Morrow and Wamsley, *Sport in Canada*, 70–77.
- MAAA: Montreal Amateur Athletic Association, "Souvenir Booklet of the Opening of the New MAAA Club House, 1905," MG 28 I 351 Volume 5, File 3, LAC; Alan Metcalfe, "The Evolution of Organized Physical Recreation in Montreal, 1840–1895", *Histoire sociale/Social History*, Vol. 11, No. 21 1978; Morrow and Wamsley, *Sport in Canada*, 64; Don Morrow, "The Powerhouse of Canadian Sport: The Montreal Amateur Athletic Association, Inception to 1909," *Journal of Sport History*, Vol. 8, No. 3 (Winter, 1981), 20–39.
- Associations regulated behaviour: Alan Metcalfe, "The Evolution of Organized Physical Recreation in Montreal, 1840–1895," *Histoire sociale/Social History*, Vol. 11, No. 21, 1978.
- Francophones and Jewish people in MAAA: Ross, *Joining the Clubs*, 14.
- OAAC opening: *Citizen*, Nov. 21, 1889.
- OAAC and OHC: Kitchen, *Win, Tie, or Wrangle*, 42–44.
- William Young: *Journal*, May 19, 1894; *Citizen*, Mar. 11, 1913.
- Young Bros.: *Journal*, Mar. 15, 1894.
- Twenty-five members: Kitchen, *Win, Tie, or Wrangle*, 44.
- Typical club structure: Kitchen, *Win, Tie, or Wrangle*, 84.
- Dey's Rink Pirates: Kitchen, *Win, Tie, or Wrangle*, 50.
- OHC clinches: *Journal*, Mar. 9, 1891.
- Rescheduling games: Kitchen, *Win, Tie, or Wrangle*, 72.
- British American Bank Note Company: Kitchen, *Win, Tie, or Wrangle*, 54.
- Ross rounds up team: Ross diary, Mar. 13 and 14, 1891; Kitchen, *Win, Tie, or Wrangle*, 54.
- Cosby Cup: *Journal*, Mar. 16, 1891.
- Gladstones: *Citizen*, Oct. 20, 1891.
- St. George's: *Citizen*, Nov. 13, 1891; *Citizen*, Dec. 3, 1891.
- Debt: *Citizen*, Oct. 20, 1891.
- Ottawa v. McGill: *Journal*, Jan. 19, 1891.
- "quit dancing": Ross diary, Jan. 21, 1891.
- Rebels: *Journal*, Dec. 4, 1890.
- Montreal: Ross diary, Jan. 8, 1892.

- "Champions of Canada": *Journal*, Jan. 9, 1892.
- $45 for home games: Kitchen, *Win, Tie, or Wrangle*, 64.
- "repatriate themselves": *Journal*, Feb. 19, 1892.
- "Grand Championship Match": *Citizen*, Mar. 7, 1892.
- Trophy idea not new: Shea and Wilson, *Lord Stanley*, 370–371.
- Stanley and Sweetland: *Montreal Star*, Dec. 29, 1896.
- Sweetland: *Journal*, May 6, 1907; *Citizen*, May 6, 1907.
- Stanley's conditions: *Gazette*, Feb. 23, 1894.
- "Condemn a man's views": *Journal*, Jul. 6, 1949.
- Lunch with Kilcoursie: Ross diary, Apr. 22, 1893.
- "also drafted": Ross diary, Apr. 23, 1893.

FIVE

- Sweetland in Montreal: *Gazette*, May 16, 1893; *Herald*, May 16, 1893; J. Andrew Ross, "Why Would a Team Refuse the Stanley Cup," LAC Blog; Montreal Amateur Athletic Association Minute Book No. 4, MG 28 I 351 Volume I, File 4, LAC.
- "handsome looking" and "appropriate speech": *Gazette*, May 16, 1893.
- Stanley's conditions: *Journal*, May 1, 1893; *Gazette*, May 1, 1983.
- Stanley was OHC fan: Roxborough, *The Stanley Cup Story*, 12.
- "continue the interest": *Gazette*, May 1, 1893.
- Kilcoursie wired MAAA: Montreal Amateur Athletic Association Minute Book No. 4, MG 28 I 351 Volume 1, File 4, p. 307, LAC.
- Gold rings and Heintzman piano: Montreal Amateur Athletic Association Minute Book No. 4, MG 28 I 351 Volume 1, File 4, 297 and 302–303, LAC; *Gazette*, May 16, 1893; J. Andrew Ross, "The 'First' Stanley Cup Rings?," Society of International Hockey Research's Behind the Boards blog, sihrhockey.org.
- "proper representatives": Montreal Amateur Athletic Association Minute Book No. 4, MG 28 I 351 Volume 1, File 4, 311, LAC.
- "unavoidable absence": Montreal Amateur Athletic Association Minute Book No. 4, MG 28 I 351 Volume 1, File 4, 315, LAC.
- MAAA-MHC dispute: *Journal*, Jan. 31, 1894; *Gazette*, Feb. 17, 1894; *Gazette*, Feb. 23, 1894; Shea and Wilson, *Lord Stanley*, 380–384; Don Morrow, "The Little Men of Iron: The 1902 Montreal Hockey Club," *Canadian Journal of History of Sport*, May 1981, Vol. 12, Issue 1, 51-65; Paul Kitchen, "They Refused the Stanley Cup," *Total Hockey*, 2d ed., 20–24.
- small loans: Don Morrow, "The Little Men of Iron: The 1902 Montreal Hockey Club," *Canadian Journal of History of Sport* 12, No. 1, 1981.
- "eyes of the general public": Montreal Amateur Athletic Association Minute Book No. 5, MG 28 I 351 Volume 2, File 1, 30–31, LAC.
- Trustees hadn't communicated directly: Montreal Amateur Athletic

Association Minute Book No. 5, MG 28 I 351 Volume 2, File 1, 33, LAC.

- Trophy in trust: Montreal Amateur Athletic Association Minute Book No. 5, MG 28 I 351 Volume 2, File 1, 36, LAC.
- Ross in Montreal: Ross diary, Feb. 16, 1894.
- Trustees' letters: *Gazette*, Feb. 23, 1894; Montreal Amateur Athletic Association Minute Book No. 5, MG 28 I 351 Volume 2, File 1, 73, LAC.
- "accidental misunderstanding": *Gazette*, Feb. 23, 1894.
- OHA dispute: *Journal*, Feb. 21, 1894; *Journal*, Feb. 23, 1894; *Citizen*, Feb. 21, 1894; *Journal*, Feb. 23, 1894; Kitchen, *Win, Tie, or Wrangle*, 74–76; Harper, *A Great Game*, 14–16.
- Toronto executives: *Journal*, Feb. 21, 1894.
- "something has to bust" and "case of hoggey again": *Journal*, Feb. 23, 1894.
- "our property": *Citizen*, Feb. 21, 1894.
- "the cup be called": *Gazette*, May 1, 1893.
- MHC v. OHC: *Gazette*, Mar. 23, 1894; *Montreal Star*, Mar. 23, 1894; *Journal*, Mar. 24, 1894.
- "tin horns": *Gazette*, Mar. 23, 1894.
- 4:45 train: Ross diary, Mar. 22, 1894.
- Ross wrote *Journal* story: Ross diary, Mar. 23, 1894.
- Ottawa focused on AHAC title: Kitchen, *Win, Tie, or Wrangle*, 92.
- Osgoode Hall: *Gazette*, Mar. 12, 1894.
- Point and cover-point: Farrell, *Hockey*, 94–95.
- Young rushing in 1893: Coleman, *The Trail of the Stanley Cup*, 6.
- Pulford goals: Coleman, *The Trail of the Stanley Cup*, 8.
- Swift story: *Gazette*, Mar. 12, 1935.
- "synonymous with homicide": *Gazette*, Mar. 23, 1894.
- Barlow: Shea and Wilson, *Lord Stanley*, 384; Jenish, *The Stanley Cup*, 14.
- "most exciting hockey season": *Journal*, Mar. 24, 1894.
- Trustees wanted leagues to handle arrangements: *Gazette*, Mar. 11, 1895.
- Queen's to play MHC: *Gazette*, Feb. 27, 1895; *Journal*, Feb. 26, 1895.
- How the game was played: Cosentino, *The Renfrew Millionaires*, 31–33.
- "puck twittering": *Journal*, Jan. 29, 1894.
- Offside rule: Iain Fyffe, "Going Sideways: The Historical Misunderstanding of Early Hockey Offside Rules," *The Hockey Research Journal*, 2015–16; *Toronto Daily Star*, Dec. 31, 1904.
- Difference between offside rule in OHA and AHAC: *Globe*, Feb. 24, 1904; *Toronto Telegram* (hereafter *Telegram*), Jan. 24, 1902; "The Origins and Development of the International Hockey League and Its Effects on the Sport of Professional Ice Hockey in North America," Daniel Scott Mason thesis, University of British Columbia, 1992, 64.
- "skate his fellow-players on side": *Globe*, Feb. 24, 1904.
- McKerrow: Coleman, *The Trail of the Stanley Cup*, 24.

- Vics win AHAC: *Gazette*, Mar. 9, 1895.
- Queen's suggested Young: untitled note, *Journal*, Mar. 6, 1895.
- MHC defeats Queen's: *Gazette*, Mar. 11, 1895.
- "excuses": *Queen's University Journal*, Mar. 16, 1895.

SIX

- Winnipeg: Morris Mott, "'An Immense Hold in the Public Estimation': The First Quarter Century of Hockey in Manitoba, 1886-1911," *Manitoba History*, Number 43, Spring/Summer 2002.
- "ambulances wait": *Manitoba Morning Free Press* (hereafter *Free Press*), Jan. 31, 1890.
- Victorias and start of Winnipeg hockey: *Free Press*, Dec. 23, 1893; H.J. Woodside, "Hockey in the Canadian North-West," *The Canadian Magazine of Politics, Science, Art and Literature*, Vol. VI, 1895–96; Iain Fyffe, "Breaking the Ice: How Big-Time Hockey Began in Manitoba," *The Hockey Research Journal*, 2015.
- "king of the Manitoba hockeyists": *Tribune*, Dec. 19, 1892.
- Armytage: *Tribune*, Dec. 30, 1896; *Tribune*, Aug. 9, 1943.
- "carried triumphantly": *Tribune*, Dec. 19, 1892.
- "orange groves": *Tribune*, Feb. 4, 1893.
- Tour: *Tribune*, Feb. 4, 1893; *Tribune*, Feb. 28, 1893; Roxborough, *The Stanley Cup Story*, 16–17.
- All-stars in Ottawa: Ross diary, Feb. 14, 1893; *Citizen*, Feb. 14, 1893; *Journal*, Feb. 15, 1893.
- "lack in team play": *Citizen*, Feb. 14, 1893.
- "unexpectedly good stand": *Journal*, Feb. 15, 1893.
- CPR station: *Tribune*, Feb. 28, 1893.
- "the public estimation": *Free Press*, Dec. 23, 1893.
- Thousand fans: *Free Press*, Dec. 26, 1893.
- Trustee's rules: *Gazette*, May 1, 1893.
- Vics tour: Roxborough, *The Stanley Cup Story*, 16–17.
- Banquet: *Tribune*, Feb. 21, 1895.
- Trophy case: Zweig, *Stanley Cup*, 319.
- Winnipeg in 1896: "The Great Wheat/Investment Boom: The Winnipeg Construction Industry, 1896–1914," Mavis Gray MA thesis, University of Manitoba, 1997.
- White sweaters: *Free Press*, Dec. 29, 1896.
- Referee: *Journal*, Feb. 13, 1896.
- Pre-match quibbling: *Free Press*, Feb. 14, 1896; *Tribune*, Feb. 14, 1896.
- "lung power": *Free Press*, Feb. 19, 1896.
- Manitoba Hotel: Sheila Grover, "The Northern Pacific and Manitoba Railway Engine House," *Manitoba History*, Autumn 1985.

- Game: *Tribune*, Feb. 15, 1896; *Gazette*, Feb. 15, 1896.
- "quick and reliable eye": *Tribune*, Dec. 30, 1896.
- "stentorian tones": *Tribune*, Feb. 15, 1896
- "a perfect shriek of delight": *Tribune*, Feb. 15, 1896; *Tribune*, Feb. 14, 1896.
- $160 share: *Free Press*, Feb. 19, 1896.
- Arrival in Winnipeg: *Free Press*, Feb. 25, 1896; *Tribune*, Feb. 25, 1896; Zweig, *Stanley Cup*, 319.
- Caretaker's tears: *Free Press*, Feb. 21, 1896.
- National news: Zweig, *Stanley Cup*, 319.
- Montreal challenge: Ross diary, Nov. 14 and 15, 1896; *Journal*, Nov. 16, 1896; *Gazette*, Nov. 17, 1896; *Journal*, Nov. 21, 1896; *Tribune*, Dec. 8, 1896; *Journal*, Dec. 11, 1896; *Tribune*, Feb. 25, 1896.
- "much be-furred": *Herald*, Dec. 26, 1896.
- Rat Portage: *Montreal Star*, Jan. 6, 1897.
- In Winnipeg: *Tribune*, Dec. 28, 1896; *Herald*, Dec. 29, 1896; *Herald*, Dec. 30, 1896; *Montreal Star*, Dec. 30, 1896.
- Higginbotham watch: *Tribune*, Feb. 28, 1893.
- Lineups: *Gazette*, Dec. 15, 1896; *Gazette*, Dec. 31, 1896.
- Capacity and seating: *Free Press*, Dec. 12, 1896; *Tribune*, Dec. 29, 1896; *Free Press*, Dec. 30, 1896.
- Gambling: *Gazette*, Dec. 31, 1896; *Montreal Star*, Dec. 30, 1896.
- "anxious crowds": *Montreal Star*, Dec. 30, 1896.
- $2 a ticket: *Herald*, Dec. 30, 1896.
- Line up, scalpers, etc.: *Free Press*, Dec. 31, 1896.
- Half the fans turned away: *Gazette*, Dec. 31, 1896.
- Montreal suggested Young: *Gazette*, Nov. 17, 1896.
- "reputation for squareness": *Montreal Star*, Dec. 30, 1896.
- Young-Nixon meeting: *Citizen*, Feb. 22, 1896.
- "take your positions": *Citizen*, Feb. 22, 1896.
- "dainty little whistle": *Free Press*, Dec. 31, 1896.
- Higginbotham death: William Humber, "Fred Higginbotham's Lasting Memorial," *The Hockey Research Journal*, 1994.
- Rink dimensions: *Montreal Star*, Jan. 6, 1897.
- "beside itself with joy": *Free Press*, Dec. 31, 1896.
- "roar of thunder": *Montreal Star*, Jan. 6, 1897.
- "damper on the crowd": *Free Press*, Dec. 31, 1896.
- "lost Valentine": *Tribune*, Dec. 31, 1896.
- "hopeless exhibition": *Herald*, Feb. 15, 1896.
- "utterly ignorant": *Globe*, Feb. 15, 1896.
- • "impartial manner": *Tribune*, Dec. 31, 1896.
- "consummate skill": *Free Press*, Dec. 31, 1896.
- "well-conducted audience": *Free Press*, Dec. 31, 1896.

- "Every move": *Free Press*, Dec. 29, 1896.
- Bulletins: *Montreal Star*, Dec. 31, 1896.
- Montreal: *Montreal Star*, Dec. 30, 1896; *Montreal Star*, Dec. 31, 1896.
- Play-by-play diction: Jenish, *The Stanley Cup*, 21.
- Newspapers: Stacy L. Lorenz, "'Our Victorias Victorious': Media, Rivalry, and the 1896 Winnipeg-Montreal Stanley Cup Hockey Challenges," *The International Journal of the History of Sport*, 2015; *Free Press*, Feb. 17, 1896.
- "victory of luck": *Gazette*, Nov. 20, 1896.
- "ounce or two of spite": *Tribune*, Nov. 24, 1896.
- "pink of condition": *Tribune*, Dec. 8, 1896.
- "effete east": *Free Press*, Feb. 15, 1896.
- "Wild and Woolly West": *Gazette*, Feb. 15, 1896.

SEVEN
- Boyle in New York and at sea: Clara Boyle, "Who Was Joe Boyle?," *Maclean's*, Jun. 1, 1938; Rodney, *Joe Boyle*, 8–11; Taylor, *The Sourdough and the Queen*, 8.
- Charles Boyle: *Hamilton Spectator*, May 2, 1919; Taylor, *The Sourdough and the Queen*, 4; Rodney, *Joe Boyle*, 4–6; Frayne, *The Queen's Plate*, 79.
- Boyle as student: Taylor, *The Sourdough and the Queen*, 6.
- "roving disposition": *Rochester Democrat and Chronicle* (hereafter *Democrat and Chronicle*), Apr. 25, 1897.
- Family yarn: Boyle, *Maclean's*, Jun. 1, 1938.
- "seas ran like mountains": *Democrat and Chronicle*, Apr. 25, 1897.
- Height and weight: Taylor, *The Sourdough and the Queen*, 16.
- Marriage: Boyle, *Maclean's*, Jun. 1, 1938; Taylor, *The Sourdough and the Queen*, 11.
- Loneliness at sea: Rodney, *Joe Boyle*, 9.
- Concerts: Taylor, *The Sourdough and the Queen*, 12.
- Boxing: Boyle, *Maclean's*, Jun. 1, 1938.
- Slavin: *Parade*, Dec. 1972, 42–43; *Victoria Daily Times*, Mar. 20, 1926.
- Boyle as manager: *Buffalo Enquirer*, Apr. 24, 1897.
- "dead broke": *Boston Post*, Feb. 10, 1897.
- National Sporting Club: *Democrat and Chronicle*, Mar. 21, 1897.
- Boyle in San Francisco: *Democrat and Chronicle*, Apr. 22, 1897; *Democrat and Chronicle*, May 17, 1897; *Democrat and Chronicle*, May 31, 1897; *Democrat and Chronicle*, Jun. 13, 1897; *Democrat and Chronicle*, Jun. 23, 1897.
- "fifty cents": Boyle, *Maclean's*, Jun. 1, 1938.
- British Columbia: *Democrat and Chronicle*, Jul. 4, 1897; *Victoria Daily Times*, Jun. 18, 1897; *Victoria Daily Times*, Jun. 22, 1897; *Nanaimo Daily News*, Jun. 23, 1897; Rodney, *Joe Boyle*, 12–16.

- "if they put up": *Democrat and Chronicle*, Jul. 4, 1897.
- "delightful voyage": *Democrat and Chronicle*, Jul. 25, 1897.
- Band playing, food and supplies: *Democrat and Chronicle*, Jul. 25, 1897.
- Banjo: Taylor, *The Sourdough and the Queen*, 31.
- White Pass: *Dawson Daily News* (hereafter *DDN*), Midsummer Number, 1899; *Democrat and Chronicle*, Aug. 24, 1897; *San Francisco Examiner*, Aug. 21, 1897.
- "tedious, tiresome and treacherous": *Victoria Daily Times*, Mar. 23, 1926.
- "unhappy mortal": *Democrat and Chronicle*, Aug. 24, 1897.
- "firm character": Rodney, *Joe Boyle*, 19.
- "to escape the annoyance": Ogilvie, *Early Days on the Yukon and the Story of Its Gold Finds*, 223.
- Tugboat: Bankson, *The Klondike Nugget*, 1.
- Headlines: "Sacks of Gold from the Mines of the Clondyke," *San Francisco Chronicle*, Jul. 15, 1897; "Rush for the Land of the Golden Fleece. Thousands Preparing for the Invasion of the Clondyke," *San Francisco Chronicle*, Jul. 17, 1897; "Reports from the Far-Away Land Where the Earth Seems Lined with Gold," *San Francisco Examiner*, Jul. 18, 1897; "Inexhaustible Riches of the Northern El Dorado," *San Francisco Call*, Jul. 20, 1987; "Gold! Gold! Gold! Gold!" and "Sixty-Eight Rich Men on the Steamer Portland," *Seattle Post-Intelligencer*, Jul. 17, 1897.
- Ad: *Seattle Post-Intelligencer*, Jul. 17, 1897.
- Claimstaking: Rodney, *Joe Boyle*, 22.
- Dredges: Neufeld and Habiluk, *Make it Pay! Gold Dredge #4*, 1–7.
- "very pleasant": *Democrat and Chronicle*, Oct. 22, 1897.
- "gold-fever patient": *Democrat and Chronicle*, Jul. 25, 1897.
- Slavin mining: *Victoria Daily Times*, Mar. 1, 1926.
- Raphael "fidgeting": *San Francisco Examiner*, Oct 10, 1897.
- Sulphur Creek claim: *San Francisco Call*, Nov. 29, 1897.
- First dog team: *San Francisco Examiner*, Aug. 21, 1897.
- Well-digger: *Seattle Star*, Jan. 5, 1905.
- Bull cook: Bankson, *The Klondike Nugget*, 98.
- "let the house have a drink": Haskell, *Two Years in the Klondike and Alaskan Gold-Fields*, 374–375.
- Gates and eggs: Berton, *Klondike*, 81–82.
- "Stillwater Willie's Wedding Night": *DDN*, Apr. 24, 1900; Robert Coutts, "The Palace Grand Theatre: Dawson City, Y.T: An Interpretative History," Manuscript Report Number 428, Parks Canada, 1981, 44.
- Jail: Taylor, *The Sourdough and the Queen*, 25.
- Temperance meetings: Berton, *Prisoners of the North*, 8.
- ironic nickname: Gray, *Gold Diggers*, 114.
- "red cravat": *San Francisco Call*, Nov. 29, 1897.

- Trip outside: *DDN*, Midsummer Number, 1899; *Victoria Daily Colonist*, Nov. 28, 1897; *Democrat and Chronicle*, Dec. 26, 1897; *Seattle Post-Intelligencer*, Nov. 29, 1897; Rodney, *Joe Boyle*, 24.
- "tough as an old rubber boot" and "trail seemed endless": *Democrat and Chronicle*, Dec. 26, 1897.
- "life of the party": *Seattle Post-Intelligencer*, Nov. 29, 1897.
- "excellent management": *Seattle Post-Intelligencer*, Nov. 30, 1897.

EIGHT

- Patrick: *Victoria Times-Colonist*, Mar. 18, 1957; Whitehead, *The Patricks*, 14–19; Lester Patrick, "When Uncle Arthur Was Little Artha," in *The Hockey Book*, 38–39.
- Scalping tickets: McKinley, *Putting a Roof on Winter*, 78.
- Turkeys: *Citizen*, Dec. 25, 1897.
- "best hat": *Journal*, Jul. 13, 1897.
- Thirteen Club: *Citizen*, Dec. 21, 1929; *Journal*, Mar. 14, 1898; *Journal*, Jan. 11, 1898.
- "shackling superstition": *Citizen*, Dec. 21, 1929
- Young v MHC: *Journal*, Jan. 21, 1895.
- "squareness": *Tribune*, Dec. 26, 1896.
- Young to BC: *Citizen*, Mar. 24, 1896; *Citizen*, Mar. 30, 1896; *Journal*, Mar. 30, 1896; *Citizen*, Nov. 10, 1896; *Journal*, Nov. 12, 1896; *Journal*, Dec. 8, 1896.
- OHC drama: *Journal*, Dec. 11, 1896; *Journal*, Nov. 13, 1896; *Globe*, Nov. 14, 1896; *Journal*, Dec. 15, 1896.
- Kirby verse: *Journal*, Dec. 13, 1909.
- "Notified Young": Ross diary, Dec. 15, 1896.
- "permanently reside": *Free Press*, Dec. 29, 1896
- "creditable manner": *Citizen*, Jan. 11, 1897.
- Ross a star point: *Citizen*, Mar. 10, 1897.
- "blood on the moon": *Journal*, Mar. 8, 1897.
- Seagram: Frayne, *The Queen's Plate*, 76–78; Canadian Horse Racing Hall of Fame site, canadianhorseracinghalloffame.com.
- Waterloo: *Journal*, Nov. 4, 1897; *Journal*, Nov. 11, 1897; *Journal*, Dec. 9, 1897; *Globe*, Dec. 14, 1897.
- "put up the necessary": *Journal*, Nov. 4, 1897.
- "nobody to resign to": *Citizen*, Jan. 15, 1897.
- Capitals challenge: *Journal*, Mar. 13, 1897.
- "trustees beg respectfully": *Journal*, Mar. 13, 1897.
- Unenthusiastic crowd: *Journal*, Dec. 28, 1897.
- "best interests of hockey": Roxborough, *The Stanley Cup Story*, 27.
- OHC: Kitchen, *Win, Tie, or Wrangle*, 111; *Citizen*, Dec. 30, 1897.

- Westwick: *Journal*, Dec. 8, 1897; *Journal*, Jan. 22, 1898.
- Chittick: *Journal*, Feb. 14, 1898.
- "What is the matter": *Citizen*, Feb. 14, 1898.
- Young in crowd: *Journal*, Feb. 14, 1898; *Citizen*, Feb. 14, 1898.
- "Disgusting scrap": "The Victorias Victorious," *Citizen*, Feb. 14, 1898.
- "great piece of stuff": *Journal*, Nov. 10, 1898.
- Injuries: *Globe*, Nov. 9, 1898; *Journal*, Nov. 25, 1898; *Citizen*, Nov. 26, 1898.
- "concussion of the brain": *Citizen*, Nov. 26, 1898.
- "worst was feared": *Globe*, Nov. 28, 1898.
- Young and Kirby: "*Journal*, Dec. 5, 1898.
- Ten-minute penalty: *Journal*, Jan. 16, 1899; *Citizen*, Jan. 16, 1899.
- "Pa Young": *Citizen*, Jan. 28, 1899.
- "unquestionably the star": *Citizen*, Jan. 30, 1899.

NINE

- San Francisco: *San Francisco Chronicle*, Dec. 4, 1897.
- "nearly as large": *San Francisco Call*, Dec. 4, 1897.
- War Department: Taylor, *The Sourdough and the Queen*, 44.
- Boyle in Ottawa: Rodney, *Joe Boyle*, 26–27.
- Sifton: Dafoe, *Clifford Sifton in Relation to His Times*, 151–188; Steele, *Forty Years in Canada*, 290.
- "Famed for their success": *Gazette*, Mar. 17, 1898, 7.
- Slavin returns: Rodney, *Joe Boyle*, 28.
- Chilkoot checkpoint: Yukon Archives genealogy records.
- Contested territory: Dafoe, *Clifford Sifton in Relation to His Times*, 180.
- Edmonton Trail: Berton, *Klondike*, 216–218.
- "species of treason": Berton, *Klondike*, 216.
- 1,150 pounds: Steele, *Forty Years in Canada*, 295.
- 90 days: Berton, *Klondike*, 154–155.
- "knee deep in mud": Steele, *Forty Years in Canada*, 290.
- "gone the other": Adney, *The Klondike Stampede*, 47.
- "make the laws": Steele, *Forty Years in Canada*, 311.
- Bouncer: Berton, *Klondike*, 364.
- Crime: Coates and Morrison, *Land of the Midnight Sun*, 113.
- "the Boys": Treadgold, *An English Expert on the Klondike*, 70.
- "far from attractive": Steele, *Forty Years in Canada*, 321.
- Charges dismissed: Rodney, *Joe Boyle*, 34–35.
- "splendid results": DDN, Midsummer Number, 1899.
- "in the front ranks": Rodney, *Joe Boyle*, 35.
- Treadgold: sources include Treadgold, *An English Expert on the Klondike*; Taylor, *The Sourdough and the Queen*; Rodney, *Joe Boyle*; *The Guardian*,

Jan. 16, 1964; Marilyn Main Thomas, "Summer at 88 Below Bonanza," unpublished memoir, Klondike History Library and Archives at the Dawson City Museum.

TEN

- Shares: *Gazette*, Oct. 28, 1898.
- "gladiators": *Montreal Star*, Jan. 1, 1899.
- Arena: Michel Vigneault, "Montreal Ice-Hockey Rinks," *The Hockey Research Journal*, Spring 1997; Shubert, *Architecture on Ice*, 63, 72; "The Arena Opening," *Montreal Star*, Jan. 1, 1899.
- "refreshment room": *Montreal Star*, Jan. 1, 1899.
- Excursions: Kitchen, *Win, Tie, or Wrangle*, 51; *Journal*, Feb. 23, 1894; *Globe*, Mar. 1, 1899.
- "make their bets": Young, *100 Years of Dropping the Puck*, 35-36.
- Sporting goods: Kidd, *The Struggle for Canadian Sport*, 17-18.
- MAAA charges admission: Paul Kitchen, "They Refused the Stanley Cup," *Total Hockey*, 2d ed., 20–24; Don Morrow, "The Little Men of Iron: The 1902 Montreal Hockey Club," *Canadian Journal of History of Sport*, 1981.
- OHA: *The Ontario Hockey Association Constitution Rules of Competition and Laws of the Game*, 1900 edition; Alan Metcalfe, "Power: A Case Study of the Ontario Hockey Association, 1890–1936," *Journal of Sport History*, Vol. 19, No. 1, Spring, 1992, 5–25; *Total Hockey*, 2d ed., 29–31.
- 1897 meeting: *Globe*, Dec. 6, 1897; *Toronto Evening Star*, Dec. 6, 1897.
- "status of any individual": *Globe*, Dec. 6, 1897.
- "to be congratulated": *Toronto Evening Star*, Dec. 6, 1897.
- Berlin: *Globe*, Jan. 7, 1898; *Globe*, Jan. 21, 1898; *Journal*, Jan. 18, 1898; Young, *100 Years of Dropping the Puck*, 38–42; Harper, *A Great Game*, 22.
- Waubaushene: *Globe*, Mar. 1, 1899.
- Liffton: *Gazette*, Mar. 2, 1898.
- Waterloo: *Globe*, Mar. 7, 1898; *Globe*, Mar. 14, 1898; *Journal*, Mar. 15, 1898; *Globe*, Mar. 15, 1898; *Globe*, Mar. 17, 1898; *Globe*, Mar. 19, 1899.
- Berlin reinstated: *Globe*, Mar. 18, 1898.
- "wrongfully used": "*Globe*, Mar. 19, 1899.
- 1898 meeting: *Telegram*, Dec. 5, 1898; *Globe*, Dec. 5, 1898; *Toronto Evening Star*, Dec. 5, 1898; *Citizen*, Dec. 5, 1898; *Gazette*, Dec. 5, 1898.
- Robertson: R. Wayne Geen, "John Ross Robertson: Hockey Czar and Humanitarian," *The Hockey Research Journal*, 2004.
- "presiding genius": *Telegram*, Dec. 5, 1898.
- "ardent British imperialist": Harper, *A Great Game*, 24.
- "purest Canadian silver": *Telegram*, Dec. 5, 1898.
- "manly nation": *Telegram*, Dec. 5, 1898.

ELEVEN

- Game one: *Montreal Star*, Feb. 16, 1899; *Free Press*, Feb. 16, 1899; *Tribune*, Feb. 16, 1899; Gazette, Feb. 16, 1899.
- Bain: Bumsted, *Dictionary of Manitoba Biography*, 12.
- Winnipeg fans: *Free Press*, Feb. 16, 1899.
- "listless": *Montreal Star*, Feb. 20, 1899.
- "vicious swipe": *Tribune*, Feb. 20, 1899.
- Referees: Roxborough, *The Stanley Cup Story*, 36–39.
- Young and Davidson: *Journal*, Feb. 28, 1898; *Citizen*, Feb. 28, 1898; *Gazette*, Feb. 28, 1898; Paul Kitchen, "Early Goal Nets: The Evolution of an Idea," *The Hockey Research Journal*, 2001.
- Nets: Hewitt, *Down the Stretch*, 32–33; Paul Kitchen, "Early Goal Nets: The Evolution of an Idea," *The Hockey Research Journal*, 2001.
- "preserved the skins": Hewitt, *Down the Stretch*, 33.
- Stocking: *Gazette*, Jun. 21, 1956; Young, *100 Years of Dropping the Puck*, 85.
- Waghorne: Hewitt, *Down the Stretch*, 190; *Globe*, Jun. 20, 1956.
- Face-off: Fred Waghorne, "The Birth of the Face-Off," in *The Hockey Book*, 5–8.
- "that punishment": Roxborough, *The Stanley Cup Story*, 38.
- Split puck: Fred Waghorne, "The First Split Puck," in *The Hockey Book*, 9–10.
- "rule book says": Waghorne Hockey Hall of Fame bio, hhof.com.
- Findlay controversy: *Gazette*, Feb. 20, 1899; *Montreal Star*, Feb. 20, 1899; *Tribune*, Feb. 20, 1899; *Journal*, Feb. 20, 1899; *Free Press*, Feb. 20, 1899; *Free Press*, Feb 21, 1899; *Tribune*, Feb. 22, 1899; Roxborough, *The Stanley Cup Story*, 24–25; Zweig, *Stanley Cup*, 313.
- Findlay-Armytage conversation: *Journal*, Feb. 20, 1899.
- "gone crazy": *Montreal Star*, Feb. 20, 1899.
- "tangled-up fizzle": *Gazette*, Feb. 20, 1899.
- "welcome to the cup": *Tribune*, Feb. 20, 1899.
- "fiasco": Ross's diary, Feb. 19, 1899.
- Trustees met again: Ross's diary, Feb. 20, 1899.
- "the betting men": *Journal*, Feb. 20, 1899.
- "unsportsmanlike action": *Free Press*, Feb. 21, 1899.

TWELVE

- General sources for Dawson include Hal J. Guest, "A History of Dawson of the City of Dawson, Yukon Territory 1896–1920," Microfiche Report Series No. 7, Parks Canada, 1981; Hal J. Guest, "A Socioeconomic History of the Klondike Goldfields 1896–1966," Microfiche Report Series 181, Parks Canada, 1985; Hal J. Guest, "Dawson, San Francisco of the North, or Boomtown in a Bog," Manuscript Report Series No. 241, Parks Canada, 1978.

- Fall colours: Berton, *Klondike*, 164.
- "offer of a good thing": *Citizen*, Aug. 24, 1899.
- "scenery along the route": Steele, *Forty Years in Canada*, 319.
- Steamers: Berton, *Klondike*, 390; Richard J. Friesen, "Theme and Resource Assessment Yukon River Recreational and Historic Waterway," Manuscript Report Number 325, Parks Canada, 1978, 154.
- Dawson in 1899: *DDN*, Midsummer Number, Sept. 1899: Margaret Archibald "Grubstake to Grocery Store: The Klondike Emporium, 1897–1907" (1972), revised and edited by Margaret A. Carter (1973), Manuscript Report No. 178, Parks Canada, 1981, 93.
- "loose characters": Steele, *Forty Years in Canada*, 323.
- "given the opportunity": Steele, *Forty Years in Canada*, 327.
- "sound constitutions": Steele, *Forty Years in Canada*, 322.
- Steele fights corruption: Gray, *Gold Diggers*, 333–338.
- "cannot understand": *DDN*, Sept. 11, 1899.
- "nefarious schemes": Gray, *Gold Diggers*, 348.
- Boyle chaired meeting: Gray, *Gold Diggers*, 348.
- Young to *Sun*: *Citizen*, Dec. 2, 1899.
- Newspapers: Bankson, *The Klondike Nugget*, 1–96; Macdonald and O'Keefe, *The Klondike's "Dear Little Nugget,"* 5–16, 111; Gray, *Gold Diggers*, 219–228; Edward F. Bush, "The Dawson Daily News: Journalism on Canada's Last Frontier," Manuscript Report Series No. 48, Parks Canada, 1971; Richard C. Stuart and William A. Waiser, "The Dawson News Publishing Company, 1899–1954," Microfiche Report Series No. 362, Parks Canada, 1984.
- "Let's get started": Macdonald and O'Keefe, *The Klondike's "Dear Little Nugget,"* 6.
- "boiling pot of hell": Bankson, *The Klondike Nugget*, 24.
- "government propaganda sheet": Bankson, *The Klondike Nugget*, 94.
- Allen sells Nugget: Macdonald and O'Keefe, *The Klondike's "Dear Little Nugget,"* 125–127.
- White: Macdonald and O'Keefe, *The Klondike's "Dear Little Nugget,"* 32–35; Les McLaughlin, "Stroller White: Newspaper Man," *The Yukoner*, Apr. 2002.
- Woodside: *DDN*, Mar. 30, 1901.
- *Sun* was government organ: *Citizen*, Dec. 2, 1899.
- Special correspondent: *Citizen*, Aug. 24, 1899.
- "mistaken idea": *Citizen*, Dec. 2, 1899.
- "turned against milk": *Citizen*, Jan. 5, 1900.
- "promiscuous dancing": *Citizen*, Dec. 2, 1899.
- Ogilvie: Gray, *Gold Diggers*, 65–68.
- "made a survey": *The New York Times*, Jul. 22, 1897.

- Related to Sifton: Hall, *Clifford Sifton Volume II*, 13.
- "deserved celebrity more": *Globe*, Jul. 11, 1898.
- "delightful companion": Steele, *Forty Years in Canada*, 319.
- Fawcett: Bankson, *The Klondike Nugget*, 106–109; Macdonald and O'Keefe, *The Klondike's "Dear Little Nugget,"* 45–47; Berton, *Klondike*, 313–317.
- "going to change things": Bankson, *The Klondike Nugget*, 108.
- *Nugget* headlines: "The Gold Commissioner Exposed," Jul. 23, 1898: "Colossal Moral Turpitude," Aug. 27, 1898; "Fawcett's Scheme," Sept. 24, 1898; "Get Him Out," Oct. 5, 1898; "Goodbye Fawcett," Nov. 9, 1898.
- "inflammatory and seditious": Edward F. Bush, "The Dawson Daily News: Journalism on Canada's Last Frontier," Manuscript Report Series No. 48, Parks Canada, 1971, 20.
- 133 days: Macdonald and O'Keefe, *The Klondike's "Dear Little Nugget,"* 112.
- Restrictive mining laws: "Dawson's Great $300,000 Fire," *Citizen*, Feb. 20, 1900.
- Corporate investment: *DDN* Midsummer Number, 1899.
- Ogilvie forecasts: "Report of the Commissioner of the Yukon Territory," Oct. 25, 1900, 5; Coates and Morrison, *Land of the Midnight Sun*, 150.

THIRTEEN
- Breakup: *DDN*, May 5, 1900; *DDN*, May 8, 1900; *DDN*, May 9, 1900; *DDN*, May 9, 1900; *Yukon News*, May 3, 2018.
- "gladness and incessant firing": *DDN*, May 8, 1900.
- "mercury frozen": *Citizen*, Feb. 1, 1900.
- Dawson Hockey club: *Klondike Nugget* (hereafter *Nugget*), Oct. 12, 1898; Firth, *An Illustrated Encyclopedia of Yukon Sport*, 137; *Nugget*, Mar. 18, 1899; Macdonald and O'Keefe, *The Klondike's "Dear Little Nugget,"* 92.
- Sports committee: *DDN*, May 8, 1900.
- Militia: *DDN*, May 9, 1900.
- "contented faces": *Citizen*, Jun. 15, 1900.
- Clarke lawsuit: Edward F. Bush, "The Dawson Daily News: Journalism on Canada's Last Frontier," Manuscript Report Series No. 48, Parks Canada, 1971.
- Young testifies: *DDN*, May 4, 1900.
- Athletic Association: *DDN*, Jul. 17, 1900; *DDN*, Jul. 31, 1900; *Citizen*, Aug. 18, 1900; *DDN*, Jul. 27, 1900.
- "up-to-date athletic association": *Citizen*, Aug. 18, 1900.
- "town boys": *Citizen*, Dec. 29, 1899.
- Hockey league: Firth, *An Illustrated Encyclopedia of Yukon Sport*, 137: *Journal*, Dec. 19, 1900.

- Woodside: *DDN*, Mar. 30, 1901; Edward F. Bush, "The Dawson Daily News: Journalism on Canada's Last Frontier," Manuscript Report Series No. 48, Parks Canada, 1971, 66.
- "no apologies": *Yukon Sun* (hereafter *Sun*), Feb. 9, 1901.
- "patriotic course": *DDN*, Mar. 30, 1901.
- League: *Nugget*, Feb. 11, 1901.
- Ad for skates and sticks: *DDN*, Feb. 27, 1901.
- Congdon: Edward F. Bush, "The Dawson Daily News: Journalism on Canada's Last Frontier," Manuscript Report Series No. 48, Parks Canada, 1971, 63.
- Senkler played against Young: *The Ontario Hockey Association Constitution Rules of Competition and Laws of the Game*, 1900.
- "pleasure of knowing him": *Citizen*, Jun. 15, 1900.
- "vouch for his honesty": Letter to Ogilvie, Weldon C. Young Government file, Yukon Archives, Dec. 19, 1900.
- Mining recorder appointment: Letter from Ogilvie, Weldon C. Young Government file, Yukon Archives, Jan. 31, 1901.
- Reimbursement: Senkler letter to Ross, Weldon C. Young Government file, Yukon Archives, Sept. 7, 1901.
- "practicable and just": *Journal*, Oct. 30, 1901.
- "a few lines": *Citizen*, Aug. 18, 1900.
- Dawson and Minto visit: Margaret Archibald, "Grubstake to Emporium: The Klondike Emporium, 1897–1907" (1972), Manuscript Report Number 178, Parks Canada; "At Dawson," *Citizen*, Aug. 18, 1900.
- "criminal administration": Hall, *Clifford Sifton Volume II*, 1.
- "our system of Government": Hall, *Clifford Sifton Volume II*, 3.
- Reluctance to allow self-government: Coates and Morrison, *Land of the Midnight Sun*, 105.
- Sifton dissatisfied with Ogilvie: Hall, *Clifford Sifton Volume II*, 13–14.
- Ogilvie "resigns": Coates and Morrison, *Land of the Midnight Sun*, 179.
- Steele not impressed with Ogilvie's partying: Charlotte Gray, "Faded Hero," *The Walrus*, Oct. 12, 2010.
- "one long nightmare": Steele, *Forty Years in Canada*, 329.
- "little whiskey": Ogilvie, *Early Days on the Yukon and the Story of Its Gold Finds*, 217.
- "pernicious kind of poison": Hal J. Guest, "Saloons, Gambling Halls and the Traffic in Liquor" in "A History of Dawson of the City of Dawson, Yukon Territory 1896–1920," Microfiche Report Series No. 7, Parks Canada, 1981.
- Libraries: Hal J. Guest, "A Socioeconomic History of the Klondike Goldfields 1896–1966," Microfiche Report Series 181, Parks Canada, 1985, 201.

- "vented their spleens": Hal J. Guest, "A Socioeconomic History of the Klondike Goldfields 1896–1966," Microfiche Report Series 181, Parks Canada, 1985, 213.
- Sports in Dawson: *Toronto Daily Star*, Jun. 14, 1901; *Yukon World* (hereafter *World*), Dec. 30, 1904; Hal J. Guest, "A Socioeconomic History of the Klondike Goldfields 1896–1966," Microfiche Report Series 181, Parks Canada, 1985, 212.

FOURTEEN

- Shamrocks: John Matthew Barlow, "'Scientific Aggression': Irishness, Manliness, Class and Commercialization in the Shamrock Hockey Club of Montreal, 1894–1901," in Wong, *Coast to Coast*; Farrell, *Hockey*, 37–39.
- "first-class players": *Citizen*, Dec. 6, 1898.
- Creation of CAHL: Don Morrow, "The Little Men of Iron: The 1902 Montreal Hockey Club," *Canadian Journal of History of Sport*, 1981.
- "fancy play": Farrell, *Hockey*, 64.
- "busiest man": Farrell, *Hockey*, 102.
- Coloured Hockey League: Adams, *Long Shots*, 22–24; Vaughan, *The Puck Starts Here*, 186–188.
- "prettiest spectacle": Farrell, *Hockey*, 71.
- "better to give": *Gazette*, Feb. 1, 1901.
- Bulletins: *Free Press*, Feb. 1, 1901.
- "as one man": *Free Press*, Feb. 1, 1901.
- Vics carried off: *Tribune*, Feb. 1, 1901.
- "feeling fine": *Free Press*, Feb. 1, 1901.
- "simply wearies": *Tribune*, Feb. 1, 1901.
- "thinking strong thoughts": *Journal*, Jan. 24, 1901.
- "dead man": *Gazette*, Feb. 1, 1901.
- "ruder, undesirable element": Farrell, *Hockey*, 42.
- Indigenous players: *The New York Times*, Jun. 25, 2018.
- Gingras stickhandler: Coleman, *The Trail of the Stanley Cup*, 57.
- French-Canadian players: Michel Vigneault, "The Catholic Connection in Montreal Hockey 1891–1917," *The Hockey Research Journal*, 1994; Kitchen, *Win, Tie, or Wrangle*, 107.
- "hammer as much as a mirror": Gopnik, *Winter*, 156–157.
- "tribal urge": Gopnik, *Winter*, 159.
- Dawson's rinks: Emil Forrest remembrance, Klondike History Library and Archives; *DDN*, Nov. 22, 1904.
- "hereby challenge": *Tribune*, Jul. 9, 1901.
- "couldn't beat a drum": quoted in Zweig, *Stanley Cup*, 308.
- "ever formed": "The Stanley Cup," *Journal*, May 1, 1893.
- 1901 Census put Dawson population at 9,142.

- "every hope": *Toronto Daily Star*, Jul. 11, 1901.
- "given a good time": *Tribune*, Jul. 9, 1901.
- McKay: *Free Press*, Oct 24, 1901.
- Trustees never heard back: *Journal*, Dec. 13, 1901.
- "enjoyable trip": *Vancouver Daily World*, Oct. 24, 1901.

FIFTEEN

- Fuller's buildings: Margaret E. Archibald, "A Structural History of the Administration Building, Dawson, Yukon Territory," Manuscript Report Series Number 217, Parks Canada, 1977; Edward F. Bush, "Commissioners of the Yukon, 1897–1918," Canadian Historic Sites: Occasional Papers in Archaeology and History No. 10; Dawson City Museum and Historical Society leaflet.
- "worked so hard": Margaret E. Archibald, "A Structural History of the Administration Building, Dawson, Yukon Territory," Manuscript Report Series Number 217, Parks Canada, 1977.
- Ross: Edward F. Bush, "Commissioners of the Yukon, 1897–1918," Canadian Historic Sites: Occasional Papers in Archaeology and History No. 10.
- Berry: Berton, *Klondike*, 62–63.
- Mulrooney: Duncan, *Frontier Spirit*, 125–131.
- Vice: Hall, *Clifford Sifton Volume II*, 9; Hal J. Guest, "Saloons, Gambling Halls and the Traffic in Liquor" in "A History of Dawson of the City of Dawson, Yukon Territory 1896-1920," Microfiche Report Series No. 7, Parks Canada, 1981.
- Newspapers: Edward F. Bush, "The Dawson Daily News: Journalism on Canada's Last Frontier," Manuscript Report Series No. 48, Parks Canada, 1971.
- DAAA: *Nugget*, Sept. 22, 1902; *Nugget*, Nov. 10; *DDN*, Jul. 20, 1909; Government DAAA file, Yukon Archives.
- Boyle was a founder: "They Knew Joe Boyle," *Maclean's*, Nov. 1, 1938.
- "pronounced chimerical": *Nugget*, Nov. 10, 1902.
- "carry on the business": Government DAAA file, Yukon Archives.
- "prosaic easterners": *Nugget*, Oct. 11, 1902.
- Boyle: *Nugget*, Oct. 8, 1902; Rodney, *Joe Boyle*, 45.
- "entirely revolutionized": *Nugget*, Nov. 18, 1902.
- Opening: *Nugget*, Nov. 25, 1902; *Sun*, Nov. 25, 1902.
- "leave their wraps": *Sun*, Nov. 25, 1902.
- Concert: *Sun*, Feb. 8, 1903.
- Boxing: Firth, *An Illustrated Encyclopedia of Yukon Sport*, 62–64; Robert Coutts, "The Palace Grand Theatre: Dawson City, Y.T: An Interpretative History," Manuscript Report Number 428, 1981, 43.
- "premier boxing club": *The Baltimore Sun*, Jan. 16, 1904.

- Curling: "*DDN*, Jul. 20, 1909.
- School enrolment: *DDN*, Oct. 9, 1902.
- Petition: *Nugget*, Nov. 15, 1902 1; *Nugget*, Nov. 21, 1902, 1; Backhouse, *Children of the Yukon*, 145–146.
- "jurists have applied": *Sun*, Feb. 24, 1903.
- Attendance at Jawbones v. Sawbones: *Sun*, Feb. 26, 1903.
- Rematch: *Sun*, Mar. 8, 1903.
- Fat men: *Nugget*, Mar. 4, 1903; *Nugget*, Mar. 11, 1902; *Sun*, Mar. 11, 1903; *Sun*, Mar. 12, 1903; *Nugget*, Mar. 12, 1903.
- "lead-pipe cinch": *Nugget*, Mar. 12, 1903.
- "pranced around like Og": *Sun*, Mar. 12, 1903.
- "$10,000": *Vancouver Province* (hereafter *Province*), Sept. 13, 1902.

SIXTEEN
- Whistle: *Telegram*, Jan. 22, 1902; *Globe*, Jan. 23, 1902; *Telegram*, Jan. 24, 1902; Roxborough, *The Stanley Cup Story*, 20.
- Auditorium Rink: Morris Mott, "'An Immense Hold in the Public Estimation': The First Quarter Century of Hockey in Manitoba, 1886–1911," *Manitoba History*, Number 43, Spring/Summer 2002.
- Wellingtons v. Vics: *Tribune*, Jan. 22, 1902; *Globe*, Jan. 22, 1902; *Telegram*, Jan. 24, 1902.
- "monopoly": *Globe*, Jan. 23, 1902.
- "hockey nabobs": *Telegram*, Jan. 24, 1902.
- Lamont: *Telegram*, Jan. 25, 1902.
- "fairly beaten": *Toronto Daily Star*, Jan. 25, 1902.
- Return: *Telegram*, Jan. 25, 1902; *Toronto Daily Star*, Jan. 29, 1902; *Telegram*, Jan. 29, 1902; *Toronto Daily Star*, Jan. 30, 1902.
- 1902 meeting: *Globe*, Dec. 8, 1902.
- "uproarious cheers": *Globe*, Dec. 4, 1899.
- Robertson: Harper, *A Great Game*, 24; Hewitt, *Down the Stretch*, 185.
- "prates and preaches": *Globe*, Dec. 3, 1900.
- London: *Globe*, Jan. 17, 1901; *London Free Press*, Jan. 19, 1901; *London Free Press*, Jan. 21, 1901; *Globe*, Jan. 28, 1901; *Globe*, Jan. 29, 1901.
- "monstrous rascality": *Globe*, Jan. 29, 1901.
- Orillia: *Globe*, Jan. 25, 1901.
- "try its fortunes": *Globe*, Dec. 9, 1901.
- "delighted with your showing": *Tribune*, Jan. 22, 1902.
- Gibson: J. W. (Bill) Fitsell, "Doc Gibson: The Eye in the IHL," *The Hockey Research Journal*, 2004; *Detroit Free Press*, Sept. 30, 1903; Bill Sproule, "Houghton: The Birthplace of Professional Hockey," *The Hockey Research Journal*, 2004; Ernie Fitzsimmons, "IHL Players: The Professional Pioneers," *The Hockey Research Journal*, 2004; Daniel Scott

Mason, "The Origins and Development of the International Hockey League and Its Effects on the Sport of Professional Ice Hockey in North America," thesis paper, University of British Columbia, 1992.

- "some of the fastest" and "make no bones": *Montreal Star*, Dec. 14, 1901.

SEVENTEEN

- OHC challenge: Ross diary, Feb. 25, 1902.
- "Declined": Ross diary, Feb. 26, 1902.
- Montreal challenge: Ross diary, Mar. 2, 1902; *Herald*, Mar. 3, 1902; *Gazette*, Mar. 4, 1902.
- "big undertaking": *Free Press*, Mar. 4, 1902.
- Referee: *Montreal Star*, Mar. 5, 1902; *Montreal Star*, Mar. 5, 1902; *Tribune*, Mar. 6, 1902; *Gazette*, Mar. 6, 1902; *Journal*, Mar. 7, 1902; *Free Press*, Mar. 8, 1902; *Gazette*, Mar. 8, 1902; Don Morrow, "The Little Men of Iron: The 1902 Montreal Hockey Club," *Canadian Journal of History of Sport*, 1981.
- "preposterous": *Montreal Star*, Mar. 5, 1902.
- "draw lots": *Free Press*, Mar. 8, 1902.
- Thirteen: *Montreal Star*, Mar. 8, 1902; *Montreal Star*, Mar. 6, 1902; *Tribune*, Mar. 6, 1902; *Montreal Star*, Mar. 10, 1902; *Tribune*, Mar. 10, 1902.
- "hoodooed us": *Montreal Star*, Mar. 8, 1902.
- CPR station: *Gazette*, Mar. 10, 1902.
- Sprints, rub downs, greeted by 800: *Herald*, Mar. 11, 1902; *Gazette*, Mar. 12, 1902; *Montreal Star*, Mar. 12, 1902.
- Preparations: *Tribune*, Mar. 10; 1902; *Herald*, Mar. 11, 1902.
- Snickers: *Montreal Star*, Mar. 22, 1902.
- MHC: Don Morrow, "The Little Men of Iron: The 1902 Montreal Hockey Club," *Canadian Journal of History of Sport*, 1981.
- Teams' styles: *Free Press*, Mar. 4, 1902.
- Boon's weight: *Tribune*, Mar. 11, 1902.
- Lineup and scalpers: *Gazette*, Mar. 14, 1902.
- "broad lake": *Herald*, Mar. 14, 1902.
- "sliding on their stomachs": *Montreal Star*, Mar. 14, 1902.
- Temperature drop: *Montreal Star*, Mar. 15, 1902.
- Second game: *Gazette*, Mar. 17, 1902; *Citizen*, Mar. 17, 1902; *Free Press*, Mar. 18, 1902.
- "enthusiastic audience": *Tribune*, Mar. 18, 1902.
- Bulletins: *Montreal Star*, Mar. 18, 1902, 2.
- "hardest fought battles": *Montreal Star*, Mar. 18, 1902.
- Montreal: *Gazette*, Mar. 12, 1902; *Montreal Star*, Mar. 13, 1902.
- "paraded the streets": *Montreal Star*, Mar. 18, 1902.
- Spanjaardt: Coleman, *The Trail of the Stanley Cup*, 73.
- "plucky little men of steel": *Montreal Star*, Mar. 14, 1902.

- "Lionmen of Iron": *Tribune*, Mar. 19, 1901.
- Return to Montreal: *Montreal Star*, Mar. 22, 1902; *Herald*, Mar. 22, 1902; *Tribune*, Mar. 22, 1902; *Free Press*, Mar. 22, 1902.
- "at least equal honors": *Tribune*, Mar. 13, 1902.
- "will never give up": *Free Press*, Mar. 19, 1902.
- Game two: *Free Press*, Feb. 2, 1903; *Gazette*, Feb. 2, 1903; *Journal*, Feb. 2, 1903; *Tribune*, Feb. 2, 1903; *Citizen*, Feb. 2, 1903.
- "rattlingly good": *Gazette*, Feb. 2, 1903.
- Meeting with trustees: *Free Press*, Feb. 2, 1903.
- "two seconds or two hours": *Gazette*, Feb. 2, 1903.
- Game three: *Tribune*, Feb. 3, 1903; *Free Press*, Feb. 3, 1903; *Gazette*, Feb. 3, 1903.
- Controversies and animosity: *Free Press*, Feb. 4, 1903; *Tribune*, Feb. 5, 1903.
- "None whatever": *Journal*, Feb. 3, 1903.
- "not properly administered": *Tribune*, Feb. 2, 1903.
- Kirby: *Journal*, Feb. 4, 1903.
- Boon shakes hands: *Free Press*, Feb. 5, 1903.
- "return the pewter": *Free Press*, Feb. 5, 1903.
- Attendance: *Gazette*, Mar. 2, 1903.
- Gate: *Journal*, Feb. 5, 1903.
- Challenges: *Journal*, Jan. 10, 1903; *Journal*, Feb. 20, 1903.
- CAHL meeting and Ross's letter: *Journal*, Mar. 2, 1903; *Gazette*, Mar. 2, 1903.
- Ross suggests MHC defend Cup: *Gazette*, Mar. 4, 1903.
- "would be absurd": *Tribune*, Mar. 4, 1903.
- Game one: *Journal*, Mar. 9, 1903; *Citizen*, Mar. 9, 1903; *Gazette*, Mar. 9, 1903.
- Westwick: *Journal*, Jan. 26, 1957; Kitchen, *Win, Tie, or Wrangle*, 102–103.
- "lightning flash": *Journal*, Jan. 5, 1903.
- Game two: *Journal*, Mar. 11, 1903; *Citizen*, Mar. 11, 1903; Kitchen, *Win, Tie, or Wrangle*, 115.
- End of the era: Don Morrow, "The Little Men of Iron: The 1902 Montreal Hockey Club," *Canadian Journal of History of Sport*, 1981.
- Attendance: *Gazette*, Mar. 2, 1903; *Journal*, Mar. 9, 1903.
- "fashionable": *Journal*, Jan. 5, 1903.

EIGHTEEN
- Labelle and Fournier: Coates and Morrison, *Strange Things Done*, 30–58; *Sun*, Jan. 18, 1903; *Province*, Jan. 20, 1903; *Whitehorse Daily Star*, Jan. 24, 1903; *Tribune*, Jan. 21, 1903; *Sun*, Jan. 25, 1903; *Nugget*, Feb. 26, 1903.
- King hanging: Report of the North-West Mounted Police, Part III, 1900.
- "amateur" with "iron nerves": *Sun*, Jan. 15, 1903.

- Dawson hangings: *Detroit Free Press*, Oct. 27, 1907.
- Banquet: *San Francisco Call*, Jan. 12, 1901; *The Morning Oregonian*, Jan. 18, 1901; *DDN*, Mar. 30, 1901.
- Eilbeck: *Gazette*, Sept. 15, 1881; *Gazette*, May 11, 1888; Humber, *Diamonds of the North*, 104–105; *The Kingston Whig-Standard*, Apr. 25, 2009; *Province*, Jun. 9, 1911; *Vancouver Daily Times*, Oct. 23, 1899; *Citizen*, Oct. 30, 1899, p3; *DDN*, Jan. 12, 1900; *Buffalo Commercial*, Jan. 7, 1902.
- "baseball crank": *Whitehorse Daily Star*, Jul. 8, 1904.
- Dust-up: *Sun*, Jun. 24, 1903; *DDN*, Jun. 24, 1903.
- Indoor baseball: *Whitehorse Daily Star*, Apr. 22, 1993; *DDN*, Sept. 20, 1904.
- Eilbeck was stocky: *DDN*, Jan. 14, 1905.
- Civil Service: *DDN*, Oct. 9, 1902.
- Athletics: *Nugget*, Oct. 11, 1902.
- McLennan: Queen's University Archives; Porsild, *Gamblers and Dreamers*, 154.
- Kennedy: *Journal*, Jun. 14, 1902.
- "something of a corker": *Nugget*, Apr. 7, 1902.
- Young with Police: *Sun*, Jan. 4, 1903.
- Civils v. Athletics: *Sun*, Mar. 1, 1903.
- "game was a stemwinder": *Nugget*, Mar. 2, 1903.
- League controversy: *Nugget*, Mar. 4, 1903; *Nugget*, Mar. 4, 1903.
- "do not consider": *Nugget*, Mar. 4, 1903.
- Eagles disbanded: *Sun*, Mar. 5, 1903.
- Challenge to Civils: *Sun*, Mar. 7, 1903.
- Dinner and opera: *Sun*, Mar. 6, 1903.
- "will be easy": *Sun*, Mar. 13, 1903.
- Tour plans: *DDN*, Mar. 11, 1903; *Nugget*, Mar. 14, 1903; *Nugget*, Apr. 28, 1903.
- "Dad" Eilbeck: *Nugget*, Mar. 14, 1903.
- Queen's tour: *Queen's University Journal*, Jan. 25, 1896.
- "replies are satisfactory": *DDN*, Apr. 28, 1903.
- Cost of trip: *Sun*, Apr. 29, 1903.
- Marriages and births: *DDN*, Aug. 10, 1903.
- Newspapers: Edward F. Bush, "The Dawson Daily News: Journalism on Canada's Last Frontier," Manuscript Report Series No. 48, Parks Canada, 1971.
- "throws out his chest": *Dawson Record*, Aug. 25, 1903.
- "greatest exhibition": "*Dawson Record*, Sept. 17, 1903.
- Accusations: Weldon C. Young Government file, Yukon Archives; *Sun*, Feb. 20, 1903; *DDN*, Feb. 25, 1903; *Province*, Feb. 25, 1903.
- "prompt action": *Sun*, Feb. 24, 1903.
- Acquittal: *Dawson Record*, Sept. 1, 1903; *Dawson Record*, Sept. 22, 1903; *Citizen*, Sep. 2, 1903; Weldon C. Young Government file, Yukon Archives.

- "wholly deprived": *Dawson Record*, Sept. 22, 1903.
- Young mining: *Sun*, Oct. 1, 1903.
- "untrammelled subject": *Dawson Record*, Sept. 22, 1903.
- Eilbeck vacation: *DDN*, Oct. 1, 1903.
- CAHL meeting: "Montreal Amateur Athletic Association, MG 28, I 351 Volume 6, File 6, Canadian Amateur Hockey League, Secretary's Book, Dec. 1898–Dec. 1905," LAC.
- "nerve to challenge": *Globe*, Dec. 29, 1903.

NINETEEN

- "perfectly parted": *Citizen*, Sept. 25, 1916.
- Thomas D'Arcy McGee: McGoogan, *Celtic Lightning*, 103–116.
- McGee: Kitchen, *Win, Tie, or Wrangle*, 105–106; *Citizen*, Sept. 25, 1916.
- "coming man": *Journal*, Feb. 25, 1897.
- "as good a forward": *Journal*, Jan. 19, 1899.
- "dodger and stickhandler": *Journal*, Jan. 18, 1900.
- Eye injury: *Citizen*, Mar. 22, 1900; *Citizen*, Sept. 25, 1916; McKinley, *Putting a Roof on Winter*, 42; Kitchen, *Win, Tie, or Wrangle*, 106.
- posthumously bestowed: Nic Clarke, "'The Greater and Grimmer Game': Sport as an Arbiter of Military Fitness in the British Empire—The Case of 'One-Eyed' Frank McGee," *The International Journal of the History of Sport*, 2011.
- "proportionately pleased": *Tribune*, Jan. 13, 1903.
- "always on the puck": *Tribune*, Jan. 19, 1903.
- "till you see them": *Journal*, Mar. 14, 1903.
- Players to Pittsburgh: *Citizen*, Mar. 14, 1903; Coleman, *The Trail of the Stanley Cup*, 76.
- OHC: Roxborough, *The Stanley Cup Story*, 27.
- Hutton: Cameron, *Hockey Hall of Fame Book of Goalies*, 21–22; *Journal*, Mar. 14, 1903.
- "cool head and quick eye": *Journal*, Mar. 14, 1903.
- Smith: Kitchen, *Win, Tie, or Wrangle*, 103–104; *Tribune*, Aug. 3, 1903.
- Pulford: *Journal*, Oct. 31, 1940; *Citizen*, Oct. 31, 1940.
- Spittal to WPHL: *Pittsburgh Press*, Feb. 13, 1903.
- Five goals: *Gazette*, Feb. 9, 1903.
- "McGee is a wonder": *Citizen*, Mar. 11, 1903.
- Dey's Rinks: Paul Kitchen, *Dey Brothers's Rinks Were Home to the Senators*, The Historical Society of Ottawa, Bytown Pamphlet Series, No. 46; Kitchen, *Win, Tie, or Wrangle*, 112.
- Capacity: *Citizen*, Nov. 25, 1903.
- "aisles were crammed": *Journal*, Mar. 11, 1903.
- "cannot be run on wind": *Journal*, Mar. 13, 1903.

- "family compact": *Journal*, Mar. 11, 1903.
- "almost blind": *Journal*, Mar. 14, 1903.
- 1,000 at second game: *Gazette*, Mar. 16, 1903.
- Lost $800: *Citizen*, Mar. 16, 1903.
- Shillington: *Citizen*, Jan. 11, 1934; *Journal*, Jan. 11, 1934; Kitchen, *Win, Tie, or Wrangle*, 118–119.
- "call ourselves the Silver Seven": *Journal*, Jan. 26, 1957.
- "animal rhythm": McGee's Hockey Hall of Fame biography, hhof.com.
- Cresceus: Nic Clarke, "'The Greater and Grimmer Game': Sport as an Arbiter of Military Fitness in the British Empire—The Case of 'One-Eyed' Frank McGee," *The International Journal of the History of Sport*, 2011.
- "checks to win": *Journal*, Mar. 11, 1903.
- "very aggressive player": *Journal*, Mar. 7, 1902.
- Finger bowl: McKinley, *Putting a Roof on Winter*, 45; *Dictionary of Canadian Biography*, www.biographi.ca.
- Minto: *Journal*, Jan. 19, 1903.
- Fans across country: Kitchen, *Win, Tie, or Wrangle*, 119–120.
- Silver Seven rarely used: Paul Kitchen, "They Weren't the Silver Seven: The Search for Ottawa's Nickname," *The Hockey Research Journal*, 2001.

TWENTY
- Game one: *Free Press*, Dec. 31, 1903; *Journal*, Dec. 31, 1903; *Citizen*, Dec. 31, 1903; *Tribune*, Dec. 31, 1903.
- "dirtiest match": *Tribune*, Dec. 31, 1903.
- "one of the bloodiest battles": *Citizen*, Dec. 31, 1903.
- Pavilion: Kitchen, *Win, Tie, or Wrangle*, 130–131; *Citizen*, Nov. 25, 1903; "Statement of Cultural Values and Heritage Impact Assessment," Submitted by Commonwealth Historic Resource Management Limited to the City of Ottawa, Aug. 2010; Aberdeen Pavilion page on National Historic Sites of Canada website, www.pc.gc.ca.
- "Cup Likely to Stay": *Journal*, Dec. 31, 1903.
- "merely shows": *Free Press*, Jan. 2, 1904.
- Game three: *Citizen*, Jan. 5, 1904.
- Ottawa v. Vics: *Gazette*, Feb. 1, 1904; *Journal*, Feb. 1, 1904; *Citizen*, Feb. 1, 1904.
- "discordant band": *Gazette*, Feb. 1, 1904.
- Ottawa leaves CAHL: *Journal*, Feb. 8, 1904; *Citizen*, Feb. 9, 1904; *Gazette*, Feb. 8, 1904; *Gazette*, Feb. 9, 1904; Kitchen, *Win, Tie, or Wrangle*, 125–127.
- "will resign": *Gazette*, Feb. 8, 1904.
- Ottawa joins FAHL: *Citizen*, Feb. 10, 1904; *Gazette*, Feb. 11, 1904; *Citizen*, Feb. 11, 1904.
- $1,500 offer: *Telegram*, Feb. 12, 1904.

- "letter went into the waste basket": *Journal*, Feb. 13, 1904.
- Rebels: *Journal*, Dec. 19, 1903; Ross diary, Dec. 23, 1903, Jan. 6, 1904, and Jan. 20, 1904.
- Married men v. single men: Ross diary, Feb. 17, 1904.
- Threat to take matter to Stanley: *Journal*, Feb. 16, 1904.
- Canard: *Gazette*, Feb. 17, 1904.
- "ordinary circumstances": *Gazette*, Feb. 18, 1904.
- Requested one Manitoba champion: *Journal*, Feb. 17, 1904.
- Berlin: *Globe*, Feb. 23, 1904; *Journal*, Feb. 23, 1904.
- Seibert: Hockey Hall of Fame biography, hhof.com.
- "tin-foil champions": *Telegram*, Feb. 27, 1904.
- "could beat anything": *Globe*, Feb. 23, 1904.
- Amherst: *Journal*, Mar. 5, 1904.
- "prepared to defend": *Journal*, Feb. 23, 1904.
- "consider we have won": *Gazette*, Feb. 25, 1904.
- 1903 meeting: *Globe*, Dec. 7. 1903; Harper, *A Great Game*, 47.
- "patriotic organization": *Globe*, Dec. 7. 1903.
- Hewitt: Peter Wilton, "Pioneer Executive," in *Total Hockey*, 29–31; *Gazette*, Apr. 16, 1932.
- Journalists: Young, *100 Years of Dropping the Puck*, 62–63.
- "if you can get enough votes": Hewitt, *Down the Stretch*, 184.
- "business was conducted": *Globe*, Dec. 3, 1900.
- Initially reluctant: Hewitt, *Down the Stretch*, 184–185.
- Informal meetings: Young, *100 Years of Dropping the Puck*, 64.
- Phillips: Hewitt, *Down the Stretch*, 214; Coleman, *The Trail of the Stanley Cup*, 77.
- "vigorous, brainy hockey": *Journal*, Feb. 24, 1904.
- "comparatively free from roughness": *Gazette*, Feb. 24, 1904.
- "actual warfare": *Telegram*, Feb. 24, 1904.
- "hammering and hammering": *Globe*, Feb. 24, 1904.
- Nelson wrote Globe article: *Journal*, Feb. 25, 1904.
- "permits downright brutality": *Toronto Daily Star*, Feb. 24, 1904.
- "trickery occurred": Hewitt, *Down the Stretch*, 188.
- Throw game rumour: *Telegram*, Feb. 25, 1904.
- "did not play roughly": *Telegram*, Feb. 27, 1904.
- "awful howl": *Citizen*, Feb. 26, 1904.
- Remaining challenges: *Journal*, Feb. 26, 1904; *Gazette*, Feb. 27, 1904.
- "O.H.A. nabobs" and "boy's club": *Journal*, Mar. 8, 1904.
- Train to Montreal: *Citizen*, Mar. 2, 1904.
- Gate share: *Tribune*, Mar. 2, 1904; Roxborough, *The Stanley Cup Story*, 30.
- Pavilion roof: *Journal*, Mar. 3, 1904.
- Ottawa v. Wanderers: *Journal*, Mar. 3, 1904; *Gazette*, Mar. 3, 1904; *Citizen*,

Mar. 3, 1904.

- "dirtiest game": *Gazette*, Mar. 3, 1904.
- "probably the dirtiest": *Journal*, Mar. 3, 1904.
- "sufficiently sanguinary": *Citizen*, Mar. 4, 1904.
- "men laid out": *Journal*, Mar. 3, 1904.
- Post-game negotiations: *Citizen*, Mar. 4, 1904; *Journal*, Mar. 4, 1904; *Gazette*, Mar. 5, 1904; *Citizen*, Mar. 8, 1904.
- "with scorn": *Journal*, Mar. 4, 1904.
- Banner: *Journal*, Mar. 9, 1904.
- Sifton: *Citizen*, Mar. 9, 1904.
- "cannot reconcile": *Journal*, Mar. 7, 1904.
- Chittick: *Tribune*, Mar. 9, 1904.
- Game one: *Citizen*, Mar. 10, 1904; *Free Press*, Mar. 10, 1904; *Tribune*, Mar. 10, 1904; *Gazette*, Mar. 10, 1904.
- "star and mainstay": *Citizen*, Mar. 10, 1904.
- Patrick at point: Elmer W. Ferguson, "The Patricks," in *The Hockey Book*, 34.
- "ability or the desire": *Free Press*, Mar. 10, 1904.
- "square hockey": *Citizen*, Mar. 10, 1904.
- Game two: *Journal*, Mar. 12, 1904; *Citizen*, Mar. 12, 1904; *Gazette*, Mar. 12, 1904.
- Injuries: *Journal*, Mar. 12, 1904.
- "considerable attention": *Journal*, Mar. 12, 1904.
- "butchers who sneak up": *Globe*, Mar. 16, 1904.
- Ottawa's record: *Citizen*, Mar. 15, 1904.

TWENTY-ONE

- Boyle delivered letter: Firth, *An Illustrated Encyclopedia of Yukon Sport*, 251.
- Club's letter: *Journal*, Sept. 10, 1904.
- Young's letter: *Journal*, Sept. 10, 1904.
- A regular at Russell House: Kitchen, *Win, Tie, or Wrangle*, 142.
- Ross acknowledged receipt: *World*, Sept. 10, 1904.
- Quebec City: McKinley, *Hockey*, 25.
- "grim and graceful": Gopnik, *Winter*, 156–157.
- "most fascinating": *The Canadian Journal of Lady Aberdeen 1893–1898*, 60–61.
- "less I like it": *The Canadian Journal of Lady Aberdeen 1893–1898*, 69–70.
- "most hair-raising finish": *Citizen*, Mar. 3, 1904.
- "radical change": *Journal*, Mar. 5, 1904.
- Written by Ross: *Free Press*, Mar. 11, 1904.
- "free from the taint": Farrell, *Hockey*, 42–43.
- "spirit of professionalism": *Gazette*, Mar. 3, 1904.
- Peel: *Globe*, Dec. 5, 1904; *Telegram*, Feb. 16, 1904.

- "dealing with boys": *Globe*, Feb. 20, 1904.
- Hern admission: *Globe*, Nov. 16, 1903.
- "not trying to dictate": *Globe*, Dec. 5, 1904.
- CAAU declared CLA professional: Harper, *A Great Game*, 57.
- "who will referee": Waghorne's Hockey Hall of Fame biography, hhof.com.
- IHL: Daniel Scott Mason, "The Origins and Development of the International Hockey League and Its Effects on the Sport of Professional Ice Hockey in North America," University of British Columbia, 1992; Bill Sproule, "Houghton: The Birthplace of Professional Hockey," *The Hockey Research Journal*, 2004; Ernie Fitzsimmons, "IHL Players: The Professional Pioneers," *The Hockey Research Journal*, 2004.
- "paramount importance": John Matthew Barlow, "'Scientific Aggression': Irishness, Manliness, Class and Commercialization in the Shamrock Hockey Club of Montreal, 1894–1901," in *Coast to Coast*, 37.
- "more than a wordy discussion": *Gazette*, Feb. 7, 1898.
- "scarcely creditable": *Tribune*, Mar. 15, 1904.
- "more hard feelings": *Gazette*, Mar. 7, 1904.
- "Sour Grapes,": *Journal*, Mar. 9, 1904.
- distraction: McKinley, *Hockey*, 35.
- fans didn't like the hypocrisy: Kitchen, *Win, Tie, or Wrangle*, 133.

TWENTY-TWO
- Sounds: Dawson residents Meg Walker and Greg Hakonson; Dorothy Whyte "Description of a Town," unpublished recollection, Klondike History Library and Archives.
- Telephone subscribers: Hal J. Guest, "Civic Amenities and Urban Utilities," in "A History of Dawson of the City of Dawson, Yukon Territory 1896–1920," Microfiche Report Series No. 7, Parks Canada, 1981.
- Carnegie Library: Gregory Tetrault, "A Carnegie Library for Dawson City," *The Beaver*, Winter 1974.
- "boy's teams": *Tribune*, Mar. 13, 1902.
- Economy: Hal J. Guest, "A History of Dawson of the City of Dawson, Yukon Territory 1896–1920," Microfiche Report Series No. 7, Parks Canada, 1981.
- Newspapers: Edward F. Bush, "The Dawson Daily News: Journalism on Canada's Last Frontier," Manuscript Report Series No. 48, Parks Canada, 1971; Richard C. Stewart and William Waiser, "The Dawson News Publishing Company, 1899–1954," Microfiche Report Series No. 362, Parks Canada, 1984.
- Congdon: Edward F. Bush "Commissioners of the Yukon, 1897–1918." Canadian Historic Sites: Occasional Papers in Archaeology and History No. 10.

- Disincorporation battle: Hal J. Guest, "A History of Dawson of the City of Dawson, Yukon Territory 1896–1920," Microfiche Report Series No. 7, Parks Canada, 1981.
- League: *DDN*, May 20, 1904.
- Denies bribery: *Dawson Record*, Jul. 19, 1903.
- Baseball scandal: *DDN*, Sept. 3, 1904; *World*, Sept. 3, 1904; *DDN*, Sept. 5, 1904; *DDN*, Sept. 9, 1904; *DDN*, Sept. 16, 1904; *World*, Sept. 16, 1904.
- "manifestly unfair and arbitrary": *World*, Sept. 3, 1904.
- Size of pennant: *DDN*, Jul. 17, 1903.
- Popular sports: *Tribune*, Jan. 19, 1905.
- "huge Irishman": Berton, *I Married the Klondike*, 47.
- Rough Riders: *Gazette*, Oct. 10, 1904.
- Boyle informed town: *World*, Oct. 13, 1904.
- "upon the condition": *World*, Oct. 22, 1904.
- Concerns about longer winter: *Citizen*, Nov. 10, 1904.
- Laurier calls election: *Gazette*, Sept. 30, 1904.
- Request for date change: *DDN*, Oct. 27, 1904; *World*, Oct. 27, 1904.
- "finest possible condition": *Gazette*, Nov. 10, 1904.
- Last steamer Oct. 22: *World*, Oct. 23, 1904.
- Players working out and skating: *World*, Oct. 13, 1904.
- Young and Boyle organizers: *Province*, Sept. 1, 1904.
- Hod Stuart: *Journal*, Nov. 12, 1904.
- Victorias interested: *Province*, Nov. 8, 1904.
- Vics won't commit: *Tribune*, Dec. 14, 1904.
- Didn't want to jeopardize amateur status: *Tribune*, Dec. 21, 1904; *World*, Jan. 1, 1905.
- New dates: *Journal*, Nov. 23, 1904; *Gazette*, Nov. 23, 1904.
- "consulting sailing dates": *DDN*, Dec. 12, 1904.
- Meeting: *DDN*, Nov. 12, 1904.
- Selection committee: *DDN*, Nov. 14, 1904.
- Practices between 7 and 8 and "hardening themselves": *DDN*, Nov. 19, 1904.
- "finally decided": *Toronto Daily Star*, Nov. 25, 1904.
- "50 to 100 miles a day": *Journal*, Nov. 25, 1904.
- Eilbeck not on either seven: *World*, Nov. 25, 1904.
- First tryout game: *DDN*, Nov. 26, 1904.
- "was in every play": *World*, Nov. 26, 1904.
- Runaway sleigh: *DDN*, Dec. 9, 1903.
- Johnstone background and "very careless": "North-West Mounted Police (NWMP)—Personnel Records, 1873–1904," Library and Archives Canada.
- Forrest: Emil Forrest remembrance, Klondike History Library and Archives.
- Played goal before: *Nugget*, Dec. 8, 1902.
- Eilbeck picked all-star team: *World*, Dec. 14, 1904.

- "warm red hue": *World*, Dec. 15, 1904.
- Boyle's advice: *DDN*, Dec. 12, 1904.
- Tickets fifty cents: *World*, Nov. 24, 1904.
- Fundraising dance and "ladies he may bring": *World*, Nov. 17, 1904.
- A.B. Hall: Berton, *I Married the Klondike*, 52.
- Dance cancelled: *World*, Dec. 2, 1904.
- Martin: *Journal*, Mar. 16, 1960; *World*, Dec. 17, 1904.
- Watt's leave of absence: Gold Commissioner's Records, Yukon Archives, 19.
- Johnstone's leave of absence: J.K. Johnstone Government File, Yukon Archives.
- Young enumerator: *World*, Jan. 17, 1905.

TWENTY-THREE
- Departure: *DDN*, Dec. 16, 1904; *Yukon World*, Dec. 18, 1904; *DDN*, Dec. 19, 1904; *Journal*, Feb. 3, 1934.
- Warm spell and little snow: *World*, Dec. 4, 1904; *World*, Dec. 5, 1904.
- "noble game": *World*, Jan. 1, 1905.
- Mush a miner's term for walking: *Montreal Star*, Jan. 10, 1905.
- Temperature on Dec. 19: *DDN*, Dec. 19, 1904.
- "More of the Beautiful . . .": *DDN*, Dec. 19, 1904.
- Overland Trail and roadhouses: Gordon Bennett, "Yukon Transportation: A History," (Canadian Historic Sites, Occasional Papers on Archaeology and History #19, Ottawa: National Historic Parks, 1978); Greg Sauce, "Historical Information Regarding the Overland Trail or the Yukon Stage Line," Dawson City Museum and Historical Society, 1994; "The Overland Trail: Whitehorse to Dawson City," Yukon Tourism Heritage Branch; *Nugget*, Nov. 7, 1902.
- "into the silent night": Berton, *I Married the Klondike*, 98–99.
- Young tells Ross players would walk: *Journal*, Sept. 10, 1904.
- Young letter to father: *Journal*, Nov. 25, 1904.
- "bicycling and sprinting work": *DDN*, Dec. 19, 1904.
- Temperature drop: *Citizen*, Jan. 13, 1905; *DDN*, Dec. 22, 1904.
- Trees: *Polk's Directory and Gazetteer, 1901*, 62.
- Distances they travelled: *Citizen*, Jan. 13, 2005.
- Distances they travelled, second account: *Province*, Jan. 7, 1905.
- Roadhouses: Murray Lundberg, "Northern Roadhouses: An Introduction," *The Yukoner*, No. 14 (no date on issue); *DDN*, Sept. 17, 1904; "Distances Overland Route—Dawson to Whitehorse," Klondike History Library and Archives.
- Wood offered posts and patrol teams: *Yukon World*, Dec. 18, 1904.
- "slept in tents": *Journal*, Feb. 3, 1934.
- "own the town": *DDN*, Oct. 4, 1902.

- Forrest telegram: *DDN*, Dec. 26, 1904.
- "badly scattered out": *World*, Dec. 27, 1904.
- RNWMP post: McKinley, *Hockey*, 32.
- Arrived in Whitehorse: *Province*, Jan. 6, 1905.
- "hardy northerners": *World*, Jan. 20, 1905.
- moving, eating and sleeping: Lifelong Dawson resident Greg Hakonson.

TWENTY-FOUR

- Whitehorse: Coates and Morrison, *Land of the Midnight Sun*, 117; *Nugget*, Jan. 31, 1900; *Whitehorse Daily Star*, Feb. 21, 1957; *Whitehorse Daily Star*, Aug. 15, 1957.
- Year-round residents: *Whitehorse Daily Star*, Mar. 26, 1904.
- White: Les McLaughlin, "Stroller White: Newspaper Man," *The Yukoner*, Apr. 2002.
- "solitary spirit" and "morose as a malamute": Service, *Ploughman of the Moon*, 310.
- "royally entertained": *World*, Jan. 1, 1905.
- WP&YR: "WP&YR," Dunnery Best, *Equinox*, Sept./Oct. 1982; WP&YR corporate history, wpyr.com/history/; Coates and Morrison, *Land of the Midnight Sun*, 117; *Whitehorse Star*, Mar. 8, 1946; Berton, *Prisoners of the North*, 260.
- "enough dynamite": WP&YR corporate history, wpyr.com/history/.
- "looked tough enough": Service, *Ploughman of the Moon*, 309.
- Train schedule: *The Daily Alaskan* (Skagway), Dec. 27, 1904.
- Snow: *Daily Alaskan*, Dec. 27, 1904; *Daily Alaskan*, Dec. 28, 1904; *Free Press*, Jan. 10, 1905.
- Missed *Amur*: *Free Press*, Jan. 6, 1905; *Journal*, Jan. 9, 1905; *Gazette*, Jan. 12, 1905.
- Skagway: *Daily Alaskan*, Dec. 30, 1904; *World*, Jan. 1, 1905.
- Dove in river: *Citizen*, Jan. 13, 2005.
- Mild weather: *Daily Alaskan*, Dec. 29, 1904.
- "half an hour's practice": *Montreal Star*, Jan. 10, 1905.
- "serious liver training": James H. Marsh, "Klondikers Challenge for the Stanley Cup," *The Canadian Encyclopedia* website, thecanadianencyclopedia.ca.
- Dolphin: *Daily Alaskan*, Dec. 28, 1904; *Seattle Star*, Jan. 3, 1905; *Daily Alaskan*, Dec. 31, 1904.
- Passengers: *Daily Alaskan*, Dec. 31, 1904.
- Thick fog: *Free Press*, Jan. 10, 1905.
- "extremely rough": *Journal*, Jan. 9, 1905.
- Fans cheered: *Journal*, Jan. 10, 1905.
- "spectacle of a team": *Citizen*, Nov. 11, 1904.

- No word: *Journal*, Jan. 4, 1905.
- "boys from the frozen north": *Citizen*, Jan. 4, 1905.
- Seattle: *Seattle Star*, Jan. 5, 1905.
- "'Swiftwater Bill'Wants Another Wife": *Seattle Star*, Jan. 5, 1905.
- Dawsonites on train: *World*, Jan. 8.
- "as hard as nails": *Tribune*, Jan. 7, 1905.
- "sturdy well-knit": *Vancouver Daily World*, Jan. 6, 1905.
- 2,786 miles: Canadian Pacific Railway Annotated Time Table: The Great Transcontinental Route, 1905, Whyte Museum of the Canadian Rockies, Banff, Alta.
- Smoking room: *Citizen*, Mar. 29, 1958.
- McLennan on chances: *Journal*, Jan. 10, 1905.
- "no further concessions": *Montreal Star*, Jan. 10, 1905.
- Boyle's telegram: *Citizen*, Jan. 11, 1905.
- Hannay joined in Winnipeg: *Tribune*, Jan. 13, 1905; *Journal*, Jan. 10, 1905; *Montreal Star*, Jan. 10, 1905. (Hannay joined in Brandon: *Free Press*, Jan. 10, 1905.)
- 8,500 people, eight grain elevators: CPR Annotated Time Table.
- Hannay: *Edmonton Journal*, Dec. 30, 1904; *Gazette*, Jan. 3, 1905; Reddick, *The Trail Less Traveled*, 172–174.
- "out of his element": *Free Press*, Dec. 28, 1904.
- Fairbairn: *Free Press*, Jan. 10, 1905.
- Majordomo: *Whitehorse Daily Star*, Jan. 10, 1905.
- Didn't sign voting lists: *Whitehorse Daily Star*, Jan. 11, 1905.
- Young on Amur: *Province*, Jan. 12, 1904.

TWENTY-FIVE
- Ketchum's: *Citizen*, Jan. 12, 1905.
- "everything but ice": *Citizen*, Dec. 10, 1904.
- Uniforms: *World*, Oct. 22, 1904.
- Light skate: *Journal*, Jan. 12, 1905.
- Forty miles in his dreams: *Journal*, Jan. 16, 1905.
- Dawson practice: *Journal*, Jan. 12, 1905; *Montreal Star*, Jan. 13, 1905; *Journal*, Jan. 13, 1905; *Gazette*, Jan. 13, 1905.
- Player weights: *Citizen*, Jan. 13, 1905.
- "not likely to walk off": *Journal*, Jan. 12, 1905.
- Photo: *Montreal Star*, Jan. 13, 1905.
- Ottawa practice: *Journal*, Jan. 13, 1905.
- Dey brothers: Kitchen, *Win, Tie, or Wrangle*, 131.
- Oswald Finnie: *DDN*, Jan. 14, 1905.
- Suddie Gilmour: *Citizen*, Jan. 6, 1905
- Jim McGee: *Citizen*, May 16, 1904.

- Family pressure: Kitchen, *Win, Tie, or Wrangle*, 140–141.
- Hannay protest: *Tribune*, Jan. 13, 1905; *Montreal Star*, Jan. 14, 1905.
- "throughout the whole country": *World*, Jan. 13, 1905.
- Rush for tickets: *Journal*, Jan. 11, 1905.
- "superior in avoirdupois": *DDN*, Jan. 14, 1905.
- "all-consuming theme": *DDN*, Jan. 13, 1905.
- Dawsonites gathered: Firth, *An Illustrated Encyclopedia of Yukon Sport*, 253.
- Fans: *Gazette*, Jan. 14, 1905.
- Lord Grey a hockey fan: *Toronto Daily Star*, Jan. 14, 1905; *Montreal Star*, Jan. 14, 1905.
- "most liberal of the spectators": *Citizen*, Jan. 11, 1905.
- Game one: *Journal*, Jan. 14, 1905; *Herald*, Jan. 14, 1905; *Gazette*, Jan. 16, 1905; *World*, Jan. 14, 1905.
- "off for two minutes": *Journal*, Jan. 14, 1905.
- Newspapermen's den: *Journal*, Jan. 16, 1905; *Journal*, Mar. 11, 1903.
- "a lot of burlesquers": quoted in *World*, Feb. 2, 1905.
- "all over with glory": *Whitehorse Daily Star*, Jan. 16, 1905.
- "first twenty minutes": *Globe*, Jan. 14, 1905.
- "met the same fate": *Gazette*, Jan. 14, 1905.
- "marvel": *Toronto Daily Star*, Jan. 14, 1905.
- "sensation": *Gazette*, Jan. 14, 1905.
- "gives promise": *Journal*, Jan. 14, 1905.
- "one great medium": *Journal*, Jan. 14, 1905.
- "not fast enough": *DDN*, Jan. 14, 1905.
- "prize fight in 'Frisco": *DDN*, Jan. 14, 1905.
- "to a standstill": *DDN*, Feb. 2, 1905.
- Boyle's comment about McGee: *Journal*, Dec. 17, 1955; *Citizen*, Feb. 28, 1957.

TWENTY-SIX

- Young in Vancouver: *Province*, Jan. 14, 1905; *World*, Jan. 15, 1905.
- "under the circumstances": *Province*, Jan. 14, 1905.
- "matches postponed": *Province*, Jan. 17, 1905.
- Young visited brother: *Regina Leader-Post*, Feb. 1, 1905.
- "may not end tonight": *Citizen*, Jan. 16, 1905.
- "will show it tonight": *Journal*, Jan. 16, 1905.
- "rather large off-sides": *Journal*, Jan. 14, 1905.
- Government purge: *DDN*, Jan. 17, 1905; *Whitehorse Daily Star*, Jan. 17, 1905; *World*, Jan. 17, 1905.
- Rumour about not playing hard: *Globe*, Jan. 16, 1905.
- "no let-up": *Herald*, Jan. 17, 1905.
- "the real thing": *Herald*, Jan. 17, 1905.

- Game two: *Journal*, Jan. 17, 1905; *Citizen*, Jan. 17, 1905; *Herald*, Jan. 17, 1905; *Montreal Star*, Jan. 17, 1905; *Tribune*, Jan. 17, 1905; *World*, Jan. 17, 1905; *World*, Feb. 2, 1905.
- "Make it larger": *Herald*, Jan. 17, 1905.
- "might have been doubled": *Citizen*, Jan. 17, 1905.
- "best centre player": *Montreal Star*, Jan. 17, 1905.
- "was a good game": *DDN*, Jan. 17, 1905.
- "hungry small boy": *Citizen*, Jan. 17, 1905.
- "a lot of tyros": *Herald*, Jan. 17, 1905.
- "skated away from them": *Globe*, Jan. 17, 1905.
- "consignment of hockey junk": quoted in *World*, Feb. 2, 1905.
- "see-saw twenty times": "Will Try it Again," *World*, undated photocopy, Yukon Archives.
- Dawson disappointed: *Montreal Star*, Jan. 17, 1905.
- Banquet and "by hook or crook": *Journal*, Jan. 18, 1905.
- CAAU controversy: *Province*, Jan. 14, 1905; *Journal*, Jan. 18, 1905; *Citizen*, Jan. 19, 1905; *Gazette*, Jan. 19, 1905.
- "resigned from the board": *Journal*, Jan. 18, 1905.
- "not ten percent": *Journal*, Jan. 18, 1905.
- Dropkicking the Cup: Roxborough, *The Stanley Cup Story*, 73–74.
- Westwick version: *Journal*, May 16, 1973; *The New York Times*, Jun. 3, 2017.
- "got to be a good story": *Journal*, May 16, 1973.

TWENTY-SEVEN
- Ahearn passes message: *Journal*, Nov. 8, 1962.
- Tried to recruit Taylor: McKinley, *Putting a Roof on Winter*, 52.
- Congdon: *World*, Jan. 19, 1905.
- No show in Kingston: *Citizen*, Jan. 20, 1905.
- Montreal: *Journal*, Jan. 21, 1905.
- British Columbia to Cape Breton: *Whitehorse Daily Star*, Jan. 17, 1905.
- "instructed to reply": Montreal Amateur Athletic Association Minute Book, MG 28 I 351 Volume 6, File 2, LAC.
- "money-making tour": *Journal*, Jan. 16, 1905.
- Arena responds: *Montreal Star*, Jan. 17, 1905.
- "friends thronged" and "hale and hearty": *Journal*, Jan. 23, 1905.
- "working like a pump": *Citizen*, Jan. 23, 1905.
- "one of the hardest fought": *Halifax Morning Chronicle*, Jan. 24, 1905.
- "Bumping into Things": *Province*, Jan. 25, 1905.
- 1,500 fans: *Journal*, Jan. 25, 1905.
- "Hockey Boys Are Making Money . . .": *World*, Jan. 26, 1905.
- Offer to pay expenses: *Journal*, Jan. 28, 1905.
- "assistance of the referee": *World*, Jan. 28, 1905.

- "deliberate steal": *World*, Feb. 2, 1905.
- Glace Bay: *Cape Breton Post*, Feb. 26, 2016.
- "admission charge": *Fredericton Daily Gleaner*, Feb. 4, 1905.
- "should not have lost": *DDN*, Feb. 24, 1905.
- Trois-Rivières: *Gazette*, Feb. 11, 1905.
- "good material": *Gazette*, Feb. 8, 1905.
- Montagnard: *Gazette*, Feb. 9, 1905; *DDN*, Feb. 12, 1905.
- Smith injured knee: *World*, Feb. 4, 1905.
- Klondikers claimed game was 2-2 tie: *World*, Apr. 15, 1905.
- Foran names Young ref: *Gazette*, Feb. 11, 1905.
- Twenty penalties: *Citizen*, Feb. 13, 1905.
- "equal to the task": *Journal*, Feb. 13, 1905.
- "applause and disapproval": *Gazette*, Feb. 13, 1905.
- "Ottawas and Weldy Young": *Journal*, Feb. 14, 1905.
- "The Killing of Alcide Laurin . . .": *Journal*, Feb. 27, 1905.
- Laurin death: *Journal*, Feb. 27, 1905; *Citizen*, Feb. 27, 1905; *Globe*, Feb. 28, 1905; *Journal*, Mar. 3, 1905; *Journal*, Mar. 29, 1905; Scanlan, *Grace Under Fire*, 54–57; McKinley, *Hockey*, 27; Proteau, *Fighting the Good Fight*, 161–162; Stacy L. Lorenz and Geraint B. Osborne, "'A Manly Nation Requires Manly Games': Hockey Violence and the 1905 Manslaughter Trial of Allan Loney," in *Putting It on Ice: Proceedings of the 2012 Hockey Conference*, 2013.
- Negotiated with Ontario teams: *Montreal Star*, Jan. 16, 1905.
- "on any ice": *Citizen*, Mar. 2, 1905.
- Lannon: *Gazette*, Feb. 27, 1905.
- Ottawa papers listed Archie Martin: *Journal*, Jan. 12, 1905, *Citizen*; Jan. 12, 1905.
- Managerial role: *Journal*, Mar. 19, 1960.
- May never have left the Yukon: Reddick, *The Trail Less Traveled*, 182.
- Brandon: *World*, Apr. 15, 1905.
- Games in Western Canada: *World*, Mar. 23, 1905.
- "firmly intend": *Province*, Mar. 27, 1905.
- Final record of the tour varies with the source. One reason is the Klondikers insisted they tied the Montreal game. Respected hockey historian Ernie Fitzsimmons determined the final record was ten wins and twelve losses. See "The Dawson City Tour," *The Hockey Research Journal*, 2001.
- "did not bring the cup": *Whitehorse Daily Star*, Apr. 6, 1905.
- Whitehorse to Dawson: "Albert is Home," *World*, undated photocopy, Yukon Archives; *Whitehorse Daily Star*, Apr. 7, 1905; *World*, Apr. 15, 1905.
- Game in Dawson: *World*, Apr. 20, 1905; "The Stars Twinkled," *World*, undated photocopy, Yukon Archives.